A FRACTURED SOCIETY

A FRACTURED SOCIETY

The Politics of London in the
First Age of Party
1688–1715

GARY STUART DE KREY

CLARENDON PRESS · OXFORD
1985

Oxford University Press, Walton Street, Oxford OX2 6DP

Oxford New York Toronto

Delhi Bombay Calcutta Madras Karachi
Kuala Lumpur Singapore Hong Kong Tokyo
Nairobi Dar es Salaam Cape Town
Melbourne Auckland

and associated companies in
Beirut Berlin Ibadan Mexico City Nicosia

Oxford is a trade mark of Oxford University Press

Published in the United States
by Oxford University Press, New York

British Library Cataloguing in Publication Data
De Krey, Gary Stuart
A fractured society: the politics of London in
the first age of party: 1688–1715.
1. London (England)—History—17th century
1. London (England)—History—18th century
I. Title
942.106   DA681
ISBN 0-19-820067-6

Set by DMB (Typesetting), Oxford
Printed in Great Britain
at the University Press, Oxford
by David Stanford
Printer to the University

For Cathy

PREFACE

———◆◆◆———

THIS book had its origin in a modest thesis proposal for a study of Corporation of London politics at the time of the Glorious Revolution. From the beginning, my research developed in unexpected directions. An earlier interest in the history of puritanism asserted itself, as did a more recent interest in the world of trade and commerce. The resulting thesis was completed at Princeton in 1978 under the rather unwieldy title of 'Trade, Religion, and Politics in London in the Reign of William III'. Readers familiar with my thesis will notice some resemblances between it and the present work, but the differences are considerable. In the course of revising the thesis, I became convinced that my original focus upon William's reign was somewhat restrictive, especially as I became interested in additional issues and questions. Among these were the connections between magisterial and popular politics and the influence upon political behaviour of the increasing circulation of all varieties of printed media.

Many historians have assisted me in the preparation of this book. The typescript benefited from a careful and exacting reading by Geoffrey Holmes, who suggested several means for its improvement. I also appreciated critical readings of all or parts of the book or my thesis from David Cannadine, Henry Horwitz, James McLachlan, John Murrin, Lois G. Schwoerer, Lawrence Stone, and John F. Wilson. I am particularly indebted to D. W. Jones for sharing the results of his London researches with me and for permitting me to make use of data from his thesis. I owe to each of these scholars my knowledge of different matters of fact and interpretation. I am indebted for others to Douglas Arnold, John Brewer, Rocco Capraro, Linda Colley, Eveline Cruickshanks, Mark Goldie, Tim Harris, Harry Payne, Nicholas Rogers, and Arthur G. Smith. I take pleasure in acknowledging my gratitude to these individuals. Any errors of fact or interpretation that remain are entirely my own.

Appreciation is also due to those institutions, societies, and archives that have supported or facilitated my work. I especially wish to thank the staff of the Corporation of London Records Office for their never failing assistance and interest. Many librarians at Colgate University and at Princeton University have also responded graciously to innumerable entreaties for rare and remote materials. Financial assistance from the Danforth Foundation and from Princeton University made possible my initial research. A post-doctoral fellowship from the Princeton history department allowed me welcome time for reflection and writing, as did a simultaneous leave from Colgate. Additional research was supported by grants-in-aid from the American Philosophical Society and from the Colgate Research Council. I am grateful to the Trustees of the British Museum for permission to reproduce 'Londons Happynes in Four Loyal-Members' as a jacket illustration. I am also grateful to the University of Chicago Press for permission to incorporate copyright material from my article, 'Political Radicalism in London after the Glorious Revolution', *Journal of Modern History*, 55 (December 1983), 585–617 (0022-2801/83/5504/01).

Several friends and scholars have aided me in personal ways of which they may not be entirely aware. Lawrence Stone has acted as a critic of my work since my first graduate seminars. No student of seventeenth-century England could have asked for a more rigorous and consistent supervisor. The late Wesley Frank Craven took considerable pains to introduce me to his own meticulous standards of historical research and scholarship. From my friends Jack and Pamela Schwandt I acquired my appreciation for London, the early eighteenth century, and much else besides. My Colgate colleagues have given me encouragement and support. Rosalie Hiam, Lois Wilcox, Mary Smith, and Thelma Mayer helped with the typescript, and Bryan Lane was an indefatigable research assistant. My parents have been interested and supportive observers of my work, and William T. Doherty gave useful advice at critical junctures.

Finally, I owe more than I can say to my wife Cathy, who has read, discussed, debated, edited, and indexed the entire book, and who has sacrificed much to see it completed. This volume is dedicated to her with thanks and joy.

London
28 May 1984

NB: Dates are given in the Old Style, except that the year is taken to begin on 1 January. The original spelling, punctuation, and italicization have generally been retained in quotations.

CONTENTS

TABLES AND FIGURES

ABBREVIATIONS

Add. MS	Additional Manuscript, British Library
BDBR	Richard L. Greaves and Robert Zaller, eds., *Biographical Dictionary of British Radicals in the Seventeenth Century*, vols. 1-2 (1982-3)
BIHR	*Bulletin of the Institute of Historical Research*
BL	British Library
Bodl.	Bodleian Library
CJ	*Journals of the House of Commons*
CLRO	Corporation of London Records Office
CSPCol	*Calendar of State Papers, Colonial Series*
CSPD	*Calendar of State Papers, Domestic Series*
De Krey, 'Trade, Religion, and Politics'	Gary S. De Krey, 'Trade, Religion, and Politics in London in the Reign of William III (Princeton Univ. Ph.D. thesis, 1978)
DND	*Dictionary of National Biography*
DWL	Dr Williams's Library
EcHR	*Ecomomic History Review*
EHR	*English Historical Review*
GL	Guildhall Library
Grey, *Debates*	Anchitell Grey, *Debates of the House of Commons, 1667-1694*, 10 vols. (1769)
HJ	*Historical Journal*
HLQ	*Huntington Library Quarterly*
HMC	Historical Manuscripts Commission, various reports
IOL	India Office Library
JBS	*Journal of British Studies*
JCTP	*Journals of the Commissioners for Trade and Plantations, 1709-18*, 3 vols. (1920-5)
Journal	Journals of the Court of Common Council, Corporation of London Records Office
KAO	Kent Archives Office
LJ	*Journals of the House of Lords*
Luttrell, *Brief Relation*	Narcissus Luttrell, *A Brief Historical Relation of State Affairs*, 6 vols. (Oxford, 1859)

PHSL	*Proceedings of the Huguenot Society of London*
POAS	*Poems on Affairs of State, 1660–1714*, vols. v–vii, eds. William J. Cameron and Frank H. Ellis (1970–5)
PRO	Public Record Office
Repertory	Repertories of the Court of Aldermen, Corporation of London Records Office
SP	State Papers, Public Record Office
TRHS	*Transactions of the Royal Historical Society*
VCH	The Victoria History of the Counties of England

INTRODUCTION

The City in an Era of Revolution

IN the seventeenth and eighteenth centuries London was frequently in the foreground of English politics. As metropolis, as chief entrepôt, and as premier parliamentary constituency, the City was an especially sophisticated political environment that was intimately connected to the larger arena of national affairs. This unique relationship between London politics and the politics of the country was permitted by the City's proximity to the seat of government at Westminster, and it was strengthened by the close ties between magisterial authorities and leading courtiers and parliamentarians. The importance of the relationship between the City and the regime was particularly evident in years of crisis or during periods of exceptional political change. One of the most important of these critical early modern political interludes was the era of party strife that occurred between the Revolution of 1688 and the Hanoverian Succession. These were years in which London and London citizens played quite significant roles in the political, religious, and economic turmoil that disturbed the state. These were years also in which London money and London 'interests' developed novel attachments to the state, attachments which themselves became the subject of strenuous political argument.

This study of the politics of London in the first age of party is addressed to four distinct questions, each of which will be outlined below. Before these questions are posed, however, the historical and the historiographical contexts of an examination of the City in this era of revolution may be further explored. The reasons for the pre-eminence of London in early modern English political and social history are many. The City's importance to monarchs and to their ministers was, in the first instance, a product of the wealth and capital of its bourgeois social orders. As London trade prospered and developed so did the influence of its commercial and trading classes. That the City could break the crown, as it did in 1640, was the greatest demonstration of its financial power. That the City could fund enormous war-time government expenditures, as the Whig Junto discovered in the 1690s, was the greatest demonstration of its financial potential. Although the country boasted several provincial manufacturing and trade centres of no mean significance, only the 'loss of the City' could threaten a ministry with loss of power. A source of envy to continental rulers, the availability of London wealth to the English regime was also a source of anxiety to Country politicians. They hoped to see the English crown supported by civic wealth, but they also feared to see it corrupted by civic wealth. Nevertheless, as every late Stuart and early Hanoverian minister was to learn, City credit, City advances, City contracts, and City influence provided the government with essential financial services even in times of peace.

Both demography and patterns of cultural change also point to London's importance in pre-industrial England. The concentration of almost one-tenth of the national population in one urban environment made London a unique English metropolis. The City received a never-ending stream of immigrants from many localities and from all degrees of society. In exchange, the London élite extended its commercial values, its bourgeois style of living and its wealth to the landed élite of the counties. Landed prejudice against commercial employments persisted; but this prejudice could not obscure an exchange of tastes, ideas, and mores that accompanied the increasingly vigorous exchange of sons and daughters between City magnates and county grandees. By the reigns of the last Stuarts, the leaders of provincial society in many counties displayed a striking absorption of the capitalist mentality and the individualistic ethos of the City. The dissemination of metropolitan styles and standards of dress, décor, and deportment was integral to the development of the more homogeneous culture of the eighteenth-century English ruling class.

London was, then, quite unusual among English localities. It invites study not because it was typical of English urban life but rather because it was so exceptional. Any study of London politics is complicated, however, by the fact that 'London' was more a geographic and social expression than a single, recognizable polity. By the late Stuart era, the habitations of some 600,000 London residents stretched in every direction from the medieval city through Westminster, the Middlesex out-parishes, Southwark, and the Surrey fringe. Perhaps only about one-quarter of the urban population resided at any given time within the area of the Corporation of London, the legally incorporated City. Nevertheless, the Corporation was at the centre of City affairs; and analysis of political developments in the Corporation will be central to this study. Many characteristics of the Corporation point to this centrality. Within the Corporation's boundaries were found London's primary facilities for overseas commerce, domestic investment, and the exchange of capital. There also were found the largest urban residential concentrations of active overseas merchants, substantial shopkeepers, and independent tradesmen. The Corporation possessed exceptionally extensive institutions of self-government; and the resident citizens of the Corporation enjoyed highly valued political and economic liberties, which they exercised in their wards, their parishes, and their livelihoods. Neither the parliamentary borough of Westminster nor Southwark rivalled the Corporation in these respects, and the inferiority of Southwark was marked by its status as a ward within the Corporation. A political concentration upon the Corporation within the larger London environment is therefore entirely appropriate. London politics in the first age of party cannot be understood at all without a focus upon the Corporation; but at the same time, an exclusive focus upon the institutional history of the Corporation would preclude attention to many important features of civic political culture. For instance, the politics of the urban crowd transcended both the bounds of the Corporation and the influence of the civic magistracy.

Civic conflict in late Stuart London was especially enlivened by changes in the nature of parliamentary politics, by increasing electoral participation, and by an enlargement in the range of divisive issues. After the Revolution of 1688, the Whig and Tory parliamentary factions of the 1680s broadened their electoral appeal, endorsed new methods of exerting local influence, and received the active assistance of local leaders who identified their prospects with those of their parties. The rapid and free development of the English press between the end of licensing in 1695 and the introduction of a stamp duty in 1712 also greatly facilitated the politicization of a growing electorate. But the electorate, as large as it may have become, was no longer the only audience for politics. In the more populous boroughs, politics were also of interest to an urban plebs who, especially by the end of Anne's reign, were as active in expressing their own sentiments as they had been in the chaotic years of the late 1640s and the early 1650s. Moreover, vigorous prosecution of the two long wars against France entailed a complete restructuring of City facilities for corporate trade and investment. The older joint stocks of the Restoration were joined and threatened by such new corporate enterprises as the Bank of England, the New East India Company, and the South Sea Company, each of which became a major government creditor. The creation of such enormous corporate concerns and of an enormous public debt not only proved divisive within the City but also divided the politicians of the nation. Finally, the period was one in which the historical religious divisions of Protestant Englishmen enjoyed their last spectacular political recrudescence before subsiding into the new eighteenth-century spirit of religious restraint.

The late Stuart party contest therefore involved critical issues, divided 'interests', and a much enlarged political public. These and other features of the competition between Whigs and Tories were signs that the status-oriented politics of a paternalistic, hierarchical society were being replaced by the interest-oriented politics of a commercial civilization. Given all these considerations, the first era of party may also be considered an era of revolution; and London was deeply involved in the revolutionary changes of 1688 to 1715. London trade fuelled the late seventeenth-century 'commercial revolution' that continued into the eighteenth century, and London capital launched the 'financial revolution' that began in the 1690s. The 'communications revolution' that issued from an unlicensed press had its greatest impact in the print capital of the country, and the numerous institutions of local self-government within the Corporation encouraged experimentation with novel forms of political organization. The rhetoric of revolution was also as much an element of London's political culture in the late Stuart decades as it had been in the 1640s and the 1650s. The concept of revolution was applied not only to the accomplished events of 1688–89 but also to the continuing effects of those events and to their anticipated results. Lastly, both City Whigs and City Tories looked to the personalities and to the myths of an earlier Revolution for symbols to express the meaning of their own conflict.

The political history of the first age of party has benefited from a scholarly renaissance that began with the publication in 1967 of J.H. Plumb's interpretation of *The Origins of Political Stability, 1675-1725* and of Geoffrey S. Holmes's study of *British Politics in the Age of Anne*. In the intervening years, these and several other historians (including especially W.A. Speck and Henry Horwitz) have developed a rich account of the competition of two mutually hostile parliamentary parties and of the evolution of Court and Country perspectives. The writings of these scholars, whose influence upon this work is frequently recorded, have enormously facilitated the comprehension of events and issues at the national level. They are, however, only beginning to be supported and supplemented by local studies.[1] In the relative absence of such work, many questions about English politics during and after the Glorious Revolution remain unanswered or only partially answered. Surviving poll books have been subjected to pioneering quantitative analysis, but too little is yet known about continuity or discontinuity in electoral attitudes over time. Party organization has been viewed from the Olympian heights of Westminster, but glimpses into mundane local political organization remain few. The sociology and the purposes of the urban crowd have received careful analysis, but the political opinions and expectations of the crowd 'within doors' are still largely hidden from sight. The impact of war upon parliamentary and ministerial decision-making has been given more consideration than the effects of war upon society and public opinion. The rise of clerical high-flyers in the Church of England has been amply studied, but the names and careers of the leading nonconformist lay spokesmen remain elusive. The investigation of such problems will be the work of several scholarly lifetimes rather than the task of a single monograph. Nevertheless, these broad problems have suggested four questions that shape the argumentation and structure of this book.

The first of these is the question of how the ideological purposes of party organization changed over time. One of the greatest

---

[1] A notable recent contribution is that of Philip Jenkins, *The Making of a Ruling Class: The Glamorgan Gentry 1640-1790* (Cambridge, 1983).

difficulties in the study of parliamentary Whigs and Tories has been
that of explaining the realignment of the parties along the Court–
Country axis that was a constant feature of Stuart politics. The
gradual reversal in the position of the party leaders on this ideological continuum after 1688 brought unswerving Court politicians
like Godolphin and unswerving Country politicians like Harley
into strange company indeed. This reversal has been as confusing
to historians as it was to contemporaries, and it cannot be entirely
clarified without attention to local politics. Can it be argued, in
particular, that the London Tories and the London Whigs experienced a similar ideological transformation? Did the 1680s' party
of magisterial prerogatives and the 1680s' party of civic opposition exchange their Court and Country connections? The answer
to these questions is an unqualified affirmative, but the explanations are as difficult and complicated as those provided by historians who have outlined the reversal of perspectives by the
parliamentary parties.

The second question of this book is concerned with the
numbers, the sociology, and the economic and political activities
of nonconformists in London after the toleration of 1689. The
passions aroused in parliamentary and clerical debates of the late
1690s about the results of toleration suggest that the limited Act of
1689 had consequences not foreseen by the Churchmen who had
agreed to it. The rage directed by the Sacheverellite crowds of 1710
against the ornamental trappings of the dissenters' religious
emancipation also suggests that urban plebs identified nonconformists with the elite Whig enemies of High-Church principles.
Was the concern of High-Church spokesmen and the anger of
High-Church crowds out of proportion to the extent of nonconformist success in the City? The evidence suggests that this was not
the case.

The third question examined here is the relationship between
party politics in the Corporation and socio-economic tensions
among the different interests who made up the 'City'. The wars of
1689 to 1713 were the single most important cause of such urban
social strains. This was because war-time taxation, war-time
trading opportunities, and war-time initiatives in public finance
had quite different consequences for active merchants, investors,
goldsmith-bankers, manufacturers, artisans, and casual labourers.
Did party disagreements, then, reflect the occupational and

economic frictions of an urban commercial society rapidly maturing in the midst of warfare of almost unprecedented dimensions? Did partisan London arguments about the constitution, about foreign policy, and about religion gain at least part of their edge from their espousal by quite different social elements within the City? These queries may also be answered in the affirmative, but the explanations are again quite complex.

The final question pursued here involves an examination of the origins and the endurance of a libertarian perspective among the London 'commons' and an examination of the relationship between popular and magisterial politics. Although the very existence of late Stuart urban 'radicalism' has been denied by some scholars, a quest for its ideological content and for its social provenance has proved intriguing to others. Urban radicalism will here be studied in the broader civic context of London politics rather than in isolation from it, and the treatment of artisan populism will necessarily be exploratory rather than definitive. What has been learned about popular political perspectives suggests that the late Stuart history of Whigs and Tories in London— and perhaps elsewhere—is incomplete without analysis of how 'the people' viewed both politics and public events.

The investigation and interpretation of these questions has posed methodological and organizational challenges. Both the course of political developments in the City and the conflicts of different groups of people clustered on opposite sides of the party divide needed to be understood. As a research task, the first of these concerns was more easily pursued than the second. The institutional records of the Corporation and of the major London joint-stock companies survive in greater quantity than the scattered and fragmentary traces of common councilmen, successful merchants, and nonconformists of different persuasions. Nevertheless, prosopographical analysis of many groups engaged in the acrimonious political life of the City is possible with the assistance of tax returns, petitions, lists of shareholders, personal inventories, and church record books. Hundreds of London party leaders, common councilmen, merchant electors, and prosperous nonconformists have been studied collectively in the preparation of this book. Although little of the biographical information gathered about these Londoners is actually presented here, it informs many interpretive judgments and supports a series of statistical portraits.

Only through the examination of such groups can the deep-seated social, constitutional, economic, and religious antagonisms that created this fractured society be revealed.

The organizational challenge encountered in the writing of this book has been that of balancing analysis of the causes and results of party conflict in London with a narrative account addressed to the four questions outlined above. The structure adopted is one that focuses attention upon the critical years at the beginning and the conclusion of the twenty-five year period under consideration. All four questions are introduced in chapters one and two. The first of these, an analysis of the historical origins of party conflict in London, emphasizes the political experiences of Londoners in the 1680s and the 1690s. Chapter two is a narrative account of the City's revolutionary crisis of 1688–90, and it dwells both upon the expression of political radicalism in the Corporation and upon the adjustment of City party leaders to the Revolution. This narrative interpretation of urban party rivalry after 1688 continues in chapter five after extensive examinations, in chapters three and four, of the politics of belief and the politics of wealth. Chapter three presents an analysis of the controversial involvement of nonconformists in late Stuart City affairs. Chapter four, which is especially concerned with the divergent characteristics of the London Whig and Tory leadership élites, also examines the commercial, occupational, and geographic antagonisms that fed the competition of the parties. With these sources of civic discord fully set forth, the history of late Stuart London politics is resumed with particular attention to the results of party conflict in the City. Chapter five explains the astonishing changes in the parties' ideological orientations between 1690 and 1710. Chapter six focuses upon the revival of urban radicalism in the last years of Queen Anne's reign; and the narrative conclusion examines the significance of the Hanoverian Succession for London politics.

I

The Origins of Party Conflict
in the City, 1679–1702

1. *Introduction: A Legacy of Factionalism*

THE residents of the 'ancient city' of London were no strangers to
political conflict at the time of the 1688 Revolution. Political disagreements, which occasionally took the form of impassioned
clashes, had been a recurrent feature of the Corporation's history
since 1640, and this was to remain the case long after Robert
Walpole's City Elections Act of 1725.[1] Stormy meetings of Common Hall, plebeian tumults, and disputes between Common
Council and the Court of Aldermen were far from novel experiences. The frequency of such incidents emphasized the existence of
abiding and fundamental questions about the formal distribution
of power in the City. The Corporation's working constitution was
in fact a chronic political irritant in the seventeenth and eighteenth centuries because it concentrated power in the hands of a
few while extending the right of political participation to many.
The irritation was most keenly felt whenever the constitutional
balance between king and parliament was also under public
scrutiny. That had been the case after 1679 when constitutional
issues had first divided Whigs from Tories. From the Exclusion
Crisis to the Revolutionary Settlement, the City constitution
remained at the heart of political disturbances in London, and

[1] Valerie Pearl, *London and the Outbreak of the Puritan Revolution* (Oxford, 1961); J. E.
Farnell, 'The Politics of the City of London, 1649-1657' (Univ. of Chicago Ph.D. thesis,
1963); Brian Manning, *The English People and the English Revolution, 1640-1649* (1976),
especially chapters 1-4; Mark A. Kishlansky, *The Rise of the New Model Army* (Cambridge,
1979), especially chapters 4 and 8; David F. Allen, 'The Crown and the Corporation of
London in the Exclusion Crisis, 1678-81' (Cambridge Ph.D. thesis, 1977); Arthur G.
Smith, 'London and the Crown, 1681-85' (Univ. of Wisconsin Ph.D. thesis, 1967);
Alfred J. Henderson, *London and the National Government, 1721-1742* (Durham, NC, 1945);
Nicholas Rogers, 'Resistance to Oligarchy: The City Opposition to Walpole and his Suc-
cessors', in *London in the Age of Reform*, ed. John Stevenson (Oxford, 1977), pp. 1-29.

these disturbances created a legacy of factionalism that was thereafter inherited by the City parties. Both the nature of Corporation
government before the Revolution of 1688 and the early history of
the City parties need therefore to be explored in order to introduce
the causes of party conflict after the Revolution.

The administrative and electoral procedures of the Corporation
had evolved in piecemeal fashion over the centuries, as dictated
by the needs of an urban society and as confirmed by royal grants
of privilege.[2] In fact and in theory, these constitutional practices
reflected the hierarchical social assumptions of early modern
England. The constitution of the City was essentially an oligarchical one in which political authority was concentrated in the hands
of the Lord Mayor and the Court of Aldermen. Chosen for life,
one from each of the City's wards, the twenty-six aldermen functioned as the supreme executive of the Corporation. The requirement that aldermanic nominees possess an estate of at least
£10,000 restricted membership to those from the highest ranks of
London society. Moreover, the Court was somewhat self-
perpetuating because the format for aldermanic elections before
1714 granted the sitting aldermen a major role in the selection of
their new colleagues.[3] In addition to their many administrative
responsibilities, the aldermen also exercised certain prerogatives
that permitted them to oversee the work of Common Council.
The latter body, consisting of 234 representatives annually elected
from the wards, acted as the Corporation's legislature. However,
the aldermen exercised a right of prior review over all matters
considered by Common Council, and individual aldermen were
appointed to all Common Council committees and directed their
work. This subordination of the Corporation's legislative agency
to its executive was ultimately preserved by the aldermen's collective privilege of vetoing acts of Common Council. Finally, the
aldermen annually selected the Lord Mayor, choosing between
two of their own number previously nominated in Common Hall,
the electoral assembly of the City's liverymen. As chief magistrate

---

[2] The best short discussion of the history and mechanics of Corporation government is
found in Pearl, *London and the Puritan Revolution*, pp. 45–68.

[3] Before 1711 the Court of Aldermen filled vacancies by choosing from two sitting
aldermen and two commoners nominated by resident ward housekeepers. Common
Council acts of 1711 and 1714 provided more popular procedures for aldermanic elections.

of the City, the Lord Mayor possessed great power and patronage
in his own right. Common Council and Common Hall met only at
his summons and could be dissolved at his pleasure. Within his gift
were several important offices in the Corporation, and before the
Revolution he customarily made a binding nomination of one of
the two Sheriffs of London and Middlesex who acted during his
mayoralty.[4]

This outline of the Corporation's constitution serves to locate
its major stress points and to explain, in part, the City's legacy of
factionalism. As the population of London grew, and as the
number of electors increased, so did dissatisfaction with a constitution that placed power in the hands of too few. The privileges
of the magisterial élite rested more upon custom than upon consent in a century in which custom was discovered to be ambiguous
and in which consent was proposed as a more certain source of
political legitimacy. Articulate critics of oligarchy suggested that a
broader distribution of authority among the organs of Corporation government was sanctioned by earlier constitutional practice,
and these critics found many precedents in the City's history to
support their view. As instances of unwarranted magisterial
authority, the aldermanic veto and the mayoral nomination to the
shrievalty were especially condemned as London analogies to the
alleged abuse of royal authority by Stuart monarchs. Eliminated
in the early years of the Long Parliament but restored after 1660,
these disputed magisterial powers became crucial sparks in the
initial 1680s blaze of urban party controversy.[5]

Other than in the Commons itself, the issues that divided the
first Whigs from the first Tories were nowhere else more vigorously debated than in London.[6] An alliance among Exclusionist
MPs, Whig magistrates, and populist London guildsmen made
the City a principal arena of anti-Court agitation from 1679 to
1683. The reasons for this London outburst of hostility to royal
government lie in the sudden convergence of national political
issues with enduring local problems. The frenzy of the Popish Plot

---

[4] Pearl, *London and the Puritan Revolution*, p. 63; Sidney Webb and Beatrice Webb,
*English Local Government from the Revolution to the Municipal Corporations Act: The Manor and the
Borough, Part Two* (1908), p. 673, n.3.

[5] Pearl, *London and the Puritan Revolution*, pp. 248-9; *CSPD 1680-81*, p. 330; Smith, pp.
33-7, 178, 187-9.

[6] Allen, pp. 130-60; J. R. Jones, *The First Whigs: The Politics of the Exclusion Crisis,
1678-1683* (1961), pp. 116-20, 198-206.

was most intense in the city of Sir Edmund Berry Godfrey, where fears of Jesuit conspiracy were fed by a sizeable Catholic population and were aggravated by the economic insecurities of artisan life. The pro-French foreign policy of Charles II, which had contributed to the rise of the new Country opposition in parliament, was equally disliked by London merchants anxious about competition from their French counterparts.[7] Royal financial administration provoked suspicions on the part of City commercial interests for whom the Stop of the Exchequer was a vivid memory. The exercise of prerogative powers during the three Exclusion Parliaments reminded London liverymen that their own electoral preferences could easily be thwarted by aldermanic obstruction. Fully aware of the constitutional implications of a parliamentary rearrangement of the succession, some London Whigs were also hopeful of seizing the occasion for an alteration of power in the Corporation.[8] However, as the Whigs became interested in electoral rights and reforms, the king's friends among the aldermen and common councilmen stood fast in defence of 'established' forms of rule in city and state. When the hysteria of conspiracy and exclusion subsided, the City party leaders engaged in a calculated struggle for mastery of the City government, revealing in the process their divergent constitutional views.

The Whigs lost this struggle, and so in the end did the Tories. A dangerous enemy for one party, the crown proved an unreliable friend for the other. As the 'popular' party, the Whigs enjoyed the support of over 60 per cent of those liverymen who appeared at Corporation polls in 1681–82.[9] However, they were unable to translate that support into effective control of the Corporation, and the strenuousness of their endeavours actually lost them the sympathy of moderate common councilmen. In their unsuccessful quest for power the Whigs saw the realization of their own worst fears about magisterial manipulation. In 1682, Whig candidates for the offices of Lord Mayor and sheriff received Common Hall majorities but were deprived of their elections through the interference of a Tory-dominated aldermanic bench and of the Tory

---

[7] Margaret Priestley, 'London Merchants and Opposition Politics in Charles II's Reign', *BIHR* xxix (1956), 205–19; Margaret Priestley, 'Anglo-French Trade and the Unfavourable Balance Controversy, 1660–1685', *EcHR*, 2nd Ser., iv (1951), 37–52.

[8] GL MS 3589, fos. 1–9; Allen, pp. 95, 120–2.

[9] Smith, p. 37.

Lord Mayor, Sir John Moore. Supported by the Common Council majority and encouraged by a gratified crown, the Tory leaders thereafter unleashed an official campaign of terror designed to rid the Corporation of the 'faction'. Tory magistrates undertook a purge of Whigs holding City offices, and the crown removed Whigs from among the London Lieutenancy commissioners and the militia officers. The new Tory sheriffs proceeded immediately to an alteration of the London grand and petty juries which boded ill for their opponents. Whig leaders who had protested against the rulings of the chair during the 1682 shrieval election were indicted, convicted, and fined for riot. The London nonconformists were subjected to a renewed policy of harassment carried out by the trained bands. Henry Cornish, an alderman and leading Presbyterian layman, was executed in 1685 for his alleged complicity in the Rye House Plot, and some outspoken Whig leaders fled the country. Finally, in the wake of Monmouth's Rebellion, 300 notable City Whigs and dissenters were arrested and temporarily incarcerated.[10]

In the meantime, the London Tories' victory had turned bittersweet. No sooner had the Whigs been defeated in the Corporation than the crown revealed its intention of destroying the Corporation. Determined to subordinate all political institutions to the monarchy, Charles made London an early target in his campaign to bring the parliamentary boroughs under royal management.[11] Some Tory common councilmen joined with moderates and Whigs in October 1683 in refusing the king's request for a voluntary surrender of the Corporation's charter, but to no avail. The charter was shortly declared forfeit in King's Bench on a royal writ of *quo warranto*, and rule of the City reverted to the crown. Mindful of the unpopularity of his action, Charles retained certain vestiges of the City's accustomed government. Whig aldermen were relieved of their offices, but a full bench of twenty-six Tory aldermen (including new royal appointees) was placed in charge of London. Old officers of the Corporation, except for Whigs, were continued

[10] CLRO London Lieutenancy Court Minute Books, 1684/85-7, fos. 24, 32-3; Smith, chapters 10-12; K. H. D. Haley, *The First Earl of Shaftesbury* (Oxford, 1968), pp. 684-704.

[11] J. R. Western, *Monarchy and Revolution: The English State in the 1680s* (1972), pp. 46-8, 69-77; Jennifer Levin, *The Charter Controversy in the City of London, 1660-1688, and its Consequences* (1969).

in their places by virtue of royal warrants. The apparatus of administration was thus retained, but the degree of electoral participation in the City's government was greatly curtailed. No elections of common councilmen were authorized, and no meetings of Common Council were summoned. Magistrates were appointed rather than elected, and the London electorate was savagely purged. Guild after guild was forced to surrender its charter, and as new charters were slowly issued, most Whigs and dissenters found their names removed from the approved lists of liveried electors.[12]

The City Tories were as surprised by this turn of events as the Whigs, and though many collaborated in the royal design at first, others were shocked by the suppression of the historic Corporation. Disillusioned London Tories who objected to the religious policies of Charles's Catholic successor received another blow when James II revamped his City government in 1686–7. Confident of the support of Whigs and dissenters for toleration, James appointed a score of them to the Court of Aldermen in place of Tory obstructionists; and he altered the livery lists again in corresponding fashion. Events were to demonstrate that these old critics of the Stuart crown would be no more co-operative than they had been in the past. The City Tories, on the other hand, had joined the City Whigs as victims of royal absolutism by the year of the Glorious Revolution. Theirs was to be the greater misfortune, because they were to suffer from the stigma of having stood by the crown in the critical years of 1679 to 1683. However much they may have disliked James by 1688, they were still subject to Whig damnation for having made the reign of a Catholic monarch possible.

The immediate flare-up of party strife in London after the Glorious Revolution was thus a resumption of the contest for power that had been curtailed in 1682–3. Moreover, disagreement over the locus of power in the Corporation was now just as much a personal matter as a constitutional problem. Dozens of Whig leaders and hundreds of Whig electors had personally experienced the loss of offices and rights in the face of Tory domination of the Court of Aldermen. Many Whigs were convinced that neither their political rights nor their lives were safe unless the City Tory leaders were made incapable of further involvement in the affairs

[12] Smith, chapters 13–14.

of the Corporation. These fears were understandable in view of the experiences of the 1680s and of the self-advertised Tory doubts about the legitimacy of the Williamite regime. A Whig pamphleteer of 1691 spoke for many when he observed that the Tory leaders in the City were 'unhang'd not because they deserv'd it not, but because they were not rewarded as they deserved'.[13]

The angry political clashes that marked the City's 'revolutionary crisis' of 1688–90 are examined in chapter two, but they will be introduced briefly here and in the subsequent sections of this chapter. One of the three principal goals of the revolutionary Whigs was that of discrediting the leaders of the City Tories. The Tories' disgrace was effected with the assistance of members of both houses of parliament, who were concerned to see the City placed in the hands of people of demonstrable loyalty to the new monarchy. Parliamentary committees made intensive examinations in 1689–90 of the political disturbances in London during Charles's reign, of the Rye House Plot executions, of the remodellings of the London livery, and of the trustworthiness of the London Lieutenancy commissioners. In the course of these investigations the past actions of several Tory magistrates and of dozens of Tory common councilmen were displayed in a most unfavourable light. Aldermen Sir John Moore and Sir James Smyth and former Sheriff Sir Dudley North were each condemned by the House of Commons for instances of unwarranted official conduct. Failing to go beyond these exemplary punishments, however, parliament did not satisfy the City Whigs' desire for revenge, and the embarrassment of the London Tory leaders failed to ensure their complete political eclipse.[14]

Nevertheless, the London Whigs repeatedly triumphed in the City elections of 1688–9, and in doing so they came within reach of another important revolutionary goal—that of gaining control of the London magistracy. A resumption of electoral activity in the City had been made possible by James's hasty restoration of the Corporation charter in October 1688.[15] This action also

---

[13] *A Petition to the Petitioners: or some queries put to the managers of the famous City Petition* (1691).

[14] DWL Morrice MS Q, 458–9, 477–8, 549 et seq., R, 129; Luttrell, *Brief Relation*, i. 500, 513–14, 560, ii. 560; HMC *House of Lords MSS, 1689–90*, pp. 109–200, 283–97; HMC *House of Lords MSS, 1690–91*, pp. 45–69; *CJ* x. 42 ff., 160, 388; Grey, *Debates*, x. 54–8, 67–73.

[15] DWL Morrice MS Q, 297, 302–3; *CSPD 1687–89*, p. 296; Richard Lapthorne, *The Portledge Papers*, eds. Russell J. Kerr and Ida Coffin Duncan (1928), pp. 47–8.

restored those aldermen who had been sitting on the bench in
1683 at the time of the charter forfeiture, eighteen of whom survived. The eight aldermanic vacancies thereby provided, plus
several additional vacancies caused by deaths and resignations
during the next year, gave the Whigs an unusual opportunity for
securing mastery of the Court of Aldermen. By vigorously con-
testing each aldermanic election, the Whigs managed to gain
effective control of the Court by October 1689. In the mean time,
Whig candidates succeeded against Tory opposition at each of
three critical Common Hall elections. In January 1689 the liverymen elected four Whigs as City MPs in the Convention Parliament. In March, Thomas Pilkington headed a poll for Lord Mayor
and was so designated by the Court of Aldermen. In June, Whig
candidates for the shrievalty and for the office of chamberlain
received the approval of the livery. Furthermore, the December
1689 wardmotes produced a Court of Common Council with a
narrow Whig majority.[16]

Finally ensconced as the dominant party within the magistracy,
the Whigs were also in a position to pursue their third revolutionary goal. This was a libertarian elimination of those oligarchic
features of the City constitution that had thwarted the Corporation electorate in the early 1680s. The Whigs failed to
accomplish this goal, though they did not fail for lack of trying. As
they knew, the passage of a statute confirming the Corporation's
privileges was made legally necessary by the uncertain legitimacy
of the charter's restoration by the writ of a dethroned king. The
City Whigs therefore submitted to parliament in March 1690
a draft bill of their own devising intended to confirm themselves
in office and to confirm the Corporation's charter.[17] As will be
demonstrated in chapter two, this draft was also intended to
secure the liberties of the electorate by transferring political power
in the Corporation from the Lord Mayor and the aldermen to
Common Council, Common Hall, and the urban electorate. Submitted to the Convention Parliament, this radical draft might

[16] One year after the restoration of the charter, the Court of Aldermen numbered
twelve Whigs and fourteen Tories; but two moderate Tories gave the Whigs an effective
aldermanic majority. For these elections, see DWL Morrice MS Q, 419-20; Luttrell, *Brief
Relation*, i. 542; *London Mercury*, 7-10 Jan. 1689; *Universal Intelligence*, 8-10 Jan. 1689. The
London Whigs also prevailed at another Common Hall in May 1689, when Sir William
Ashurst was elected to the Convention Parliament to replace the deceased William Love.

[17] Journal 51, fos. 33-6.

have won favour; but submitted to the 1690 Parliament, it stung the sensibilities of Tory MPs quickly recovering from their near paralysis during the Revolution. Suspect to many for making the City 'independent from Monarchy', the Whig draft received scant consideration, and in May 1690, parliament passed a Corporation of London Act much more to the City Tories' liking.[18]

The Whigs had lost in parliament, but the Tories were now to lose again in the City. The London Act required immediate elections, following traditional procedures, of a new Lord Mayor, chamberlain, sheriffs, and common councilmen. However, because of a defect in its language, the act did not technically require replacement of the fifteen sitting aldermen elected since 1688, although that had been the clear intention of the parliamentary Tories. In the elections held pursuant to the act, the London Tories regained superiority on the Common Council; but the Whigs narrowly retained the mayoral and shrieval offices which, with their existing aldermanic majority, sustained their magisterial dominance.[19] In terms of its stated purpose of 'settling' the Corporation, the London Act quickly proved a failure. Its passage was followed by a six-month period of rhetorical violence and political quarrelling in which the Tory leaders in the Corporation attempted to impede the management of City business by Whig magistrates whose authority they refused to acknowledge. This constitutional impasse was broken only after the defeat, in a close division, of a petition by the Tory Common Council majority to the House of Commons.[20]

By rejecting the petition of the City Tories, parliament dealt a blow to their confidence while at the same time confirming the legitimacy of the City Whigs' domination of the magistracy. As Tory enthusiasm ebbed, the London Whigs resecured their hegemony in the Corporation, complementing their working aldermanic majority with effective control of the Common Council by 1692. However, the Whig leaders accomplished but part of their revolutionary agenda in the early 1690s. They came to govern the Corporation under the same oligarchic constitution they had once

---

[18] *Statutes of the Realm* (1819), vi. 171–3 (2 W&M c8); Grey, *Debates*, x. 43; Henry Horwitz, *Parliament, Policy and Politics in the Reign of William III* (Manchester, 1977), pp. 56–7.

[19] Journal 51, fo. 45; DWL Morrice MS R, 151, 161; Luttrell, *Brief Relation*, ii. 47.

[20] DWL Morrice MS R, 222–3; Luttrell, *Brief Relation*, ii. 140–1; Horwitz, *Parliament, Policy and Politics*, p. 64.

condemned. Moreover, chastened by their experiences during the City's revolutionary crisis, the Whig leaders gradually discovered after 1690 that the possession of office was sweeter than the sponsorship of constitutional amendments. This surreptitious apostasy of the Whig magistrates from their erstwhile political principles could not fail to become obvious in time. In 1695 the grumblings of disillusioned liverymen broke into the open after a glaring instance of manipulation of Common Hall by the Whig magisterial élite. By then the Whig City leaders had clearly divorced themselves from the tradition of populist opposition in the Corporation. That tradition was to be inherited in Anne's reign by the City Tories who, with new leaders and new issues, would perpetuate the urban legacy of factionalism in the early eighteenth century.

2. The Nonconformist Presence

The volatile nature of the City's political life in the late Stuart era stemmed from a combination of social, economic, and religious conflicts. In the remaining sections of this chapter, each of these conflicts will be isolated and analysed in order to explain the origins of the factionalism that matured into the partisan competition of the 1690s and the 1700s. Pride of place must be accorded to the issue of religion, the most enduring and visible cause of contention in London. Unlike the Corporation's constitutional problem, which fluctuated enormously in its intensity over time, the friction between nonconformists and Church-Tory leaders was an abiding political irritant. This was so in part because the character of the national religious settlement long remained an open question, despite the intended finality of the early religious acts of the Cavalier Parliament. Neither the ecclesiastical establishment nor the principal dissenting spokesmen were happy with the Restoration settlement of religion or with such revisions as the 1673 Test Act or the 1689 Toleration Act. Churchmen and nonconformists of different persuasions hoped for further revisions of various sorts, and this diversity of intentions sowed much distrust among clerical leaders and lay representatives of all positions within and without the Church. Moreover, the conformity of many Civil War Puritans during the Restoration, whether sincere or not, left both the episcopal order and the dissenting remnants with the difficult task of re-defining their identities. In any case, religious tension was inevitable under a regime that had abandoned the objectives of religious uniformity without relinquishing the means of religious persuasion.

The uncertainty produced by this peculiar situation was nowhere more evident than in London, where nonconformists were concentrated in astonishing numbers. The size of the nonconformist population in the City and its environs may have approached 100,000, and the likelihood is that dissenters were increasing rather than declining in number in the last years of the seventeenth century.[21] If the numerical strength of dissent in London was exceptional, the wealth and social respectability of the dissenting élite were even more so. Whether one looks at the Court of Aldermen, or at the directorates of the great joint-stock companies, or at the magnates of London's overseas trade, one finds not just a few important dissenters but multitudes of them. These men and their families frequented the most flourishing of the eighty or more dissenting meeting-houses licensed in and about London in the decade after the Revolution. Anxious Tory squires at Westminster had not far to look, therefore, to see new tabernacles rising which appeared to challenge and overshadow those of the established church. By the middle of Anne's reign several of these City meeting-houses rivalled adjacent parish churches in the splendour of their fittings and in the opulence of their congregations.[22] Sir John Pakington, the long-serving Worcestershire MP, complained loudly in the Commons in 1705 about the visibility of nonconformist congregations in the City, noting that, 'Their Conventicles are now fuller than any of our Churches, and more attendance of coaches about them.'[23]

The Tory litany of complaint was inspired not merely by the social prominence of dissenters but also by an outburst after 1688 of political activity by nonconformists in London and in the provincial

---

[21] Geoffrey Holmes, *Religion and Party in Late Stuart England* (1975), pp. 13–14; Geoffrey Holmes, *The Trial of Doctor Sacheverell* (1973), p. 37.

[22] Geoffrey Holmes, 'The Sacheverell Riots: The Crowd and the Church in Early Eighteenth-Century London', *Past and Present*, 72 (1976), 63–4. Sources bearing upon the number of nonconformist churches established in the City and adjacent parishes after the Revolution include: BL Add. MS 32057, fo. 11; GL MS 9579; and Walter Wilson, *The History and Antiquities of Dissenting Churches and Meeting Houses in London, Westminster, and Southwark*, 4 vols. (1808–14).

[23] W. A. Speck, ed., 'An Anonymous Parliamentary Diary, 1705–06', *Camden Miscellany*, xxiii (Camden Society, 4th Ser., vii, 1969), appendix, 83.

towns. This development was only too reminiscent of the political activism of a more revolutionary generation of Puritans. In London, the revival of nonconformist political energy can be traced to the first clashes between parliamentary Whigs and Court followers during the Exclusion Crisis. Already the victims of a punitive ecclesiastical programme, the London dissenters were particularly fearful about the consequences of a Catholic succession, and were therefore hopeful that Shaftesbury's faction might prove amenable to a redress of their grievances.[24] Born amidst these great expectations, and confirmed in the days of their miscarriage, the Whig–nonconformist alliance bore its first fruit during the meeting of the Convention Parliament. In March 1689 the London dissenters subscribed in great numbers to a petition thanking William for his sympathy, in hopes of eliciting royal action on their behalf. In June the nonconformists pushed through Common Hall a petition to the Commons calling for a repeal of the sacramental test. Although the limited Toleration Act that had received crown assent by then continued the Test Act, toleration nevertheless proved a stimulant to the religious and political expressions of dissent in the city. The widespread practice of occasional conformity, or 'catholic communion', to use the nomenclature of the nonconformists, permitted many dissenters in London to overcome the legal obstacles to their enjoyment of civil office.[25] In fact, nonconformist political assertiveness and office-seeking were so pronounced after 1688 as to suggest that the Revolution inaugurated a veritable political renaissance for London dissenters.

The first hint of this development came before the Common Council elections of December 1688, when the London dissenters sought to have laid aside the oaths of supremacy and allegiance which were obnoxious to some among their number. This endeavour was unsuccessful, but over thirty known nonconformists who had no objections to the oaths were nevertheless elected, and, according to Presbyterian diarist Roger Morrice, potential common councilmen among the dissenters exceeded their Anglican

[24] Douglas R. Lacey, *Dissent and Parliamentary Politics in England, 1661-1689* (New Brunswick, NJ, 1969), pp. 121-9.

[25] DWL Morrice MS Q, 387, 524, 579-80; Luttrell, *Brief Relation*, i. 551; *A Seasonable Caution to all Loyal Subjects against Antimonarchical Principles* (1690); *True Account of the Proceedings of the Common-hall* (1689); John Flaningam, 'The Occasional Conformity Controversy: Ideology and Party Politics, 1687-1711', *JBS* xvii (1977), 38-62.

counterparts in number as well as in wealth.[26] Additional non-conformists were selected as common councilmen in subsequent years, and in most of the years of the 1690s at least 15 per cent of the Common Council can be connected to dissent. The presence of nonconformists among the magisterial élite was even more noticeable. In 1693, for instance, the Presbyterian Sir William Ashurst was chosen as one of several nonconformist Lord Mayors of William's and Anne's reigns. Ashurst took the occasion of his installation in office to defend the political conduct of his dissenting brethren, among whom were not a few of his aldermanic colleagues.[27] Indeed, in 1693 eight of the twenty-six sitting aldermen were either nonconformists or persons who had close family ties to dissent. These nonconformist office-holders were assisted in their quest for places by the large number of dissenting London electors who were especially concentrated among the overseas merchants and the 'middling sort' of traders and shopkeepers.

The vigour of nonconformist participation in Corporation affairs, together with its rather remarkable results, suggested to many that the Whig party and the dissenting electorate were virtually interchangeable political interests. The dissenters provided the Whigs with their most reliable political constituency, and the Whigs were quite often referred to as the 'dissenting party', and even as the 'fanaticks', in the first years after the Revolution. The triumph of the Whigs in the Corporation in the early 1690s thus secured for the London nonconformists precisely the political emancipation, though *de facto* in nature, that had been denied them by the cautious framers of the Toleration Act. This development, which also occurred in some provincial towns with sizeable dissenting populations, contributed to the genesis of such Anglican phobias as those voiced by Pakington.[28] In London the reaction against the nonconformist challenge was discernible as early as the March 1690 parliamentary election in which the 'church party' succeeded in electing four Tory City MPs in place of the four Whigs who had sat in the Convention. The successful Church candidates benefited in the poll from the exertions of

---

[26] DWL Morrice MS Q, 350, 387.

[27] Bodl. MS Carte 233, fo. 287; Luttrell, *Brief Relation*, iii. 197.

[28] Judith J. Hurwich, '"A Fanatick Town": The Political Influence of Dissenters in Coventry, 1660-1720', *Midland History*, 4 (1977), 15-47; John T. Evans, *Seventeenth-Century Norwich: Politics, Religion, and Government, 1620-1690* (Oxford, 1979), pp. 318 ff.

London parochial clergy resentful about the competition, now legal, of dissenting divines for the attention of their parishioners.[29] Such concerns grew more pronounced in the early 1690s in view of the mounting political success of dissent, and they were especially apparent in the London mayoral election of 1692. A Whig broadside put out before the 1692 mayoral election, for instance, complained about '*a lying Doctor* about *Aldgate*, running up and down under pretence of *a Circular Letter*, and crying out, *the Church, the Church; O the Church is betray'd into the hands of false Loons!*'[30]

Once established as an issue, the religious question was to persist as a fundamental element of London's political culture during the reigns of the last Stuarts. Here was a permanent cleft in the City's electorate and in its political leadership, a division that was always operative beneath the surface, even in such years as the mid-1690s and the first part of Anne's reign, when the Corporation was relatively free from overt partisan turmoil. Religious belief remained a significant factor influencing the electoral choices of London citizens in Common Hall and in the wards. Beginning in the last years of William's reign, religious feeling on both sides in the Corporation became demonstrably more intense. The 1697–8 mayoralty of the militant occasional conformist Sir Humphrey Edwin enlivened religious passions in the City, ignited the literary controversy on the subject of occasional conformity, and thereby contributed to the accelerating High-Church revolt of the parish clergy. After 1697 nonconformist activities in London and in other parliamentary boroughs rekindled the national debate over the ecclesiastical settlement. Infected by the religous rancour in these corporations, parliament and Convocation in turn stoked the fires of local religious animosity. Because the City had become the pre-eminent stage for a revived puritanism that placed 'the Church in danger', the Corporation of London became the *bête noire* of the Anglican apocalypse.

3. The Spoils of Trade

Second only to nonconformity as a source of discord in City life was a series of quarrels over foreign trade and investment oppor-

---

[29] Lapthorne, p. 67; *A Letter to a Friend in the Country* (1690); Henry Horwitz, 'The General Election of 1690', *JBS* xi (1971), 81, 84.

[30] *A Letter from a Country Gentleman, to an Eminent but Easy Citizen* (1692). Also see: KAO Chevening MS 78, R. Yard to A. Stanhope, 11 Oct. 1692; *Advice to the Livery-Men of London, in their Choice of a Lord-Mayor, on Michaelmas Day, 1692* (1692).

tunities. From their beginnings in the late 1670s these commercial disputes raised important political and even constitutional questions, and for that reason they fed, and were in turn fed by, the political factionalism in the City. These mercantile tensions arose at least in part from the fact that the 1688 Revolution was preceded by an era of unprecedented prosperity for the London overseas traders.[31] As the volume of London commerce expanded in the Restoration decades, old issues about the organization and direction of the country's trade were again debated. One of these issues was the legitimacy of commercial monopolies sanctioned by royal charter but not endorsed by parliament. A related question was that of freedom of access to those trades that had been assigned either to joint-stock companies like the East India and Royal African Companies, or to closed regulated companies like those that traded to the Levant and to Russia. In the latter trades, participation could be limited by restrictive admissions policies, while in the former trades access was circumscribed by the finite size of the companies' stocks. A third concern was whether trade was best conducted by means of such corporate bodies at all, or whether the nation's commerce would not better be advanced by opening trades to all comers, a situation already characteristic of the flourishing colonial sector. The first of these problems was overtly a constitutional one, while the others also touched upon the crown's prerogative of regulating trading activities as it deemed best.

The discussion of these issues by London merchants and by interested MPs was further enlivened by two additional considerations. The first of these was a desire that foreign policy be made in a manner that facilitated the expansion of overseas commerce. In London this matter was explicitly addressed in the days of Charles II's pro-French machinations by fourteen mercantile petitioners who astutely foresaw the danger from increased French commercial competition.[32] Their petition reflected broader concerns among City merchants about the crown's regard for trade, concerns that could easily be inflamed by crown critics. A second factor bearing on the discussion of trading issues was the enlargement of the number of active merchants in the City, an

[31] Ralph Davis, 'English Foreign Trade, 1660-1700', *EcHR*, 2nd Ser., vii (1954), 150-66.
[32] Priestley, 'London Merchants and Opposition Politics'.

increase that was directly attributable to the expanding opportunities of a vigorous commercial economy. By 1680 the size and the wealth of the London mercantile community had grown to such an extent that the existing merchant companies were no longer adequate to satisfy the demand for investment and trading opportunities.[33] This situation encouraged criticisms of the restrictive privileges of such corporate bodies, and it also stimulated interloping activities by enterprising private merchants. All that was necessary to transform these budding commercial problems into political issues was for the privileged joint stocks to adopt a defensive posture in closer alliance with the crown, and for dissatisfied merchants to look to the parliamentary opposition for redress. This division of the London merchants along the emerging Whig–Tory axis was a natural one in view of the constitutional implications of their central concerns, and the division had become apparent by the time of the Revolution.

The progressive politicization of merchant opinion can best be seen in the public dispute over the conduct of the lucrative East India trade, a dispute which gained momentum in the 1670s and which continued unabated for the next quarter century.[34] Foes of the Company who complained that its capital stock was too small and that its policies were determined by too few investors launched a capital subscription for a new company in 1681–2, only to be disappointed by the old Company's receipt of a new royal charter in 1683. Meanwhile, the governing clique of Sir Josiah Child and friends outmanœuvred Deputy Governor Thomas Papillon, a leading City Whig, and other internal critics who were prepared to bring in additional investors through a new capital subscription.[35] Indebted to the Court for the security of their new charter, Child and the East India Company's directorate thereby wedded themselves to the Tory position of support for the crown. Selling out of the stock, Papillon and a number of followers joined the

[33] Kenneth G. Davies, 'Joint-Stock Investment in the Later Seventeenth Century', *EcHR*, 2nd Ser., iv (1952), 283–301.

[34] D. W. Jones, 'London Overseas Merchant Groups at the End of the Seventeenth Century, and the Move against the East India Company' (Oxford D. Phil. thesis, 1971); P. Loughead, 'The East India Company in English Domestic Politics, 1657–88' (Oxford D. Phil. thesis, 1981); Arnold A. Sherman, 'Pressure from Leadenhall: The East India Company Lobby, 1660–1678', *Business History Review*, 50 (1976), 329–55.

[35] Loughead, pp. 163–74; William R. Scott, *The Constitution and Finance of English, Scottish and Irish Joint-Stock Companies to 1720* (Cambridge, 1910), ii. 139–49.

Company's external critics in making disenchantment with the East Indies trade a characteristic of London whiggism. By the time of the Revolution, then, the East India controversy was beginning to assume the proportions of a party wrangle, at least as far as many London merchants and investors were concerned. A body of established investors, largely Tory in sympathy, monopolized the East India stock to the near exclusion of new men with money to invest, who largely drifted towards the Whigs. Although discernible, this division was not absolute because the Company's stockholders continued to include a sizeable number of Whig and nonconformist investors.[36]

What was true of the East India Company was also true of two other stocks, the African and the Hudson's Bay Companies. Like the larger Indian concern, each of these companies continued to include some Whig traders and financiers, but they were also exposed to Whig attack because of their royal charters and because of the Tory proclivities of their principal investors. That attack came in the City and in parliament from 1689 on, as the nation considered the commercial implications of the Revolutionary Settlement.

The East India Company at first managed to retain its standing, doing so despite repeated parliamentary scrutiny of its operations and despite the opposition of a rival London mercantile syndicate. William granted the Company a new royal charter in 1693, and the Company offered an additional capital subscription to the public for the sake of bringing in new investors. Among those who subscribed for stock at this juncture were many former City critics, but neither the issuance of the new charter nor the floating of the new subscription silenced the Company's many remaining mercantile opponents. Similarly, in the wake of the Revolution, the Royal African Company sought to re-anchor its monopoly on the sound bottom of a parliamentary grant, but its efforts were repeatedly frustrated by the diverse criticisms of several hostile interests. The Hudson's Bay Company did manage to secure statutory confirmation of its privileges, but its enemies succeeded in limiting the grant to seven years. Only the moribund Eastland Company fell completely as the easiest sacrifice to arguments for freer trade. It lost its monopoly by action of parliament in 1689, and thereafter it declined into virtual non-existence.[37]

[36] See chapter 3, section 3 and chapter 4, section 2.
[37] Kenneth G. Davies, *The Royal African Company* (1957), pp. 101 ff., 122 ff.; Kenneth G.

Little if any co-ordination lay behind the activities of the London antagonists of these different corporate concerns in the 1690s, but their opposition was nevertheless linked through a common commercial rationale and through a common whiggish perspective. The dominant City critics of the old monopolies came from the ranks of the Whig magistracy and of the great Whig merchants, while many of their chief City defenders were Tory aldermen and Tory common councilmen. In other words, many of the party men who competed for power in the Corporation in the 1690s were concurrently wrestling with one another for trading rights and opportunities. Political rivalries in the City were reinforced by commercial jealousies.

The rivalries within the City's trading and investing élite became even more obviously partisan as the decade wore on and as William's war dragged on inconclusively. Among the domestic complications of the Nine Years War were two problems that contributed further to the Whig sympathies of many active London merchants and that also strengthened the bonds between them and the Whig ministerial Junto. The first of these was the wartime disruption of trading activities by French naval operations and privateering. Shipping losses were exceptionally severe under the Carmarthen–Nottingham ministry, and by 1694 the City reputations of these and of other Tory statesmen were badly damaged.[38] Secondly, the dislocation of trade produced a capital glut in the City, as many traders withdrew their stock from commercial employment. This served both to aggravate the previous dissatisfaction with alternative investment opportunities and to fuel the joint-stock boom of the 1690s, an event which saw the number of national stock ventures increase by 1695 from eleven to almost one hundred.[39] The most important of these new stocks was the Bank of England, which was authorized by parliament in

Davies, 'Introduction' to *Hudson's Bay Copy Booke of Letters Commissions Instructions Outward 1688–1696*, ed. E.E. Rich (Hudson's Bay Record Society, xx, 1957), xxvi–xxxvi; E. E. Rich, *The History of the Hudson's Bay Company, 1670–1870* (Hudson's Bay Record Society, xxi, 1958), i. 266–9; Henry Horwitz, 'The East India Trade, the Politicians, and the Constitution: 1689–1702', *JBS* xvii (1978), 1–7; R. W. K. Hinton, *The Eastland Trade and the Common Weal in the Seventeenth Century* (Cambridge, 1959), pp. 156–61.

[38] KAO Chevening MS 78, R. Yard to A. Stanhope, 1 Aug. 1698 and 21 Nov. 1693; Bodl. Newdigate Newsletters for 17 June 1693 and 4, 22, 27 July 1693; HMC *House of Lords MSS*, New Ser., i. 190–3; Luttrell, *Brief Relation*, iii. 141–2; 225; Horwitz, *Parliament, Policy and Politics*, pp. 116, 126, 132.

[39] Davies, 'Joint-Stock Investment', p. 292.

1694 at the instigation of Charles Montagu, the Junto's 'projector-general'. Created to facilitate the public finance of the extraordinary expenses of war, the new institution rested upon a stock subscription that was quickly taken up with the idle capital of the City's merchant community. Furthermore, from the Bank's inception, its directors were drawn from the same commercial interests that dominated the Whig magistracy in the Corporation, and its subscription also marked the beginning of the entrenchment of the Whig 'moneyed interest' in the new public debt.

The public debt was enlarged by other Junto measures that culminated in a complicated 1698 attempt to turn the East India trade to public advantage. In that year the East India Company was outmanœuvred in the Commons by a newly organized syndicate of City merchants who, with the encouragement of the Junto, succeeded in securing a parliamentary charter to conduct the East India trade. The act that authorized the incorporation of this New East India Company did not automatically deprive the Old Company of its existence and resources, but its future was nevertheless jeopardized. The New Company, like the Bank, was created through a public subscription of capital that was lent in its entirety to William's financially pressed government. Like the Bank, the directorate and shareholders of the New Company were overwhelmingly Whig in their political sympathies.[40] Other important changes in the organization of trade that pleased the City's Whig merchants were also authorized by parliament before the century's end. In 1697 and in 1698, the Hudson's Bay Company and the Royal African Company respectively were deprived by parliament of their exclusive privileges. In the following year, the stagnant Russia Company also found its monopoly broken by an organization of tobacco re-exporters, Whigs almost to a man, who had gained support at Westminster and at the court of Peter the Great.[41].

This rapid transformation of the City's trading and financial institutions in the 1690s signalled the successful rise of a new Whig mercantile and financial oligarchy. Once the party of popular opposition in the Corporation, by the mid-1690s the City Whigs

[40] Horwitz, 'East India Trade', pp. 8-12.
[41] Davies, *African Company*, pp. 132-5; Rich, *Hudson's Bay Company*, i. 355-67; Jacob M. Price, *The Tobacco Adventure to Russia* (Transactions of the American Philosophical Society, New Ser., li. part 1, Philadelphia, 1961), 37-47.

were becoming the party of new wealth. Their commercial successes were envied and resented by Tory investors whose wealth
and status were damaged through the defeats suffered by the Old
East India Company and by other long-established trading concerns. This resentment was expressed in both Corporation and
parliamentary politics in the last years of William's reign. In
those years, the politics of the City reflected a fairly clear division
between a City Whig–Bank–New Company complex, on the one
hand, and a City Tory–Old Company complex, on the other.
This division was certainly modified by other considerations, but
the City's political rivalries and its commercial jealousies overlapped to a much greater extent from 1698 to 1702 than had
previously been the case. For instance, the Whigs' effective aldermanic majority, which had depended upon the co-operation of a
few maverick Tory aldermen, dissolved after 1698 when these
Tories, all three directors of the Old Company, became far less
reliable allies. This alignment of City Whigs and City Tories on
opposite sides of the East India issue was paralleled in the Commons, where the same question also became a clearly partisan one
by 1698.[42]

The centrality of the new joint-stock rivalry in the City's politi-
cal life was also evident in the first general election following the
Old Company's triumph in securing parliamentary support. In
London, the election of January 1701 saw the keenest contest for
Commons seats since the parliamentary election of 1690. Two
New Company directors were among the Whigs' four Common
Hall nominees, three of whom were also directors of the Bank of
England. The four Tory candidates defeated by those put up by
the Whigs included three directors of the Old East India Com-
pany, one of whom, Sir John Fleet, was also its past governor.[43]
In other constituencies, as in London, the New Company was by
far the more successful in returning its directors and sympathizers

---

[42] Horwitz, 'East India Trade', pp. 12–18. The three maverick Tory aldermen were
Sir John Fleet, Sir Francis Child, and Sir William Hedges.

[43] The City MP candidates promoted by the parties in January 1701 were: (1) Whig
(elected): Sir William Ashurst (Bank), Sir Robert Clayton (Bank), Gilbert Heathcote
(Bank, New Company), Sir William Withers (New Company); (2) Tory: Sir Francis
Child (Old Company), Sir John Fleet (Old Company), Sir William Prichard (Old Company), Sir Charles Duncombe. Sir William Withers, promoted by the Whigs in this election, was actually a Tory; but his involvement in the New East India Company made him
acceptable to the Whigs.

to the 1701 House of Commons, though not without a noticeable resort to bribery. Thereafter, some of the steam went out of the East India controversy. The two companies entered into serious negotiations in the summer of 1701, and they agreed in January 1702 upon terms for their subsequent merger.[44] Nevertheless, the City parliamentary elections of November 1701 and of July 1702 both followed that of January 1701 in exhibiting the association of Whigs with the New Company and the Bank, and the association of Tories with the Old Company.

Some observers hoped that the 1702 accord between the two India Companies would lead to a fading of the East India issue from London affairs and to a moderation of political differences in the City.[45] Such hopes were, however, far too sanguine. The East India accord did lead to a lessening of City tensions in the first years of Anne's reign, but friction between adherents of the two Companies did not cease before their 1708 merger. In any case, the dismantling of old monopolies, the creation of new joint stocks, and the establishment of a public debt were already by 1702 nurturing the 'moneyed interest' that would be so strenuously attacked by the popular Tory civic opposition of the early eighteenth century.

4. War and Peace

England's involvement in the Nine Years War began almost unnoticed in the first months after the 1688 Revolution, but the war was soon to have dramatic repercussions at home. The war interrupted a period of exceptional prosperity for London's overseas merchants. It also drained the country of money, drove up prices, required a variety of new taxes and revenue schemes, and made necessary a national re-coinage. Each of these domestic consequences of the war contributed to the seriousness of parliamentary debate about its prosecution, and altogether they made the success of the allied armies a matter of utmost concern in the City. Moreover, the war directly affected the development of party conflict in post-Revolutionary London. The vulnerability of the country to French attack in the early years of the war placed a

---

[44] Robert Walcott, 'The East India Interest and the General Election of 1700–1701', *EHR* lxxi (1956), 223–39; Horwitz, 'East India Trade', p. 17; Scott, i. 367–8, ii. 168–71.
[45] *Flying Post*, no. 1154, 26–9 Sept. 1702.

high premium on the attainment of internal quiet and order, especially in London—vital as it was to the crown's finances. This was realized very quickly by the country's new warrior king, and somewhat belatedly by the City magistrates of both parties. Although this war and its successor ultimately increased the tensions in late Stuart party conflict, the Nine Years War nevertheless led to five years of relative political peace in the Corporation (under Whig aegis), beginning in 1691.

That this would prove the case was scarcely predictable in the first years of William and Mary's reign. Far from inducing Londoners to forget their party quarrels, the war seemed before the autumn of 1690 merely to provide them with additional reasons for venting their distrust of one another. Among the factors in the revival of factionalism after the Revolution was the Whig belief that London could not be secure in wartime unless those Tory leaders who had co-operated with the exiled James II were excluded from City government. The Whigs became even more fearful when they discovered that William was not only oblivious to such suspicions but was also prepared to promote a party balance in London.[46] The king relied upon the subscription loans sponsored by the Corporation to provide short-term credit for war expenses, and his chief concern for the City by 1690 was to prevent the party conflict there from interfering with his money-raising efforts. By establishing his impartiality towards the London parties William hoped to ensure the active support of both Whig and Tory lenders for his campaigns; but his steps in this direction, misread by each party, served only to inflame further the political passions in the City in the summer and fall of that year. The Whigs became more desperate for fear of losing royal support, while the Tories became more determined in expectation of gaining it.

Tory determination and Whig desperation were especially evident in the climactic constitutional impasse that interrupted Corporation activities after the passage of the defective City of London Act. The more the Tories struggled to achieve the original purposes of the London Act, the more they encouraged Whig portrayals of themselves as irresponsible abetters of the country's enemies. The resort to a petition to the Commons by over one hundred Tory stalwarts among the aldermen and com-

---

[46] Horwitz, *Parliament, Policy and Politics*, p. 50.

mon councilmen eventually forced a parliamentary resolution of this crisis in December 1690. The Tory petitioners, however, succeeded only in confirming the fears of Whigs who believed that their efforts were a ruse to distract the attention of MPs from the more important task of supplying William's campaign against the 'Universal Despotic Monarchy' of Louis XIV. According to one pamphleteer, as the eyes of foreign Protestants turned to the English parliament for succour, the Tory petitioners were indulging in 'a *Propense Contrivance*, to renter *Abortive* the *Wistful Expectation* of All *Europe*'.[47] The diarist Narcissus Luttrell agreed when he wrote, after the failure of the petition, that it 'would have obstructed the publick affairs of the nation, in giving money, and the like weighty matters'.[48]

The disappointment of the City Tories at Westminster also dashed their reviving political fortunes in the Corporation. Already vulnerable to charges of acceding to Stuart absolutism, the Tory leaders could no longer afford factious behaviour that might be construed as disloyalty in time of war. The City Whigs suffered from no such handicaps for the moment, and William was aware by 1690 that the Whigs were far more generous in responding to his appeals for money than were the Tories. As the London Whigs established their hegemony over the Corporation, they did so as the party best equipped for fashioning the war-time alliance between City money and the revenue departments of the government. The success of the Whigs, the embarrassment of the Tories, and the uncertainties of war therefore combined to weaken the party enthusiasm of 1689–90. Perhaps to the discomfiture of intemperate Tory veterans, younger moderate Churchmen like Sir John Fleet and Sir Francis Child acquiesced in the Whig ascendancy. These Tory aldermen and many of their Whig colleagues hoped now to avoid divisive confrontations in the Corporation for the duration of the war. Agents of the commercial élite, they became devotees of political order, subordinating, though not abandoning, the dictates of partisanship to those of magistracy. In 1695, when many liverymen revolted against magisterial manipulation of shrieval elections and thereby imperilled political order in the Corporation, Whig aldermen had no reason to suspect the complicity of their Tory colleagues. The

[47] *Reflections upon the Late Famous Petition, and the Well Timing of It* (1691).
[48] Luttrell, *Brief Relation*, ii. 141.

same war-time concern for political stability may account for the failure of any City figure to exploit immediately the financial crisis of 1695–6, an interval of economic instability which terminated the prospects of dozens of the new minor stocks. Not until 1697, the year of the war's end, was the Corporation again disturbed by Whig–Tory conflict to the same extent as in the early 1680s or in the two years that followed the Revolution. The attainment of peace provided Londoners with the security to indulge anew in political debate, and the political disappointments and the economic injuries suffered by populist guildsmen during the first 'Whig' war then began to have partisan consequences.

The impact of the war of William's reign upon politics in the City and at Westminster was in fact far more extensive than this mid-1690s' diminishment of partisanship in London. The war also made necessary the establishment of a public debt, and the City made available the capital to fund the debt. Raising many suspicious eyebrows in parliament before 1697, this new debt was to prove a source of recurrent argument thereafter. Its very existence was unacceptable to country gentlemen who argued, with little exaggeration, that the public debt was in reality an intolerable burden owed by themselves to London merchants and financiers of the Whig persuasion. Furthermore, in the City, as Whig investors profitably tied their financial futures to that of the government, they also unintentionally dovetailed the party division in London with an important urban sociological rift. Beginning at the time of the debt's creation during the Nine Years War, there first became detectable an evolving split of the urban electorate between prosperous Whig retailers and overseas traders, with money in the Bank or the funds, and declining or immobile Tory shopkeepers and petty tradesmen, with marginal prospects. Once established, this pattern was to endure as a stable feature of late Stuart London politics.[49]

The war of this reign and that of the next also wrought a fundamental change in the relationship between the City and the national regime. The Corporation became but one agency in a proliferating matrix of City institutions, most of them financial or commercial in nature, and most of them related in one way or another

[49] Dame Lucy Sutherland, 'The City of London in Eighteenth-Century Politics', in *Essays Presented to Sir Lewis Namier*, eds. Richard Pares and A. J. P. Taylor (1956), pp. 49–74; Rogers, 'Resistance to Oligarchy'.

to the debt, which bound Londoners and their money to the government. As these new links were established between the City and the state, the Corporation lost some of its importance in the eyes of government ministers and of commercial magnates who aspired to national influence. William was the last English monarch who needed to rely upon the Corporation to organize public credit, and by the end of Anne's reign Bank directors wielded more influence in national affairs than did City aldermen. Nevertheless, the Bank, the India Companies, and the other London stocks remained associated with the Corporation in a single City polity. Feuds in the Corporation spilled over into other spheres of City activity and vice versa, and the entire archipelago of enterprises rising from the sea of debt became objectionable to simple freeman who derived no advantages from them and who resented the wealth of those who did. The metamorphosis of the City, which was initiated by the war of the 1690s, and which created the power and wealth of the eighteenth-century London Whig élite, therefore also prepared the way for the Tory alliance between urban plebs and country squires.

In the years of the Peace of Ryswick (1697–1702), these ramifications of the concluded war of William's reign were only dimly foreseen even by perceptive Londoners; but the conduct of foreign policy nevertheless proved more controversial than before. By 1701 the possibility of another war separated resolute City Whigs from restrained City Tories, and the contradictory perspectives of the parties on foreign policy gave added impetus to their contest in the Corporation. For instance, dismayed by William's resort to a Tory ministry, the London Whigs promoted in 1701 a City address to the crown on the state of the nation, finally carrying it against Tory opposition after Louis XIV's recognition of the Pretender.[50] This incident, and others like it, suggest that the coming of the War of the Spanish Succession contributed as greatly to the revival of London party spirit at the end of William's reign as the duration of the Nine Years War had previously discouraged it. Nevertheless, as the war of 1702 began, the party conflict in London ebbed, just as it had after 1691. The magisterial consensus of mid-1690s was

[50] Journal 53, fo. 123; BL Add. MS 40775, fo. 79, J. Vernon to William III, 19 Aug. 1701 and fo. 221, J. Vernon to William III, 30 Sept. 1701; Luttrell, *Brief Relation* v. 94; *Post Boy*, 27–30 Sept. 1701; *Flying Post*, 30 Sept.–2 Oct. 1701; Horwitz, *Parliament, Policy and Politics*, p. 295.

re-established in the early part of Anne's reign, as patriotism took precedence over party divisions without removing them. When this consensus disintegrated again after 1707, disagreement over the purposes, scope, and financing of Britain's continental military endeavours was among the causes of Whig–Tory acrimony. War was an issue and an economic reality that affected all Londoners regardless of their wealth, and its ultimate impact upon London politics was divisive rather than cohesive.

5. *Whitehall and Westminster*

This discussion of the origins of party conflict in London has several times called attention to the larger political environment of which the City was a part. Partisanship could not have taken root in London unless it had sprouted from indigenous seeds of conflict, but neither could it have flourished unless it had been fertilized frequently with the rich national humus of constitutional debate and political instability. Because of its size, its location, and its economic importance, the City of London was uniquely exposed to political pressures and suggestions emanating from Whitehall and Westminster. The crown and its ministers, the Commons and the Lords, intervened now and again in London politics with varying degrees of success. Even without intending to do so, ministers and MPs might substantially influence political discussion in the Corporation because the very issues of their own debate were promptly aired in the City. Moreover, the meeting of each new parliament and the nature of each major ministerial change led to adjustments in the relationship between London and the regime as well as to alterations in the political climate within the City. The politics of London were so closely bound to those of the nation that parliamentary figures and ministers could become principal actors in the political processes of the City. The presence of such extra-metropolitan agents or influences was especially disruptive in those years when one party dominated the City magistracy while the other party dominated the ministry.

Perhaps these generalizations will gain in clarity through an investigation of a few late seventeenth-century examples of royal, ministerial, and parliamentary involvement in City politics. The most controversial form of executive intrusion in the affairs of the Corporation was the calculated interference by the crown or its agents in elections or other political processes. James, for instance, had unsuccessfully sought to stem the erosion of his popular support in London by discouraging Lord Mayor Sir John Chapman from summoning a meeting of Common Council after the restoration of the Corporation's charter. Shortly thereafter, at the time of the December 1688 wardmotes, William or his chief noble supporters attempted, over the objections of Chapman, to promote the return of sympathetic nonconformists as common councilmen.[51]

Ministers also interfered in Corporation affairs, with or without royal authorization, in order to secure their own ends in the City. Lord Nottingham, Secretary of State in the early 1690s, was especially inclined to do so. His political intrusions in London affairs well illustrate, however, the uncertain outcome of ministerial intervention in the City. By the time of his 1693 dismissal, the Church-Tory Secretary had good reason to regret his confrontations with the Whig magistrates, who had by then come to see him as a more formidable opponent than the flagging City Tories. Nottingham first intervened in the City in July 1690 on behalf of the Tory alderman of Dowgate ward, whose recent contested declaration of the election of several Tory common councilmen was voided by the Whig-dominated bench. On behalf of his Whig colleagues, Lord Mayor Sir Thomas Pilkington refused to comply with an order from the Secretary that reinstated the Dowgate Tories. Pilkington also wasted little time in treating Queen Mary to a personal display of verbal pyrotechnics and in firing off a 'very briske Letter' to the Secretary himself. A second order from Nottingham concerning a similar dispute in Aldersgate ward was treated with equal contempt by the Whig magistrates. By the end of the summer the aldermanic decisions regarding the Common Council representation of these two wards had become a principal grievance of the Tory common councilmen who obstructed the conduct of Corporation business for the remainder of the year. Seeking to defuse the developing political confrontation in the City in 1690, Nottingham had instead embroiled himself in the controversy.[52]

---

[51] DWL Morrice MS Q, 328-9, 387; *London Courant*, 18-22 Dec. 1688.

[52] DWL Morrice MS R, 161, 176, 183; Repertory 95, fos. 153-4 et seq.; BL Add. MS 61690, fos. 76-7; *CSPD 1690-91*, p. 80; *The Case of Dowgate and Aldersgate Wards, and the matters in question between the Court of Aldermen, and the Common Council thereupon* (1690).

Similar scenes occurred in the Corporation in the autumn of 1692 when the Secretary again unwisely ventured into City politics on the occasion of the mayoral election. Nottingham suffered a 'great disappointment' when two strong Churchmen among the aldermen fell behind their Whig-sponsored rivals in the mayoral poll.[53] Lending his assistance to the friends of episcopacy in the City, the Secretary ordered the arrest of two liverymen responsible for circulating printed sheets critical of the Church-Tory candidates. His action was not well received in the City, where at the next Common Council a motion was debated for a petition against this infringement upon the Corporation's legal jurisdiction. The matter was eventually dropped after the appointment of a committee of investigation, but it was not without important consequences. The affair prompted the City Whigs to show their support for Nottingham's enemies in the ministry and in parliament by publicly feasting the most prominent of those critics, Admiral Edward Russell, the future Junto Lord.[54] Moreover, by making the Secretary so odious in the City, this new incident, following those of 1690, helped establish the popular assumption of his culpability for the series of wartime mishaps that culminated in the mangling of the unprotected Smyrna trading fleet by French naval squadrons in 1693. The outburst against the Secretary in the City on that occasion added to the pressures that obligated William to dismiss him in November 1693. Nottingham's meddlings in the affairs of the Corporation are thus model illustrations of how ministerial encroachment might upset those affairs and might even have repercussions affecting the ministry itself.

Subtler means for exerting influence or for cultivating support in London were available to the government, but these also could have unintended results. The appointment of individuals prominent in the Corporation to coveted places and honours could easily be given a partisan bias by the crown and its ministers in order to inform the London electors of those who presently enjoyed royal confidence. For instance, during William's initial year of reliance upon the Whigs, he made clear his approval of the City Whig leaders in his deliberate appointments of some of them to the

---

[53] BL Loan 29/186, fo. 139, P. Foley to R. Harley, 1 Oct. 1692.

[54] Journal 51, fos. 221-3; Luttrell, *Brief Relation*, ii. 616, 620, 624, 631; HMC *Finch MSS* iv. 496; Henry Horwitz, *Revolution Politicks: The Career of Daniel Finch, Second Earl of Nottingham* (Cambridge, 1968), pp. 130-9.

Customs and Excise Commissions and in the knighthoods he conferred upon others at Sir Thomas Pilkington's mayoral show.[55] Because many liverymen, even sophisticated ones, had as great a regard for the crown's wishes as for those of partisan City leaders, they were quite sensitive to such signals apparent in the distribution of royal favour.

The surest guide to the monarch's pleasure was the composition of the London Lieutenancy, held in commission under the crown, and seven times altered between 1689 and 1715. The commissions of William's reign, announced in 1689, 1690, and 1694, followed the formation of new governments and placed the City's trained bands in the hands of persons well disposed towards the king's ministers. Each alteration of the Lieutenancy also reversed the party preponderance on the commission in the expectation of influencing the outcome of electoral decisions in the Corporation. The commissions of 1689 and of 1694, which added many City Whigs to the Lieutenancy and which removed many leading Tories, promoted the interests of Whig magistrates and office-seekers and harmonized well with the prevailing Whig mood of the electors.[56] The issuance of the 1690 commission with its preponderance of Tories, however, became another factor in that year's party confrontation in the Corporation. It angered the City Whigs without weakening their zeal, and it stimulated the reviving spirits of their Tory rivals. It influenced the outcome of the 1690 City MP election, which was carried by the Tories, and it provoked debates in the Commons and an investigation in the Lords.

Just as the crown and its ministers could upset the tranquillity of the Corporation, so could members of parliament by their individual or collective actions. Because so many City merchants sat for other constituencies, and because so many MPs were well versed in the affairs of the City, the potential for overlapping political disputation was great. In years of political crisis, like 1640–2 or 1679–81, the boundaries between politics at Westminster and politics in London dissolved, as parliamentary politicians inflamed political tempers in the City through their encouragement

---

[55] *CSPD 1689–90*, p. 53; Luttrell, *Brief Relation*, i. 597.

[56] Members of the 1689 Lieutenancy commission are in HMC *House of Lords MSS, 1690–91*, pp. 45–7. Members of the 1690 commission are in *A List of the Commissioners of Lieutenancy of the City of London* (1690). (The list in *CSPD 1689–90*, pp. 501–2 is defective.) Members of the 1694 commission are in *CSPD 1694–95*, p. 21.

of extra-parliamentary demonstrations and petitions. Even in less extraordinary times, parliamentary feuds spilled over into the Corporation, as when ambitious politicians like Admiral Russell solicited civic support. Moreover, the frequent necessity for parliamentary adjudication of the City's commercial and political problems provided many opportunities for the exploitation of those problems at Westminster. That this would happen in 1690 was almost inevitable, since the uncertain legal status of the Corporation after the Revolution made its very existence dependent upon parliamentary action. The nature of that action was in turn determined by the results of the 1690 general election which, more than any other event, delayed the establishment of Whig control over the Corporation that had seemed so assured in 1689. The City Whigs had in that year been able to count upon the sympathy of the Convention Parliament, but in 1690 they were nearly undone by the enmity of Church-Tory MPs. By their votes on the London Act, the Tories in the Commons gave their City friends grounds for hope; by their oversights in preparing a defective bill, they made certain the confusion in the City that followed the sudden May adjournment of the session.

Parliament's attention to the City's constitution in 1690 became another precipitant of the partisan stand-off in London because it was inflammatory without being conclusive. Having demonstrated its capacity for unhinging public affairs in the Corporation, parliament was incapable of putting things straight until it was recalled to work in October. Meanwhile, the City parties railed against each other for several months without parliamentary adjudication. Neither William, who was absent in Ireland, nor Nottingham proved capable of dealing with the party conflict in the capital. Resolution of the crisis depended upon a clarification by parliament of its own intentions in the London Act, a clarification that did not come until December, and which then came in a manner that surprised many observers.[57] Within its first year of existence, therefore, the 1690 Parliament had both generated and sustained party conflict in the City through action followed by inaction.

No other episode in the City's history until Walpole's 1725 City Elections Act so starkly revealed the influence of Westminster

[57] Horwitz, *Parliament, Policy and Politics*, p. 64.

upon London's political life, and that influence remained detectable through the following years in sundry guises. Lingering
anxiety over the London Lieutenancy led to a renewal of the
Lord's investigation of that body in 1693, but the investigation
was too brief to have serious repercussions in the Corporation.[58]
The virtual bankruptcy of the City's Chamber required an act of
parliament in 1694 to regulate Corporation finances, but this
problem had little partisan significance.[59] It was really in its
regulation of commerce rather than in its oversight of the Corporation *per se* that parliament decisively intruded upon City political
affairs for the rest of the 1690s. By facilitating the establishment of
new trading concerns at the expense of obsolete monopolies, parliament re-fashioned the organization of London commerce. These
improvements, together with parliament's creation of the Bank
and the government funds, altered the institutional fabric of City
politics as the commercial revolution continued and as England's
'financial revolution' began. Finally, by the end of the decade, the
politics of London were clearly showing the first effects of a novel
departure in parliamentary politics. The unprecedented series of
frequent general elections that began in 1698, three years after
William's hesitant acceptance of the Triennial Act, regularly permitted the electors of London and those of other constituencies to
express their attitudes towards the personalities and the issues
that dominated discussion in the Commons. In London, where
the selection of Corporation office-holders provided the liverymen
with much electoral excitement, the contests for the City's places
in parliament now became howling vortices in the partisan
tempests that periodically blew through the City.

6. *The People in Politics*

A final ingredient of party conflict in London was the large, articulate, and restless City electorate, which was accustomed to regular
participation in Corporation affairs. Informed, increasingly sensitive to constitutional and economic issues, and enthusiastic in
defence of their 'antient rights', the people were an independent
variable in the development of party politics. The people could be

[58] Ibid., p. 111; Luttrell, *Brief Relation*, iii. 39, 41; *LJ* xv. 238-40.
[59] John R. Kellett, 'The Financial Crisis of the Corporation of London and the
Orphans' Act, 1694', *The Guildhall Miscellany*, ii (1963), 220-7.

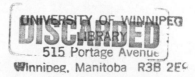

cajoled by the City party leaders. They could be guided and even inflamed by them, but they could not be controlled by either party. Popular support was the greatest asset in the contest for political power in London, but it could not be taken for granted, as the Whigs were to discover in the 1690s. The electorate were quick to detect betrayal at the hands of self-interested magistrates and quick to discover threats to their traditional political independence. This was especially true of London's 8,000 or more liverymen, who enjoyed the fullest measure of civic privilege, and who were therefore the most zealous guardians of the historic liberties of the London citizenry. The people in politics were suspicious, jealous, and stubborn. The reasons for such political behaviour need to be explored further in order to appreciate fully the role of the people in the conflict of the City's parties.

Insight into that role may be gained by considering the size of the electorate. The potential for disorder in the Corporation was great because the number of people capable of participating in Corporation affairs was great. Simply stated, the electorate included the entire rate-paying adult male population of the City, divided into three status categories with unequal rights. The lowest category consisted of 'mere' inhabitants, who were, strictly speaking, not citizens at all because they had failed to assume the freedom of the City by entering one of the guild companies. But these inhabitants were nevertheless entitled both to a voice in the selection of the petty officers of their precincts and wards, and to hold those offices themselves. Above the mere inhabitants in this civic hierarchy, and vastly outnumbering them, were the freemen of the Corporation, those individuals who had chosen, or who had been obliged, to take up membership in a guild. Comprising 80 per cent or more of the resident householders of the incorporated wards,[60] the freemen elected common councilmen at the annual

[60] Valerie Pearl suggests that 'roughly three-quarters of the adult male householders in the City were freemen' in mid-seventeenth century London. See her 'Change and Stability in Seventeenth Century London', *London Journal*, 5 (1979), 13. The proportion of householders who were freemen is likely to have been higher by the later part of the century because the annual number of admissions to the freedom was increasing while the population of the Corporation was declining. See J. R. Kellett, 'The Breakdown of Gild and Corporation Control over the Handicraft and Retail Trade in London', *EcHR*, 2nd Ser., x (1958), 389n. Estimates of the number of City householders and of the number of freemen vary. A figure of somewhat more than 20,000 householders is supported by the poll tax returns for 1692 and accords with the population and household size estimates in David V. Glass, 'Introduction' to *London Inhabitants Within the Walls 1695*, London Record

St. Thomas's Day wardmotes, and they also nominated aldermanic candidates whenever their wards experienced vacancies.
Every freeman of a company with a livery was also eligible to be
called to the livery, and he usually did enter that body, the third
and most select electoral category, after gaining a measure of
substance or after continuing in his vocation for a sufficient length
of time. Regarded as the most responsible of the freemen, the
liverymen in Common Hall elected the City's parliamentary
members, the Lord Mayor, the sheriffs, and other high Corporation officials. What is again most noteworthy about this electoral
élite is its comparatively large size. Resident liverymen made up
at least 35 per cent of the City's householders at any given time.[61]
Moreover, in the half-century since the 1640s, the livery seems to
have doubled in number, even though the overall population of
the Corporation had actually declined.[62] Finally, the continuous
replenishment of the livery from the guilds meant that many
freemen who were not actual Common Hall parliamentary electors were potential Common Hall electors in waiting.

That precinct meetings, wardmotes, and Common Halls were
only occasional events in the Corporation's annual calendar is
true. They were also often poorly attended in quiet years. Nevertheless, these assemblies could easily be disturbed by partisanship, and even minor electoral disruptions like those in Aldersgate
and Dowgate in 1690 could become major irritants in the continuing friction between the parties. Rowdiness was an ever present
possibility because of the numbers of people who might appear at
electoral events, and the likelihood of disorder was increased by
the difficulty of excluding from the crowd those who did not have
the right to be present. Such considerations were part of the

Society Publication, ii (1966) and P. E. Jones and A. V. Judges, 'London Population in
the Late Seventeenth Century', *EcHR*, vi (1935), 45–63. The figure of 12,000–15,000
resident freemen provided by Sidney Webb and Beatrice Webb in *English Local Government*,
p. 584, is surely too low.

[61] This proportion is based upon a total livery of about 8,200 (a figure reached by 1700
and stable for some time thereafter), several hundred of whom, at least, were no longer
City householders. GL and BL, *The Poll of the Livery-Men of the City of London, at the Election
of Members of Parliament* (1710); GL, 'Index to the Liverymen of London in 1700 . . . 1710',
comp. T. C. Dale (typescript, 1933); William A. Speck and William A. Gray, 'Londoners
at the Polls under Anne and George I', *Guildhall Studies in London History*, i (1975), 253;
Rogers, 'Resistance to Oligarchy', pp. 23–4, n. 5 and n. 8.

[62] Valerie Pearl estimates the size of the mid-century liveried electorate as about 4,000
in her *London and the Puritan Revolution*, p. 50.

rationale for those magisterial prerogatives designed to prevent electoral assemblies from degenerating into democratic anarchy. The size of the electorate also became an issue between the parties, as Whig and Tory leaders alternated in encouraging or discouraging full electoral participation to suit their own changing circumstances.

The propensity of Londoners for clamorous political behaviour was also due in part to their exceptional articulateness. As has been previously noted, the political awareness of the urban population could not but be stimulated by its exceptional exposure to national political events. Moreover, both the high London literacy rate and the concentration of the English printing trade in London made for a vigorous popular political culture.[63] These features of the urban environment, together with the City's superior educational facilities,[64] created a mass audience that was notoriously receptive to political journalism of any description. Even in entertaining themselves, Londoners fed their political appetites, imbibing suggestive and even inflammatory morsels in plays, drolls, and ballads.[65] Finally, popular assertiveness was bred in the wards and in the livery companies, each of which provided its members with the experience of limited self-government and with opportunities for the active enjoyment of historic rights. Literate, informed, and inquisitive, the freemen and liverymen of London were the despair of those who extolled the importance of customary deference in an orderly society.

The importance of the livery companies as active agents in the political education of the people has been overlooked in discussions of the continuing decline of the guild's commercial monopolies. Certainly, the ability of the guilds effectively to control handicraft production in the City was deteriorating, and certainly, the presence of many overseas traders in some of the most prestigious companies had eroded the correlation between vocation and guild membership. However, to concentrate upon these and other signs of the material decline of the guilds is to overlook their continuing

---

[63] For London literacy, see David Cressy, *Literacy and the Social Order: Reading and Writing in Tudor and Stuart England* (Cambridge, 1980), pp. 72–5, 146–7; and Lawrence Stone, 'Literacy and Education in England, 1640–1900', *Past and Present*, 42 (1969), pp. 101–3 et seq.

[64] Pearl, 'Change and Stability', p. 6.

[65] Peter Burke, 'Popular Culture in Seventeenth-Century London', *London Journal*, 3 (1977), 148 ff.

vitality, together with the wards, as schools of popular, participatory political experience. Guild members, especially among the liverymen, were accustomed to assuming responsibility for promoting their collective welfare, and the guildsmen were also the interested recipients of a rich medieval heritage of craft pride, of corporate rights, and of charter privileges. Although authority within most guilds was concentrated in the hands of a few, the guilds nevertheless perpetuated a tradition of civic participation and of self-interested collective association. Here the London liverymen absorbed a populist political and economic perspective that emphasized the possession and exercise of 'antient rights' in guild, ward, and Corporation alike. The attachment of the London citizenry to these historic rights arose in the guilds and the wards, where they were accustomed to undertaking their own business. In the guilds, Londoners practised forms of delegated authority and of fraternal self-discipline. Here they grew resentful of magisterial arrogance, of electoral manipulation, and of corruption. Here was bred the restlessness of the 'commonality' of London—a democratic restlessness that punctured the oligarchic pretensions of the commercial élite and that found one outlet in partisanship. Instinctively inculcated in the guilds and wards, this populist attachment of the London electorate to personal rights and to civic autonomy was to propel many liverymen towards the party of opposition, which the Whigs were at first but which the Tories were to become.[66]

The centrality of the livery companies in shaping the political attitudes and expectations of their members must be recognized, but it also must not be exaggerated. As they participated in the affairs of their companies and of the Corporation, the liverymen were exposed to certain assumptions about their socio-political environment, but these assumptions did not constitute a distinct guild ideology or *mentalité*. Neither were these assumptions fully absorbed by all liverymen, least of all by cosmopolitan merchants and prosperous retailers. Only lower in the social and electoral pyramid, within the great body of the *artisanat* and petty tradesmen, did populist notions of participatory rights readily circulate. And even here, among the *menu peuple* of the City, subscription to this popular creed was often latent rather than active, tacit rather than expressed. In the political crises that recurred at

[66] For the continuing vitality of the guilds, see Pearl, 'Change and Stability', pp. 8–13.

regular intervals after 1679, however, agitated liverymen time and again moved to defend traditions of inviolate corporate rights that seemed jeopardized by constitutional and commercial innovations.

In the 1680s, when both the constitution of the Corporation and the integrity of the guilds were violated by the crown, thousands of liverymen found themselves erased from the rolls of their companies and ejected from the electorate. This traumatic invasion of London liberties by the monarchy became the single most important formative episode in the late Stuart political education of the London electorate. Aroused by this gross affront to their civic heritage before 1689, the people of the Corporation— the freemen and the liverymen—had every reason to be vigilant in their political choices after 1689. That vigilance was immediately noticeable in the popular support for the City Whigs' post-Revolutionary campaign to punish the City Tory leaders and to diminish the authority of the magistracy. The whiggism of many London electors was a reflection of their sensitivity to the recent encroachments upon their accustomed rights, and it was also an expression of the resonance between the Whigs' rhetoric of political rights and the guildsmen's own operating assumptions. Once alerted to the vulnerability of their rights, however, many of these same electors would be prepared to repudiate the Whig leadership if it should become unfaithful to popular assumptions about the Corporation's constitution. The opening of precisely such a rift between the Whig City leaders and many of their erstwhile popular supporters explains at least part of the confusion in City politics in the mid-1690s. Just as clearly, the rabidly intense party conflict that erupted in London about a decade later may be attributed partially to the rise of the Tory party in defence of 'antient rights', a popular civic constitution, and the interests of small craftsmen jealous of the new Whig aristocracy of finance and trade. In London, during Anne's reign, 'the people in politics' became the Tory party.[67]

---

[67] Gary S. De Krey, 'Political Radicalism in London after the Glorious Revolution', *Journal of Modern History*, 55 (1983), 585–617; Linda Colley, 'Eighteenth-Century English Radicalism Before Wilkes', *TRHS*, 5th Ser., 31 (1981), 1–19.

II

The Revolutionary Crisis in London Politics, 1688–1690

———◆———

1. The Constitution

THE first two years that followed the Revolution of 1688 constitute a distinctive period in London's history. Beginning with the flight of James II in December 1688, the City was convulsed by a fitful series of party paroxysms that stilled only in December 1690 with the failure of the petition of the London Tories to the Commons. These years marked a crisis in the City's politics, a short and traumatic period of acute political affliction that saw the climax of an older pattern of City politics and the gestation of a new party paradigm. On the one hand, the crisis of 1688–90 saw the ultimate resolution of the party conflicts that had arisen in the early 1680s. On the other hand, this crisis established the terms and the structure of London's political system in the classical age of party politics that followed the Revolution. In the wake of the Revolution, the City parties re-defined themselves after the five-year hiatus of direct crown rule of the Corporation. The London party leaders refined the tools and the techniques of partisanship, and they greatly enlarged the boundaries of acceptable party activities. Moreover, aspiring City politicians of each party now realized that the success of the Revolution might require dramatic adjustments in the ideological premises and the polemical postures of the past.

The origins of this crisis in London politics are to be found in the ambiguity of the 'Glorious' Revolution. The act of revolution in 1688–89 left its meaning still uncertain, especially since this most peculiar of all revolutions was an act of party compromise. In the City, as in parliament, clarification could come only through a power struggle because Whigs and Tories disagreed with each other, and even among themselves, over precisely what the Revolution implied. Parliamentary clarification of the constitutional significance of the Revolution was slow in coming, and City leaders therefore had little choice but to work out its meaning for the Corporation on their own. This work was fraught with difficulty for two reasons. Firstly, the initial signals from Westminster and Whitehall were mixed, if not contradictory. Secondly, the Corporation suffered from a constitutional malaise of its own after the hasty return of its charter through the dubious royal fiat of a soon-to-be-dethroned monarch. The aftermath of the Revolution in the City was thus a period of extreme confusion, an awkward time in which the ambiguity of the national constitution was matched by painful uncertainty over the status of the Corporation's charter.

What turned confusion into crisis were the still unresolved issues of the early 1680s and the sudden increase in intensity of all the major causes of party conflict outlined in chapter one. Partisan and personal hatreds stemming from a decade of unhappy political experiences in the Corporation burst into the open as party leaders re-engaged in the old contest to vindicate their conflicting interpretations of the civic constitution by controlling the magistracy. The struggle gained exceptional force as urban nonconformists clamoured for freedom, as royally-chartered stocks floundered, as war commenced, as parliamentary statesmen jostled for influence in the City, and as the people of London returned to politics with a passion. In less extraordinary years, when the constitutional parameters of politics were respected, these problems could become the catalysts of party competition; but when both the constitution of the nation and that of the City were open to revision, the catalysis produced chaos rather than competition. The revolutionary 'unsettlement' that distracted parliament and the administration beginning in 1689 was thus matched by a similar unsettlement of City politics.

This revolutionary crisis in London shared several characteristics with such earlier critical intervals in the City's history as 1640–2 and the Exclusion Crisis. As with those episodes, the years from 1688 to 1690 saw the circulation of a notable body of pamphlet literature and political ephemera, the active participation of the electorate in Corporation affairs, and the organization of a variety of extra-constitutional public activities—mass demonstrations, petitions, and the like. But the crisis of 1688–90 also had a few unusual aspects that distinguish it from other politically turbulent periods in London history. The constitution of the City, the framework of Corporation politics, clearly hung in the balance as each party strained to influence the parliamentary act that legally restored the City's charter. The necessity for such an act afforded parliament a unique opportunity to tamper with the City's government under the guise of restoring it. In other words, Londoners were utterly dependent upon parliament for a resolution of their constitutional problems. The citizenry were also provided with ample opportunity to influence magisterial decision-making during these critical years. The extraordinary series of events that began in England in the autumn of 1688 made necessary an unusual number of elections in the City between October 1688 and June 1690. In that twenty-month period most London liverymen were presented with twelve or thirteen electoral opportunities. Wardmote elections of common councilmen took place four times, and Common Hall was summoned eight times. In addition, the unusual turn over on the aldermanic bench (twenty-one vacancies) led to more aldermanic elections than were conducted altogether in the remaining twelve years of William's reign. In an ordinary year most liverymen participated in only three important civic elections (those of Lord Mayor, sheriffs, and common councilmen); but in the first twenty months of the City's revolutionary crisis, the typical London liveryman was confronted with an electoral choice on the average of once every seven weeks. No other period in the Corporation's history is equivalent in this respect. The popular excitement generated by these frequent elections was no doubt further stimulated by the fact that *no* elections had been conducted in the City during the previous five years of royal management—another period without parallel in the Corporation's history. The principal effect of this unique run of elections was to encourage party competitiveness and organization, as can be seen from the fact that most elections were contested.

The revolutionary crisis in London's politics was thus a multi-faceted one that involved the constitution, extra-parliamentary happenings, and the composition of City government. The second and third of these aspects will be treated in the following sections of this chapter. Here, the focus will be upon the constitutional problem, the core of the crisis. James's assumption of the right to restore the City's forfeit charter in October 1688 revived the constitutional arguments heard before and after the King's Bench judgement of 1683. The Whigs argued now, as they had earlier, that both the King's Bench judgement and the suspension of the charter were illegal. What was needed, according to the Whigs, was an act of parliament specifically declaring this to be so and also giving the restoration of the charter the security of statutory enactment. For the City Tories, however, the matter was otherwise. Contending that the King's Bench judgement had in fact legally dissolved the Corporation, the Tories had grave doubts about the legitimacy of James's restoration of the charter and of all municipal elections held since that time. An act of parliament was needed, according to the Tories, in order to reverse the judgement, to re-establish the Corporation, and to provide for the selection of new municipal office-holders to replace the cadre of Whigs elected after the Revolution.[1]

The constitutional dispute therefore became entangled with the question of offices and who should have them. It was also complicated by the determination of the Whigs to seize this opportunity to ensure that the electors would never again be banned from politics as they had been during the Stuart 'invasion' of the Corporation. The best way to prevent this in the future was to provide for the elimination of those constitutional practices that had recently diminished popular oversight of the magistracy, and to see that the rights of the London electorate were henceforth underwritten by statute. The City Whigs had every reason to believe that the moment was propitious for such a project, especially in view of the Convention's adoption of a Declaration of Rights that formally clarified the balance of authority between the crown and parliament and that catalogued the rights of English subjects. The City Whigs' first step in the direction of constitutional revision was taken in January 1689 when the Court of Aldermen requested the advice of a triumvirate of prominent Whig legal authorities—Sir George Treby (Recorder of the Corporation), Sir John Holt, and Henry Pollexfen.[2] Their advice was incorporated into the draft statute prepared by May 1689 by a Whig-dominated committee of Common Council. This draft, the first of two written by the City

[1] Levin, *Charter Controversy*; CLRO Misc. MS 141.10 No. 9; *The State of the City of London*; *Considerations upon the Act of Parliament, for reversing the Judgment in a Quo Warranto against the City of London* (1690).

[2] Repertory 94, fo. 93; Lois G. Schwoerer, *The Declaration of Rights* (Baltimore, Md., 1981), pp. 43–7, 55–6.

Whigs, was presumably the same as that which received two readings in the House of Commons in the summer of 1689. The most
notable feature of this draft was its clause for safeguarding the electoral rights of the liverymen. The elections of magistrates were to be
determined by the majority of voices in Common Hall, and the
electoral clause made no mention of the mayoral claim of right to
make a binding nomination of one sheriff.[3]

These and other clarifications of Common Hall procedures
revised recent constitutional practices, but the draft of May 1689
did not provide for similar revisions in the relationship between
Common Council and the Court of Aldermen, or in the procedures
for ward elections. Further revisions, and these of a rather startling
nature, came only in a second draft. This was prepared by March
1690 by another Whig-dominated Common Council committee.[4]
If the second draft represents the ultimate constitutional objectives
of the Whigs, then their initial moderation is somewhat puzzling.
The most likely explanation of the Whigs' restraint is their failure
to obtain a clear Common Council majority until December 1689
and their over-confidence in the first months after the Revolution.
Not until the winter of 1689–90 did the Whigs learn how exceedingly optimistic were their expectations of a ready implementation
of 'revolution principles'. Their expectations then became clouded
by a series of political reverses that included the king's shift to the
Tories in his ministerial appointments, the uncertain complexion
of the new parliament, and the loss of London's Commons seats
to four Tories. Much worried, but still dominant on the aldermanic bench and in Common Council, the City Whigs seem to
have decided that the Revolution could now be secured in the
Corporation only through the passage of a far more detailed statute. The second draft act therefore took the form of a blueprint for
radical, populist adjustments in the Corporation's constitution.
The 'people', or the large City electorate, were to be entrusted
with safeguarding their own greatly extended liberties.[5]

Like the earlier draft, that of March 1690 guaranteed the
autonomy of Common Hall in shrieval elections, and it ignored

---

[3] Journal 50, fos. 366, 374–7; *CJ* x. 211, 215.
[4] Journal 51, fo. 12.
[5] A copy of this draft has been preserved in Journal 51, fos. 33–6. Also see, CLRO Misc.
MS 141.10 and GL MS 5099. I have previously commented upon this draft in 'Political
Radicalism in London', pp. 591–3.

the mayoral prescription of one sheriff. The Common Hall clauses of the 1690 draft further specified that the liverymen should exercise absolute freedom in the annual mayoral election. In the City's recent past, the Court of Aldermen had elected the Lord Mayor from two aldermanic candidates chosen by Common Hall, and the senior alderman below the chair could usually expect to succeed to the mayoralty in this manner. However, the new Whig draft act, citing authoritative 'antient Charters', called for the direct election of the Lord Mayor by the liverymen. Had this clause actually been implemented, the mayoral election would have become as popular in nature as was the election of City MPs.

The redefinition of the magistracy apparent in this popular formula for the mayoral election was but part of a broader scheme for turning the Corporation into a participatory civic commonwealth, a democratic polity in which the magistrates were to be true representatives of the people. This at least would have been the effect of the suffrage provisions of the Whigs' 1690 draft. The wardmote suffrage for the election of both aldermen and common councilmen was defined to include all ward housekeepers paying scot and lot, and the language of the draft failed to specify that such housekeepers must also be freemen. Moreover, the Whigs wished to place aldermanic elections on the same popular foundation as the mayoral election. Disregarding the previous procedures whereby wardmotes nominated four aldermanic candidates, one of whom was then elected by the sitting aldermen, the draft proposed that ward housekeepers directly elect their aldermen. Although the aldermen would now be chosen according to democratic procedures, the Court of Aldermen was nevertheless to relinquish its ascendancy in Corporation affairs to Common Council. The latter body was to be released from those impediments that had subordinated it to the aldermen—the aldermanic veto, the aldermanic right to prior review of all Corporation business, and the mayoral prerogative of summoning or dismissing the common councilmen at will. Common Council was to meet on eight specified occasions during the year, an increase over the number of annual sessions in recent times. Extraordinary sessions could be initiated by either the Lord Mayor or a certain number of common councilmen, and adjournments were to require the consent of a majority of those present.

Considered together, these provisions effected a stunning transformation in the prospective status of Common Council. No longer to be a pliant rubber stamp for the magistracy, Common Council was instead envisaged as a representative forum in which popularly elected delegates of the people were to conduct the major business of the Corporation. The Court of Aldermen would have retained its position as the City's executive agency, still entrusted with a great variety of important administrative tasks, but it would no longer have functioned as a senior legislative partner of Common Council. The proposed direct election of aldermen emphasized the accountability of the City government to the people, while the draft's failure to prescribe the possession of a £10,000 personal estate for election as alderman promised to weaken the oligarchic composition of the aldermanic bench. The anti-élitist intent of the Whigs in 1690 was also evident in a clause prohibiting the buying and selling of City offices. Here, then, was the City Whigs' interpretation of the meaning of the 1688 Revolution for London—the establishment of what can only be described as a functioning civic republic.

Who were the City Whig spokesmen who prepared and promoted this democratic document, and how can their radical political views be explained? These questions may be answered by investigating the careers of twenty-five Whig leaders in the Corporation who were either elected or restored to the Court of Aldermen between 1688 and 1690, or who were members of the Common Council committee that drafted the proposed statute.[6] These individuals may be regarded as the prime movers behind the Common Council's decision of 27 March 1690 to approve the measure and to forward it to the House of Commons for parliamentary consideration.

Although the political perspective of the authors of the draft statute was clearly populist, the social status of these twenty-five radical Whig leaders was just as clearly not. Of those whose occupations can be determined, fourteen were active overseas merchants at the time of the Revolution, and three others were retired merchants. Some were more successful entrepreneurs than others, but as a group, these revolutionary Whigs were drawn not from the City's 'lesser merchants' but rather from the City's

[6] Ibid., p. 594 n. 28 for the names of these leading revolutionary Whigs.

commercial élite.[7] Among the twenty-five were six future directors of the Bank of England, including Sir John Houblon (the Bank's first governor) and Gilbert Heathcote, the greatest City magnate of the early eighteenth century. Five of the Whigs were past or future directors of the Old East India Company or of the rival East India corporation chartered by parliament in 1698. Among those Whig leaders not involved in overseas trade, the most prominent was Sir Robert Clayton, a former Exclusionist MP and the City's pre-eminent private banker. Despite his phenomenal wealth, Clayton had scarcely shown oligarchic tendencies during his 1679–80 mayoralty. In the 1690s he moved in free-thinking circles, and he was a friend and patron of the political and religious radical John Toland.[8]

The endorsement of a radical draft statute by these wealthy and respectable Whig commercial leaders is rather surprising. Nevertheless, several reasons may be offered for the libertarian sentiments they exhibited in 1688–90.[9] One noticeable characteristic of this Whig leadership group was its lack of sympathy for the established church. Seventeen of the twenty-five were either known nonconformists or individuals with close family ties to dissent. Sir William Ashurst and his brother Sir Henry Ashurst were scions of one of the pre-eminent Presbyterian families in the country. Sir William clearly had a reputation for radicalism in Billingsgate ward, for which he served as alderman after the Revolution. When he attended the ward's 1689 inquest, the Tory questmen accused him of 'beginning a health to our Soveraigne Lord or Lords ye people'.[10] Other leading dissenters among the promoters of the radical draft included former Lord Mayor Sir Patience Ward, current Lord Mayor Sir Thomas Pilkington, and future Lord Mayor Sir Humphrey Edwin. The political heritage of these dissenters was not inherently republican or radical, but

---

[7] J. H. Plumb, *The Growth of Political Stability in England 1675-1725* (1967), p. 37.

[8] Basil D. Henning, *The House of Commons 1660-1690* (The History of Parliament, 1983), ii. 84–7. Clayton's radical 1690s' friendships are noted in Margaret C. Jacob, *The Newtonians and the English Revolution 1689-1720* (Ithaca, NY, 1976), pp. 220-2, 226. Houblon and Heathcote were also directors of the New East India Company of 1698. Other joint-stock directors among the Whig leaders were Sir William Ashurst (Bank), Sir Robert Clayton (Bank, East India), James Denew (Bank), Sir Humphrey Edwin (East India), Sir James Houblon (Bank), Thomas Papillon (East India).

[9] Another approach to City radicalism is provided in Mark Goldie, 'The Roots of True Whiggism 1688-94', *History of Political Thought*, 1 (1980), 195-236.

[10] BL Sloane MS 203, fo. 60.

their theology and ecclesiology did have individualistic tendencies. Moreover, the experiences of dissenters since the Restoration had engendered a suspiciousness of authority and a self-interested desire for the extension of political liberties.

If nonconformity was one source of Whig radicalism, recent political events seem to have been another. Few of the revolutionary Whig leaders who fashioned the new popular framework for City government were new to the politics of the Corporation. In fact, twenty of the twenty-five had been elected to, or deprived of, a City office during the Exclusion Crisis and had suffered some form of personal political harassment since the revocation of the City's charter. Many of them had been arrested, imprisoned, or subjected to a house search at the time of Monmouth's Rebellion.[11] Pilkington had been both fined £100,000 and imprisoned for four years on the charge of *scandalum magnatum* for intemperate speeches against the Duke of York. Ward and Exclusionist MP Thomas Papillon had found a Dutch exile congenial during the Tory 'reign of terror', as had John Wildman, the irascible republican, one-time Leveller, and associate of both the Duke of Monmouth and Algernon Sidney.[12] In other words, the City's radical Whig leaders had shared fully in the heady early days of the Exclusion movement, and had also shared fully in its dismal political failure. Their prediction that a Catholic monarch would undermine the country's 'balanced' constitution and jeopardize personal liberties had become a self-fulfilling nightmare. Embittered by the City Tories' connivance in their humiliation, these Whig leaders saw the purpose of the Revolution as more than merely to confirm rights and privileges violated by the crown in the 1680s. The radical changes they proposed for the City's government were designed to ensure that the power of the City magistracy would never again be used to frustrate the popular will.

Also likely to have influenced the framers of the Whig draft were the radical justifications of the Revolution that had circulated in

---

[11] See biographical details in Smith, pp. 392–401 and J. R. Woodhead, *The Rulers of London 1660–1689* (1965). For persons suspected of complicity in Monmouth's Rebellion see Smith, pp. 413–15; and CLRO, Lieutenancy Court Minute Book, 1684/85–1687, fos. 24, 32–3, 37–44.

[12] Henning, iii. 202–5, 247, 721–3; Irene Scouloudi, 'Thomas Papillon, Merchant and Whig', *PHSL* xviii (1947), 49–72; Maurice Ashley, *John Wildman, Plotter and Postmaster* (1947).

the Convention and in print by 1690.[13] Drawing upon a contractual theory of government, these arguments shared the
assumption that the Revolution represented a defence of the
historic rights of Englishmen lately threatened by the Stuart
crown. If the Revolution was construed generally as a recovery of
popular rights, then the City Whig draft was merely an application to the Corporation of the principles of the Revolution. With
so much discussion of an 'original' contract in the air, many supporters of the draft no doubt regarded it as resembling in spirit the
City's original or 'antient' constitution. Moreover, if the objection was made that the draft granted novel freedoms to the citizenry, the answer could be made that it actually restored to the
people rights that had once been theirs but that had somehow
been lost in recent generations.

These ideas met with little enthusiasm among City and parliamentary Tories. City Tory leaders resented the draft because it
impugned their anti-populist conduct in the last years of Charles
II. Prominent Tories in the Commons were apprehensive about a
document that, as Sir Edward Seymour charged, would convert
the Corporation into a 'commonwealth'.[14] They feared the potential repercussions in other boroughs if the government of London
was altered along such democratic lines. According to the Tory
author of a pamphlet critical of the draft, its authors were 'State-
Mountebanks' who hoped 'to spread their Contagion into all
Corporations through the Kingdom'.[15] The draft thus raised
familiar fears among Tory politicians at Westminster, fears that
the City was again becoming a dangerous hotbed of political
radicalism. Seymour, Sir Thomas Clarges, and other parliamentary Tories understandably perceived the City Whigs as irresponsible republicans or levellers and as the direct descendants of the
mid-century radicals who had overturned the country's traditional
institutions. The cordial ties between City Whigs and parliamentary radicals seemed to confirm that impression. So did Whig
complaisance at the return to London of Edmund Ludlow, the

[13] J. P. Kenyon, *Revolution Principles: The Politics of Party 1689–1720* (Cambridge, 1977),
pp. 5 ff., 35 ff.; Mark Goldie, 'The Revolution of 1689 and the Structure of Political Argument: an Essay and an Annotated Bibliography of Pamphlets on the Allegiance Controversy', *Bulletin of Research in the Humanities*, 83 (1980), 473–564; Schwoerer, *Declaration of
Rights*, pp. 155–6, 159–60, 176–9, 287.

[14] Grey, *Debates*, x. 43–5, 54–61.

[15] *Reasons humbly offered, for the Lords ready Concurrence with the House of Commons, in the Bill
for reversing the Judgment in the Quo Warranto, and restoring the City-charter in status quo, etc.* [1690].

unreconciled regicide, and the elevation to the aldermanic bench of the former Leveller leader Wildman.[16] Moreover, the public behaviour of the London Whig leadership in the first months after the Revolution accorded with the popular intentions announced in their draft statute. The apprehensions of Tory squires about those intentions were further raised as they observed the City Whigs' involvement in popular extra-parliamentary political activities. These events need now to be considered in order to understand both the resolution of London's political crisis and its significance for the future.

2. Politics Out of Doors

The attempt of the London Whigs to define the meaning of the Revolution for the City in a draft statute was part of a broader post-revolutionary programme of political propaganda, party organization, and orchestrated agitation. The collapse of press licensing at the time of the Revolution released a flood of William-ite printed material, most of it published in the capital and exten-sively circulated there.[17] Though miscellaneous in origin, this literature had the general purpose of arousing popular support for the Revolution. This it seems to have succeeded in doing, and in London the people found ample occasions, both ordinary and ex-traordinary, for participating in revolutionary politics. The great number of elections in the City presented the citizens with numerous opportunities for influencing the direction of Corpora-tion affairs. These opportunities for political participation were supplemented during London's revolutionary crisis by an array of extra-constitutional incidents, which were initiated by Whig and nonconformist leaders or by the people in imitation of established Whig patterns. Such episodes may be interpreted as a revival by the Whigs of the 'theatre of street politics' they had directed in the early 1680s.[18]

---

[16] Grey, *Debates*, ix. 397-8; Luttrell, *Brief Relation*, i. 582, 603, 607; Thomas B. Macaulay, *The History of England from the Accession of James II*, ed. C. H. Firth (1914), iv. 1770-1; A. B. Worden, 'Introduction' to Edmund Ludlow, *A Voyce from the Watch Tower*, Camden Society, Fourth Series, vol. 21 (Royal Historical Society, 1978).

[17] Lois G. Schwoerer, 'Propaganda in the Revolution of 1688-89', *American Historical Review*, 82 (1977), 843-74.

[18] For this phrase see Nicholas Rogers, 'Popular Protest in Early Hanoverian London', *Past and Present*, 79 (1978), 70.

As the City Whigs sought to establish a popular definition of the Revolution *on paper*, they therefore sought also to implement the definition *in practice* through politics out of doors. This effort added to the sense of urgency in the City, suggesting to the people that the results of the Revolution might depend upon their own continuing exertions. The revival of extra-constitutional politics by the Whigs was both genuine and enthusiastic, and the obvious Whig commitment to populism was precisely what so frightened the Tory MPs who had reluctantly accepted William as king. As the Whigs and the people demonstrated their participatory conception of the Revolution out of doors, they provoked an intervention in the City by conservative parliamentarians that can legitimately be described as counter-revolutionary in intention.

No sooner had the Convention met in late January 1689 than the City Whigs and their radical friends at Westminster launched their first popular petition. Calling for the speedy settlement of the crown on William and Mary, the petition of 2–4 February 1689 was provoked by the hesitation of the House of Lords to concur with the Commons' declaration of a vacant throne. Although the petition's sponsors discreetly sought to avoid the appearance of any coercion of parliament by the people, the membership of both Houses nevertheless construed it in those terms and refused to accept it. Another petition, one widely subscribed to by City dissenters, similarly miscarried in late March 1689. It was circulated shortly after the defeat of proposals for comprehension and for repealing the Test Act, and it was formulated as an expression of gratitude to the new king for his stated sympathy for his nonconformist subjects. At the suggestion of dissenting spokesmen at Westminster, however, the London nonconformists' petition was withdrawn for fear of further hardening the position of Church MPs.[19]

Two further petitions were initiated in the City in June 1689 in hopes of favourably influencing parliamentary business. Signatures were gathered early in the month in support of a proposed Commons' address to the throne against the employment of ministers who had served under James. This petition was dropped when MP Jack Howe and other radical Whig proponents of the

---

[19] DWL Morrice MS Q, 454–5, 524; Lois G. Schwoerer, 'Press and Parliament in the Revolution of 1689', *HJ* xx (1977), 552; Schwoerer, *Declaration of Rights*, pp. 210–12; Horwitz, *Revolution Politicks*, pp. 87–94.

address failed to proceed with it. It also drew criticism from those who believed that such a petition ought to have been formally adopted by Common Council rather than privately circulated. This consideration may have influenced the tactics of nonconformist leaders who succeeded, through a combination of luck and chicanery, in pushing a petition for repeal of the sacramental test through Common Hall on 24 June 1689. Following a predetermined design, the petition was adopted after the conclusion of the shrieval election, the main business of the day, by which time many liverymen not in the secret had gone home. Printed 'by authority', or so it was claimed, the petition was distributed in other boroughs as an encouragement to their nonconformist electors. The Common Hall petition was accepted by the Commons, but only after the House had 'spent two hours in fierce objections and Wranglings', and it was consequently abandoned by the Whig leadership.[20]

Despite their very limited success, the London petitions of 1689 were reminiscent in several ways of the 'monster' City petitions of the 1640s and of 1679. The February petition for settling the crown upon William and Mary was said to have gained fifteen thousand signatures over a single weekend, and those of March and early June were also reported to have been subscribed to by 'thousands'. Moreover, the radical intentions and the popular character of the petitions outraged Church-Tory MPs. Sir Thomas Clarges did not hesitate to point out the frightening parallels with the 'strange' City petitions of the past.[21] Although the City Whigs' petitions demonstrated their ability to organize public opinion and to maintain popular enthusiasm, they also touched off the parliamentary reaction against the Whig leadership.

The revival of mass petitioning by the City Whigs and nonconformists had one other unintended consequence. It inspired the unruly presentation of a genuinely plebeian petition at Westminster. The descent of angry Spitalfields' silkworkers on parliament in August 1689 was the one event of the critical post-Revolutionary years with potential for crowd violence. This protest of several thousand workers and their wives was provoked by

[20] DWL Morrice MS Q, 575, 579–80; *A Seasonable Caution*; *True Account of the Proceedings of Common-hall*; *CJ* x. 197; Luttrell, *Brief Relation*, i. 542, 551; Grey, *Debates*, ix. 280 ff., 362–5; Horwitz, *Parliament, Policy and Politics*, p. 31.

[21] Grey, *Debates*, ix. 362.

a bill designed to encourage the wearing of woollens at the expense of silk. Popular rather than partisan in its origins, the silkworkers' 'demonstration' none the less revealed the continuing rapport between radical Whig leaders and the London 'mobile'. This relationship is a mysterious one, but the contacts established between old Exclusionists and the crowd were seemingly still intact after the Revolution. The agitated workers were addressed by three Whig spokesmen, apparently chosen because of the regard in which they were held by the people. They were the Earl of Monmouth, freethinker and former confidant of Algernon Sidney, Dr Edward Fowler, a City vicar inclined towards comprehension (and soon to be a Low-Church bishop), and Thomas Firmin, antitrinitarian and sponsor of private charities for the poor. The three speakers skilfully commended the silkworkers' cause without encouraging their demonstration, and the crowd retired to the City's out-parishes without further incident. Monmouth and Firmin were to appear again in the City's extra-constitutional politics of 1689-90.[22]

The silkworkers' petition raised a new and perhaps unwelcome question for the City Whigs as they worked out the practical implications of the Revolution. Although the Whigs regarded active citizens as the best defenders of their own rights and interests, they could not condone crowd behaviour that threatened to overstep the bounds of civil order. The Spitalfields mob was all too reminiscent of the violently anti-Catholic throngs that had taken to the streets in the autumn of 1688 as James's government collapsed.[23] If the Whig leaders were to be successful in the City, they needed to sustain popular enthusiasm for the Revolution but to discipline it as well. Three mass *événements* of late 1689 served both to assemble the people in support of the Whig cause and to exhibit the popular will in a respectable and orderly manner.

The first of these was the Lord Mayor's show, staged as was customary on 29 October. The mayoral installation of Sir Thomas Pilkington, perhaps the most acerbic of the Whig magistrates, was celebrated by the Whigs as 'London's Great Jubilee', a tribute to the Revolution and to the rescue of the City from oppression. The affair was rich with symbolism, studded

---

[22] DWL Morrice MS Q, 596; *Corporation of Weavers at London and Canterbury* (1689); Luttrell, *Brief Relation*, i. 568-9; Horwitz, *Parliament, Policy and Politics*, p. 35.

[23] William L. Sachse, 'The Mob and the Revolution of 1688', *JBS* iv (1964), 23-40.

with Whig talent, and most importantly, open to the people. The 1689 show featured, as usual, a festive procession by foot and by barge of the Lord Mayor and his official entourage from the City to Westminster for the administration of the oaths. Participation was extended vicariously to the guildsmen, drawn up by company along the way, and to the people, who lined the streets and crowded the balconies. On his return from Westminster, the Lord Mayor officially reviewed four pageants presented in Cheapside and left standing until dark for the people's edification. An added attraction of 1689 was the stunning entrance of William and Mary in a cavalcade headed by the Earl of Monmouth and including members of both Houses, the judges of the courts of law, and the foreign ambassadors.

According to one observer, the show 'out-did all that had been seen before on the like occasion', but what was most striking was the Whigs' use of the pageants to represent visually the political message of the day. The iconography of each pageant presented a variation on the theme of the country's deliverance from popery and slavery. One pageant featured a splendidly arrayed Augusta, a personification of the City of London, who saluted the lately imprisoned Lord Mayor as a defender of the City's rights and privileges. Another presented a collection of wild animals and an ominous figure who reminded his auditory that 'London's a den where savage beasts do lurk.' The line referred in this critical year not only to the ever present fear of social anarchy, but also to the continuing presence of dangerous Tories in the City magistracy and the royal ministry. The Lord Mayor's show of 1689 was thus an enormously successful piece of orchestrated street theatre. The entire City became a *tableau vivant* of the 'glorious' Revolution. Traditional civic ritual was adeptly employed by the Whigs to legitimate the change of regime *in the presence* of the people whose rights had thereby been preserved.[24]

The show was undoubtedly a hard act to follow, but followed it was within a week by the celebration of a double holiday on 4-5 November. The first day was the king's birthday. The second was the date of the customary Gunpowder Plot celebration, now much enhanced as the first anniversary of the country's 'second

[24] DWL Morrice MS Q, 637; Matthew Taubman, *London's Great Jubilee* (1689); Lapthorne, p. 62; Luttrell, *Brief Relation*, i. 594, 597; Frederick W. Fairholt, *Lord Mayors' Pageants* (1843), i. 107-9; Peter Burke, 'Popular Culture', pp. 151-2.

Redemption' from popery by William's landing at Torbay. Officially sponsored by the City government, the celebrations nevertheless allowed for much initiative from below. Work ceased on both days, sermons were attended 'every where', and popular enthusiasm was expressed in the ringing of bells and in bonfires at night.[25]

A month later came the most interesting of these popular happenings. The first anniversary of William's arrival in the capital was celebrated by the crowd in a fashion that suggests prior organization by someone, but that also derived much of its inspiration from the people themselves. Little is known about either the social composition or the size of the crowd of 18 December 1689. More is known about its activities. As bonfires were lit in different parts of town, a slow and orderly procession with 'a 1000 Lights' moved through the City from Whitechapel in the east to Fleet Street in the west. The crowd carried a dozen effigies of loathsome characters from the last reigns, including Lord Chancellor Sir George Jeffreys, Sir Roger L'Estrange, and the foremen of the Russell, Sidney, and Cornish juries. With the effigies was carried a triple gallows, which was set up at Temple Bar. Assembled there, in the vicinity of the country's legal institutions, the crowd itself assumed the authority of a court and proceeded with a mock trial of the figures it had borne aloft. After numerous speeches these detested personages were found guilty of treason by acclamation, hung from the gallows, and consumed by the flames of a 'monstrous' fire. The evening's solemnities ended with cheers for the new sovereigns, William and Mary.[26]

What had the crowd done? It had staged a highly theatrical rite on a spot that could not have been better chosen for the purpose. At Temple Bar the Lord Mayor recognized the sovereignty of the crown on the occasions of royal visits to the City. This he did by briefly surrendering to the monarch the sword of the City, a symbol of its independence and of his own authority. Temple Bar was therefore a juridical site. It was popularly associated with the recognition of authority and with the transfer of power. Convening there, the crowd adopted the judicial authority of its superiors, ritually claiming the sovereignty said to reside in the people by some of the defenders of the Revolution. So endowed,

[25] Luttrell, *Brief Relation*, i. 600.
[26] DWL Morrice MS R, 53–4; Lapthorne, p. 66.

the people voiced their approbation of the Revolution and of their own role in it. The rule of William and Mary was now popularly accredited through the recitation and punishment of the misdeeds of the previous reigns. The mock trial was thus a fitting popular counterpart to the official legitimization of the Revolution on 29 October. Then the Whig magistrates had instructed the people in the meaning of the Revolution. Now the people responded with a pageant largely of their own making.[27]

The processions of 1689, much like the petitions which preceded them, underlined the cordial relations between the Whig leaders and the people. They also suggested the existence of cordial relations between the City Whigs and the crown. By the time of the festive Lord Mayor's show, however, that idea was little more than a polite fiction. William's growing misgivings about the Whigs, both those in parliament and those in the City, were many. He had no patience for their vindictive self-righteousness. He grew weary of their attacks upon his Church-Tory ministers, and he grew fearful about their attitude towards his prerogative. He singled out two of the City members, Sir Robert Clayton and Sir Patience Ward, as being among those whose support fell short of his expectations. Becoming suspicious that many Whigs were crypto-republicans, he fixed upon the City as a potential trouble spot, and came to regret the military authority he had conferred upon the London Whigs in the 1689 Lieutenancy commission. Among those he most suspected was Monmouth, whose City connections had given him charge of a voluntary regiment raised by the London Whigs to serve as an occasional royal bodyguard. As early as June 1689, William confided to Halifax that 'my Ld Mordaunts [Monmouth's] Regt. in the city, perhaps [is] for a Commonwealth'.[28]

As the strain between William and the Whigs worsened, some party leaders in parliament seized the expedient of employing the money of their allies in London to increase Whig leverage on the crown. Since the Revolution, London Whigs of every social description had shown much generosity in lending their money to the king. The immense resources of some Whig lenders and the enthusiasm of others made their money a potential asset in the

---

[27] Temple Bar had not yet attained its eighteenth-century notoriety as a traitor's golgotha. See James Holbert Wilson, *Temple Bar: The City Golgotha* (1853).

[28] H. C. Foxcroft, *The Life and Letters of Sir George Savile, Bart.* (1898), ii. 222 et seq.

mounting party struggle for William's confidence. Financial coercion of the crown had been effective in 1640, and Whig leaders therefore had reason to believe that the trick might work again. Although the intention of the ensuing financial manœuvres was strictly utilitarian, the Whigs were actually initiating yet another popular extra-constitutional political technique, because the loans affected were raised by mass subscription. In the end, however, the Whig resort to financial pressure proved a dismal failure. The Whigs succeeded only in further annoying William and in giving Tory MPs further cause for concern.

The principal parliamentary organizer of financial pressure upon the crown was the wily and reckless Earl of Monmouth, whose Westminster associates included the Duke of Bolton and Richard Hampden. In the City, Lord Mayor Pilkington seems to have been an interested party, as were Thomas Firmin and Sir Humphrey Edwin, the notorious dissenting Lord Mayor of 1697–8. The first in a series of incidents involving London money came in November 1689, but whether it was part of a premeditated design cannot be said. When approached by the crown to exert themselves on behalf of a new loan, the City Whig leaders expressed considerable reluctance. Echoing parliamentary voices, Thomas Firmin declared that money would be lent more readily if the ministry was purged of former servants of James.[29] This resistance was reversed in a financial tack of the opposite sort by Monmouth just before the holiday adjournment of parliament. The earl surprised the king with a Christmas gift of some £300,000 in City advances on various revenues, emphasizing that 'it was mostly Fanaticks and Wiggs money'.[30]

The London Whigs' next attempt to use City money for political purposes came in the spring of 1690. By that time, however, great changes had taken place both at Westminster and in London. In February 1690 William had dissolved the Convention Parliament and begun an alteration of the ministry in favour of the Churchmen. At the urging of Carmarthen and Nottingham, he also decided upon a reconstruction of the London Lieutenancy commission, a decision that kindled rumours and much comment in the City. These developments were unmistakable indications that the London Whigs no longer enjoyed the crown's favour.

[29] DWL Morrice MS R, 1.
[30] Ibid., 58.

This fact was absorbed quickly by the liveried electorate who, in Common Hall on 4 March 1690, voiced their respect for the crown's wishes. The four sitting Whig MPs were defeated by four City Tory leaders. The City Whigs were understandably upset to discover that their popular support could prove so fleeting. Worse was to follow on 15 March, when the names of the new Lieutenancy commissioners were discovered to include 'the most violent Tories in the City'.[31]

Just before the commission was released, Lord Mayor Pilkington, himself one of the defeated Whig MPs, was summoned before the Privy Council to hear the crown's wish for magisterial assistance in organizing another public loan. Understandably irate, the Lord Mayor noted that the Lieutenancy alteration would scarcely encourage the generosity of those citizens who had previously lent most. He was right. The money for this loan, as well as that for another in May, came in rather slowly and from fewer individuals. All the same, the amount of money from Whig sources was still greater than that from City Tory hands.[32] Those Whigs who abstained from the two loans, or who adjusted their contributions, had no shortage of political reasons for doing so. In April and May, parliament debated both the City Whigs' draft and the Lieutenancy alteration at great length before reaching decisions that shocked and disappointed the Whigs. Parliamentary consideration of City affairs produced a confrontation between London's revolutionary Whigs and the Tory MPs that left the Corporation in a feverish political condition. The existence of a crisis in City affairs became clear to all, although the outcome was still in doubt.

3. Climax and Resolution

The impression of radicalism that the London Whigs had made upon many in parliament surfaced repeatedly in the debates on the Lieutenancy and on the bill for restoring the City government. The Whigs' revival of politics out of doors and their desire to re-make the Corporation as a model of popular government could scarcely be interpreted as anything other than radicalism by

---

[31] Ibid., 117; Gilbert Burnet, *History of his Own Time*, 2nd edn. (Oxford, 1833), iv. 72; Horwitz, *Parliament, Policy and Politics*, p. 50.

[32] DWL Morrice MS R, 124; CLRO MSS 40/36, 40/43.

royalist MPs. The Whigs' draft was consequently condemned in
the Commons as the work of a 'cabal', and their former command
of the militia was portrayed as a military threat to William
himself. Mindful of the City's stormy past, Clarges spoke for
many Church-Tory MPs when he argued that 'the King could
not go with any security out of London without that change of the
Lieutenancy'. He sadly remembered 'what they did in *Charles I's*.
time, and the consequences'.[33] The Tories' fears of nonconformist
radicalism were again reflected in a Commons' address to William
approving the Lieutenancy alteration. The king was thanked for
his 'great Care . . . *of the Church of England*' in depriving the City
dissenters of the influence they had enjoyed on the 1689 commission. The Commons' response to the London Whigs' draft
statute showed equal hostility to them. The recently elected Tory
City MPs declined to present the draft at Westminster after its
adoption by Common Council, and the Commons refused on
party votes to accept the draft from the hands of the London
sheriffs or to hear the pleas of City counsel. Instead, the Commons
appointed a committee to prepare a bill of its own, a committee
that included the four Tory City MPs.[34]

The Commons' bill, approved in early May 1690, was totally
unacceptable to the City Whigs. It incorporated the Tory argument that the King's Bench judgement against the Corporation
charter was valid until reversed by the enactment of the bill, an
interpretation that assumed the irregularity of the City's current
government. The Commons bill called for immediate elections of
magistrates and common councilmen, and it provided that if
these elections were not held, the heavily-Tory magistrates and
common councilmen of 1683 should resume their places. Finally,
the bill included no definition or clarification of what privileges or
constitutional practices were being restored to the Corporation.[35]
As Sir Christopher Musgrave had argued in debate, entering
upon 'the Sea of the ancient Rights of the City' was too hazardous
a voyage.[36] Although the City Whigs carried a petition in Common Council to the House of Lords against the Commons bill, the
Lords nevertheless passed the Corporation of London Act without
any alterations.

[33] Grey, *Debates*, x. 55.
[34] *CJ* x. 388; Grey, *Debates*, x. 54-8, 67-78.
[35] *CJ* x. 372 et seq.; *LJ* xiv. 491 ff.; *Statutes of the Realm*, vi. 171-3 (2 W&M c8).
[36] Grey, *Debates*, x. 60.

The response of the City's revolutionary Whig leaders to the miscarriage of their proposals for constitutional reform was surprisingly tame. Despite some discussion of petitioning William against accepting the bill, the London Whig leaders made no attempt to influence him and inclined instead towards introducing reforms in the Corporation later through alterations in the City by-laws.[37] In other words, when they perceived that the parliamentary bill threatened their own tenure in office, the Whig magistrates became more concerned about their places than about an immediate enlargement in the rights of the Corporation electorate. They had already been rudely shocked by the electorate's unexpected preference for Tory MPs in March 1690. Now, the Whig magistrates found the legitimacy of their rule in the City denied by parliament in such a way as to encourage the electors to deprive them of their offices. This left the Whig leadership in an extremely awkward situation. On the one hand, they claimed to be champions of the citizenry, and they had made good that claim since the Revolution. On the other hand, their objections to the London Act and their grumbling acquiescence in its terms placed them in direct opposition to 'the sense of the people' voiced in the City and elsewhere in the general election of 1690. As the Whigs redoubled their efforts to retain power, efforts that would prove successful in the end, they were faced with an entirely new dilemma. In seeking to secure their control of the magistracy, would they act in accordance with the principles they had lately espoused out of doors and in their rejected draft act? Would they respect the wishes of the people even if the people wished them out of office?

The Whig leaders did not have the leisure to think out their dilemma in these abstract terms. The London statute required them to act immediately. Magisterial elections were scheduled within a week of the act's passage; wardmote selections of common councilmen came within three weeks. The Common Hall summoned on 26 May saw the liverymen divide almost evenly between the parties, but the Whigs nevertheless won the day. Two Whig nominees were narrowly chosen as sheriffs in preference to two Tories. Lord Mayor Pilkington and the Whig chamberlain retained their offices, but these victories were obtained despite the apparent Common Hall leads of their opponents. The Whig

[37] DWL Morrice MS R, 146.

authorities turned indecisive results in their favour by utilizing magisterial powers they had condemned in their recent draft, although they cloaked their behaviour within traditional Common Hall procedures. The Tory leaders understandably believed they had been cheated of the offices of Lord Mayor and chamberlain. The Whigs were much less successful at the wardmotes of 10 June. The strenuous exertions of City Tory leaders encouraged the freemen to return three Tory common councilmen for every two Whigs.[38]

Like the 1690 London parliamentary poll, the City elections held pursuant to the London Act suggest a weakening of the revolutionary Whig leaders' rapport with the citizenry. Paradoxically, no sooner had the London Whigs pressed for electoral reforms than they offended the very electors who would have benefited most from reform. How can this puzzling development be explained? Several new factors in the City's revolutionary crisis seem to have cost the Whigs critical votes.

First, the issue of nonconformity as a threat to the established church had already been manipulated skilfully by Tory propagandists. The aggressive tactics of the London dissenters in 1689 had prepared the way for a backlash, directed from above, against a Whig leadership so closely connected to the nonconformist cause. Bishop Henry Compton of London and the parochial clergy made religion a critical issue in the 1690 London parliamentary poll, and once raised, the issue is likely still to have alarmed some liverymen and freemen in May and June.[39] Secondly, since the dissolution of the Convention Parliament, the London electorate had received a series of clear and unmistakable signals both from Whitehall and from Westminster that the London Whig leaders no longer enjoyed the confidence of the crown or of its ministers. Thirdly, the political loyalties of the promoters of the radical Whig draft had been impeached not only in parliament but also in the public prints. Six Whig aldermen who had also been members of the Convention (four of them for the City) were among those MPs blacklisted in Tory electoral

---

[38] Ibid., 151, 161; Journal 51, fo. 45; *The Case of the Lord Mayor and Aldermen of London, upon the petition of some of the Common-council Men* (1690); Luttrell, *Brief Relation*, ii. 47, 49–50; Lapthorne, p. 76.

[39] Horwitz, 'General Election of 1690', p. 84.

propaganda as 'commonwealthmen'.[40] The charge was certainly one that would have influenced moderate Anglican electors already aroused by the religious question. Finally, by the time of the Corporation elections in May and June, the City Tories had overcome the paralysis that afflicted them immediately after the Revolution. Politically rehabilitated by the Lieutenancy alteration, leading Tory aldermen and common councilmen of the City expected to regain power under the favourable terms of the new London Act. In 1689 the London Tories had given the City's Whig leadership a relatively poor contest, but in 1690 the City Tories struggled for power with a new-found relish.

Given this revival of popular respect for the City Churchmen, the Tories could probably have regained control of the magistracy if a new aldermanic bench had also been chosen in 1690. In fact, the clear intention of the Tory MPs who had drafted the London Act was that every aldermanic position filled since the Revolution should be refilled. This did not happen, however, because the language of the act failed specifically to designate the aldermen as among those officers of the Corporation who should now be re-elected. This deficiency was discovered too late in the parliamentay session to be corrected before adjournment, and the sitting Whig aldermen thereby retained offices to which the London Tories claimed they had no right.

The crisis in London now reached its summer climax. For the next several months a discordant fugue was played out in the politics of London. In an extended political movement, the point of one party was quickly matched by the counterpoint of the other, as both parties hastened the City's crisis towards its ultimate resolution. Six Tory City leaders sued for the offices of Lord Mayor, alderman, and chamberlain on the grounds of Whig non-compliance with the London Act and of Whig interference in the Common Hall of 26 May. The Whig aldermen not only refused to relinquish their places but also sought to recover lost Common Council seats through partial adjudication of two disputed wardmote returns. The Tory aldermen solicited and received ministerial directives in support of their displaced common councilmen. The Whigs responded to intervention from Whitehall by organizing further extra-constitutional demonstrations of dissatisfaction

---

[40] Ibid., pp. 82–4; *Some Queries concerning the election of Members for the ensuing Parliament* (1690); Andrew Browning, *Thomas Osborne* (1951), iii. 164–72.

with the ministry. When indignant Tory common councilmen refused to choose the City's ordinary committees in the autumn, the government of London collapsed amidst a shambles of constitutional uncertainty.[41]

As these jarring motifs were sounded one against the other, they threatened to prevent the crown from efficiently tapping the resources of London in the escalating war against Louis XIV. The distractions in the City coincided with William's critical Irish campaign and with the invasion scare that followed the French naval victory off Beachy Head on 30 June. The leaders of both parties in the City hastened to assure the queen of their support when the prospect of a French descent on behalf of James II materialized, but the Whigs' offer of assistance now came with several strings attached. With every reason to dislike and to distrust the present government, Monmouth and the City Whigs seized upon the invasion scare to harass the ministry and its City friends in the London Lieutenancy. William's absence in Ireland at this juncture left Mary vulnerable to Whig pressure. With this in mind, the London Whigs, perhaps acting in concert with parliamentary radicals, pursued political manoeuvres in July 1690 with two purposes. On the one hand, they sought to embarrass Tory opponents whose loyalty they genuinely suspected. On the other, they sought to present themselves to the queen as worthy of her confidence. In accomplishing these objectives, the Whigs continued to rely upon the novel forms of public pressure that had proved so useful to them in the past.

As financial difficulties threatened to obstruct the government's defence preparations, the Earl of Monmouth stepped forward on 14 July to end the queen's embarrassment with an offer of ready funds. Presumably drawing upon his customary City sources, the Earl offered £200,000 available immediately, *provided* that Mary dissolve the parliament that had demonstrated so much dislike for the City Whig leaders. Rejecting this scarcely veiled attempt at blackmail, Mary instead requested the Corporation to sponsor another loan from the London citizenry. Angered by the queen's rebuff, Monmouth, the Duke of Bolton, and others of 'that party' intervened in the City to impede the progress of the loan. This time their efforts met with less success than had been the

[41] Journal 51, fos. 58, 62; Repertory 95, fos. 142-8 et seq.; BL Add. MS 61690, fos. 56-7, 76-7; *Case of Dowgate and Aldersgate Wards*; *CSPD 1690-91*, pp. 80, 131.

case in the spring. Most Whig lenders in the City seem to have feared that financial recriminations might only assist William's enemies.[42]

This consideration did not, however, prevent the City Whigs from sparring with the government over the military defence of the capital. At the height of the panic that followed the defeat off Beachy Head, the Tory Lieutenancy had proposed raising six regiments of auxiliaries to supplement the City's nine-thousand-man militia. For their part, the Whig magistrates promoted a plan for the raising of volunteer regiments of horse and dragoons by the Corporation. Both ventures collapsed because of the mutual distrust between the Tory Lieutenancy commissioners and the Whig magistrates. When Lord Mayor Pilkington was called before the queen in council on 15 July to discuss military preparations, he took the occasion to lecture Mary on the necessity of eliminating untrustworthy persons from the ministry and the Lieutenancy. Intentionally or not, Pilkington's speech seconded Monmouth's brazen attempt at coercion on the previous day, and his remarks left several councillors spluttering about throwing a sitting Lord Mayor in the Tower.[43] A week later, following Pilkington's lead, the Whig citizenry expressed their dissatisfaction with the Tory Lieutenancy in the streets—or, rather, off the streets. When Mary reviewed the City militia at Hyde Park on the 21st, 'few housekeepers came in person'. According to Morrice, many of them instead sent servants and porters in their own arms and clothes or hired substitutes, 'so that the Appearance was far less numerous and magnificent than it has many times been'.[44] On the other hand, the London Whigs were quite enthusiastic about the City's volunteer regiments. They raised some £15,000 for their support in the expectation that the queen would provide them with reliable commanding officers. Suspicious of the Whigs' motives, however, the ministry became cautious about the establishment of what appeared to be a party militia, and in mid-August the queen suggested that the regiments were

---

[42] CLRO MSS 40/36, 40/43; DWL Morrice MS R, 158, 171; HMC *Finch MSS* ii. 371; Sir John Dalrymple, *Memoirs of Great Britain and Ireland* (1790), iii. part ii, Book v. appendix, 21, 98, 101, 117–18.

[43] Journal 51, fos. 48–9; DWL Morrice MS R, 171; Luttrell, *Brief Relation*, ii. 75–7; Lapthorne, p. 79; *A List of the Names of the Field-Officers, Captains, Lieutenants and Ensigns in the Auxiliaries of the City of London* (1690).

[44] DWL Morrice MS R, 173.

no longer necessary, by which time the invasion scare had passed. [45]

The country's escape from invasion, and William's return from Ireland in September, eased the political tension in the City but resolved none of its causes. Resolution of the City's crisis came only late in the year. After parliament had re-assembled for its 1690-1 session, some 120 City Tory stalwarts petitioned the Commons for redress against the Whig magistracy. Their list of grievances included the allegedly illegitimate tenure of many Whig magistrates and the interference of Whig aldermen in the Common Council's right to final arbitration in disputes over its own membership. [46] The City Tories had every reason to expect a sympathetic response from MPs who had already expressed their distrust of the Whigs. But the Tories' cause was lost in December when a narrow Commons vote suspended debate on their petition after four days of heated discussions. [47] This action was instrumental in the re-establishment of political order in the Corporation under Whig auspices.

The revolutionary crisis in London politics was now over. But what were the lasting effects of the crisis upon the City's politics? The answer to this question emerged gradually as London's party leaders absorbed their experiences of 1688-90, but some indications of revised perspectives were already apparent by December 1690.

The political behaviour of the City Whigs was no longer entirely consistent with the constitutional principles or with the rhetorical posture they had articulated since the Revolution. They had interfered with the freedom of the liveried electorate. They had utilized the same magisterial prerogatives they had criticized for a decade. They had successfully obstructed the legislative intention of the parliamentary majority. In the midst of the new regime's first serious military trial, they had smeared the Tories as a disloyal faction. Above all else, the Whigs had learned to take for granted neither of their revolutionary bases of support. They had been disappointed by the crown. They had been disappointed by

[45] Ibid., pp. 176-7, 183, 192; Luttrell, *Brief Relation*, ii. 90; HMC *Hastings MSS*, ii. 216.

[46] *To the Honourable, the Knights, Citizens, and Burgesses, in Parliament . . . the humble petition of the members of the Common-council . . . hereunto subscribing* (1690).

[47] BL Add. MS 42952, fos. 107-13; DWL Morrice MS R, 22-3; *CJ* x. 492, 503; Luttrell, *Brief Relation*, ii. 140-1; Horwitz, *Parliament, Policy and Politics*, p. 64.

the people in the 1690 City elections. The electorate was regarded in Whig political argument as the embodiment of native shrewdness, but in turning to Tory candidates, some electors had demonstrated more independence than virtue. The City Whig leaders may well have concluded from their reverses of 1690 that the people were not yet the best judges of their own interests. Were the Whig magistrates any better judges? As the Whigs groped towards an affirmative answer, they placed themselves in an ambiguous situation also confronted by other revolutionary elites—namely, the fine line between instructing the people and manipulating them.

As London's revolutionary crisis passed, therefore, it left the Whigs as chastened revolutionaries more interested in the consolidation of power than in its distribution. Realizing that their advocacy of popular constitutional revisions had nearly cost them control of the City, the Whigs gradually lost interest in constitutional revision in the early 1690s. They came to regard their own possession of office as the best safeguard of the rights of the people. The City Whig leaders continued to speak of the Revolution as having re-established popular liberties; but as they took increasing care to prove their competence and respectability to anxious MPs, they abandoned the 'theatre of street politics' they had hitherto endorsed. Such political expedients were inappropriate as the Whigs became more concerned with the maintenance of political stability and with co-operation between the City and the executive in the promotion of trade and investment opportunities. The people were not again to be 'invited' by the London Whigs into the politics of the Corporation in the first age of party. The revolutionary crisis in London was thus formative in the City's early eighteenth-century political structure because it began the transformation of the Whigs from the party of electoral liberties into the party of the social and economic élite.

The experiences of 1688–90 were equally critical in the transformation of the London Tories. They too were behaving in an unfamiliar manner by 1690 and were developing an unfamiliar vocabulary in their apologetics. Having obstructed the will of the City electorate in the early 1680s, and having shown no sympathy for the popular provisions of the London Whigs' draft statute, the Tories nevertheless donned the ill-fitting raiment of civic opposition. These defenders of tradition in state and of hierarchy in

church had expeditiously appropriated many of the techniques of
opposition politics. For instance, in their petition to the Commons, the Tories presented themselves as the champions of an
electorate threatened by a Whig clique seeking to 'usurp . . . all
Power in the City'. Moreover, these once staunch royalists not
only petitioned the House of Commons but also petitioned
against Whig 'Defiance of *Parliamentary Priviledges*'![48] Once above
appeals to the multitude, the City Tories now addressed the people
in persuasively argued tracts and circulated their printed petition
for public inspection. Once the party of instinctive obedience to
authority, the Tories had disrupted the work of Common Council
in October 1690 'in a very rude and clamorous manner'.[49] Further,
in claiming a right for Common Council to judge the elections of
its own members, the City Tories found precedent in a single case
of 1642, an episode from another revolutionary crisis in
London.[50] In seeking to gain power in the crisis of 1688–90, the
Tories had thus shed the character of an oligarchical clique and
had begun to put on that of an organized political party. As the
crisis passed, therefore, it left the Tories as chastened monarchists
now as much interested in the techniques of party advancement as
in the political traditions of the past.

And what of the people? What of the City's large and volatile
electorate? What was the meaning of the City's crisis for them?
This question is difficult to answer because the people ceased to
speak so emphatically for themselves in the early 1690s. The
extraordinary run of civic elections was now ended, and the extra-
constitutional opportunities for political participation passed with
the resolution of the crisis. The people seemed to acquiesce in the
Whigs' hegemony in the Corporation after 1690, or so the party's
gradual recovery of seats in Common Council would suggest. The
ultimate popular residue of the crisis was probably not complac-
ency, however, but raised expectations—expectations of which
the Whig leadership would eventually run foul. The elections,
processions, petitions, and general excitement of 1688–90 enriched

---

[48] My italics. *A Caution to the Inhabitants of Every Ward* (1690); *To the Honourable, the Knights, Citizens, and Burgesses, in Parliament* (1690).

[49] *The Case of the Lord Mayor and Aldermen of London* (1690). Also see, *A New Years Gift for the Tories, alias rapperrees* (1690).

[50] Pearl, *London and the Puritan Revolution*, pp. 137–8. This Common Hall attracted the participation of only slightly more than half the City's liverymen. Two-thirds of the liveried electorate, however, had polled for City MPs ten weeks earlier.

the political experience of the City electorate and gave the people practical instruction in what the Revolution had accomplished. Imbibing the discussion of rights rescued from arbitrary government, and internalizing that message through their own return to civic politics, the freemen and liverymen of London probably became even more sensitive to encroachments upon their traditions than in the past. For the time being, such sensitivity was expressed in the folk cult of William as a conquering hero and in the general popularity of the Revolution.[51] But in time many London citizens whose political expectations had been stimulated by the Whigs in 1688–90 would come to see the Whig leadership as the principal threat to restored popular freedoms.

[51] For William's status as a popular folk hero I am indebted to a talk by Peter Burke at the Institute of Historical Research, 1975.

III

The Politics of Belief

━━━━◆◆◆◆◆━━━━

1. Introduction: The London Dissenting Interest

No issue was more important than religion in creating and sustaining party enthusiasm in late Stuart England. The critical role of the religious question in the politics of William's and Anne's reigns makes the social composition of the nonconformists and their political activities among the most intriguing historical questions of the period. Nevertheless, investigation of late Stuart dissent has remained a rather frustrating scholarly pursuit. Although the dissenting clergy are well known through their rich legacy of sermons, treatises, and letters, the case is quite otherwise with the dissenting laity whose religious and political attitudes were shaped, in part, by the same sermons and treatises. Indeed, as one scholar has recently lamented, 'Our knowledge of the political role of dissent actually decreases as its impact becomes the more pronounced.'[1] Analysis of the political behaviour of nonconformists has been retarded by the persistence of a textbook stereotype of a stagnant dissenting population, declining in the social calibre of its leadership and lacking in political energy. One frequently reprinted text maintains that as late as the reign of Queen Anne the nonconformists were 'content to remain on the defensive', preferring to 'sacrifice their political rights' in order 'to safeguard the sanctity of their meeting houses'.[2] Even so astute a scholar as Sir John Plumb once relegated dissent to a 'minor' position among the precipitants of late seventeenth-century political conflict.[3] More recent attention to the Augustan High Church movement and to the tensions which produced it have

---

[1] Richard R. Johnson, 'Politics Redefined: An Assessment of Recent Writings on the Late Stuart Period of English History, 1660 to 1714', *William and Mary Quarterly*, 3rd Ser., 35 (1978), 716–17.

[2] Maurice Ashley, *England in the Seventeenth Century*, Hutchinson University Library (1978), pp. 247–8.

[3] Plumb, *Political Stability*, p. 38.

corrected this view, though still without satisfying the 'crying need' for local investigations of nonconformity.[4] The present chapter is a response to that need and is intended to explain why the London dissenters had become a favourite phobia of high-flying parsons and squires by the end of Anne's reign.

Recent attempts to estimate nonconformist numbers in late seventeenth-century England have supported the contemporary Anglican view that dissenters made up at least 10 per cent of the population. If the assumption is made that dissent was especially strong among the 'middling sort' in London and the provincial towns, the conclusion may be drawn that dissent was substantially over-represented within the parliamentary electorate. Geoffrey Holmes has tentatively suggested that 15–20 per cent of the early eighteenth-century electorate may be regarded as nonconformist.[5] For reasons not fully understood, dissent remained a much stronger force in some boroughs and counties than in others. London was the foremost local centre of dissent. The City's 100,000 nonconformists numbered 20 per cent of all English dissenters and 15–20 per cent of the greater London population.

This large dissenting minority was found throughout urban society, but the reasons for the strength of dissent varied from one social order to another. London was a socially unsettled and congested urban environment, and like other such environments, it had much potential as a breeding ground for restrictive and self-conscious plebeian creeds. This potential was greatest in the crowded tenement districts without the walls to the east and to the west, where a large annual influx of country immigrants jostled with thousands of other labourers, both skilled and unskilled. In these areas, the pressing population overwhelmed the parochial system of religious and social order, leaving the ecclesiastical establishment an exceedingly remote institution for workmen, apprentices, and casual labourers. Large numbers of such persons seem to have found relief from their precarious circumstances in the Baptist and Independent fellowships that thrived in the peripheral City wards and out-parishes. The parliamentary Tories sought to remedy the Church's urban handicaps through the 1711

---

[4] Holmes, *Religion and Party*, p. 34; Holmes, *Sacheverell*; G. V. Bennett, *The Tory Crisis in Church and State 1688–1730: The Career of Francis Atterbury, Bishop of Rochester* (Oxford, 1975).

[5] Holmes, *Religion and Party*, p. 21.

Fifty New Churches Act, but this Anglican response was late in coming and rather slowly implemented.

Dissent also attracted a strong following from the City's pre-eminent social order of overseas merchants. Nonconformity was especially characteristic of the colonial traders (examined in section three), and it was also widespread among the rising Iberian merchants and the élite Levant houses. The ties between the colonial trades and nonconformity were forged from 1625 to 1650 when competing political–religious perspectives also came to express rivalries within the London merchant class.[6] The continuing dissent of many colonial merchants was undoubtedly reinforced by personal contracts and business dealings with Puritans and Quakers in New England, the middle colonies, and the West Indies. The dissent of many London merchants was also a family affair. The Ashursts, Lanes, Joliffes, Sambrookes, and Westerns —pre-eminent dissenting commercial families of the late Stuart era—had each been active in the Levant or colonial trades in the mid-century decades of revolution. The nonconformity of these and other families was supported and sustained from generation to generation by the extensive marriage and business alliances that permeated the overseas trading community. Each of the families mentioned above was related to other dissenting families of City or national prominence. For instance, Sir Henry Ashurst Bt. and his brother Sir William Ashurst, both of whom were aldermen and MPs, had family ties to the celebrated Presbyterian martyr Henry Cornish, to Commons Speaker Paul Foley, and to John and Richard Hampden. Similarly, alderman William Joliffe was tied by marriage to the Foleys and to the Papillons, a leading London Huguenot family with a strong electoral influence in Dover.

Continuing work on the socio-economic background of early Stuart puritanism has supported established generalizations about a close relationship between religious activism and the 'middling sort'.[7] Prospering through their own pains, petty-bourgeois shopkeepers and craftsmen came to express a political and religious assertiveness that matched their economic independence. Self-employed and self-confident, these serious and sober persons

---

[6] Robert Brenner, 'The Civil War Politics of London's Merchant Community', *Past and Present*, 58 (1973), 53–107.

[7] Christopher Hill, *Society and Puritanism in Pre-Revolutionary England*, 2nd edn. (New York, 1967), pp. 124–44; Manning, pp. 152–62.

rejected ecclesiastical ceremony and hierarchy as superfluous and extravagant. Turning instead to Calvinist theology and discipline, they found doctrines that sanctioned their earnest behaviour and invited their active leadership in fashioning a spiritual kingdom on earth. Neither the moral easiness of the restored monarchy nor the political subservience of the restored episcopate is likely to have impressed industrious Puritans who became industrious dissenters after 1660. Indeed, as will be suggested below, the social core of London nonconformity was to be found within the City's prosperous interior retail wards.

The strength of dissent in London can be explained, then, by pointing to social factors that sustained nonconformity among the poor, the middle class, and the commercial élite. Two additional encouragements also merit notice. One of these was the supportive presence in London of large non-English churches whose Calvinist traditions were closer to those of the nonconformists than to those of the Church of England, and whose members frequently intermarried with dissenting families. The most important of these churches were the French Reformed Church at Threadneedle Street, the Dutch Reformed Church at Austin Friars, and the Scots Presbyterian Church at Founders' Hall. The London dissenters were also fortunate in the quality of their ministerial leadership. At the hub of English commercial and political life, London attracted the talents of the ablest nonconformist preachers and organizers—Richard Baxter, John Howe, Daniel Burgess, Timothy Cruso, Daniel Williams, William Penn, Benjamin Keach, and Joseph Stennet, to mention only a few. Encouraged alike by the friendship and patronage of wealthy merchants and by the opportunity of exerting considerable influence through preaching and the press, these clerics were indispensable in maintaining nonconformist enthusiasm in London during the dark years of Caroline tribulation and the ensuing era of renewal.

Both the resilience of late Stuart dissent and the continuing importance of religion as a public issue make the relative dearth of scholarship on the dissenters somewhat surprising. Two obstacles, however, have retarded analysis of the dissenting community in London and elsewhere. The first of these is that of making positive identifications of prominent nonconformist lay families who, before 1689, had little reason to leave behind records of their dissent. Even those sources available after 1689 are scanty, incomplete, and occasionally misleading. Although most nonconformist churches did keep records, few membership books beginning before the mid-eighteenth century survive, and those that do survive frequently record members by surname only. This obstacle is compounded by a second difficulty, that of establishing a satisfactory definition of dissent, an undertaking as problematic as that of defining puritanism. The practice of occasional conformity and the passions it produced among both dissenters and Anglicans point to the difficulty of making a neat separation between the one and the other. How, for example, should the historian regard the successful entrepeneur of dissenting parentage who conformed in mid-career or late in life? Similarly, in the absence of other information, should the Whig draper whose wife or whose brother was a nonconformist also be regarded as one? Should Presbyterians be treated together with Independents or with 'Infidels, Turks, Hereticks, Quakers, Anabaptists, Latitudinarians, and Free-thinkers', to repeat a typical high-flying refrain? Consideration of these problems may be illuminated further by providing a few biographical illustrations.

What, for instance, is to be made of the religious position of Sir Gilbert Heathcote, Whig City leader, merchant MP, and the greatest commercial magnate of his day? No direct evidence suggests that he was a dissenter, and no recent historian has described him as one. Heathcote was characterized as 'a zealous Church-of-England man' by the contemporary printer John Dunton, but Dunton's testimony is frequently more facetious than truthful. Supporting this description, however, is the fact that Sir Gilbert's New York brother Caleb was a leader in the partial establishment of the Church of England in that colony, and was an active enemy of the New York Presbyterians. On the other hand, Sir Gilbert and his brother came from a once strongly Puritan Chesterfield family, and their London cousin George Heathcote was a Quaker. Sir Gilbert's closest business associate in the early 1690s was Arthur Shallett, an Independent wine merchant and MP. A list of the 1690s members of the Devonshire Square Baptist Church includes a 'sister Heathcott', and the surname is so rare, even in London, that a family relationship between this woman and Sir Gilbert is quite likely. Moreover, his son John was intimate in 1715 with young Dudley Ryder and with that future attorney-general's Hackney circle of dissenting friends. Finally, in March

1731, when Heathcote was nearly eighty, he introduced a bill in the Commons to prevent suits for tithes, a measure that would have been especially beneficial to the Quakers. This evidence certainly suggests that Heathcote was strongly interested in dissent, but is it sufficient to describe him as a crypto-nonconformist?[8]

Other examples of the difficulty of ascertaining religious convictions may be found in the cases of Sir Henry Hatsell and his brother Lawrence. Sons of an 'active roundhead' of Devonshire who sat in Cromwell's parliaments, the first Hatsell was an Exchequer Baron under William, and the second was a scrivener and Million Bank director. The marriages of the brothers strongly suggest that they inherited their father's hostility to the Anglican Church establishment. Sir Henry Hatsell married a daughter of the foremost merchant member of the Dutch Church, Austin Friars, and the name of Lawrence Hatsell's wife was recorded in the membership book of the Devonshire Square Baptists.[9] Unfortunately, no direct evidence proves that either brother ever attended a dissenting meeting.

These problems of identification and of religious ambiguity make detailed analysis of the London dissenters a hazardous venture. The historian must either remain content with impressionistic generalizations or be prepared to take many risks in interpreting fragmentary data. The latter course has been taken here with full awareness that attaining statistical precision about something as elusive as religious belief is extremely difficult.

The measurements and interpretations of City dissent in the following sections of this chapter rest both upon the concept of a London 'dissenting interest' and upon prosopographical analysis of some 800 persons who have been included in it. More than three-quarters of the London dissenting interest were definite nonconformists, though only dissenters whose wealth, occupation, or political activity marked them as substantial citizens have been

---

[8] *DNB*; Romney Sedgwick, *The House of Commons 1715–1754* (The History of Parliament, 1970), ii. 123; Devonshire Square Baptist Church, Stoke Newington, MS Minutes, *Lib.* A; Dudley Ryder, *Diary 1715–16*, ed. William Matthews (1939), p. 52; Joseph Besse, *A Collection of the Sufferings of the People Called Quakers* (1753), i. 462, ii. 259; *CSPD 1691–92*, pp. 322–3; John Dunton, *Life and Errors* (1818), p. 354; Dixon R. Fox, *Caleb Heathcote, Gentleman Colonist* (New York, 1926); Henry G. Hood, Jr., 'A Study of the Occasional Conformity and Schism Acts, their Effects, and the Agitation for their Repeal' (Univ. of Pennsylvania Ph.D. thesis, 1956), p. 35.

[9] *BDBR* ii. 73; Devonshire Square MS Minutes, *Lib.* A.

considered. Their names were recovered from all the surviving London nonconformist church books, from accounts of the prosecutions of London and Middlesex dissenters in the 1680s, and from the records of the earliest nonconformist organizations.[10] The remainder of the dissenting interest is made up of probable dissenters, like Sir Henry Hatsell and Lawrence Hatsell, and possible dissenters or persons strongly interested in dissent, like Sir Gilbert Heathcote. The family histories and careers of these individuals are so closely tied to those of known nonconformists as to make their sympathy for dissent obvious and their occasional participation in nonconformist social and religious life quite likely. Moreover, quite a few of these individuals probably were indeed dissenters—dissenters whose names simply do not appear in the patchy records of London nonconformity.

The conception of a London dissenting interest also mirrors late Stuart discussion of the religious problem. The phrase 'dissenting interest' was one employed by contemporaries, and one with a somewhat ambiguous meaning similar to that introduced above. Dissenters applied the label to themselves, but Anglican usage was closer to the definition used here. High-Churchmen regarded definite dissenters and persons of doubtful commitments as but different varieties of the same religious species. As far as they were concerned, the Church of England was endangered as much by nominal Anglicans, who had been corrupted by or even won over to nonconformist political and religious perspectives, as it was by the stalwart nonconformist minority itself. Dr Henry Sacheverell, for instance, was gravely concerned about the political influence of actual dissenters, but he was even more concerned about false brethren 'who are for a *Neutrality in Religion*, who *really* are of *none*, but are a *secret* sort of *Reserv'd Atheists*, who always pretend to be *of* the *Church*, join in the *Herd*, and will sometimes frequent Our *Publick Communion*, as long as the *Government* appears on Our side; but if anything is to be got by it, can with as *safe a Conscience* slide privately into a *Conventicle*, and look as *Demure* as the slyest Saint amongst 'em.'[11]

---

[10] Church record books are listed individually in the bibliography. Early nonconformist organizations are discussed below. For 1680s' persecutions, see: GL MS 9060; CLRO Conventicles Boxes 1 and 2; *Middlesex County Records (Old Series)*, ed. John C. Jaeffreson, iv (1965).

[11] Sacheverell, *Perils of False Brethren* (1709), pp. 10–11.

Such High-Church perceptions frequently led to rabid rhetorical flights of fantasy, but they were grounded in reality. This was so because the differences between nonconformists and the Church of England did not produce, either in practice or in argument, a simple polarization between two mutually hostile camps. Instead, as the burning issue of occasional conformity reveals, the boundary between dissent and moderate conformist piety was an extremely fluid one. Though some dissenters found occasional conformity incompatible with their principles, and though others suffered it only as a necessary evil, still others may have regularly divided their worship between a parish church and a favourite meeting-house. Moreover, the traffic between church and conventicle clearly moved in both directions and at varying paces. For some persons of dissenting origins, occasional communion provided a quick route to full conformity, but for others it was a long-term half-way house which required neither the repudiation of dissenting family and friends nor the loss of nonconformist identity. Similarly, the preaching reputations of some nonconformist divines probably enticed some moderate conformists into their auditories. This may especially have been true of persons of Puritan stock who had shied away from dissent only because of the disabilities inflicted upon nonconformists before 1689.

The London dissenting interest is not, therefore, merely a convenient concept. It incorporates the very religious confusion that so disturbed the schematic ecclesiastical notions of the high-flyers. On the one hand, it cautiously extends beyond the parameters of proven dissent to include those persons closest to known dissenters in the late Stuart religious spectrum. On the other hand, it is much narrower in definition than the 'low-church party', the equivalent of the Whig following in church and society. Study of the dissenting interest also invites joint analysis with the English nonconformists of 'French Presbyterians', like the Houblon, Delmé, Dubois, and Lethieullier mercantile families, and of similarly denizened Dutch traders. However, only those non-Anglican Protestants of foreign extraction with clear nonconformist ties have been considered as sufficiently interested in dissent to merit inclusion in the dissenting interest.

A final question of definition that must be considered is that of the internal cohesion of the London dissenting interest. Does the conflation of Presbyterians, Independents, Baptists, Quakers,

possible dissenters, and sympathizers render the dissenting interest an artificial grouping that would have been totally unrecog-
nizable to those included within it? Were the different bodies of
dissenters so divided against one another as to be incapable of
concerted political endeavour? These questions are most appro-
priately asked in reference to the Quakers, who scrupulously
maintained their separate identity, and whose beliefs were no
better liked by other dissenters than they were by the established
clergy. Nevertheless, if Church-Tory accounts of critical City
elections of the last years of Anne's reign are to be credited, the
London Quakers gave welcome assistance to the main body of
dissenters in promoting Whig candidates.[12] Although the peculiar
position of the Quakers needs to be acknowledged, Quakers and
other dissenters do appear to have recognized their common interests. The same may be said of the Baptists who, though divided
amongst themselves and somewhat lacking in collective identity,
were subsequently to join with Presbyterians and Independents in
establishing the Dissenting Deputies.

The Presbyterians and Independents were, in any case, the
predominant persuasions within the dissenting interest, accounting for most of the dissenters' political visibility and for most of
their commercial capital. Although the differences between these
groups were important and will be discussed below, the many
connections between them require attention here. The issues that
had originally divided their Puritan progenitors were still aired,
but a general softening in the Presbyterian and Independent positions on church organization occurred once such organization was
permitted. Unable to perfect their earlier models of national ecclesiastical discipline, both bodies borrowed from each others's tenets
in establishing functional church polities under the terms of the
1689 toleration.[13] The adoption of similar forms of congregational
self-government enlarged a consensus that already included many
doctrinal and liturgical questions. In London, the Revolution
was actually followed by a union of Presbyterian and Independent
congregations which, though short-lived, promoted an awareness
of a common heritage and of common prospects. Furthermore, this

[12] *Post Boy* no. 2881, 24–7 Oct. 1713 and no. 2928, 11–13 Feb. 1714; *Supplement*
no. 573, 12–14 Sept. 1711.

[13] Russell E. Richey, 'Effects of Toleration on Eighteenth-Century Dissent', *Journal of
Religous History*, 8 (1975), 350–63.

temporary union brought together many leading London Presbyterian and Independent laymen as managers of a fund for the support of clerical education and the augmentation of clerical stipends.[14] Although the responsibilities of the managers of this Common Fund were entirely charitable, Common Fund meetings facilitated the association of dissenting representatives also active in secular affairs. For instance, sixteen of the forty-one Common Fund lay managers or proposed managers (1690–3) were elected during their careers to London offices ranging from common councilman to City MP.

The demise of this fund and the establishment in 1694 and 1695 respectively of separate Presbyterian and Congregational Funds is unlikely to have greatly marred the appreciation of common interests among City dissenting leaders and office-holders. Although now divided, the two funds continued to draw together from different congregations lay figures of the same calibre as those of the Common Fund, and each functioned somewhat as a London denominational steering group. Together, the funds constituted a dissenting leadership élite whose contacts surely carried over into other fields of concern.[15] Moreover, many London Presbyterian and Independent fund managers remained in association with one another and with other dissenting spokesmen in still another common enterprise. This was the New England Company, a Puritan missionary society created in 1649, which survived the Restoration to become the most distinguished nonconformist organization prior to the formation of the Dissenting Deputies in 1732.

The nonconformist character of the New England Company has not previously been emphasized so strongly.[16] The original members of the concern, who were drawn overwhelmingly from London, were entirely Puritan and largely Independent. This composition was modified, however, by its 1662 royal charter, which removed several persons politically active during the Interregnum and replaced them with reliable peers and courtiers. During the long governorship of Robert Boyle (1662–89), the moderate

---

[14] Alexander Gordon, *Freedom After Ejection* (Publications of the Univ. of Manchester, cxiv), Manchester, 1917; Charles G. Bolam, *et al., The English Presbyterians: From Elizabethan Puritanism to Modern Unitarianism* (1968), pp. 99–102, 119–23.

[15] DWL MS Minutes and Index of the Presbyterian Fund Board, i; DWL Microfilm Minutes of the Congregational Fund Board, i–ii.

[16] William Kellaway, *The New England Company, 1649–1776* (1961).

conformist natural philosopher, the company assiduously devoted itself to the non-controversial task of converting the American Indians. However, the company continued to sponsor nonconformist missionaries exclusively, and after 1689 its co-opted membership recovered much of its original religious character during the governorship of Presbyterian Sir William Ashurst (1695–1720). The Company also excited the jealousy of the episcopal establishment, which in 1701 organized its own missionary society, the more broadly concerned Society for the Propagation of the Gospel in Foreign Parts.

Analysis of the composition of the New England Company from 1681 to 1715 reveals that two-thirds of its membership may be identified from other sources as dissenters. The remainder could not have accepted election to the body without being interested in dissent. Joined together for a distinctive spiritual venture, the membership was so interconnected by business and marriage alliances as to suggest its recruitment from a recognized coterie of leading Presbyterian, Independent, and foreign Protestant families. Moreover, the combined political accomplishments of the members marked them as men of exceptional influence in the City. Twelve of the forty-five members of 1698 once served as London sheriffs; nine were aldermen, of whom five were elevated to the Lord Mayor's chair; four were directors of the Bank of England; and Sir Henry Hatsell, as noted above, was a Baron of the Exchequer. Although the concerns of the company's members were largely apolitical, the body was nevertheless the most interesting expression of London nonconformist identity and unity across sectarian lines. Presbyterian and Independent spokesmen of the dissenting interest gained from the New England Company not only greater familiarity with one another, but also greater experience in working together for shared objectives.

This introductory sketch of the London dissenting interest has admittedly revealed it to be a heterogeneous body of persons. Reflecting the fragmented nature of dissenting religious life, it was far from being a phalanx of regimented political cadres. Nevertheless, the dissenting interest was a distinct element within City politics, and it may be considered the irreducible core of the London Whigs. Expressing their unity most visibly in Corporation polls, the London dissenters were also linked by the institutional expressions of a reviving Puritan community. Having lived in something of a political wilderness from 1660 to 1689, the dissenters found in toleration the promise of renewed engagement in a secular world they could still influence if no longer remake. The significance of this engagement may better be judged by examining the sociology of dissent and the presence of the London dissenting interest in late Stuart commerce, investment, and politics.

2. Dissent and Society

A. Patterns

If dissenters of all persuasions were clearly found at every level of urban society, differences in the social quality of the dissenting bodies in London were equally apparent. These differences may best be outlined through an analysis of the dissenting interest restricted to those persons of known or probable sectarian preferences. Because this information is available for only half the dissenting interest, the social comparisons made here rest on rather small numbers of individuals. The difficulties of identification again make this unavoidable, but generalizations may be strengthened by examining several indices of sectarian social character. To these limited statistical comparisons will be joined a more impressionistic but still informative biographical examination of dissenting notables of differing backgrounds. These personal studies will be helpful in measuring the calibre of dissenting lay leadership in London.

Table 3.1 Nonconformist Church Organizations in London, 1715

	Presbyterian	Independent	Baptist	Quaker	Unknown	Total
City Within the Walls	12	5	4	2	1	24
City Without the Walls	3	7	9	2	1	22
Adjacent Parishes Within the Bills of Mortality	13	11	14	3	2	43
Total	28	23	27	7	4	89

Based on transcript of 1715 list of London dissenting meeting-places in BL Add. MS 32057, fo. 11. I have counted congregations rather than meeting-places.

The geographical distribution of London dissenting congregations, surveyed in Table 3.1, may be supplemented with additional information in order to suggest a few social patterns. Presbyterian meetings were most numerous in vicinities of concentrated wealth—within the London walls, in the fashionable West End, and in detached centres of élite settlement like Hackney and Stoke Newington. Baptist and Independent churches were also found in these areas, but in noticeably smaller numbers. Accounting for only one-sixth of the nonconformist meetings within the walls, the Baptists were instead probably the largest sect outside the walls. That the Baptists were somewhat plebeian in their social composition is also indicated by the concentration of their congregations in manufacturing areas to the east and in the western ward of Farringdon Without. Many Independent congregations were also found in such industrial environments.

This geographical distribution of dissenting churches in 1715 seems, therefore, to correspond well with some mid-seventeenth-century urban religious profiles. Although lacking the perfection of its classical model, Presbyterianism still offered orderly notions of church organization and social relations to well-to-do bourgeois families. The more democratic polity of the Baptists, on the other hand, had much less support from the social élite and much more support from economically marginal, but religiously independent, artificers and craftsmen. Though also attracting many such producers, the Independent congregations probably included many more middling and substantial traders than did the Baptists. This fact is not entirely evident, however, from the nonconformist church census analysed above, which may under-represent the number of Independent congregations within the walls.[17]

The greater social respectability of the City Independents, and the greater scarcity of prominent men among the Baptists, both become more apparent from the data recorded in Table 3.2. If the accumulation of offices may be taken as indicative of relative social standing, Presbyterianism again commanded the loyalty of the most distinguished group of dissenting office-holders. Half these late Stuart London office-holders were Presbyterian, and more citizens who possessed the social respect required for election

---

[17] Examination of other sources supports the accuracy of the 1715 list except for the number of Independent congregations within the walls. As many as twelve appear to have been established in the decade after 1689. See GL MS 9579; Wilson, *Dissenting Churches*.

Table 3.2 Office-holding by Late Stuart London Dissenters of Known or Probable Persuasion, 1685–1715

	Common Council	City Magistrate	House of Commons	Government Place(s)	Total Office-holders
Presbyterians	31	12	19	12	52
Independents	24	6	6	1	29
Baptists	8	7	9	4	20
Quakers	2	0	0	0	2

Dissenting office-holders who held more than one office have been counted under each appropriate column, but they have only been counted once in the column of totals. The City magistrate column includes persons who held one or more of the following offices: alderman, chamberlain, Sheriff of London and Middlesex, and Lord Mayor.

to magisterial office adhered to that dissenting persuasion than to any other. Independents, however, were also quite numerous among dissenting common councilmen of known persuasion. Moreover, the much greater success of Independents than of Baptists in obtaining that office certainly suggests that Independency was stronger within bourgeois social ranks, and it may also suggest that Baptist electors within the Corporation were somewhat fewer in number. The almost complete absence of Quakers among London office-holders was more a product of their religious ethos of withdrawal than of any lack of prosperous followers, as may be seen from Table 3.3.

Dissenters of known or probable persuasion account for only one of every eleven London merchants actively trading in 1695 or 1696. Nevertheless, except for an over-representation of Quaker merchants, the patterns in Table 3.3 are unlikely to be misleading. What the table most clearly indicates is again the superior social quality of the London Presbyterians. Not only did Presbyterian merchants probably outnumber their Independent counterparts, but they also included more traders operating with large annual business volumes. This may account for the greater numbers of City Presbyterians chosen for magisterial office and returned to the House of Commons. Because of their greater representation within the upper ranks of the bourgeoisie, Presbyterians were more successful in attaining positions of political power or influence. If leading Presbyterians were clustered at the apex of dissenting

Table 3.3 Trade Turn-overs of Dissenting London Merchants of Known or Probable Persuasion in 1695 or 1696

	£500-£2500	£2500+	£5000+	£10,000+	Total Merchants Active in 1695 or 1696	Average Turn-overs (£)
Presbyterians	11	9	1	3	24	4,666
Independents	6	2	3	0	11	3,044
Baptists	1	1	0	1	3	——
Quakers	15	8	6	1	30	3,519

Trade turn-overs taken with permission from D. W. Jones, 'London Overseas Merchant Groups', Appendices B(1) to B(11), pp. 388–468. Because the records of the London Quakers are greatly superior to those of other dissenting bodies, more Quaker merchants have been identified. The total number of Quakers trading in 1695 or 1696 may not may have greatly exceeded thirty.

mercantile society, prominent Baptist merchants were relatively few. The London Quakers, on the other hand, included many smaller and middling merchants whose turn-overs matched those of Independent houses, and several Quaker merchants were among the City's commercial élite.

The nonconformist presence in London commerce and investment will be considered more fully in sections three and four below, but the social patterns presented here are again supported by the data presented in Table 3.4. Although the Quakers and Baptists included some men of considerable wealth, comparatively few persons from these persuasions joined other dissenters in seeking to influence the crown through generous lending in the critical post-revolutionary year of 1689. Instead, Presbyterians and Independents had more money to lend and were more eager to employ their resources for political purposes. In subsequent years, the capital of wealthy and respected City Presbyterians and Independents would mark the intersection between the dissenting interest and the new 'moneyed interest' of public investors.

B. Presbyterians and Independents

These social patterns of late Stuart City nonconformity not only reflect differences among dissenting persuasions but also suggest that London Presbyterians and Independents shared more with each other than either religious body did with the Baptists or the

Quakers. The temporary London union and the abortive Common Fund of the early 1690s expressed the common intellectual heritage of Presbyterians and Independents, their common objections to the established church, and their common position as the English brethren of the 'reformed churches' of the continent and of Scotland. Although the differences between their 'élitist' and 'democratic' notions of church polity also carried over into their social followings, Presbyterians and Independents nevertheless recognized their religious kinship. Some dissenting City families gave belief to both persuasions, and intermarriage between Presbyterian and Independent mercantile families was commonplace. Examples might also be given of dissenting clergy, and even of entire congregations, who straddled the ecclesiastical fence between these dissenting church bodies. But who were the City Presbyterians and the City Independents? Only a look at the actual lives and careers of some of the persons who cut these patterns will bring them to life.

Table 3.4 Nonconformist Subscriptions to a Corporation Loan to the Crown, July 1689–February 1690

	£500 or less	£500+	£1000+	£2000+	Total Subscribers	Total Subscription (£)
Presbyterians	18	5	3	3	29	19,300
Independents	19	7	2	1	29	12,950
Baptists	6	1	0	0	7	1,350
Quakers	5	1	0	0	6	1,000

CLRO MS 40/36.

There is no doubt about the identity of the premier Presbyterian family in late Stuart London. Sir Henry Ashurst Bt. (1642–1711) and Sir William Ashurst (1647–1720) were the sons of a Civil War and Restoration Levant merchant who was also an intimate friend of the venerable Richard Baxter. Both Ashursts were leading Turkey merchants of their day and men of notable wealth. The brothers' distinguished political careers made them spokesmen not only for City Presbyterians but also for dissenters across the country, including those of the family's native county of Lancashire. An Exclusionist MP, Sir Henry became an alderman under

James II and continued his parliamentary career after the Revolution, also serving briefly as an Excise Commissioner. Sir William Ashurst was Alderman of Billingsgate Ward for thirty-three years, obtaining the mayoralty in 1693–4. Like his brother, he sat in several parliaments and was a Commissioner of the Excise.[18]

The Ashursts were especially active in nonconformist affairs. Sir Henry was a manager of the Presbyterian Fund, and as noted above, Sir William acted as governor of the New England Company for twenty-five years. Sir William supported young dissenting clergymen as chaplains, and Sir Henry left the Presbyterian divine, Matthew Henry, £800 to use 'for the glory of God'. The brothers also commanded the respect of the Congregationalist establishment of the Massachusetts Bay Colony. In 1689 Sir Henry was charged by Boston's revolutionary provincial government with the trust of re-securing confirmation of the original Massachusetts charter from the new English regime. He served as agent for the colonies of Massachusetts, Connecticut, and New Hampshire at various dates over the next twenty years. As governor of the New England Company, Sir William Ashurst was also interested in the affairs of North Americans, both red and white. He was a Proprietor of West Jersey, and in 1710, he was requested by Massachusetts to follow his brother as agent but declined for reasons of health. The influence of the family continued far into the eighteenth century. A son of each brother sat in the House of Commons, and seven Ashursts of succeeding generations were members of the New England Company.[19]

Among Sir William Ashurst's aldermanic colleagues in the last years of Anne's reign was Presbyterian John Fryer (1671–1726). Fryer's absorption as an apprentice of the preaching of Timothy Cruso and Daniel Williams, as well as his presence at the execution of 'ye pious Mr. Cornish', informed his mature religious and political outlook. A pewterer by trade, Fryer was aided in his rise to the magistracy and to directorships in the United East India Company and the South Sea Company by notable inheritances.

---

[18] The surname is also spelled Asshurst. Henning, i. 558–60; Bodl. MS Rawlinson D 862, No. 19, fo. 37, T. Preston to Sir Thomas Rawlinson, 20 Oct. 1689.

[19] GL Microfilm New England Company Letterbook, 1688–1760, fos. 92–3, Joseph Dudley to Sir William Ashurst, 15 Nov. 1710; CSPCol vii. No. 739; Sedgwick, i. 423; Kellaway, pp. 167–8, 289–90; Lacey, p. 376.

Chosen alderman in the year of Sacheverell's impeachment, Fryer came to believe that the 'Protestant interest' was imperilled by the Church-Tory revival that occurred thereafter: 'All things lookt very dismall by ye wicked arts of an ill Ministry: who were indeavoring to bring in ye Pretender, and thereby would have restored Popery amongst us . . . '. But the Protestant Succession was preserved through the vigilance of its supporters, and Fryer himself assisted in the suppression of Jacobitism as Sheriff of London and Middlesex during the 1715–16 tumults. He had by then become one of the first Hanoverian baronets, a reward he attributed to his refusal to resign as alderman after the passage of the Occasional Conformity Act.[20]

Not all City Presbyterians were as wealthy and prominent as the Ashurts or Sir John Fryer, but Presbyterianism does seem to have been more widespread among successful urban professionals than were other dissenting perspectives. For instance, two-thirds of the late Stuart London medical men identified as dissenters were of Presbyterian sentiments. Among them was Henry Sampson (1629–1700), whose daybooks reveal him to have been quite familiar with other Presbyterians in learned professions.[21] Sampson was an ejected clergyman who after 1662 had turned from the cure of souls to the cure of bodies, and after the 1688 Revolution he represented the Silver Street Presbyterian meeting on both the Common Fund and the Presbyterian Fund. Sampson and his half-brother Nehemiah Grew (1641–1712), also a physician, walked in the spiritual footsteps of Sampson's step-father, Dr Obadiah Grew, the Presbyterian Civil War divine. Among their Presbyterian medical colleagues were Edward Hulse (1631–1711) and George Howe (1655?–1710).[22]

Presbyterianism seems to have been the most pronounced persuasion among London dissenting legal men and booksellers, several of whom were also friends or acquaintances of Henry Sampson. For instance, one of Sampson's Presbyterian clients in the 1690s was Sir Thomas Rokeby (1631–99). Rokeby and

[20] GL MS 12, 017 with quotations from fos. 14, 28. Fryer inherited a portion of the estates of Restoration magnate Sir John Cutler through his dissenting uncle Edmund Boulter, a London grocer and Boston MP.
[21] BL Add. MS 4460. Extracts from Sampson's papers are printed in *Gentleman's Magazine*, New Ser., xxxv (April, 1851), 381–8; ibid. (July, 1851), 11–17; *Christian Reformer or Unitarian Magazine and Review*, New Ser., xviii (1862), 235–47.
[22] *DNB* on each individual.

his City merchant brother Benjamin, a director of the New East
India Company, were the sons of a Cromwellian officer. Sir
Thomas was an active proponent in 1688 of the Prince of
Orange's interest in his native York, and he was rewarded there-
after with judgeships of Common Pleas and of King's Bench.[23]
Henry Sampson may also have known the Presbyterian civilian
Sir Edward Abney, who was MP for Leicester from 1690 to 1698.
Sir Edward was the elder brother of London Alderman Sir Thomas
Abney (1640–1722) who, like Sampson, was a member of the
Silver Street Presbyterian congregation, and who was also a
leading London dissenting spokesman.[24] As a patron of the London bookstalls, Sampson was also familiar with many dissenting
bookdealers. One of them was Thomas Cockerill who, like Sampson, served as a manager of the Common Fund. Another was
Thomas Parkhurst, also a member of the Silver Street meeting,
who was reputed to be 'the most eminent Presbyterian Bookseller
in the Three Kingdoms'.[25]

The wealth, status, and reputations of the London Presbyterians
mentioned here make understandable the complaints of high-flying
squires, like Sir John Pakington, about the weekly crowding of
coaches near London dissenting conventicles. The City Presbyterian meetings were assemblies of families of obvious social
substance. The same may be said of several Independent congregations, or at least of those Independent congregations within
the walls, which also attracted many followers from the ranks of
successful merchants and tradesmen. Although no known Independent families possessed the prestige of the Ashursts, City
Independents like the Boddingtons, Brooksbanks, Fleetwoods,
Hackshaws, and Hollises were nevertheless men of superior standing. The chance survival of the diary of George Boddington
makes him the most interesting of these.

George Boddington (1646–1719) was the eldest son of a
Lothbury packer of the same name. In 1666, when the younger
Boddington came of age, his father set him up in the Levant trade
with an original capital of £1,000. In the same year, Boddington

---

[23] *DNB*; Sir Thomas Rokeby, 'A Brief Memoir of Mr. Justice Rokeby', *Publications of the Surtees Society*, xxxvii (1861), 58, 62.

[24] *DNB*; Edmund Calamy, *Memoirs of the Life of . . . John Howe* (1724), p. 210; Edmund Calamy, *An Historical Account of My Own Life* (1829), ii. 245–6.

[25] Dunton, i. 205, 214; Gordon, pp. 162–3; Henry R. Plomer, *A Dictionary of . . . Printers and Booksellers . . . 1688 to 1725* (1922), p. 76.

was accepted as a member of the gathered congregation of Thomas Vincent which met at the Three Cranes, Thames Street. He must have prospered quickly because four years later he married a bride with a £2,000 portion. She was the daughter of William Steele (d. 1680), Recorder of the Corporation during the Common-wealth and Cromwellian Lord Chancellor of Ireland. Despite his commercial success, Boddington remained an exceptionally scrupulous Independent. He left the Thames Street church when it abandoned the congregational way of admitting members only upon a public profession of faith. Admitted to the Lime Street meeting, Boddington represented it on the board of the Common Fund, and from 1695 to 1702, he served as treasurer of the Con-gregational Fund. In 1689 he was elected to the London Common Council, 'but not being qualified by the Sacramental test only appeared to Act for about two months'. Chosen governor of the minor Greenland Company in 1693, Boddington was elected a Bank of England director the following year. Finding that Bank business claimed too much of his time, he disqualified himself for the office by selling his stock. In 1702 Boddington was elected MP for Wilton; but his election was challenged, and he was dis-qualified for again refusing to comply with the Test Act.[26]

George Boddington's acquaintances included Joseph Brooks-bank (1655–1726), who provides another illustration of the calibre of leading London Independents. Like Boddington, Brooksbank represented the Lime Street Independent meeting on the Congre-gational Fund board after the Revolution. A merchant and ware-houseman of Cateaton Street, he counted among his relations by marriage the Whig Lord Mayor Sir Thomas Stamp (1628–1711), whose surname became the given name of Brooksbank's son. Again like Boddington, Brooksbank was an original subscriber to the Bank of England. Other investments included a pro-prietorship in West Jersey and estates in his native Yorkshire. Stamp Brooksbank (1694–1756), son of Joseph, was one of the foremost nonconformist spokesmen of the next generation. A successful Levant trader, the younger Brooksbank was also a member of parliament, a director and governor of the Bank of

---

[26] GL MS 10,823/1 with quotation at fo. 44; PRO PROB 11/569 (Browning), fo. 99; History of Parliament Trust microfilm of Robert Walcott, 'MPs Tempus Anne'; J. R. Woodhead, *The Rulers of London 1660–1689* (1965), p. 33.

England, a dissenting deputy, and a New England Company member.[27]

C. Baptists

The social and religious milieu of the London Baptists was greatly different from that of the Presbyterians and the Independents. Contentious and democratic, the Baptists showed fewer signs of denominational consciousness than dissenters of other persuasions. Arminian and Arian, general and particular, seventh day and 'monerkey judmentt', the Baptists expressed every opinion from plebeian scepticism and anti-clericalism to expectant millenarianism. This lack of consensus was the cause of frequent disciplinary disputes and of congregational schisms and secessions. With the exception of the Devonshire Square church, which was located near wealthy City parishes, the Baptist congregations were made up primarily of cloth-workers, artisans, and tradesmen of the humbler sort. Typical was the church meeting at White's Alley, which counted only one well-to-do member in the 1690s out of a total adult male membership of 150. The congregation had recurrent difficulty in raising the meeting-house rent and suffered a schism in 1699 over the question of Arminian teaching.[28]

The 'mechanick' composition of the London Baptists was also characteristic of their clergy. Some of these pastors had mediocre educations; others maintained themselves through an industrial trade; few were well equipped to act as dissenting spokesmen. What the London Baptists may have lacked in social quality, however, they compensated for in their numbers. An abiding political irritant to the monarchy after 1660, the London Baptists also numbered some West Countrymen who aroused suspicions during Monmouth's 1685 rising. Although the Baptists produced few civic leaders after 1688, Baptist tradesmen free of the Corporation joined other dissenting electors in supporting the political rebirth of City nonconformity in William's reign.

Chief among the exceptional Baptist merchants, investors, and office-holders who appear in Tables 3.2, 3.3, and 3.4 were several Devonshire Square meeting habitués. The social respectability of

[27] PRO PROB 11/609 (Plymouth), fo. 117; Ryder, p. 259; Gordon, p. 224; Kellaway, p. 291; Sedgwick, i. 495.
[28] GL MS 592.

that congregation was due at least in part to the reputation of its clergyman, William Kiffen (c. 1616–1701), the aged Civil War Baptist spokesman who served briefly as alderman under James II. Joining his pastor on the bench in 1687–8 was Sir John Eyles (d. 1703), a West Indies trader and the last Lord Mayor during the suspension of the charter. The sons of a Wiltshire wool-stapler, Eyles and his brother Sir Francis Eyles Bt. (c. 1650–1716) ranked among the foremost merchants of their day. Sir Francis followed Sir John as alderman in Anne's reign, also serving for a long time as director of the Bank of England and as a director (at different times) of the Old, the New, and the United East India companies. Three sons of the two brothers maintained the family interest in City politics, in the stocks, and in the Commons.[29]

Other prominent Devonshire Square Baptists included Alder-man Gregory Page (d. 1693) and his son of the same name. The second Gregory Page (c. 1668–1720), created baronet in 1714, was a director of the Old and the United East India Companies, and a New Shoreham MP who left a fortune estimated by con-temporaries at over £500,000.[30] Page is likely to have known the scrivener Lawrence Hatsell, who has also been tied to Devonshire Square. Another City Baptist of note was Sir Gregory Page's friend Joseph Collett (1673–1725), who was chosen governor of Madras by the United East India Company and was a member of the strongly Arian Baptist church at Paul's Alley, Barbican.[31] Drawn from the ranks of the City élite of traders and investors, these men were scarcely typical of the Baptist social following.

More representative of the Baptist congregational leadership were three Baptists elected to the Common Council in William's reign. Richard Bristow (1630–1709), a grocer of All Hallows Bread Street, was a common councilman for most of the years between 1672 and 1701. Rated at £70 per annum in 1692, Bristow was a member of the Particular Baptist church that met in Petty France. In 1689 he was a representative for that church at the first general assembly of Particular Baptists, and he was a trustee for a projected fund designed to support the Particular Baptist clergy.[32]

---

[29] Henning, ii. 285–6; Sedgwick, ii. 20–2; Woodhead, p. 66.

[30] Sedgwick, ii. 319–20; Woodhead, pp. 124–5.

[31] Joseph Collett, *Private Letter Books*, ed. H. H. Dodwell (1933); William T. Whitley, 'A Baptist Governor of Madras in 1716', *Baptist Quarterly*, vii (1934–35), 123–37.

[32] Alfred C. Underwood, *History of the English Baptists* (1947), p. 129; Woodhead, p. 38, where Bristow is described as a Tory.

Another Baptist who served briefly on the Common Council was the Cripplegate cheesemonger Abraham Hickman, a member with his wife of the Devonshire Square church. Living with him as an apprentice in the 1690s was Benjamin Stinton, who became a leading Baptist pastor in Anne's reign. An inventory of Hickman's estate compiled in 1706 showed that he owned a sugar house, ten property leases, and shares in seven ships; but after his debts were subtracted, he was worth a mere thousand pounds.[33] Finally, the William Russell who served on the Common Council in 1702 for St. Bride's parish is believed to have been the Baptist Dr William Russell (1634–1703) who lived there. He was a chemist, a medical author, and a messenger among the City General Baptists.[34]

D. Quakers

Although numerically the smallest of the dissenting bodies in London, the Quakers were socially the most distinctive and organizationally the most sophisticated. The Friends' meetings of the urban area acknowledged the administrative and financial supervision of the Six Weeks Meeting for London and Middlesex. The hundred-odd members of that body, both men and women, were drawn from the households of substantial Quaker shopkeepers, craftsmen, and merchants.[35] By 1689 the London Friends already exhibited the unusual Quaker fusion of piety and prosperity. However, the wealth of the London meetings should not be exaggerated. Those scholars have been misled who have followed Charles Leslie's claim of 1696 that the central Gracechurch Street meeting was composed of some of 'the *Richest* Trading Men in London'.[36] Although it was the wealthiest assemblage of London Friends, the Gracechurch Friends numbered many poor and marginal families, as did the other meetings. Leslie rightly noted the large proportion of City Quakers engaged in trades that led to comfortable circumstances; but many more substantial Quakers

[33] CLRO Assessment Box 32, MS 15; CLRO Common Serjeant's Book 5, fo. 158b (Inventory Box 41).

[34] Underwood, p. 126; William T. Whitley, *The Baptists of London, 1612–1928* (1928), p. 114; Thomas Crosby, *History of the English Baptists* (1740), iv. 240-4.

[35] Society of Friends' Library, MS Minutes of the Six Weeks Meeting for London and Middlesex, ii–v.

[36] Charles Leslie, *The Snake in the Grass*, 3rd edn. (1698), p. 362; William C. Braithwaite, *The Second Period of Quakerism* (1919), p. 499; Frederick B. Tolles, *Quakers and the Atlantic Culture* (1960), p. 58.

were drapers, clothiers, and shopkeepers than were overseas merchants or goldsmith-bankers. Moreover, although a few exceptionally wealthy men frequented the London meetings, the more
modest wealth of many middling Quakers was the source of the
community's reputation for frugality and industry. These sober
traders drew inspiration and encouragement from such resident
Quaker spiritual authorities as Stephen Crispe, William Crouch,
William Mead, Daniel Quare, and George Whitehead. The London Quakers were clearly the most distinguished society of
Friends in England or in the New World.

The wealthiest London Quakers were those engaged in overseas
trade. Among them was Edward Haistwell, once a travelling com-
panion of George Fox and by the 1690s a major tobacco import-
exporter. In 1695 Haistwell had a turn-over of £17,000, and he
subsequently made sizeable investments in the Bank of England,
the Old East India Company, and the Royal African Company.
Other Quaker tobacco merchants of note were Benjamin and
James Braine and Josiah Bacon, a major subscriber for New East
India stock in 1698.[37] The stock purchases of these London
Quakers were quite exceptional, however. Despite the accumulation of Quaker wealth in the City by the 1690s, the London
Friends took very little part in the epoch-making capital subscriptions and public loans of that decade. Only one Quaker merchant,
an Old East India Company investor, served as a joint-stock
director in the late Stuart period. Furthermore, Quakers were
equally uninvolved in the affairs of the Corporation. Only two of
their persuasion are believed to have been chosen for the Common Council, both in the early 1690s.

Two reasons may be offered for this disparity between Quaker
wealth and Quaker participation in the business of the City. First,
the Quakers refrained on principle from active engagement in
secular affairs. Their perception of themselves as a separated godly
society inhibited involvement in the public politics and the public
corporations of the world about them. Moreover, the propagation
of images of Quaker peculiarity, whether desired or not, was so
extensive that few people outside their ranks were likely to regard
Quakers as suitable for such employment. Secondly, by the time

---

[37] George Fox, *Short Journal and Itinerary Journals*, ed. Norman Penny (Cambridge,
1925), p. 327; Jacob M. Price, *Capital and Credit in British Overseas Trade* (1980), p. 120;
Price, *Tobacco Adventure to Russia*, pp. 105–6.

of the Revolution, the London Quakers were already deeply involved in colonial enterprises of their own which satisfied both
their need for investment opportunities and their thirst for
spiritual community. A score of wealthy London Quaker families
of William's and Anne's reigns, for instance, had been among the
'First Purchasers' of land in Pennsylvania. Others, like the
Brassey family of goldsmiths, were investors in the Free Society of
Traders in Pennsylvania, which was organized to direct the colony's economic development.[38] The Jerseys also attracted the
interest of London Quakers. Among ten London Quaker proprietors of East Jersey was Gilbert Mollison, an Aldersgate hood
and scarf seller and a close marriage relation of Friends' apologist
Robert Barclay.[39] The Quaker proprietors of West Jersey included
the wife of Lombard Street merchant Henry Gouldney, whose
religious life may be followed in his published correspondence.[40]

This devotion to their particular interests was characteristic of
London Friends of all social stations. Easily distinguished by their
peculiar speech, costume, and social habits, the Quakers emphasized their separateness through their endogamous marriages and
their noticeable preference for dwelling near one another. About
half the Quakers in the dissenting interest resided in one of three
Quaker 'colonies' in the City, each with a meeting-house at its
centre. One concentration was to the north-west in the parishes of
St. Bartholomew the Great and St. Botolph without Aldersgate,
near the Quaker meeting-house at the Bull and Mouth, Smithfield
market. Another concentration was to the north-east in several
parishes near the Devonshire House meeting. The third concentration, the densest of all, was in the heart of the City near the
Gracechurch meeting in four wealthy adjacent parishes. Quakers
made up 20 to 25 per cent of the population there, totally domin-
ating some streets.

Although the Quakers' preference for residential segregation
and their trans-Atlantic interests expressed a desire to be a people

[38] Samuel Hazard, Annals of Pennsylvania, 1609–82 (Philadelphia, Pa., 1850),
pp. 637–42; 'Free Society of Traders in Pennsylvania', Pennsylvania Magazine of History and
Biography, xi (1887), 175–80.

[39] Arthur Raistrick, Quakers in Science and Industry (New York, 1968), p. 250; John E.
Pomfret, The Province of East New Jersey, 1609–1702 (Princeton, NJ, 1962), pp. 137, 358,
397–9.

[40] Quaker Post-Bag, ed. Sophie Felicité Locker Lampson (1910), pp. 47–109; John E.
Pomfret, The Province of West New Jersey, 1609–1702 (Princeton, NJ, 1956), p. 287.

apart, they could not completely effect a divorce from London politics. The outward signs of their inward withdrawal made them especially visible to their detractors, and their persistent efforts to avoid oaths and tithes brought them unwanted attention. Their quest for saintly perfection on earth, their repudiation of clergy and sacraments, and their novel forms of worship attracted the hostile pens of Anglican detractors. Charles Leslie, Francis Bugg, and the noted Quaker apostate George Keith portrayed the Quaker separation as an unsightly fracture in English society. This theme was mimicked in street literature and popular prints that cheaply caricatured the Friends as unstable visionaries, as unchristian Shylocks, and as pious hypocrites.[41] The Quakers unwittingly provided easy grist for the High-Church propaganda mill so concerned with the perils of religious permissiveness. However much other dissenters professed their moderation, the Tories sought still to paint them all with the brush of Quaker 'fanaticism'.

The animosity of the Church and the gullibility of the curious thus combined to make the beliefs of the Quakers a political issue. Moreover, the competition of benevolent Whigs and malevolent Tories brought the London Quakers perforce into the City's political life. Despite their unwillingness to accept Corporation offices, the Quakers showed no reluctance to vote for dissenters and Whigs who would. Indeed, no sight was better calculated to provoke paroxysms of ire in the Tory press than the trouping of black-frocked Friends to London's parliamentary polls.[42]

3. Dissent and the City

As the preceding section has suggested, generalizations about the social quality of late Stuart nonconformists must take careful account of local variations in the followings of the different dissenting persuasions. Little is revealed by scholarly restatement of the seventeeth-century association of dissent with the 'trading

---

[41] British Museum, Department of Prints and Drawings, *Catalogue of Prints and Drawings in the British Museum, Division I: Political and Personal Satires* (1873), ii. no. 1536-7; *The Bagford Ballads*, ed. Joseph Woodfall Ebsworth (Hertford, 1878), i. 30-1, ii. 729-33; *The Pepys Ballads*, ed. Hyder Edward Rollins (Cambridge, Mass., 1931), vii. 278-80.

[42] *Supplement* no. 573, 12-14 Sept. 1711; *Post Boy* no. 2875, 10-13 Oct. 1713 and no. 2928, 11-13 Feb. 1714.

interest' of the nation. Certainly dissent found a strong social base
among the 'industrious sort', but in urban localities like London,
dissenting spokesmen were drawn as frequently from the social
élite as from industrious 'middling' occupations. This fact has
been obscured by the tendency to identify dissent too exclusively
with the petty-bourgeoisie and to deny that dissent could long
have attracted merchant families of the first rank. These assumptions, and the difficulty in identifying individual dissenters, have
left unanswered the question of the extent of nonconformity among
the late Stuart London élite of overseas traders and joint-stock investors. The question nevertheless remains an important one both
because of the great expansion of English trade and English trading
capital after 1660, and because of the initiation of momentous
experiments in war-time public finance in the early 1690s.
Although Tory critics pictured the new 'moneyed interest' that
arose from the commercial and financial revolutions as tainted by
dissent, students of these related developments have made little
progress in studying nonconformist involvement. In his superb
history of the development of English public credit, for instance,
P. G. M. Dickson was forced for lack of evidence to draw a cautious
conclusion about dissenting contributions to the beginnings of
the financial revolution: 'The likelihood is', he wrote, 'that . . .
most domestic Nonconformists were artisans or tradesmen, and
their ownership of securities was probably therefore insignifi-
cant.'[43]

The isolation of the dissenting interest is helpful in overcoming
the problems that have retarded investigation of nonconformity
and the City élite. Two questions will be addressed here in order
to reveal the social quality of the leading London dissenting families and to measure their contribution to the commercial and financial changes that transformed the City in the late Stuart period.
Firstly, the distribution of dissenters among the different London
overseas trading specializations will be examined. Secondly, the
stock lists and directorates of several corporate enterprises will be
investigated in order to measure dissenting involvement and
leadership in the joint stocks. Analysis will focus on the City in
the 1690s.

---

[43] P. G. M. Dickson, *The Financial Revolution in England: A Study of the Development of
Public Credit, 1688–1756* (1967), p. 259.

A. Dissent and Trade

At least 17 per cent of the London merchants active in 1695–6 were dissenters or persons from families with strong ties to nonconformity. Because of the difficulties in identifying non-conformists, the figures in Table 3.5 may safely be said to under-represent the actual number of dissenting traders. To argue that 20 to 25 per cent of the late Stuart London merchants were dissenters would not unduly strain the available evidence. The survey of mid-1690s overseas traders in Table 3.5 also reveals that dissenters were far more numerous among the colonial sugar and tobacco traders than among the European and Near Eastern traders. The forty-six colonial merchants of 1695–6 who can be tied to dissent accounted for half the volume of the sugar and tobacco trades, and four of the five colonial traders with the largest turn-overs in 1695–6 were dissenters.[44]

Table 3.5 The Dissenting Interest and London's Overseas Trade, 1695–6

	All Merchants	Dissenting Interest	
European and Near Eastern Trade	560	69	12%
Colonial Trade	127	46	36%
All Overseas Trade	687	115	17%

Table 3.5 is based on the lists of merchants active in 1695 and/or 1696 in D. W. Jones, 'London Overseas Merchant Groups', Appendices B(1)–B(11), pp. 388–468.

Some European and Near Eastern trades also proved more attractive to London dissenters than other trades. This is suggested in Fig. 3.1. It compares the known trading specializations of some 160 late Stuart merchants interested in dissent with the known trading specializations of over 700 other contemporary London traders. The percentages of each group trading to six geographical areas are juxtaposed, with merchants who specialized in more than one trade counted in each appropriate area. Finally, the distribution of London trading volume among the area specializations is indicated, using D. W Jones's calculations for 1698.[45]

[44] Ibid., pp. 458–68. [45] Ibid., p. 259.

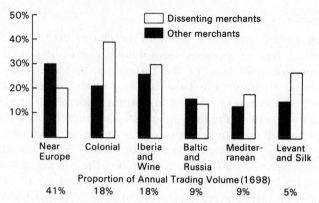

Fig. 3.1 Specializations of London Dissenting Merchants
Compared with those of other London Merchants

The striking connection between the colonial trades and non-conformity is again revealed in Fig. 3.1. The relative disinterest of merchants from dissenting backgrounds in the Near European trade is also striking. That trade, largely in cloth, still accounted for over 40 per cent of London's commerce; but only one-fifth of the dissenting merchants were involved in it. (London Puritan merchants of the 1640s had been similarly disinterested in the trade to northern Europe.[46]) On the other hand, late Stuart dissenting merchants were disproportionately active in the Levant trade, and their import of Spanish and Portuguese wine was also notable, though perhaps not exceptional. The visibility of the dissenting interest in these trades is also indicated by the number of definite or likely dissenters among the wealthy silk and wine importers who participated in the initial capital subscriptions to the Bank of England (1694) and to the New East India Company (1698). Almost one-half (46 per cent) of the Turkey merchants who made such stock investments were of dissenting backgrounds, as was the case for almost one-quarter (24 per cent) of the wine importers.[47]

How may these concentrations of dissenters in particular branches of London's overseas trade be explained? The strong connection between dissent and the colonial trades may perhaps be traced to

---

[46] Brenner, pp. 82–5.

[47] These figures are derived from several sources, the most important of which is D. W. Jones, 'London Overseas Merchant Groups', Appendices C(1)-C(2), pp. 470–81.

their inception in the colonizing schemes of Puritans and Country MPs in the 1620s. Two decades later the London colonial merchants were staunchly parliamentarian in sympathy, and one scholar has convincingly argued that the colonial traders were a vital element within the Independent grouping that gained power in the City in 1648-9.[48] By the time of the Interregnum, London's colonial commerce was dominated by merchants comfortable with republicanism and congregationalism and convinced that the future expansion of the country's trade depended upon their own unimpeded individual enterprise. The survival of this distinctive religious and economic mentality among the colonial merchants after 1660 is one explanation for the prevalence of dissent among them in the reigns of the last Stuarts.

Another explanation for the strength of dissent among the colonial traders was the emergence in the late seventeenth century of an Anglo-American Quaker community. A preference for the colonial trade was far more noticeable among Quaker merchants than among dissenting merchants of other persuasions. Many London Quakers had family ties with Friends in Pennsylvania and the Jerseys, and as has been noted previously, some London Quakers purchased land and proprietary shares there. But the principal colony with which most London Quakers traded was neither Pennsylvania nor the Jerseys but rather the tiny colony of Barbados. The number of Quakers among that island's English inhabitants was noteworthy, and many of the Barbados Friends owned plantations and slaves.[49] A well-developed commercial partnership seems to have existed between Quaker sugar importers in London and Quaker planters in Barbados and other West Indian colonies.

Explanations for the concentration of dissenters among the Turkey merchants and the Iberian merchants are more difficult to provide. The most substantial Levant traders of the 1640s were largely royalists,[50] and the Iberian wine trade developed too late in the century to have been strongly marked by the commercial and religious disputes of the Civil War and Interregnum. The Levant trade seems to have attracted many of the City's leading traders of French ancestry like the Delmés, the Houblons, and the

---

[48] Brenner, pp. 76-82, 91-7.

[49] Richard S. Dunn, *Sugar and Slaves: The Rise of the Planter Class in the English West Indies, 1624-1713* (Chapel Hill, NC, 1972), pp. 103-6.

[50] Brenner, p. 85.

Lethieulliers. Intermarriage between such naturalized trading families and English dissenting families was natural and extensive, and it may have facilitated the entrée of younger dissenting merchants into the Turkey trade. However, no general explanation may be given for the significant dissenting presence in the Levant trade until more work has been done on London merchants during the Restoration decades.

This noticeable dissenting involvement in the colonial, silk, and Iberian wine trades has several implications of importance. First, it may be argued that merchants who were dissenters were disproportionately involved in the expansion of English trading volume in the late seventeenth century. That expansion was closely related to the dramatic rise in colonial imports and colonial re-exports, according to Ralph Davis,[51] and those were the very trades pursued most vigorously by dissenting merchants. Moreover, if dissenting merchants were highly visible in the commercial revolution, they were equally instrumental in the beginnings of the financial revolution. D. W. Jones has demonstrated that wine merchants were especially active in the original capital subscriptions of the Bank and of the New East India Company,[52] and the subscriptions of the Levant merchants were also disproportionately large. The heavy dissenting presence in the new stocks, which will be discussed below, may therefore be attributed in part to the extraordinary investments of dissenting Turkey and Iberian traders.

The large number of dissenters among the Levant traders is also significant for an additional reason. The Levant merchants were the wealthiest traders in London on a per capita basis,[53] and their incomes and status granted them greater political respect in the City and at Westminster than other trading groups. The prevalence of dissent among the Turkey traders enhanced the political influence of the dissenting interest, therefore, and the London dissenters found notable magisterial and parliamentary spokesmen in such Levant merchants as Sir William and Sir Henry Ashurst, Sir Humphrey Edwin, and Thomas and Philip Papillon. However, neither the exceptional influence of some dissenting merchants nor the exceptional stock investments of others should be taken to

---

[51] Davis, 'English Foreign Trade, 1660–1700'.
[52] D. W. Jones, 'London Overseas Merchant Groups', pp. 239, 249.
[53] Ibid., pp. 256–7.

indicate that dissenting merchants in general were wealthier than other traders.

The strong association between dissent and the sugar and tobacco trades also gave London nonconformists an exceptional role in other colonial affairs. Five London merchants interested in dissent served as colonial agents at various dates in William's and Anne's reigns—Sir Henry Ashurst (Massachusetts, Connecticut, New Hampshire), Sir Gilbert Heathcote (Jamaica), Sir Bartholomew Gracedieu (Jamaica), Sir Francis Eyles (Barbados), and Bastian Beyer (Leeward Islands). As men of influence both at home and in the colonies, these dissenting agents routinely advised the Council of Trade about appointments of colonial personnel and about the war-time defence of island plantations. Other London dissenters became involved in colonial affairs in a variety of official and private capacities. For instance, Edward Reisheir was a leading Jersey proprietor of Anne's reign, and he was also the brother of a Bermuda governor of William's reign.[54] Richard Merriweather's extensive trade and properties on Nevis and St. Christopher made him a natural spokesman both for the planters of those islands and for the London merchants who imported their products. Also a trader to New York, Merriweather became the London business agent for Hudson River magnate Robert Livingston.[55] Edward Haistwell, the largest London Quaker tobacco trader of the 1690s, appeared before the Council of Trade from 1699 to 1702 on behalf of Maryland Quakers who felt threatened by an act of that colony's assembly.[56]

London traders from the dissenting interest were also engaged in two new corporate efforts that grew out of the colonial trade in the 1690s. One of these was the West Jersey Society, whose members were proprietors of that colony from 1692 to 1703. Dissenting sympathies, predominantly Presbyterian and Independent, can be established for one-third of the society's original forty-eight members, including its president Sir Thomas Lane.[57] Another group that included many dissenting traders was the 1698

[54] *CSPCol* viii. no. 2638; *CSPCol* xx. no. 568.

[55] *CSPCol* ix. no. 2084-5; *JCTP 1708-9 to 1714-15*, pp. 419-20; Lawrence H. Leder, *Robert Livingston, 1654-1728, and the Politics of Colonial New York* (Chapel Hill, NC, 1961), pp. 106, 110-2.

[56] *CSPCol* xii. no. 90; *CSPCol* xx. no. 874.

[57] Pomfret, *West New Jersey*, pp. 170-89; *New Jersey Archives*, 1st Ser., ii (Newark, NJ, 1881), 65-6.

syndicate that discomfited the Russia Company by gaining a contract from Peter the Great to supply the Russian tobacco market. One-third of the original sixty-five contractors were interested in dissent, and most of the tobacco which the syndicate sent to Russia in the first years of operation was supplied by three dissenting re-export firms—John and Thomas Cary, Sir Thomas Lane and Company, and Edward Haistwell.[58] Commercial opportunities rather than religious interests brought together both the West Jersey proprietors and the tobacco contractors. However, the colonial trades were so strongly permeated by dissenting family ties and business connections that any new colonial venture was bound to re-assemble leading City dissenters. Indeed, the importance and prosperity of the colonial trades supported the influence of the dissenting interest as a whole.

B. Dissent and Investment

An unparalleled expansion in the City's facilities for private investment and public credit occurred during William's reign, despite the commercial depression of the 1690s. Through a series of financial expedients, the Whig Junto yoked the government's need for massive war-time credit to the London merchants' demand for additional investment outlets. The Bank of England and the New East India Company were the institutional centre-pieces of a panoply of short-term and long-term funds that supported war-related expenditures until the peace of 1713. The Tory ministries of Anne's reign relied upon these sources of City credit as strongly as did the Junto; but as war weariness spread among Country Tories after 1707, so did a Country fear that the new public creditors might gain undue influence upon the executive. This fear was rooted not only in Country tradition but also in the sensitivity of the Anglican squirearchy to any evidence of dissenting influence in government. Given the proportion of London trading capital in the hands of dissenting merchants, the suspicions of Tory MPs about the origins of the mounting public debt were not without foundation. City dissenters were quite visible among lenders, and they were even more visible among the directors of the major London stocks.

That this would be the case had been indicated earlier by dissenting participation in the short-term loans arranged for the

---

[58] Based on analysis of biographical appendix to Price, *Tobacco Adventure*, 105–10.

crown by the City Chamber before the establishment of the Bank. The raising of such loans from the citizens of London was not an innovation of William's reign, but both the reliance of the crown upon the City for stop-gap loans and the large sums involved were distinctive elements of government finance during the early years of the War of the Grand Alliance. Because a greater proportion of these subscriptions came from City residents than was the case with subsequent joint-stock investments, they may be the best guide to the proportion of London capital in dissenting hands.

For political reasons, Whig spokesmen selectively encouraged and discouraged subscriptions; but dissenting contributions remained fairly steady despite the politics of lending. The subscriptions of the dissenting interest to the five largest loans made through the Corporation Chamber during the first two years of William's reign are presented in Table 3.6. Persons known to have been interested in dissent accounted for 16 to 20 per cent of the subscribers to each loan, and they subscribed 27 per cent of the money lent. This is an index not only of the willingness of dissenters to lend to the government, but also of their ability to do so. Moreover, the actual proportion of dissenting money was probably considerably higher. Diarist Roger Morrice, whose familiarity with City dissent surpasses that of the modern historian, reported that 'upon strict observation' some £148,000 (80 per cent) of the first loan could be traced to dissenting sources.[59] This figure is almost certainly exaggerated, but it suggests that the indices of dissenting investments that follow are cautious rather than excessive.

Although short-term public loans arranged through the Corporation were an important source of government credit in the early 1690s, they were unsatisfactory for several reasons. They were open to political manipulation; the loans were frequently undersubscribed; and the proceeds of new subscriptions were needed as much for the repayment of old loans as for the payment of new expenses. These inconveniences were overcome through the establishment of the Bank of England. Its nominal original capital of £1.2 million was lent to the government at 8 per cent, with repayment scheduled over several years. Enlargements of its stock, the absorption of other public creditors as stockholders, and continuing loans to the government made the Bank the most

[59] DWL Morrice MS Q, 419.

Table 3.6 The Dissenting Interest and Corporation Loans, 1689–1691

		SUBSCRIBERS		SUBSCRIPTIONS	
	Total	Dissenting Interest (%)	Total (£)	Dissenting Interest (%)
1. January–March 1689	1,300	17	185,675	22
2. July 1689–February 1690	800	19	242,205	31
3. February–March 1690	450	20	86,230	29
4. November 1690– February 1691	410	16	154,617	29
5. February–April 1691	740	19	170,500	24
			839,227	27

CLRO MS 40/35–6, 40/44.

influential corporate public creditor of Anne's reign. Some 18 per cent of the original Bank stock subscription can be traced to over 150 persons with dissenting connections (Table 3.7). This figure is comparable with dissenting contributions to the Corporation loans because as much as one-quarter of the 1694 Bank subscription appears to have come from outside London.

Table 3.7 The Dissenting Interest and Joint-Stock Investment in the 1690s

	TOTAL STOCK (£)	DISSENTING INTEREST		
		Investors	Stock (£)	Proportion (%)
Bank of England, 1694	1,200,000	158	215,000	18
Million Bank, 1695	200,000	29	32,150	16
New East India Company, 1698	1,685,000	111	248,000	15
Old East India Company, 1699	1,514,609	118	217,964	14
Royal African Company, 1693	438,850	27	49,650	11

Bank of England, Archives Section, Index to the Book of Subscriptions, 1694; IOL Home Miscellaneous Series, iii., List of Adventurers, 1699, and Parchment Records 54 (New East India Company); PRO C 114/16 (Million Bank) and T 70/188, fos. 113–21 (Royal African Company).

Table 3.8 The Dissenting Interest and Joint-Stock Directorships, 1688–1715

	ALL DIRECTORS	DISSENTING INTEREST	
		Directors	Proportion (%)
Bank of England, 1694–1715	89	38	43
Million Bank, 1695–1715 (partial)	71	19	27
New East India Company 1698–1708 (partial)	64	21	33
Old East India Company, 1688–1708	100	17	17
United East India Company, 1708–1715	55	17	30
Royal African Company, 1688–1712	142	14	10
South Sea Company, 1711–1715	55	9	16

Table 3.8 rests upon analysis of lists of joint-stock directors found in the following sources: Bank of England: W. Marston Acres, 'The Directors of the Bank of England', *Notes and Queries*, clxxix (1940), 38–41, 57–62, 80–3; Million Bank: PRO C 114/14/1, C 114/15/1; New East India Company: IOL B/42, B/45, B/47, B/49, and Edward Chamberlayne, *Angliae Notitia*, 19th edn. (1700), p. 597 and 20th edn. (1702), pp. 617–18; Old East India Company: IOL B/39–41, B/46, B/49; United East India Company: IOL B/49–53; Royal African Company: Davies, *African Company*, pp. 377–90; South Sea Company: John Carswell, *The South Sea Bubble* (Stanford, Calif., 1960), pp. 273–85.

Other evidence also suggests that the dissenting presence in the Bank was greater than is indicated in the original stock subscription. For instance, one-quarter of the individuals who held at least £4,000 of Bank stock in 1694, 1701, and 1705 were definite, probable, or possible nonconformists.[60] Dissenters are easier to identify among larger stockholders than among smaller ones, and these figures may therefore be the best guide to overall nonconformist investment in the Bank. The influence of nonconformist stockholders is indicated even more dramatically by the large number of persons from the dissenting interest who appear among the Bank's directors. Ten of the original twenty-four

[60] *A List of the Names of All the Subscribers to the Bank of England* [1694]; *A List of the Names of All the Proprietors in the Bank of England* (1701); *A List of the Names of All the Proprietors in the Bank of England* (1705).

directors were from the dissenting interest, and over two-fifths of all Bank directors from 1694 to 1715 were known nonconformists or persons from dissenting backgrounds (Table 3.8). Moreover, if all directors from Huguenot, Dutch, or Lutheran families are also taken into consideration, over half the Bank's late Stuart directorate was non-Anglican.

In no other late Stuart fund or corporation did London nonconformists take so keen an interest as in the Bank of England; but wherever sound investment opportunities existed, dissenting money was found. When another financial enterprise, soon known as the Million Bank, was incorporated in London in 1695, the dissenting interest accounted for 16 per cent of its original stock subscription. When the New East India Company was launched by the Junto in 1698, at least 15 per cent of its initial share capital, which was also lent to the government, was subscribed by persons interested in dissent. Furthermore, a full third of the persons known to have served as directors in the decade of the company's existence were definite, probable, or possible dissenters. This fact probably indicates that actual dissenting ownership of New Company stock was higher than can be demonstrated. Nonconformist investment in the Old East India Company during William's reign was also considerable, but some evidence suggests that dissenting influence in the Old Company waned in the late 1690s. Only seventeen of the one hundred post-Revolution Old Company directors had dissenting connections. Moreover, in 1698, the year of the New Company's creation, all seven sitting Old Company directors linked to dissent were among those removed at the annual General Court,[61] and in the next decade only six nonconformist share-holders ever sat on the directing Court of Committees. After the two companies merged in 1708, however, dissenting stockholders were almost as well represented among the directors of the United Company as had formerly been the case in the New Company. Finally, several prominent City men with dissenting allegiances or connections were included by Robert Harley in the initial South Sea directorate.

This survey of nonconformity and City investment has emphasized the importance of the London dissenting interest as a body of public creditors. The Bank of England and the New East India

---

[61] IOL B/41, fo. 278.

Company were each founded upon the national debt, and the investment of Million Bank capital in government annuities made it another important corporate creditor by the end of Anne's reign. Nonconformists seem, therefore, to have been most attracted to those stocks with a secured return from government interest paid on borrowed stock. Towards stocks without such a guaranteed return, like the Old East India Company, dissenting investors appear to have exercised an increasing degree of caution. This restraint is also illustrated in the record of dissenting participation in the Royal African Company which, at the beginning of William's reign, was second only to the Old East India Company as a major City corporate enterprise. During the next fifteen years, however, the African Company was threatened by external attacks upon its monopoly and by internal manipulations of its stock, which together depressed the value of its shares and contributed to its financial collapse in Anne's reign.[62] As the African Company declined, so did dissenting ownership of its stock, which fell from 11 to 5 per cent between 1693 and 1703. Moreover, although fourteen of its 142 directors from 1689 to 1712 were interested in dissent, only three of these served on the company's Court of Assistants after 1702. London dissenters showed a similar disinterest in the land bank schemes of 1695–6 and in Sir Humphrey Mackworth's Mine Adventure, each of which apparently was perceived as unsound.[63]

In contrast to these 'adventures', the investment of nonconformist money in the major City stocks gave the London dissenting interest and its leaders a new arena for the exercise of influence. The point has frequently been made that the number of nonconformists elected to the parliaments of William's and Anne's reigns was never high. Although confirmation of this interpretation must await further biographical research on the membership of the late Stuart Commons,[64] the suggestion may be offered that the joint stocks provided nonconformists with an alternative means of taking part in important national affairs.

---

[62] Davies, *African Company*, pp. 79–87, 135–52.

[63] PRO T 52/19, fos. 1–25; *List of the Names of the Subscribers of Land and Money towards a Fund for the National Land-Bank* (1695); *List of the Names of the Subscribers to the Land-Bank* (1695); *List of All the Adventurers in the Mine-Adventure* (1700).

[64] See Henning, i. 11–13, 50–3 for a disscussion of nonconformists among the Commons members of the Restoration Parliaments.

The directors of the Bank and of the East India Companies were frequently consulted by ministers about financial, commercial, and even diplomatic questions. They were, moreover, well placed to secure government contracts and government places for themselves and their friends. In this way, City leaders from the dissenting interest were perhaps able to exert as much influence on ministerial decision-making from without parliament as they were from within the Commons. For precisely this reason, the issues of religion and public finance became closely linked in the minds of High-Church Country Tories. The new economic order of the early eighteenth century, which was so strongly criticized by Bolingbroke and other Tory spokesmen, was clearly as beneficial to the London dissenters as it was threatening to the lesser gentry. The landed interest had many reasons for disliking the moneyed interest, not the least of which was the steady rise of the dissenting interest on the swelling national debt.

4. Dissent and London Politics

Although the wealth and influence of nonconformist merchants and investors gained the hostile notice of City Tories and landed squires, the political consequences of the legalization of public dissent aroused the most fear in the Church-Tory camp. Acceptable to the Church party only as an indulgence to scrupulous consciences, the restricted toleration of 1689 was quickly perceived as inimical to the security of the religious establishment. Everywhere the erection of permanent meetings produced alarm, but nowhere were those meetings frequented by more respectable company than in London. And though the Revolution catapulted dissenters into office in some boroughs and confirmed them in office in others, the Corporation overshadowed all other constituencies in providing political power for its militant dissenting élite. Nonconformist office-holding in the City is the best indicator of the role of the dissenting interest in late Stuart London politics, and it also assists in explaining why City dissent had such a remarkable impact on the tempestuous political society of which London was a part.

The discovery that eighteen of sixty-four late Stuart London aldermen (1688–1715) were definitely not Anglicans, and that six others were strongly interested in dissent, provides the clearest evidence of nonconformist political strength in the Corporation. Some 120 common councilmen of the period were also definite dissenters or persons with dissenting connections. Several factors contributed to the prominence of the dissenting interest in the Corporation. Among these were a deliberate pursuit of office in defence of the Revolution, the initial encouragement of William III, and the large number of nonconformists with the requisite social background for magisterial office. As important as all these factors, however, was a peculiarity of the political structure of the Corporation that facilitated nonconformist office-holding.

Twelve small adjacent wards in the centre of the City, with only one-quarter of the ratepaying population, elected almost half the London common councilmen and aldermen. These wards composed a geopolitical 'inner city' with a population significantly wealthier than that of the remaining wards within the walls and vastly wealthier than that of the wards without the walls. Socially distinctive throughout the seventeenth century, the inner city wards drew over half their ratepayers after 1689 from the ranks of prosperous craftsmen, shopkeepers, wholesale traders, and merchants.[65] These same wards also yielded the great majority of dissenting office-holders. Two-thirds of the common councilmen and over half the aldermen from the dissenting interest were chosen from the over-represented inner city. Urbane and commercially oriented, the electors of the inner wards included the most enthusiastic Whigs in the Corporation, and their noticeable partiality for dissenting office-holders suggests that the inner city electorate was also heavily infused with dissenting principles. Sixty years earlier, the London inner city had provided the original political and mercantile élite of Puritan Boston.[66] In William's and Anne's reigns, it remained the social matrix of urban dissent as a political interest. Resident throughout the Corporation, but concentrated within the inner city, the nonconformists were thus well placed to secure the election of dissenting and Whig candidates.

The extent of nonconformist office-holding in London strongly coloured the City Tories' perception of their whiggish adversaries. Beginning in the early 1690s, London Churchmen claimed that

---

[65] CLRO Assessment Boxes: 1694 4/- Aid Returns; GL 1710 Land Tax Returns.

[66] Bernard Bailyn, *The New England Merchants in the Seventeenth Century* (New York, 1964), pp. 36–8.

the Whig party and the dissenting interest were indistinguishable. Even an impartial observer of the 1690 City parliamentary poll believed that three-quarters of the liverymen who favoured the Whig candidates were dissenters.[67] Edmund Bohun, Tory press licenser in the early part of William's reign, was among the most outspoken early exponents of a strong identification between post-Revolution City whiggery and religious sectarianism. The Church party had a natural majority in the City, he contended, but it was handicapped by the superior electoral tactics of its opponents and by the political naïvety of some of its friends: 'Mark and avoid those busie seditious Agents . . . those Sycophants who, tho' they dissent from and despise our Established Religion; yet can fawn, and flatter and run up and down wheedling our Members by Awe, Interest, or Influence, to incline, and dispose them to chuse such Persons as may most favour of their Faction.'[68] Once articulated, the idea of a dissenting conspiracy behind the Whig party became a staple ingredient in Tory diatribe and a useful theme in appealing to those electors who resented dissenting wealth and who feared dissenting intentions.

Church-Tory disquiet about dissenting influence in London politics was aggravated by the exceptional incidence of occasional conformity within the City's social élite. Although the literary controversy about the subject did not always make specific reference to the City, the Corporation was the scene of the episode that ignited the dispute, and London remained the chief eyesore in a Church-Tory vision of despair. As much a City–Country issue as the new public debt, occasional conformity was responsible for some of the choicest vocabulary of High-Church polemic.

Tory panic about the dissenting presence in the Church's communion erupted in 1697 after Lord Mayor Sir Humphrey Edwin's stunning public processions from morning prayer at St. Paul's to afternoon sermons at dissenting meetings. Attempting to advertise and to legitimize occasional communion by employing the full regalia of his office, Edwin was instead 'abused in the streets by Ballad-singers, Hawkers, and raskally Fellows', and he was quickly restrained by an anxious magisterial bench.[69] Edwin was

---

[67] *Letter to a Friend in the Country* (1690).

[68] Cambridge University Library, Sel 3.232[81], 'A Coppy of a Printed Paper which was Published in Guild-hall on Wednesday ye 24. June 1691.'

[69] Repertory 102, fo. 11; *A Rowland for an Oliver* (1698); Luttrell, *Brief Relation*, iv. 303, 309.

not, however, the eccentric Cromwellian killjoy caricatured in some contemporary ephemera. The son of a Puritan mayor of Hereford, Edwin's Turkey treasure secured a bride for his eldest son from the progeny of an earl. Moreover, what frightened Church critics and some dissenting critics alike was not the singularity of Edwin's behaviour but the regularity with which City dissenters conformed to the Anglican sacramental rite in order to satisfy the Test Act. Indeed, as one defender wrote, this Lord Mayor had simply exhibited 'more Courage than some of his Predecessors' in openly avowing his dissent.[70]

Edwin's actions were also feared by his detractors as signalling a new dissenting initiative for Anglican concessions. Both the theatrical display of his processions and the endorsement of them by such City dissenting divines as John Howe (who shortly there after preached in favour of comprehension) suggest that this may have been the case.[71] Edwin's sabbath drama merely outraged his Tory audience, however, as did a similar mayoral show in 1702 by Edwin's Presbyterian colleague and John Howe's friend, Sir Thomas Abney. Not surprisingly, the defeat of Abney and other Whigs in the 1702 parliamentary poll was celebrated by one partisan pen as the triumph of Canterbury over Geneva, or as 'the Restauration' of pious rule after thirteen years of schismatic chaos.[72] When Jonathan Swift complained in 1704 that 'Jack's Tatters' had lately come 'into Fashion in . . . [the] City', he therefore echoed many Churchmen who believed that dissenters among the magistracy made Guildhall a dangerous rival to the Cathedral of Saint Paul.[73]

The London dissenters were obnoxious to their Church-Tory opponents not only because of the number and the importance of the offices they held, but also because of the political ideas they were believed to maintain. In the political creed of the high-flyers, the Church and the monarchy were twin institutions 'Twisted and Interwoven into the very Being and Principles of each Other' as 'One entire compounded Constitution, and Body Politick'.[74]

[70] [George Ridpath], *A Dialogue betwixt Jack and Will* (1698).

[71] John Howe, *Sermon Preached on the Day of Thanksgiving* (1697).

[72] *The Restauration; or: A change for the Better* (1702).

[73] Jonathan Swift, *A Tale of a Tub* in *The Prose Writings of Jonathan Swift*, ed. Herbert Davis (Oxford, 1957), p. 131.

[74] Henry Sacheverell, *The Political Union* (1702), p. 9.

Because the dissenters gave no allegiance to the former, they could scarcely give any loyalty to the latter. The confrontation between Church and meeting was thus also an ideological contest between rival theories of government, or so the episcopal party believed.[75] The Tory doctrines of passive obedience and of non-resistance guarded the state against the Genevan system of contractual government, limited monarchy, and the right of resistance—a system that had wrecked the English constitution once and that threatened to do so again. As Swift argued in the *Examiner*, the nonconformist quest for a '*Dominion of Grace*' had led to an unnatural rebellion, the murder of a king, the destruction of monarchy and episcopacy, and a release of the forces of social anarchy.[76] The case was put even more bluntly by Doctor Henry Sacheverell:

Presbytery and Republicanism go hand in hand, They are but the Same Disorderly, *Levelling Principle*, in the Two Different Branches of Our State, Equally Implacable Enemies to *Monarchy* and *Episcopacy* . . . It may be Remember'd, that they were the *Same* Hands that were Guilty Both of *Regicide* and *Sacriledge*, that at once Divided the *King's* Head and Crown, and made Our *Churches* Stables, and *Dens of Beasts, as well as Thieves*.[77]

A warm issue at the time of Anne's accession, the argument about the politics and principles of the nonconformists was stoked to white-hot intensity by 1709. The literary polemics and the popular tracts in which the controversy raged extended the furor throughout the country, but the furor was greatest in London both because of the size of the audience for political print and because of the power of the dissenting interest. The Tory critique of dissenting republicanism became the most effective rhetorical weapon in the High-Church armoury because it could be used to discredit not only the dissenting minority but also the entire Whig party. For instance, this critique enlivened the annual commemoration in the City's churches of the death of Charles I who, as monarch and High-Church saint, personified the union of institutions threatened by the Whigs. Such practised City performers as Luke Milbourne, rector of St. Ethelburga, marked the feast of Charles the Martyr with political catechisms of obedience and with political exorcisms of the spirits of Calvinist resistance.[78]

---

[75] Kenyon, *Revolutoin Principles*, pp. 83–101.
[76] *Examiner*, i. no 37, 5–12 Apr. 1711.   [77] Sacheverell, *Political Union*, pp. 50–1.
[78] Luke Milbourne, *The People not the Original of Civil Power . . .* (1707); Luke Milbourne, *A Sermon preach'd at St. Ethelburga's . . .* (1708).

The same anxiety about dissenting principles made Benjamin Hoadley, the Low-Church rector of St. Peter-le-Poor, the most despised City cleric of his day. Hoadley's offence lay in his enunciation of the dissenting principle of resistance from within the doors of the Church. Savagely caricatured in the London prints, Hoadley provided the Tories with his physical lameness as a symbol of the spiritual malady contracted through the whiggish adoption of the Puritan political heritage.[79] Another symbol of dissenting political delirium was that of the calf's head, which was widely propagated through Ned Ward's *Secret History of the Calves-Head Club*. Appearing in new editions in most years between 1703 and 1714, this undistinguished work recounted the mock masses allegedly celebrated with calves' heads and wine by a club of London dissenters on the thirtieth of January. Ward's exposé of an annual sabbath of political witches lent credibility to charges that the most fashionable City meetings observed the martyrdom of Charles I with blasphemous republican incantations and with psalms of praise.[80] Not without reason has one historian suggested that the execution of Charles I was the fulcrum of late Stuart controversial literature.[81]

The impact of these jaundiced images of dissent upon London politics was jarringly apparent in the Sacheverell affair, which was as important a watershed in the politics of the City as it was in those of the country. Henry Sacheverell's famous sermon of 5 November 1709 was preached at the invitation of a London Lord Mayor and to a London audience. Chief among his intentions was to set right 'the *Deluded* People in this . . . *Metropolis*', especially 'its *Rich* and *Powerful Inhabitants*', about their '*Notions of Government*, both in *Church*, and *State*'.[82] The explicitness of Sacheverell's message also clarified the party contest in the Corporation, and the drama of his impeachment confirmed and advertised Tory fears about a whiggish design against the Church.

---

[79] For instance, see British Museum, *Catalogue of Prints*, ii. no. 1503, 280–2.

[80] *POAS* vii. 355–6; *Rehearsal*, i. no. 29, 10–17 Feb. 1705 and no. 33, 10–17 Mar. 1705; *Observator*, iii. no. 90, 21–4 Feb. 1705; *Flying Post* no. 1531, 22–4 Feb. 1705; Kenyon, *Revolution Principles*, pp. 76–7; Howard W. Troyer, *Ned Ward of Grubstreet* (Cambridge, Mass., 1946), p. 108 ff. For the membership and intellectual context of the 'Calves-Head' republican circle of the 1690s, see A. B. Worden, 'Introduction', to Edmund Ludlow, *Voyce from the Watch Tower*.

[81] Kenyon, *Revolution Principles*, p. 66.

[82] Sacheverell, *Perils of False Brethren*, p. 3.

Beginning in 1710, the Tory press conducted the campaign against the Whig magistracy as a religious crusade to drive the beast of dissent from its civic den. A purge of dissenting common councilmen at the 1710 wardmotes was celebrated by the arch-Tory *Post Boy* as a fruit of Sacheverell's triumph, and the same paper accused dissenters of resorting to electoral bribery on the eve of the 1711 wardmotes. This charge came in the aftermath of a dispute over the election of a new alderman for the inner city ward of Broad Street, which had been preceded by a Church-Tory campaign to deprive the Whigs of the seat. The miscarriage of this attempt was attributed by the Churchmen to the influence of the Pinners' Hall Independents, who met in the ward, and to the exertions of dissenters of all persuasions.[83] In the same year, the doughty doctor himself spearheaded a ministerial assault on the sitting Whig-dissenting Bank directorate at the annual General Court of shareholders. The rout of a Church-approved ticket of directors was blamed upon 'Infidels and Hereticks, Quakers, Anabaptists, Independents, Presbyterians, Latitudinarians, Free-thinkers, Modern Whiggs, Low Churchmen, etc'.[84] Despite these failures, London Churchmen could take much satisfaction in the wake of Sacheverell's City intrusions. Evicted in dozens from Common Council, the Whigs were also threatened with a loss of the magistracy, and the party's dependence upon the dissenting electors of the inner wards was made especially apparent.

The public impact of the Sacheverell affair upon the politics of the Corporation was matched by its impact upon the City's electorate and *artisanat*. The political persecution of Sacheverell and his popular apotheosis brought to full flower a budding thicket of anti-nonconformist pamphlets, poems, and prints. This printed material was nowhere more fully absorbed than in London where it was produced and initially disseminated. Its rich imagery, its provocative iconography, and its aggressive rhetoric not only reflected the public High-Church outlook on dissent but also informed and impressed the receptive urban crowd. Several of the themes of popular Sacheverellite literature have already been introduced, and what is most noteworthy about the entire corpus

---

[83] *Post Boy* no. 2436, 21–3 Dec. 1710 and no. 2591, 18–20 Dec. 1711; *Supplement* no. 573, 12–14 Sept. 1711.

[84] *Post Boy* no. 2486, 17–19 Apr. 1711; Holmes, *Sacheverell*, p. 258.

is the manner in which Church propaganda vividly placed the early eighteenth-century religious divide in a mid-seventeenth century context. Borrowing from the dissenters' own apocalyptic heritage, Church apologists repeatedly juxtaposed the varieties of dissent with the seven-headed beast of the Book of Revelation. The Solemn League and Covenant again became a representation of binding political conspiracies hatched in the crowded confines of London conventicles like the opulent Lincoln's Inn Fields' meeting of Daniel Burgess. The political heresies of Augustan free-thinkers and contractual apologists were damned by association with the revolutionary words of Harrington, Sidney, and Milton. Most evocative of all was the figure of Oliver Cromwell, who leared from prints and leapt from pages as a choice symbol of dissenting deceptiveness, of military ambition, and of republican tyranny.[85]

The effectiveness with which High-Church propaganda made the events of Anne's reign rhetorically contemporary with the events of the 1640s and 50s gave it both its cutting edge and its popular appeal. This dissenting demonology was creatively internalized by City plebs who sought explanations and redress for their war-time political disillusionment and for their social despair. The marriage of Anglican controversia and plebeian dissatisfaction was celebrated in the furious crowd catharsis that turned Sacheverell's ordeal into an even greater ordeal for the London dissenters. Consummated in the 1710 pillage of City dissenting temples, this union endured even without active nurture from above. Three years later, Daniel Burgess, who was recently deceased and whose meeting had been among the first crowd targets of 1710, was burned in effigy during the celebrations of a Long Acre mob for the Tory peace of Utrecht. Five years later the Jacobite crowd of the Hanoverian Succession crisis was convinced that George I was merely a dissenting mannequin. They also pointedly included effigies of Cromwell among those they maligned in Cheapside and Smithfield while crying 'Down with the Rump' and 'No Presbyterian Government'.[86] As on many other occasions, the people

[85] British Museum, *Catalogue of Prints*, ii. no. 1502 (208), no. 1508 (285-7), no. 1541 (329), no. 1545 (331-2); F. F. Madan, *A Critical Bibliography of Dr. Henry Sacheverell*, ed. W.A. Speck (University of Kansas Publications, 1978), no. 963 (266-7), no. 965 (267), no. 982 (272-3); *Examiner*, i. no. 21, 14-21 Dec. 1710, no. 38, 12-19 Apr. 1711, and no. 40, 26 Apr.-3 May 1711.

[86] Holmes, 'Sacheverell Riots'; *Flying Post* no. 3373, 9-12 May 1713; Rogers, 'Popular Protest', pp. 72, 82, 89-92.

appealed to the past and embellished the slogans of their betters in order to lend legitimacy to their intervention in the 'high' politics of the élite.

The political strength of the London dissenting interest therefore lent credibility to a Tory revival of a highly polemical antipuritan mythology. However distorted Church propaganda may have become, it was effective because it was believable; the political and commerical industriousness of the City's dissenters contributed to the success of their adversaries' high-flying rhetoric. The emancipation of London dissenters in William's reign could not be reversed, but it was increasingly limited in Anne's reign by the rise of a popular Tory party that pilloried dissenting pretensions to power and respectability. In London, dissenters became the scapegoat for plebeian disenchantment with a Whig war, a Whig successsion—and Whig wealth. The party of dissent from 1679, the Whigs became the party of City wealth in the 1690s. This development further fractured London politics in ways that will be explained in the following chapter.

IV

The Politics of Wealth

1. Introduction: Enterprise, Investment, and Leadership in Late Stuart London

THE politics of late Stuart London were influenced by three distinct but related revolutions that produced both divisive issues and a divided City leadership. The Glorious Revolution was accompanied by remarkable alterations in the organization and conduct of English overseas commerce and of government finance. So novel and far-reaching were these changes that historians of trade and finance have written of both a 'commercial revolution' and a 'financial revolution'. The first of these revolutions, which antedated the political crisis of 1688–9, involved an unprecedented expansion in the scope, volume, and personnel of London's long-distance trade, and the enlargement of mercantile capital in City hands before 1688 sustained a series of experiments after 1688 in massive government borrowing.[1] The creation of this public debt, which was owed to thousands of individual creditors and which was destined to become permanent, was the centre-piece of England's financial revolution. Made necessary by the burden of financing the wars of William's and Anne's reigns, the public debt was interwoven with new City stocks that answered the demand for additional investment opportunities from the moneyed families of the commercial revolution. The Bank of England (1694) and the New East India Company (1698) were floated through capital subscriptions lent to the government, and the South Sea Company (1711) incorporated the numerous subscribers to other previously disparate components of the government debt.

The period from 1688 to 1715 thus saw not only a division within the Corporation over critical political issues, but also the taking of

[1] Davis, 'English Foreign Trade'; Davies, 'Joint-Stock Investment in the Later Seventeenth Century'.

critical initiatives in the founding of the modern eighteenth-century City. The short-term financial expedients of seventeenth-century government were replaced by a sophisticated apparatus for long-term public indebtedness. Reliance upon the advances of goldsmith-bankers and popular credit subscriptions gave way to reliance upon corporate institutions which served needs in addition to that of government finance. The few restricted Restoration joint stocks were suddenly joined in the 1690s by dozens of new corporations, some of them sound and some fanciful. Business transactions at the Royal Exchange increased in volume and in complexity and were accompanied by the first serial publications devoted to business affairs. Brokers became so numerous and bothersome as to require regulation by statute in 1697 and again in 1708. Finally, the new facilities for credit and investment, which absorbed the ready capital and savings of thousands of wealthy and middling families, created a recognizably new status group in English society, the ominous 'moneyed interest' of Tory rhetoric.

These commercial and financial transformations of the City have been the subject of numerous historical studies. The London overseas merchant community, both as a whole and as subdivided by trade specializations, has been examined by historians of commerce.[2] Individual joint stocks have been analysed in several company histories, and the revolution in City finance that began in the 1690s has been fully treated by P. G. M. Dickson.[3] Historians of City business have been interested in the political orientations of the corporations or trading groups of their studies, and historians of late Stuart politics have also been concerned to judge the politics of City interests which had parliamentary influence. The consensus of historical opinion supports two statements

[2] D. W. Jones, 'London Overseas Merchant Groups at the End of the Seventeenth Century'; D. W. Jones, 'London Merchants and the Crisis of the 1690s' in Peter Clark and Paul Slack, eds., *Crisis and Order in English Towns 1500–1700* (1972); Price, *The Tobacco Adventure to Russia*; Hinton, *The Eastland Trade*; H. E. S. Fisher, *The Portugal Trade: A Study of Anglo-Portuguese Commerce 1700–1770* (1971); Davis, *Aleppo and Devonshire Square: English Traders in the Levant in the Eighteenth Century* (1967).

[3] Dickson, *The Financial Revolution*; Scott, *Joint-Stock Companies to 1720*; Davies, *African Company*; Rich, *Hudson Bay Company*; Carswell, *South Sea Bubble*; K. N. Chaudhuri, *The Trading World of Asia and the English East India Company, 1660–1760* (Cambridge, 1978); Sir John Clapham, *The Bank of England: A History*, 2 vols. (Cambridge, 1944); John G. Sperling, *The South Sea Company: An Historical Essay and Bibliographical Finding List* (Kress Library of Business and Economics Publications, no. 17) Boston, Mass., 1962.

about the relationship between City business and politics. First, the older City companies with royal associations were Tory, and the newer institutions of the financial revolution were Whig. Secondly, London merchants and financiers of the early eighteenth century have been described, as a body, as inclined to the Whigs. These observations have generally been based upon contemporary opinion, upon earlier secondary authorities, or upon the examination of prominent London figures who spoke for the City in parliament. Discussions of the politics of City business have not been based, however, upon political analysis of large bodies of London merchants and investors. Moreover, particular trading groups and stocks have been studied in isolation from one another rather than studied together, and the reasons for the apparent political preferences of different occupational or commercial groups have not always been adequately explained. Although a characterization of late Stuart London merchants as rather whiggish is accurate, this assertion explains neither when the development became apparent nor whether the various trading groups in the City differed in the degree of their politicization. Finally, attempts to identify the politics of different sectors of City business have not explained how the sometimes conflicting interests of those sectors affected the character of City politics.

The object of this chapter is to disassemble and to analyse politically the complicated set of business interests and institutions that made up the City. The central question is that of explaining how the momentous commercial and financial developments of the late Stuart period contributed to the fracturing of London's political life. In other words, what did the party labels of Whig and Tory mean in the context of trade and investment, and what changes took place in those meanings as City trade and investment also experienced change? The chapter is not an examination of City enterprise and business *per se*, but rather a study of the *politics* of London enterprise and business, or the politics of wealth. The emphasis will be primarily upon the reign of William, because his reign saw the establishment of a new relationship between London politics and London wealth. If the London Whigs were the party of the Glorious Revolution at the beginning of William's reign, they were also, by the end, the party of the commercial and financial revolutions. Moreover, among the sources of party competition in London after 1688 was the dissatisfaction of younger Whig merchants with long-established Tory joint stocks, while among the sources of party competition by 1702 was the jealousy of Tory craftsmen for the newly-established Whig empire of corporate enterprise.

The politics of London wealth may be surveyed by isolating and analysing a single London leadership élite with overlapping interests in politics, enterprise, and investment. One hundred and ninety-eight persons have been considered 'City leaders' for the purposes of this analysis. The City leaders include all persons who served as alderman, sheriff, chamberlain, or City MP between 1688 and 1715, and all persons who were promoted for one of these offices by either party during the same period. Many but not all of these City leaders were also active as directors of the London joint stocks during their careers. Additionally, all directors of important joints stocks between 1688 and 1715 who were also elected to the London Common Council at any time between 1688 and 1720 have been counted as City leaders. Finally, several appointed aldermen of James's reign who retained the honorary designation of alderman after 1688, and who remained active in the joint stocks in William's reign, have also been counted as City leaders.

Defined in this manner, the City leaders are not simply a sample of the London socio-economic élite. The group, instead, encompasses all Londoners whose business and political interests led them to accept positions of influence or responsibility in *both* the Corporation and the stocks. They were not all of paramount importance, and not all important late Stuart Londoners are among those designated here as City leaders. For instance, many merchants and financiers who were influential in the City, in the Commons, or in Whitehall are not counted among the City leaders because they took no part in Corporation affairs. By the same token, some London magistrates and magisterial nominees among the City leaders were never elected to joint-stock offices. Nevertheless, the assembling of this City élite group permits a clear answer to the question of who were the leaders of the City Whigs and of the City Tories. Identification of the City leaders also assists in judging the political orientation of the directorates of the major corporate enterprises of the City. Table 4.1 provides an occupational survey of the late Stuart City leaders of each party, and Table 4.2 compares the joint-stock offices held by Whig and Tory City leaders.

Although the numbers of Whig and Tory City leaders were almost equal, the occupational profiles of the two groups are quite

Table 4.1 City Leaders by Party and Occupation

	Occupation			Whigs	Tories
I.	Active overseas merchants			60	29
	Principal trade(s) of above:				
	A. Baltic/Russia	10	3		
	B. Colonies	14	5		
	C. Iberia/Wine	18	5		
	D. Italy/Mediterranean	7	4		
	E. Levant/Silk	24	9		
	F. Near Europe	9	4		
II.	Rentiers and retired overseas merchants			11	19
III.	Domestic traders and industrial employers			20	32
IV.	Money-lenders: goldsmiths and scriveners			7	12
V.	Other and Unknown			4	4
				102	96

Active overseas merchants have been counted in Part I under each geographic area to which they are known to have traded.

Table 4.2 Corporate Directorships held by City Leaders

Offices	Whigs	Tories
Bank of England, 1694–1715	30	3
Old East India Company, 1698–1708	13	26
New East India Company, 1698–1708 (partial)	16	3
United East India Company, 1708–15	15	3
Royal African Company, 1689–1712	17	30
South Sea Company, 1711–15	10	8
Million Bank, 1695–1715 (partial)	12	4
Land Banks, 1695	6	3
	119	80

The records of the New East India Company and those of the Million Bank permit the identification of most, but not all, of their late Stuart directors.

different. Almost three in five of the Whigs were active overseas merchants, but this was true of fewer than one-third of the Tories. Whigs greatly exceeded Tories among City leaders drawn from every sector of London's overseas trade. On the other hand, among those City leaders who were *rentiers* or retired overseas merchants (in 1688), Tories significantly outnumbered Whigs, and such individuals were much more evident in the leadership of the Tory party in William's reign than they were among the Whigs. In the 1690s especially, the Tories were handicapped by a rather ageing leadership, while the Whigs benefited from a younger and more dynamic leadership which was heavily recruited from the active trading community. Among other occupational groups the domestic traders and industrial employers were the most numerous, but the proportion of such City leaders among the Tories was much greater than among the Whigs. Indeed, slightly more Tory City leaders were drawn from domestic and industrial trades than from overseas commerce. The importance of these leaders in City Tory councils was especially evident in Anne's reign, by which time many of the leading Tory *rentiers* and retired men of commerce had passed from the scene. The early eighteenth-century London Tory party leadership included some merchants, but it was dominated by domestic traders, industrial employers, and also by money-lenders. Although the money-lenders among the City leaders were few, the Tory money-lenders were at the heart of their party after 1702.

The Tories were a party not only of older men, but also of older money. Two out of every three corporate directorships held by late Stuart Tory City leaders were in the Old East India Company and the Royal African Company, and all but one of these fifty-six directorates were first obtained in William's reign. These older joint stocks deserved the Tory label not only because of their controversial royal monopolies but also because the leadership of the Tory party in the Corporation was so heavily interlocked with their directorates. These stocks were, however, only relatively Tory and not absolutely so, since Whig City leaders also had thirty directorships in them. If the London Tories were tied to the old stocks at the time of the Revolution, they were increasingly divorced from the City stocks by the time of the Hanoverian Succession. As the Old East India Company gave way to the United Company, and as the African Company declined in importance, the Tory presence in City corporate enterprise declined notice-ably. Few persons active in the new stocks of the financial revolu-tion became Tory party leaders, and the complex of City trading and financial institutions became a Whig preserve.

Unlike their Tory counterparts, the Whig City leaders were drawn in number from all these corporations, and during the entire period from 1688 to 1715 they held almost 50 per cent more directorships than the Tories. This difference is especially apparent among those persons who first assumed positions of leadership in the City during Anne's reign. Twenty-five Tory leaders first prominent after 1702 held only eleven corporate directorships, but twenty-six new Whigs held thirty-one. The London Whig leadership was most intimately associated with the directorate of the Bank of England. However, between 1698 and 1708, New East India Company directors were also quite notice-able in City Whig councils, as were United Company directors after 1708. The number of Whig and Tory leaders among the South Sea Company directors was roughly equal.

The City leaders examined here spoke not only for the parties which promoted them for office, but also for the stocks which they directed and for the socio-occupational groups from which they came. The subsequent sections of this chapter will be devoted to the politics of these different City occupational groups which the City leaders represented. Section 2 explores the origins of the predominantly whiggish inclinations of London's active late Stuart merchants, and section 3 examines the politics of the dif-ferent trading sectors of the London mercantile community. Sec-tions 4 and 5 seek to explain why domestic traders, industrial employers, and money-lenders were more prominent in the leader-ship of the City Tory party. The careers of some City leaders will be investigated in sections 3, 4, and 5 in order to illustrate pat-terns and trends characteristic of the politics of London wealth. A final section is addressed to the question of how City parties which diverged in the character of their leaderships also came to diverge in the nature of their social followings.

2. The 1690s: Patterns of Trade and Politics

The 1690s were a rather unusual period in the organization and development of London trade. The decade was one in which the momentum of commercial expansion was temporarily interrupted by the hazards of trading during a war of unprecedented dimensions for the English nation. Far from discouraging the enterprising spirit of the London mercantile community, however, the war of William's reign accelerated the modernization of City trade. Before the end of the decade, the monopolies of the East India, African, Russia, and Hudson's Bay Companies had either been eliminated or irreversibly weakened by their opponents among the active overseas traders. The ambitions and capital accumulations of dissatisfied merchants not only shattered established corporate privileges but were also harnessed effectively to the engines of government finance. Moreover, the 1690s were a decade in which commercial questions were of importance in clarifying the terms of both party competition in London and party debate at Westminster. The thesis will be advanced here that during the 1690s a new relationship was established between trading wealth and City politics. The patterns of trade and politics that emerged during the 1690s also endured for the remainder of the first age of party, changing only after 1715 when the issues of political debate also changed.

The ensuing analysis of the patterns of trade and politics rests upon the identification of 1,339 merchants believed to have been active during the reign of William III.[4] Of these, 559 who were definitely London liverymen, and who were thereby eligible to participate in all City electoral choices, have been chosen for study. The fact that at least 42 per cent of the known merchants of William's reign were liverymen is significant in itself. This proportion is sufficient to suggest that the issues of Corporation politics were generally of interest to the overseas traders. Moreover, among merchants whose geographic areas of specialization are known, the proportion on the livery was even higher. In other words, the separation between the sphere of City business and the sphere of Corporation affairs that is so evident by the mid-eighteenth century had yet to develop.[5] Whigs among

[4] Procedures employed for identifying merchants, for discovering those on the livery, and for determining partisanship are explained in De Krey, 'Trade, Religion, and Politics', iii. 463–72.

[5] Rogers, 'Money, land and lineage; the big bourgeoisie of Hanoverian London', *Social History*, 4 (1979), 438–9. Admission to the livery of a City guild is admittedly not an entirely satisfactory index of the political interests or activities of the London overseas merchants. All that is argued here is that the merchants on the livery had greater oppor-

merchants on the livery greatly outnumbered Tories. 60 per cent of those merchants on the livery (337) were Whig. Only 132 or 24 per cent were Tory, and the evidence for the remaining merchants on the livery is unavailable or inconsistent. In other words, the greater number of active overseas traders among the Whig City leaders reflects a corresponding bias among all merchants involved in City politics.

How is this overwhelming bias to be explained? Can the divide between Whig and Tory merchants be connected to any significant commercial variables? These questions will be addressed by examining several factors that might have had a bearing upon the political inclinations of London merchants—geographical specializations, volume of trade, joint-stock investments, and duration of trading activities.

Do the partisan preferences of active 1690s' merchants reflect the different interests of those who traded to different geographical areas? The data analysed in Table 4.3 reveal that a Whig political perspective was prevalent among the liveried merchants who specialized in every area of London trade. Although the ratio of Whigs to Tories among the merchants trading to different areas varied considerably, Whigs outnumbered Tories by about two to one or considerably more in each group. The Whig bias of the London traders of the 1690s must therefore have arisen from factors that affected all merchants regardless of their specializations. This is not to deny that the characteristics of different geographical trades are important in explaining the degree of politicization of each group of merchants and in explaining the relative preponderance of Whigs within each group. These matters will be deferred here, however, and considered in section 3 of this chapter.

Does the political division between Whig and Tory merchants reflect the jealousy of smaller traders for the wealth of the great magnates, a pattern that has been detected in the politics of mid-eighteenth-century London merchants?[6] The data analysed in Table 4.4 suggest that this was not the case. The number of Whigs greatly exceeded the number of Tories among merchants trading with smaller, medium-sized, and larger volumes. The

tunities to become involved in City politics and that they provide a useful guide to the political inclinations of all London merchants.

[6] Sutherland, p. 70; Rogers, 'Resistance to Oligarchy', p. 6.

Table 4.3 Geographical Specializations and Partisanship of 1690s'
Merchants on the London Livery

	Whig	Tory	Whig to Tory Ratio
Near Europe	56	20	2.80
Colonial	80	23	3.48
Iberia and Wine	67	26	2.58
Baltic and Russia	47	10	4.70
Mediterranean	43	22	1.95
Levant and Silk	62	21	2.95
Specialization Unknown	79	34	2.32
All Liveried merchants	337	132	2.55

Merchants have been counted under each geographic area to which they are known to have traded. Sources employed in determining geographical specializations include D. W. Jones, 'London Overseas Merchant Groups', Appendices B(1) to B(11), pp. 388–468 and others listed in De Krey, 'Trade, Religion, and Politics', iii. 463–72.

Table 4.4 Trading Volumes (1695–6) and Partisanship of 1690s'
Merchants on the London Livery

	Whigs	Tories	Whig to Tory Ratio
£5000 and more	48	26	1.85
£2,500 to £5,000	45	14	3.21
£500 to £2,500	84	34	2.47
Others on livery	160	58	2.76
All on livery	337	132	2.55

Trading volumes are derived from D. W. Jones, 'London Overseas Merchant Groups', pp. 388–468.

data suggest both that the medium-rank merchants were especially partial to the Whigs, and that Whig sentiments were somewhat less pervasive—but still predominant—among merchants trading with the greatest volumes.

Another index of the scope of merchants' trading activities is the number of geographical trades in which they were involved. Table 4.5 reveals that Whig inclinations were more widespread

Table 4.5 Multiple Geographic Specializations and Partisanship
of 1690s' Merchants on the London Livery

	Whigs	Tories	Whig to Tory Ratio
Two or more areas	71	21	3.38
One area	187	77	2.43
Number of areas unknown	79	34	2.32
All liveried merchants	337	132	2.55

For sources, see note to Table 4.3.

among merchants known to have pursued multiple geographic specializations. Investigation of the relationship between partisanship and the scope of trading activities indicates, therefore, that the medium-sized traders were particularly partial to the Whigs and that geographical diversification was more noticeable among Whig merchants than among Tory merchants.

Does the party division among London merchants reflect antagonisms between those traders who invested capital in the old 'royalist' joint stocks and those traders who invested in the new stocks launched by the Whig Junto? The data presented in Table 4.6 bear upon this question, and also suggest another question. A greater number of active Tory traders of the 1690s were investors in the older monopoly joint stocks than in the new 'parliamentary' stocks. However, active Whig traders outnumbered active Tory traders among the investors in all four of the corporate enterprises considered here, although Whig merchants invested less money in the old companies than in the new. The City Tories frequently turned to the old companies for their political leaders, but the principal shareholders of those companies nevertheless included both many Whig merchants and many nonconformists, as was indicated in chapter three. Moreover, the ratio of Whigs to Tories is so much greater among merchants who made investments than among merchants who did not make investments as to suggest an intimate relationship between mercantile investment and Whig principles. Explaining the precise nature of this relationship is, however, rather problematic. Had those merchants who responded to the new investment opportunities of the 1690s previously

Table 4.6 Joint-stock Investments and Partisanship of
1690s' Merchants on the London Livery

	Whigs	Tories	Whig to Tory Ratio
A. OLD 'ROYALIST' COMPANIES			
1. *Old East India Company, 1694*			
Under £2,000	32	11	
£2,000 to £4,000	7	4	
£4,000 and more	1	8	
All	40	23	1.74
2. *Royal African Company, 1693*			
Under £2,000	20	12	
£2,000 to £4,000	6	6	
£4,000 and more	0	1	
All	26	19	1.37
B. NEW 'PARLIAMENTARY' COMPANIES			
3. *Bank of England, 1694*			
Under £2,000	45	2	
£2,000 to £4,000	23	7	
£4,000 and more	11	1	
All	79	10	7.90
4. *New East India Company, 1698*			
Under £2,000	34	8	
£2,000 to £4,000	22	2	
£4,000 and more	24	4	
All	80	14	5.71
Total Investors	162	50	3.24
Others on Livery	175	82	2.13
All on Livery	337	132	2.55

Merchants who invested in more than one stock company have only been counted once among the total investors. IOL, East India Company, Home Miscellaneous Series, ii, List of Adventurers, 1694, and Parchment Records 54; PRO T 70/188, fos. 113–21; Bank of England, Archives Section, Index to the Bank of England Subscriptions, 1694.

adopted Whig principles? Or did merchants who were excluded from the old stocks, and who bought stock in the new companies, become Whigs as a result? That is to say, did Whigs make investments, or did investments make Whigs?

To answer these questions, an attempt must be made to explain *when* the Whig bias of the London mercantile community became evident. Dating the development will also clarify *why* merchants —and especially why those merchants with money to invest— exhibited so strong a partiality for the Whig party. Table 4.7 presents a comparison of the partisanship of three relative age groups among the active London merchants of William's reign. Those merchants active in the 1690s who began their trading careers before 1675 show only the slightest Whig bias. These individuals were the survivors of a generation of merchants whose attitudes were shaped by vivid memories of the anarchy of the civil wars and the uncertainties of the Interregnum. Moreover, they had little reason to be dissatisfied with joint stocks reorganized or launched under royal charters.

Table 4.7 Partisanship of 1690s' Merchants on the London Livery: Duration of Trading Activity as an Indication of Relative Age

	A. Numbers			B. Distribution	
	Whigs	Tories	Whig to Tory Ratio	Whigs %	Tories %
Before 1675	29	28	1.04	9	23
1675–1690	157	58	2.71	49	48
After 1690	134	36	3.72	42	30

A few merchants who cannot be placed in one of the three categories with any confidence have been omitted from Table 4.7. Procedures employed to determine the duration of trading activity of 1690s' merchants are described in De Krey, 'Trade, Religion, and Politics', iii. 471.

On the other hand, a strong Whig bias is evident among those merchants of the 1690s who are believed to have begun trading in the fifteen-year period culminating in the Glorious Revolution and its parliamentary settlement. They were all active in the 1680s, which was the most prosperous commercial decade of the Restoration, a decade that also saw the development of two new commercial problems. One of these problems was the fear that the expansion of English trade might be jeopardized by French competition, a fear that was scarcely relieved by the French sympathies of Charles II and James II. The second problem was that the expansion of investment facilities in the City lagged far behind the accelerating accumulation of capital, as K.G. Davies noted some time ago.[7] Much dissatisfaction about the existing joint stocks was understandably expressed in the 1680s, and many of those who expressed such dissatisfaction identified with the political opposition to monarchs who protected privileged and limited stocks. As D.W. Jones has argued, dissatisfaction with the old stocks became even more intense in the early 1690s, when the war-time interruption of trade created an unprecedented glut of idle capital in the City.[8] Merchants who commenced their trading careers after the Revolution both shared the frustrations of their slightly older trading brethren and were relieved by the Whig Junto's solutions to these frustrations. Not surprisingly, the new London merchants of the 1690s were overwhelmingly whiggish, and many of the Whig merchants who initiated their trade after the Revolution were investors in the new stocks.

The Whig bias of London merchants who began their careers after 1675 seems, therefore, to have been related to rising mercantile frustration over finding outlets other than trade and land for surplus profits. In the 1690s, a substantial body of mature merchants still outside the old stock companies was joined by many younger men who quickly came to share their dissatisfaction with the old stocks. From the merchants' point of view, what was wrong with these companies was not that they had non-parliamentary charters and monopolies (although that was a useful argument after the Glorious Relvolution), but simply that they were too small and too few. Pressure from these merchants contributed directly to the expansion of the old companies in the early 1690s, to the boom in minor joint stocks from 1689 to 1695, and to the establishment of major new joint stocks. In other words, those who were Whigs in the context of City trade perceived the Revolution of 1688 as an opportunity to restructure and enlarge the existing facilities for investment. This attitude was an important component of the definition of what being a Whig meant in London, and it is equally important in explaining the role of the Whig party in the politics of the Corporation. Whig traders made investments in the 1690s because the desire for investment opportunities was by definition a London Whig concern.

---

[7] Davies, 'Joint-Stock Investment in the Later Seventeenth Century'.
[8] D.W. Jones, 'London Overseas Merchant Groups', chapter 7.

The interpretation advanced here of the relationship between the politics of wealth and the politics of party rests entirely upon the active mercantile community of the 1690s. Because no complete reconstruction of the active merchants of the preceding Restoration decades has been made, the extent of Whig bias among *all* merchants active in the 1680s must be considered cautiously. Those merchants who began their careers between 1675 and the Revolution and who remained active for all or part of William's reign were clearly heavily Whig, but the development of a Whig bias among the London merchants as a whole may have been quite gradual. Some evidence suggests that this Whig bias may not have been readily apparent before 1688. For instance, active merchants chosen for Corporation offices between 1675 and the Revolution were fairly evenly divided between the parties.[9] Furthermore, in 1682, those City livery companies that included large numbers of merchants were evenly divided between Whig and Tory mayoral candidates.[10] In other words, although reasons for the predominance of Whigs among the active 1690s merchants can be traced to the preceding decade, the new relationship between City wealth and City whiggism seems not to have been firmly established until the time of the Revolution.

The London Whigs of the 1690s were thus the party of established merchants whose hopes of participating in corporate ventures had previously been thwarted. They were also the party of a growing body of younger merchants whose expectations for investment outlets could be met only by depriving old investors of their exclusive hold on corporate profits and privileges. Obversely, the Tories were a minority party among the London merchants; but the City Tories did include some merchants who had entered the old stocks through luck or connections, and others who were suspicious of the novelty of joint stocks established on a national debt. As Table 4.7 (B) also suggests, the active Tory traders of the 1690s included a significantly larger proportion of older men and a significantly smaller proportion of younger men than their Whig counterparts. Once the connections among new trading wealth,

[9] This argument is based on analysis of biographies in Woodhead.

[10] Bodl., *A List of the Poll of the Several Companies of London for a Lord Mayor* (1682). On the other hand, the number of London and provincial merchants in the House of Commons increased somewhat in the Exclusion Parliaments. When compared with other family type groups among the members, these merchant MPs were notably hostile to the Court. See Henning, i. 7–8, 54–5.

new men, and the new stocks had been established in the 1690s, the City Whig merchant investors became an enduring and critical interest in the politics of late Stuart England. Moreover, as the moneyed interest established itself in the City, the London Whigs completed a quick transformation from being the party of opposition to being the party of trade and corporate enterprise.

3. The London Mercantile Community

Examination of the politics of London wealth has revealed striking differences in the occupational profiles of Whig and Tory City leaders. An important new alliance between rising younger merchants and Whig parliamentary figures has also been dated to the 1690s. Both these features of London politics may be further studied by looking at the different trading groups that made up the London mercantile community. Much overlap among these groups resulted from the number of merchants with diverse geographical trading interests. Nevertheless, some groups of geographical specialists had distinctive histories. The political inclinations of many merchants on the livery were probably informed by experiences they shared with trading colleagues who pursued the same specializations. Moreover, the City leaders from mercantile backgrounds spoke not only for their parties, and not only for merchants and investors, but also for the geographical trades from which they were drawn. The circumstances of different groups of traders and the careers of corresponding City leaders should also reveal, therefore, that the Whigs were the party of trade and corporate enterprise, and that among those merchants attached to the older stocks were many leading London Tories.

The convergence between City trade and City politics varied from specialization to specialization. A guide to these variations is provided in Table 4.8, which measures the proportion of the active merchants of William's reign from each geographical trade who were London liverymen.

A. The Colonial Merchants

A rather large proportion of the colonial traders of William's reign were liverymen (Table 4.8), and the proportion of Whigs among those on the livery was also exceptional (Table 4.3). These

Table 4.8 1690s' Merchants on the London Livery According to
Trading Specializations

Area	All Merchants	Merchants on the Livery	Percentage on the Livery
Near Europe	248	97	39
Colonial	215	119	55
Iberia and Wine	250	115	46
Baltic and Russia	139	66	47
Mediterranean	132	76	58
Levant and Silk	156	107	69
Area(s) Unknown	454	155	34
All Merchants	1339	559	42

Merchants have been counted under each area to which they are known to
have traded. For sources, see note to Table 4.3.

political characteristics were probably related to two other distinctive features of the colonial merchants. Dissent was especially
widespread among them, as has been explained in chapter three.
Furthermore, many colonial traders were active opponents of
three trading corporations that possessed privileges inimical to
their own activities. The place of dissent among colonial merchants requires no further comment, but their antagonism to
privileged trading concerns does.

Instrumental in the expansion of English trade in the decades
after the Restoration,[11] the colonial merchants were accustomed
to an exceptional degree of independence. From their inception,
the colonial trades had been characterized by easier access than
those trades that were the preserves of regulated companies or of
joint-stock corporations. The colonial merchants seem to have
credited the expansion of their trade in sugar and tobacco to the
freedom they enjoyed, and because of this 'whig' attitude, they
were unsympathetic to monopolies they perceived as hindrances
to their own continuing expansion. Among these obstacles were
the Royal African Company and the Hudson's Bay Company,
two of the Restoration joint stocks, and the much older regulated
Russia Company.

Chartered in 1672, the African Company had originally included
a preponderance of active merchants among its shareholders.

[11] Davis, 'English Foreign Trade'.

By the 1690s, however, the company's slave trade monopoly
was acceptable neither to many colonial planters, who complained of a short supply of Africans, nor to some interloping
colonial traders, who were able to undersell the company. Repeatedly attacked before parliament by these allied interests, the African
Company could not count on support from other active merchants because its limited capitalization had prevented the acquisition of shares by younger traders. Although parliament
restricted the company's privileges in 1698, the West Indies merchants remained dissatisfied and were among those whose complaints prompted a parliamentary termination of the company's
monopoly in 1712.[12] Conducting a less essential trade, the
diminutive Hudson's Bay Company attracted less opposition.
Nevertheless, its 'boundless charter', which gave it control of
the northern fur trade, aroused the jealousy of London merchants
who traded to New York and to New England. Only 13 per cent
of the Hudson's Bay stock was held by active traders in 1690.
Although the company secured a short-term parliamentary
renewal of its privileges in that year, this grant was vigorously
opposed by a body of active Whig merchants headed by the
Presbyterian alderman and tobacco magnate, Sir Thomas Lane.
Seven years later the Hudson's Bay Company lost its parliamentary monopoly in a contest with the same colonial interests.[13]
Similarly, in 1699, several of the City' largest colonial traders
were among the Whig leaders of the new syndicate that gained
parliamentary cancellation of the Russia Company's privileges in
the Narva trade.[14]

   As a group, the colonial traders well illustrate, therefore, the
opposition of enterprising and independent Whig merchants to
privileged corporations established before the Revolution.
Although many of these sugar and tobacco importers were trading
with rather small volumes,[15] many colonial specialists were nevertheless subscribers to the Bank of England and to the New East
India Company. They were also well represented among the

[12] Davies, African Company, pp. 44–6; De Krey, 'Trade, Religion, and Politics', i.
100 n. 97.
[13] HMC House of Lords MSS, 1690–91, p. 73. Also see the Hudson's Bay Company
stock list in Edwin E. Rich, ed., Hudson's Bay Copy Booke of Letters Commissions Instructions
Outward, 1688–1696, Hudson's Bay Record Society, xx (1957), 314–15.
[14] Price, Tobacco Adventure, pp. 105–10.
[15] D. W. Jones, 'London Overseas Merchant Groups', pp. 256–7, 458–68.

directorates of these new stocks, and they counted some of the wealthiest City leaders among their number. Mention will be made here of the careers of four colonial City leaders, each of whom typifies one or more patterns in the relationship between trading wealth and late Stuart politics.

Sir Gilbert Heathcote (1652–1733) is the best known of these City leaders. He was perhaps the most successful merchant of his day, and his political career was equally noteworthy. In William's and Anne's reigns, Heathcote and his six brothers, all newcomers to the City, established a family trading empire that dwarfed the scale of many corporate concerns. Primarily a West Indies and Baltic merchant, Heathcote also traded to Spain, the Mediterranean, New York, and—as an interloper—to the East Indies. Two of his brothers went to Jamaica, a colony that Sir Gilbert served as agent, and another brother established himself in New York. Three brothers with trading interests similar to Sir Gilbert's remained with him in London. In Anne's reign, Heathcote became a personal symbol of the moneyed interest that reached from the stocks into the politics of the City and the nation. He was a member of the Bank directorate from its organization in 1694 until his death forty years later, and he was also a director of the New East India Company for most of its existence. As governor of the Bank in 1710, Heathcote headed the delegation of City magnates who sought to dissuade Anne from dismissing her Whig ministry. Despite his anti-populist behaviour as Lord Mayor in 1710–11, Heathcote had once been a radical Whig who supported the 1690 design to democratize the Corporation. His career perfectly mirrors the ideological volte-face that accompanied the City Whigs' acquisition of power in the Corporation and in the stocks.[16]

Equally revealing is the career of Robert Heysham (1663–1723), a colonial City leader who is usually considered a Tory but who eventually proved attractive to the Whigs. A Barbados trader, Heysham served as agent for that colony and as MP for his native Lancaster from 1698 to 1715. Although a brother was a one-time Barbados agent for the African Company, Heysham was the largest African separate trader of Anne's reign, and in 1712 he

---

[16] *The Marlborough–Godolphin Correspondence*, ed. Henry L. Snyder (Oxford, 1975), iii. 1371; N. Tindal, *The Continuation of Mr Rapin de Thoyras's History of England*, 2nd edn. (1751), ii. 273; Woodhead, pp. 87–8; Sedgwick, ii. 121–4; Dunn, 208, 220–1.

appeared before the Council of Trade on behalf of those who sought the dissolution of the African stock. The following year he deserted the Oxford ministry in the Commons because of its unpopular commercial treaty with France, and he was adopted as a parliamentary candidate by the City Whigs, who hoped to exploit the French treaty issue. By 1713, then, Heysham's position with regard to the African trade paralleled that of many Whig colleagues among the colonial merchants; and he seems to have been modifying his Hanoverian toryism into Country whiggism. Two years later, in the first parliamentary poll of George I's reign, the London Whigs secured his election as City MP. Unlike many London Whig City leaders, however, Heysham made few investments, was never elected to the directorate of a major London joint stock, and kept most of his capital in trade; and he died worth a modest £20,000. He was the epitome of the independent colonial trader.[17]

The careers of two Tory colonial City leaders were interwoven with the history of the African trade in a somewhat different fashion. Alderman Sir Jeffrey Jeffreys (1652–1709) was the most successful tobacco merchant of the late Stuart decades. He was an agent for the Leeward Islands and for Virginia, and he sat in several late Stuart parliaments for Brecon. The heirs of an original member of the African Company Court of Assistants, Jeffreys and his brother John (also a Tory MP) were directors of the company in the 1680s and the 1690s.[18] Jeffreys' Tory aldermanic colleague Sir John Fleet (1648–1712), a City MP for much of William's reign, was the only other colonial City leader of either party with ties to the African Company. Trading to the West Indies as early as 1677, Fleet was a long-serving director of both the African Company and the Old East India Company. Like Heysham, Fleet modified his politics in mid-career. Elected alderman and sheriff in 1688, Fleet at first joined interest with the City Whigs, although he was a moderate Tory rather than a revolutionary Whig. After the mid-1690s, however, Fleet's investments increasingly tied him to the Tory side in the disputes over

---

[17] CLRO Common Serjeant's Book, vi. fo. 114; *JCTP 1708–9 to 1714–15*, p. 335 et seq.; *A Collection of White and Black Lists* (1715), p. 29; Sedgwick, ii. 136; Davies, *African Company*, pp. 298, 372; Horwitz, *Parliament, Policy and Politics*, p. 348; Holmes, *British Politics in the Age of Anne* (1967), p. 280.

[18] Walcott, MPs tempus Anne; Woodhead, p. 98; Davies, *African Company*, pp. 295, 385; Horwitz, *Parliament, Policy and Politics*, p. 349.

the East Indies and African trades. He appears as a Tory in parliamentary division lists from 1696.[19] The investments of Fleet and Jeffreys were exceptional for colonial merchants, and those investments also seem to have strongly influenced their politics.

B. The Levant Merchants

The Turkey merchants were somewhat fewer in number, but they clearly occupied a distinctive position in City politics and City enterprise. Two-thirds of the Levant traders of William's reign were liverymen (Table 4.8). This was the greatest proportion for any group of geographical specialists, and it may reflect the Levant Company's requirement that its London members be free of the Corporation. Still, the magnitude of the Levant merchants' involvement in City affairs is rather astonishing. Over one-third of all merchant City leaders were trading to the Near East (Table 4.1), and no fewer than one-fifth of all Levant merchants who were active in William's reign became City leaders. These and other Levant traders were highly visible among the late Stuart directors of the London stocks. On a per capita basis, the Turkey traders were the wealthiest merchant group in London, and their contributions to the initial subscriptions for Bank and New East India Company stock were second only to those of the more numerous wine importers.[20] Strongly Whig, the Levant livery-men were significantly more so than the liveried mercantile community as a whole (Table 4.3).

The pre-eminence of the Levant merchants in the late Stuart City was not a recent development. After depriving the Near European merchants (the old Merchant Adventurers) of their commanding role in the Corporation in the reign of Charles I, these Near Eastern merchants dominated London affairs for the remainder of the century, with the exception of the decade of the Interregnum. As long as the Levant trade flourished, so did the careers of those who conducted it. The Levant Company enjoyed a monopoly, but its privileges were not challenged until the reign of George I, when signs of decline in the trade became apparent. In the ensuing decades the English market for Ottoman silk, cotton, and yarn constricted, and the number of younger merchants

---

[19] William Foster, 'Sir John Fleet', *EHR* li (1936), 681–5; Luttrell, *Brief Relation*, ii. 289, 569; Woodhead, p. 70; Horwitz, *Parliament, Policy and Politics*, p. 346.
[20] D. W. Jones, 'London Overseas Merchant Groups', pp. 256–7.

entering the trade fell off sharply. By the mid-eighteenth century, the civic empire of the Turkey traders had also vanished.[21]

The political visibility of the Levant traders in the late Stuart period may be attributed in part to their wealth and to the social respect their wealth commanded, but their heavy involvement in City affairs was also prompted by a need to protect what they had gained in the past. The first twenty years of the Restoration were a golden age for the Levant trade. Thereafter, however, the Turkey merchants encountered the beginnings of foreign competition from their French counterparts in the Near East, and they complained of domestic competition from the 'royalist' East India Company. French competition in the Levant was more a perceived threat than a material one before 1700, but it was sufficient to make the London Levant traders suspicious about the French proclivities of Charles II and James II. As early as 1670, the Levant Company also objected to competition in the English silk market from the Indian and Persian imports of the East India Company. By 1680 this dispute had reached parliament, and a year later counsel for the two companies argued their cases before the privy council. The crown's partiality for the East India Company on this occasion was not forgotten by the Levant traders or by the East India Company's other critics.[22] Although some Levant merchants of both parties were Old East India Company shareholders or directors in the next decades, the hostility between the Levant Company and the Old Company made many Turkey traders enthusiastic supporters of the Whigs' 1698 plan for reorganizing the India trade.

Both the Levant traders' fears about French competition and their irritation with the Old East India Company fed their Whig inclinations. Furthermore, by the middle of the 1690s they had yet another reason to be suspicious of Tory ministries. The Levant trade was severely disrupted in the early years of the War of the Grand Alliance, and the Levant merchants blamed their difficulties, whether fairly or not, upon the Carmarthen–Nottingham Church-Tory ministry.[23] Little trade was possible until 1693 when the government at last provided a naval convoy for a

[21] Brenner, pp. 54–65; Alfred C. Wood, *A History of the Levant Company* (Oxford, 1935), pp. 136 ff.

[22] Loughead, 'East India Company', chapter 4; *The Allegations of the Turkey Company and Others against the East-India Company* (1681); Wood, pp. 101–5.

[23] The quantity of English cloth exported to Turkey in exchange for Near Eastern

Turkey fleet. Unfortunately, the four hundred merchantmen which sailed for Smyrna in May 1693 lost the protection of the allied main fleet prematurely. The interception of the Turkey-bound ships in July by two French squadrons cost London traders an estimated £1,000,000. The Levant merchants protested bitterly to the crown, complaining of Nottingham's mishandling of naval affairs. Although the Secretary was dismissed a few months after this episode, the Symrna fleet disaster was not quickly forgotten, and it contributed to a belief within the London mercantile community that trade was unsafe in the hands of parliamentary Tories. Like the colonial merchants, the Levant merchants had good reason, therefore, for adopting a Whig posture in politics. They found the War of the Spanish Succession less disruptive in the short-term, but during the war-time decades their French rivals established the groundwork for a capture of the European trade to Turkey in the first half of the eighteenth century.[24]

Bound together by their wealth, status, common economic interests, and small numbers, the Levant traders were also a highly inbred and endogamous mercantile élite. Few of the thirty-three City leaders who traded to the Levant came from obscure backgrounds. The fathers of at least sixteen of them were London merchants, many of whom had also traded to Turkey.[25] Additional leading Levant traders were the sons of a Wiltshire clothier, a mayor of Hereford, a Staffordshire squire, and an influential Civil War Puritan divine.[26] Sir George and Sir Charles Thorold were fourth generation Levant merchants, and Huguenot families long active in the English silk trade were represented by Sir Edward and Sir Christopher Des Bouverie, Sir James and Sir

products between 1691 and 1695 suggests that the trade has fallen to its lowest level between 1666 and 1735. Davis, *Aleppo and Devonshire Square*, p. 42.

[24] PRO Levant Company Court Minutes, SP 105/155 esp. fo. 256; HMC *House of Lords MSS*, New Ser. i. 190-3; Bodl. Newdigate Newsletters LC 2194 (4 July 1693), LC 2200-1 (22, 27 July 1693); Luttrell, *Brief Relation*, iii. 141-2, 225; Horwitz, *Revolution Politicks*, pp. 128-46; Davis, *Aleppo and Devonshire Square*, pp. 28-9.

[25] See Woodhead, chiefly, for the merchant fathers of the following Levant City leaders: Sir Henry Ashurst Bt., Sir William Ashurst, Sir John Buckworth, Sir Peter Delmé, Sir Christopher DesBouverie, Sir John Eyles Bt., Sir James Houblon, Sir John Houblon, Sir Randolph Knipe, Sir Christopher Lethieullier, Sir Gabriel Roberts, Sir Charles Thorold, Sir George Thorold Bt., Sir Samuel Dashwood, Sir Thomas Vernon, Sir Thomas Webster Bt.

[26] Ibid. for the fathers of Sir Francis Eyles Bt. (Wiltshire clothier), Sir Humphrey Edwin (mayor of Hereford), Obadiah Sedgewick (Puritan divine); and see Sedgwick, ii. 73 for the father of Sir Richard Gough (Staffordshire squire).

John Houblon, and Sir Christopher Lethieullier. Thirteen of the Levant City leaders were returned to the Commons in the late Stuart period. The wealth and continued influence of these families are indicated by the fact that no fewer than thirty of their relatives (excluding marriage relations) and direct descendants (male lines only) were also elected to the House of Commons between 1702 and 1754.[27] The sons or nephews of several Levant City leaders succeeded them in trade, but in the first half of the eighteenth century, many Levant families responded to commercial changes and to the customary route of London wealth by exchanging the silk market for the land market. Although they remained active in London affairs into the reign of George I, these élite families thereafter abandoned City politics for county politics. Only one of the families of the leading London Levant merchants of the first age of party was still among the largest London silk importers of the 1730s.[28]

C. The Near European Merchants

As the Levant merchants rose to the top of London mercantile society in the seventeenth century, the Near European merchants—numerically one of the two largest trading groups—slipped farther from their former position of civic leadership. The proportion of Near European merchants on the livery was the lowest for all groups of geographical specialists (Table 4.8). Near European traders were about as wealthy on a per capita basis as the colonial merchants, but they took much less part in London and national politics and invested little in the great stock flotations of the 1690s.[29] Despite their great numbers, they provided relatively few City leaders, and the trade turn-overs of many of them were modest.

The Near European merchants of the 1690s were mostly cloth exporters, and this has much to do with their relatively inconspicuous role in City affairs. The dwindling of the continental market for England's old draperies earlier in the seventeenth century had reduced the prosperity and the City influence of London cloth exporters, even though cloth remained the country's largest

[27] This figure is derived from the genealogical information in Walcott, MPs tempus Anne, and from Sedgwick.
[28] Davis, Aleppo and Devonshire Square, p. 60.
[29] D. W. Jones, 'London Overseas Merchant Groups', pp. 256-7.

export commodity. The development of new draperies was beneficial for the cloth industry, but it seems not to have enabled the London cloth exporters to recover their former position in the mercantile community. Foreigners or recent denizens accounted for one-third of those who exported £500 or more in old draperies in 1695, according to D. W. Jones.[30] Although their knowledge of foreign markets and their international contacts may have advanced England's cloth export trade, these traders were especially unlikely to take much interest in Corporation affairs. The London cloth exporters were, then, on the side-lines of Corporation politics during the first age of party; they contributed less to the financial revolution than other trading groups; and they accounted for little of the continuing expansion of English trade.

The thirteen Near European merchants whose wealth, investments, and political commitments made them City leaders were exceptional in all these respects to most cloth exporters. Whig Near European leaders of note included Peter Godfrey, Sir Thomas Scawen, and Sir Henry Furnese. Godfrey (1665–1724), a trader with diverse interests, was the son of a Whig merchant and a nephew of the mysteriously murdered Sir Edmund Berry Godfrey. He was an original director of both the Bank and the New East India Company. One of four merchants unsuccessfully promoted by the Whigs in 1713 for the City's parliamentary seats, Godfrey was elected City MP in 1715, joined Walpole in opposition, and was re-elected to the Commons in 1722.[31]

Sir Thomas Scawen (c.1650–1730) and his elder brother Sir William Scawen (1647–1722) were leading cloth traders in William's and Anne's reigns. Sir William was a long-time MP and Bank director, but like many Near European merchants, he took no part in Corporation politics. Sir Thomas, on the other hand, was chosen alderman in 1712, and he was another of the four Whig City parliamentary candidates defeated in 1713 but triumphant in 1715.[32]

Sir Henry Furnese Bt. (1658–1712) is the best known of the Near European City leaders. The son of a bankrupt Sandwich grocer, Furnese rose from his apprenticeship as a stocking-seller to become a major linen and lace importer in the 1690s. Strategically

---

[30] Ibid., pp. 181–2, 188.
[31] Sedgwick ii. 65–6; Henderson, p. 24.
[32] Sedgwick ii. 410–11.

placed in the Flanders trade, he secured his first contract for army remittances in the 1690s, and between 1705 and 1710, the trust of Godolphin and Marlborough gained him the lion's share of continental remittances. Furnese was among the original directors of the Bank of England and of the New East India Company, which he was instrumental in creating. Chosen MP for his native Sandwich in 1701, he was one of ten New Company directors expelled from that parliament on charges of bribery. Re-elected the same year, he held the Sandwich seat until his death, and in 1711 he capped his City career with an election to the Court of Aldermen. His reputation as a war profiteer and his active membership in the Kit-cat Club earned Furnese a place in the satire of Swift and of Defoe.[33]

Two of the four Tory City leaders who traded to northern Europe also merit comment. Sir William Gore (1643–1708) was one of only three late Stuart Tory City leaders who served as Bank directors. Sir William Withers (1653–1721) was one of only three late Stuart Tory City leaders who served as directors of the New East India Company. The unusual corporate investments of Gore and Withers gave their political careers some unusual twists.

With a trade turn-over of some £64,000 in 1695, Gore was one of the great merchant princes of his era, and he served as governor of the Hamburg Company (once known as the Merchant Adventurers). A City alderman from 1690, his court connections gained him contracts as a supplier to both the army and the navy in the war of William's reign. Gore's extensive Old East India shares earned him a directorship in that concern beginning in 1693, and the following year he also joined the Bank directorate. His interests in the Bank made him more acceptable to the Whigs than other Tory City leaders, but as one observer wrote in 1701, 'They do not think him much of their party'. In that year, the Whig leaders successfully promoted Gore for Lord Mayor, doing so not because they liked his principles, but because every Whig alderman save one had already been Lord Mayor. Between his

[33] BL Add. MS 5752, fo. 236; BL Add. MS 33512, fos. 179–90, Henry Furnese to Corporation of Sandwich, various dates, 1701–8; *Examiner*, i. no. 41, 3–10 May 1711; *POAS* vi. 406; HMC *Portland MSS* iv. 637, 655; *Marlborough–Godolphin Correspondence*, ii. 609 et seq.; Holmes, *British Politics*, pp. 156, 191; Horwitz, *Parliament, Policy and Politics*, p. 282; Pat Rogers, 'Matthew Prior, Sir Henry Furnese and the Kit Cat Club', *Notes and Queries*, New Ser. xviii (1971), 46–8.

mayoralty and his death, Gore was less visible in London affairs, but two sons reasserted the family's City influence, both as South Sea directors and one as a member of the parliamentary October club.[34]

Sir William Withers, the son of a Cheapside linen-draper and Common Council loyalist during the Exclusion Crisis, first came to prominence in City affairs in 1697–8. He was then chosen as an African Company assistant, a New Company director, and an alderman. In the first 1701 City parliamentary election, Withers was included by the City Whigs in the Bank–New Company ticket which they successfully promoted against Tory–Old Company candidates. Not re-elected to the New Company directorate in that year, he was also dropped by the London Whigs, who again carried the City's parliamentary seats in the second 1701 general election. His brief flirtation with the Whigs over, Withers was a Church-Tory candidate at every City parliamentary election between 1705 and 1715, actually holding one of the City seats from 1707 until his defeat in 1715. An original director of the United East India Company, he was dumped in 1710 and figured in an unsuccessful Tory-ministerial effort to recover control of the United Company in 1711.[35]

D. *The Baltic and Russia Merchants*

Relatively few London merchants traded to Scandinavia, Russia, or other Baltic lands in the late seventeenth century. Four small, overlapping clusters of traders have been combined in this category: (1) Eastland cloth exporters (some of whom were also importers), (2) the small membership of the Russia Company, (3) importers of Baltic flax, hemp, timber and other naval stores, and (4) colonial merchants who also traded to the Baltic, chiefly as tobacco re-exporters. Despite this heterogeneity, the Baltic and Russia merchants on the livery exhibit a very distinctive political composition. The ratio of Whigs to Tories among them is much higher than that of any other group of merchants on the livery (Table 4.3). The strength of Whig sentiment among the Baltic and Russia liverymen is difficult to explain, but it seems to be

[34] BL Add. MS 40775, fo. 221, James Vernon to William III, 30 Sept. 1701; HMC *Portland MSS* iii. 632; D. W. Jones, 'London Overseas Merchant Groups', Appendix B(1); John Ehrman, *The Navy in the War of William III, 1689–97* (Cambridge, 1953), pp. 61–4, 66; Sedgwick, ii. 71–2; Carswell, p. 278.

[35] Walcott, MPs tempus Anne; Woodhead, p. 179.

related to a 1690s influx of younger enterprising merchants into trades previously monopolized by the declining Eastland Company and by the restrictive Russia Company. More than half the liverymen in this group were colonial-Baltic traders or Baltic importers, and they in particular included a number of influential merchants who were unhappy with the monopoly privileges of the Russia Company. As in other sectors of late Stuart London trade, therefore, monopoly was at the heart of political divisions among the Baltic and Russia merchants. In this case, the 'tory' Russia Company included very few active traders. Its opponents, on the other hand, included many merchants involved in the dynamic colonial sector, where whiggish opposition to monopolies was most pervasive.

This controversy, which has been analysed by J. M. Price, merits some attention here.[36] The issue that politicized the Northern trades in the late seventeenth century was the opening of a new market for colonial tobacco in Russia. The exclusive contract offered by Peter the Great for supplying his domains with tobacco prompted dreams of an inexhaustible new outlet for a crop already being over-produced in the mainland plantations. The merchants who projected these heady visions found their prospects dimmed by the antique Marian monopoly of the Russia Company. Moreover, the policies adopted by the Russia Company after the Revolution gave its opponents many grounds upon which to object to its privileges. Governed in the 1690s by the Tory merchant and MP Sir Benjamin Ayloffe, the company tightened its monopoly after 1691 by discouraging new admissions. Its small size, its restrictive policies, and the nominal impositions that the company levied on non-members who wished to trade to the Narva were all offensive to its critics. In 1698-9, the issues that divided the Russia Company and its opponents were aired in the press and in parliament after a newly organized trading syndicate secured the tsarist tobacco contract. Victory in this debate was claimed by the new tobacco combine when parliament disobliged the company by opening its trade to all merchants upon payment of a forty shilling admission fee.

The sixty-five 'tobacco contractors' who challenged the Russia Company were mostly active London merchants. Their expecta-

---

[36] Price, *Tobacco Adventure*, esp. pp. 37–47. Also, see GL MS 11,741, Russia Company Court Minutes, ii. 123, 147 et seq.

tions about the future of the Russia trade were not fulfilled, but the composition of the group reveals in microcosm the emerging relationship among Whig politics, commercial enterprise, and new corporate investments. Thirty-seven of forty-one whose politics can be determined were Whigs, and twenty-one of these Whigs were dissenters or persons interested in dissent. Fifteen of the contractors became Bank of England directors during their careers; sixteen became New East India Company directors; and fifty-nine of the sixty-five invested in either the Bank or the New Company.[37] The contractors were thus a vanguard group, including some of the most diversified and ambitious merchant-investors in the City. Ten of the sixty-five were City leaders. Among them were several persons whose careers have already been noted—Sir Gilbert Heathcote (three of whose brothers were also tobacco contractors), Sir Thomas Scawen (and his brother Sir William Scawen), Sir Henry Furnese, and the Tory tobacco magnate Sir Jeffrey Jeffreys. Of the other City leaders among the tobacco contractors, Presbyterian Sir Owen Buckingham (1650–1713), who was also a London alderman and Reading MP, deserves mention as a leading Baltic-colonial trader.[38]

E. The Iberian Merchants

The first age of party coincided with a critical period in the history of English trade with Spain and Portugal. In the last decades of the seventeenth century, the Iberian wine trade grew at an exceptionally rapid rate because of lengthy embargoes on French wines and because of tariff preferences given to Spanish and Portuguese wines. In the 1690s the Spanish wine trade surpassed the Portuguese, but the Portuguese trade gained its lasting eighteenth-century supremacy during the disruption of Anglo-Spanish trade in the war of 1702–13. Indeed, the Portuguese market for English textiles also expanded considerably as the Portuguese economy was invigorated by the growing English demand for Portuguese wines. London exports of cloth and of other commodities to Portugal increased dramatically in the decade after the Peace of 1697. The continued development of Anglo-Portuguese commerce

---

[37] These figures are based on analysis of Price's biographical directory of the contractors in *Tobacco Adventure*, pp. 105–10.

[38] Walcott, MPs tempus Anne; Woodhead, p. 40; Holmes, *British Politics*, p. 482 n. 6.

thereafter was an important factor in the English commercial revolution, as was the revival of Anglo-Spanish trade after 1713.[39]

The Iberian traders of William's reign thus enjoyed an exceptional degree of prosperity, and they played a correspondingly exceptional role in the beginnings of England's financial revolution. The number of London merchants trading to Spain and Portugal in the 1690s is noteworthy in itself. Some 250 City merchants were active in the trade in William's reign, two-thirds of them as wine importers and the remainder as exporters of cloth and other products. Despite the relative newness of the trade, the Iberian merchants outnumbered the colonial traders and matched the number of Near European merchants. Spanish and Portuguese merchants on the livery in William's reign exhibited typical Whig preferences, but they took an atypical role in City affairs. Indeed, the striking contributions of many Iberian traders to the new stock flotations of the 1690s involved them more deeply than any other group in the Whig Junto's war finance.

The importance of the Iberian traders and of their capital in the public finance of William's reign has been demonstrated and explained by D. W. Jones.[40] He has also established that merchants involved in the Iberian trade were increasingly visible in the organized opposition to the Old East India Company in the 1690s. His analysis of the initial Bank and New Company subscriptions reveals that 30 per cent of the investments in these stocks which were made by merchants came from wine importers.[41] This proportion is significantly greater than that for the élite Levant merchants or for any other trading group. Heavy investments in the Bank and in the New East India Company catapulted many Iberian merchants into positions of leadership in the City. More late Stuart stock directors came from the Iberian trades than from any other geographical specialization, and the Iberian merchants were second only to the Turkey merchants in the number of City leaders from their ranks.

The careers of three Iberian City leaders are noteworthy for what they reveal about the politics of wealth. Sir James Bateman (c.1660–1718) and Samuel Shepheard sen. (1648–1719) were major stock investors of the 1690s, and although they were mercantile Whigs,

[39] Fisher, Introduction and chapter 1.
[40] D. W. Jones, 'London Overseas Merchant Groups', pp. 111, 239–50, 256–7.
[41] D. W. Jones, 'London Merchants and the Crisis of the 1690s', p. 341.

each has also been described with some reason as a 'tory' after 1711. Their City activities were parallel in several respects. Moreover, their biographies serve as useful illustrations of the fact, sometimes obscured by party labels, that the Whig 'moneyed men' were not entirely the undivided regiment decried by their adversaries.

Like other wine importers looking for investment opportunities, both Bateman and Shepheard emerged in the 1690s as notable critics of the Old East India Company's limited capitalization. Both were original directors of the New East India Company, and Bateman was also an original and continuing Bank director. Each was strongly tied to the Junto, and Bateman was personally involved in public finance as a long-time trustee for the circulation of Exchequer bills and as a lender on the land tax. Each was also chosen as a director of the United East India Company in 1709 and 1710.[42]

Both Bateman and Shepheard entered Corporation politics as Whigs in Anne's reign. Chosen sheriff in 1702 and alderman in 1708, Bateman was one of the defeated Whig candidates in the City's 1710 parliamentary poll. Shepheard first sat in the Commons in 1701 for Newport, Isle of Wight, but he was expelled and imprisoned for bribing electors in six constituencies on behalf of New Company men. Although he declined to become a candidate for the London Whigs in the next parliamentary election, Shepheard was among those who ousted the Tory City MPs of Anne's first parliament in the 1705 City poll.[43]

Scarcely the stuff from which Tories were made, these wine traders nevertheless figured in the early history of the 'tory' South Sea Company, having fallen out in 1710–11 with their Whig colleagues among the Bank and East India directors. In May 1711, when the directorate of Harley's South Sea Company was announced, Bateman was named sub-governor and Shepheard was named a director. Did these curious City friends of Harley also become Tories through their enlistment in his new corporate rival to the Bank–East India complex? The question cannot be answered fully without exploring the City context of the establishment of the South Sea Company, an endeavour best deferred to

---

[42] HMC *Portland MSS* iv. 559; Sedgwick, i. 443; Dickson, pp. 370, 429; Walcott, MPs tempus Anne; Holmes, *British Politics*, p. 171.

[43] HMC *Portland MSS* iv. 26; Woodhead, pp. 25, 147; Walcott, 'East India Interest', pp. 235-6, 238.

chapter six. However, the argument may be offered here that Bateman and Shepheard's involvement in the South Sea Company did not represent a radical break with their past careers as Whig stock directors and government creditors. Although the company was launched under Tory parliamentary auspices, Harley's intention in promoting the scheme was to preserve public credit, and that was an intention that City magnates like Bateman and Shepheard could heartily endorse. Certainly they parted company in 1711 with opponents of Harley's government, like Sir Gilbert Heathcote and Sir Henry Furnese, but in so doing they simply demonstrated more flexibility than some Whig leaders in accommodating themselves to the Tory triumph of 1710. Their behaviour thereafter suggests that they were pragmatic Whigs rather than renegade Whigs.[44]

In the early 1690s, when Bateman and Shepheard were pursuing the wine trade, one of their leading colleagues in that trade was Tory City leader Sir Basil Firebrace (1652–1724). A High-Churchman and the son of an officer of the households of Charles I and Charles II, Firebrace was appointed to the offices of alderman and sheriff by James II. After the Revolution, his political interests and his trading interests were initially somewhat contradictory. With other rising wine importers, Firebrace was involved in the 1691 syndicate that unsuccessfully challenged the Old East India Company. However, when the Old Company gained a renewal of its charter in 1693 and enlarged its share capital, he bought into the Company, acquiring some £10,000 stock and serving as a director in 1694–5. He was a target in the 1695 parliamentary enquiry into the bribery of MPs by the Old Company. Firebrace did not become a major government creditor, but he was active in negotiations between the two India companies after 1700 and was handsomely rewarded by the Old

[44] Bateman did not adopt a Tory posture in Corporation politics after 1711; after the Hanoverian Succession, he voted in the Commons with other Whig oligarchs for the Septennial Act. Less is known of Shepheard's subsequent career. As a common council-man for Bishopsgate Within, he was trusted by the City Whig club that sought to influence Corporation politics from 1714 through 1717. Although his son of the same name ingratiated himself with the Cambridge Churchmen as their MP, Samuel Shepheard sen. has been identified as a dissenter by several historians. Holmes, *British Politics*, pp. 17, 27, 164, 498 n. 62; Sedgwick, i. 442, ii. 420–1; Hood, p. 34 et seq.; 'Minutes of a Whig Club 1714–1717', ed. H. Horwitz, in *London Politics 1713–1717* (London Record Society Publications, xvii), 1981, 29 et seq. Samuel Shepheard sen. is also described as of 'no church' in BL Stowe MS 354, fos. 161–2, *A Numerical calculation of the Honourable Mem—rs as were elected for the Ensuing Parl—nt* [1705].

Company with stock and money. In Anne's reign he suffered severe business losses and attempted suicide, but he lived to see the establishment of an enduring family interest in Suffolk.[45]

The careers of these three leading wine importers of the 1690s point again to the intimate involvement of the City Whigs in the financial revolution, and to the ties between City Tories and the old stocks. The three case studies also reveal, as did several previous ones, that patterns of wealth and politics were sometimes qualified by the pursuit of influence and income by individual City leaders. The interests of London merchants and investors sometimes cut across the lines of party debate without disrupting them.

F. The Mediterranean Merchants

The Italian and other Mediterranean merchants made up one of the smaller trading groups within the London mercantile community, and like the Baltic and Russia traders, they were a heterogeneous lot. With the exception of the Mediterranean grocery importers, most of these merchants also traded to other areas. Mediterranean trade seems to have been especially attractive as a secondary specialization for those who imported silk and wine from the Levant and Iberia. For instance, all seven Whig City leaders involved in Mediterranean trades were also active silk or wine importers. On the other hand, three of the four Tory City leaders in this group (Sir Joseph Herne, Sir Benjamin Newland, and Jeremiah Gough) were grocery importers not known to have pursued other specializations. Indeed, the small number of merchants on the livery who were primarily Mediterranean grocery importers were strongly Tory. This political preference, unique among London trading interests, may have reflected competition between Mediterranean fruit importers and the élite Levant merchants, who also imported some fruit.[46] London merchants trading to Leghorn were similarly discomfited by the Turkey merchants' position in the English silk trade, and they challenged the Levant Company's Near Eastern silk monopoly in the early Hanoverian period.[47]

[45] *DNB*; Luttrell, *Brief Relation*, v. 43 et seq., vi. 178; Woodhead, p. 69; Horwitz, *Parliament, Policy and Politics*, pp. 151–2; Sedgwick, ii. 36.

[46] The Tory sentiments of the Mediterranean fruit importers explain the relatively low Whig-to-Tory ratio among Mediterranean merchants on the livery (Table 4.3).

[47] Davis, *Aleppo and Devonshire Square*, pp. 37, 179–80; Wood, p. 139.

Sir John Ward (1650–1726) may be singled out from among the City leaders in this group for the light his career sheds on City politics. Exporting cloth to both Iberia and the Mediterranean from the late 1670s, he was the nephew and heir of another City leader, the dissenting Sir Patience Ward (1629–96), who was deeply involved in City affairs during the Exclusion Crisis.[48] In 1710 John Ward reflected that 'my aim has always been to have no byass or obligation', and his career in the stocks and in the Corporation suggests that, although he was a consistent Whig, he was also a rather independent one. An opponent of the Old East India Company in the early 1690s, his objection was to its limited capitalization rather than to its royal monopoly. When the Company enlarged its stock in 1693, Ward was among its new shareholders. In 1694 he invested in the Bank, and he acted as a director for most of the next thirty years. Ward also acted as an Old Company director from 1696 to 1698; but he subsequently transferred his interest and his money to the New Company, of which he was a director in Anne's reign. Like other Bank and New Company directors, he was a major private lender to the government in the first decade of the eighteenth century.[49]

In view of his career in the stocks, Ward's promotion by the City Tories in 1708 for one of London's Commons seats is rather curious. In that election, the London Church party sought to siphon votes from a strong City Whig ticket by advancing Ward and Sir William Withers (both with New Company connections) and two Tory goldsmiths. This ruse proved partially successful when Ward and Withers were elected, but Ward was still considered a reliable Whig by the parliamentary Junto. He was chosen alderman from a strong Whig ward in 1709, but he was defeated with other Whigs in the 1710 City parliamentary poll. A leading figure in the City's readjustment to the Tory triumph of 1710, Ward again acted as an independent Whig, making early overtures to Harley. He was instrumental in distancing the Bank from the uncooperative stance of Sir Gilbert Heathcote, while turning back the 1711 attempt of Sir James Bateman and Samuel Shepheard to bring many ministerial supporters into the Bank and East India directorates. Again unsuccessfully promoted by

[48] Whether Sir John Ward was also a dissenter is unknown, but he has been counted within the dissenting interest on the basis of this and other nonconformist connections.
[49] Holmes, p. 358; Dickson, pp. 266, 279–80.

the Whigs for London MP in 1713, Ward regained his City seat after the Hanoverian Succession.[50]

G. Rentiers *and Retired Merchants*

This examination of the politics of the London mercantile community may be completed with a brief consideration of those City leaders who had retired from active trade by 1689 or who were *rentiers* in William's reign. Both labels are applicable to most of the thirty City leaders who have been included in this group, the majority of whom had been overseas traders before the Revolution and whose capital was by then invested in land and in the stocks. In age at least, these individuals were truly the City's fathers. Most were in their sixties or seventies during William's reign; several had been prominent in the Corporation as early as the 1670s; and many did not survive the turn of the eighteenth century.

Two-thirds of these ageing and experienced City leaders were Tories. This fact points to the preponderance of *rentiers* and retired merchants in the highest City Tory councils in the first years after the Revolution. Eleven of the Tory aldermen who returned to the bench in 1688 were *rentiers* or retired merchants, and in the parliamentary elections of 1689–95 the London Church party drew several of its candidates from their ranks. The stock connections of these City leaders, both Whig and Tory, also illustrate the convergences between party rivalries and stock politics. All but two of the nineteen Tory *rentier* City leaders of the 1690s were one-time investors in the Old East India Company or in the Royal African Company, and most of them were also past or present directors of these stocks. Only one of them was a Bank investor in 1694. Four of the eleven Whigs among the leading City *rentiers* and retired merchants were also one-time directors of the Old East India Company or of the Royal African Company, but four of them were also Bank investors in 1694.

Of the older Tory City leaders of William's reign, Sir William Prichard (*c*.1632–1705) was perhaps the foremost. The son of a

[50] *Daily Courant* no. 1947, 14 May 1708; *Post Boy* no. 2482, 7–10 Apr. 1711; H. L. Snyder, 'Party Configurations in the Early Eighteenth-Century House of Commons', *BIHR* xlv (1972), 65; J. G. Sperling, 'The Division of 25 May 1711, on an Amendment to the South Sea Bill', *HJ* iv (1961), 194 n. 22; B. W. Hill, 'The Change of Government and the "Loss of the City", 1710–11', *EcHR*, 2nd Ser., xxiv (1971), 407 n. 6; Holmes, *British Politics*, p. 178n.; Sedgwick, ii. 520.

Southwark rope-maker, Prichard was a supplier of cordage and match to the Ordinance Office in the reign of Charles II, but little else is known of his business activities. An alderman from 1672, he was a leading City loyalist during and after the Exclusion Crisis. Having gained the mayoralty in 1682, Prichard presided over the demise of the City's charter, but he subsequently broke with James II and was discharged as alderman. He was reinstated on the bench in October 1688, and resuming his leadership of the City Churchmen, he figured in their 1690 attempt to unseat Whig magistrates. Prichard was promoted for City MP at every parliamentary election except one between 1685 and 1702, actually serving in three parliaments. A long-time investor in both the Old East India Company and the Royal African Company, he served as director of each in William's and Anne's reigns. Prichard's High-Church inclinations were commemorated at his funeral service by the clerical brother of high-flying Francis Atterbury.[51]

4. Money-lenders: Goldsmith-Bankers and Scriveners

The City's financiers were the only professionals whose wealth and status rivalled those of the great merchant princes. Although they were vastly fewer in number, the money-lenders were remarkably visible within the City's political élite. Thirteen goldsmith-bankers and six scriveners were among the late Stuart City leaders. The greatest among them had as much claim to be City representatives as the leading London traders, and their resources and influence gave them entrée to the highest ministerial councils. Like the mercantile leaders, the financiers could present themselves as spokesmen for important sectors of City business and opinion. They had ties with the City's working goldsmiths, from whose activities their own were not yet entirely differentiated. The trust of their depositors and clients also contributed to the political credibility of the premier City financiers.

The financiers among the Tory City leaders conspicuously outnumbered their Whig counterparts. Among the goldsmith-bankers in the group, all but three were Churchmen. Analysis of the political careers of the money-lenders also reveals that financiers were at the centre of the City Tory leadership, but that important Whig money-lenders were merely in the wings of their party's

---

[51] Henning, iii. 291–2; *Daily Courant* no. 900, 5 Mar. 1705.

élite. Of the seven Whig financiers only Sir Robert Clayton (1629–1707), the most successful scrivener of his or of any other day, was either an alderman or a City MP.[52] On the other hand, ten of the twelve Tory City leaders who were financiers were either aldermen or were promoted for City MP at one election or another. Indeed, one or two financiers were among the Church-Tory candidates at each parliamentary poll in the City between 1701 and 1715.

How may the Tory proclivities of so many leading City financiers be explained? The attitudes of some Tory financiers active in William's reign or earlier were probably influenced by connections to the old monopoly joint stocks, but on the whole the Tory financiers did not make unusual investments in any of the late Stuart corporate enterprises. The partisan breakdown of the leading City financiers does correspond, however, to the partisan breakdown of all City goldsmith-bankers, working goldsmiths, and scriveners. For instance, in the 1710 and 1713 parliamentary elections, about 60 per cent of the liverymen of the Goldsmiths Company were inclined to the Tory candidates. The liverymen of the much smaller Scriveners Company favoured the Tories in these elections by an even greater ratio. These facts suggest that broader occupational considerations may have contributed to turning leading money-lenders into leading Tories.[53]

Several such considerations assist in explaining why so many goldsmiths and scriveners preferred Tory candidates. The artisan goldsmiths were greatly inconvenienced by the outflow of bullion from England in the early stages of William's war, by the ensuing monetary crisis of 1695, and by the recoinage of 1696. Each of these difficulties could be attributed to the financial expedients of Whig ministers. Perhaps of greater importance was the fact that working goldsmiths, scriveners, and goldsmith-bankers were all threatened after the Revolution by important changes in the City that were also encouraged by the Junto. The enlarged opportunities for joint-stock investment must, in some instances, have absorbed wealth that might otherwise have passed through their hands into plate, jewellry, lands, and deposits. Moreover, the financial revolution spawned new corporate agencies and new occupations, like that of the growing breed of stock-jobbers, which

[52] Henning, ii. 84–7; *BDBR*, i. 151–2.
[53] Goldsmiths and scriveners on the Common Council were also overwhelmingly Tory.

encroached upon the customary business of goldsmiths and money-lenders. Those scriveners who specialized as brokers, middlemen, and mortgagees in the land market now found themselves on the periphery of a City increasingly devoted to corporate trade and government securities. Not surprisingly, among the early applicants for stock-broker's licences were many goldsmiths seeking to preserve their business by acquiring new credentials.[54]

If the scriveners were displaced by the financial revolution, the goldsmith-bankers were at least disturbed by it. They were greater in number than the scriveners and had more to lose from a joint-stock bank and from a broadly diffused public debt. The private bankers themselves had no compelling reason to invest in the stock of the Bank of England. They could reasonably expect to realize greater profits from private lending than from the dividends of an unproven joint-stock organization. They could also command greater respect by lending directly to the government as individuals than by joining the host of new corporate public creditors. Nevertheless, because of the proliferation of institutions and securities which supported the public debt, the government had less need for the goldsmiths' services than it had during their 'golden age' in the reign of Charles II. Furthermore, the Bank of England soon came to compete with the goldsmiths for deposits and for exchange and remittance contracts, and the Bank eventually acquired a reputation for soundness that the goldsmiths, with much smaller assets, could no longer match. As the Bank and its proprietors prospered, the goldsmith-bankers declined, at least numerically. Forty-four London goldsmiths and partnerships are believed to have kept running cashes in 1677; but by 1725, the number of private bankers in London had apparently fallen to twenty-four.[55]

In view of these circumstances, the money-lenders emerged as natural spokesmen for many in London who resented both the Bank's intrusion upon City affairs and the power it wielded in Corporation and national politics. In giving voice to their own

[54] Goldsmiths Company, Court Minute Books, x, fos. 85-8, 93, 103; *Considerations upon the Bill for better Discovery of Clippers* (1694); Donald C. Coleman, 'London Scriveners and the Estate Market in the Later Seventeenth Century', *EcHR*, 2nd Ser., iv (1951), 221-30; D.W. Jones, 'London Overseas Merchant Groups', p. 101.

[55] *The Little London Directory of 1677* (1863); F.G. Hilton Price, *A Handbook of London Bankers* (1890-1), pp. 182-6; David M. Joslin, 'London Private Bankers, 1720-85', *EcHR*, 2nd Ser., vii (1954), 173.

professional envy of the Bank, the private lenders found reservoirs of sympathy among City electors suspicious of the oligarchic tendencies of the Bank's Whig spokesmen. By Anne's reign, then, the Church party was not only the party of those who feared the Bank's influence, but was also a party that found a disproportionate share of its leadership from among those financiers who were particular rivals of the Bank's directorate.[56]

Several late Stuart City financiers were nevertheless Whig leaders, but they seem to have been attracted to that party for reasons extraneous to their professional concerns. For instance, the Whig politics of Sir John Sweetapple, Lawrence Hatsell, George Caswall, and John Blunt were at least in part attributable to their dissenting backgrounds, and Sir Robert Clayton's political views were more strongly shaped by events prior to the Revolution than by developments after 1689. Clayton and Sweetapple were the only Whig financiers who invested either in the initial stock subscription of the Bank or in that of the New East India Company. Indeed, the stock investments of leading Whig financiers contrasted sharply with those of Whig City leaders who were merchants. Five of the seven Whig financiers had African Company connections, and three of them had Hudson's Bay Company connections. Caswall and Blunt played important parts in the genesis of the South Sea Company. In fact, although Caswall and Blunt were nonconformists, and although they were Whigs in Corporation politics, they were as strongly antagonistic to the Bank of England's corporate banking monopoly as any of the Tory goldsmith-bankers. Both were prominent in the history of the Sword Blade Company, and under their auspices that company briefly intruded into the field of joint-stock banking in the first half of Anne's reign. Barred from further banking by the 1708 statutory confirmation of the Bank's monopoly, the Sword Blade directors eagerly thrust themselves into the widening breach between the Bank and the new Tory government in 1710–11.[57]

The three leading Tory goldsmith-bankers of the late Stuart period were Sir Francis Child, Sir Charles Duncombe, and Sir Richard Hoare. The career of each may be considered in turn in

[56] KAO Chevening MS 78, R. Yard to A. Stanhope, 7 May 1696; *CSPD 1696*, pp. 178-9; Clapham, i. 29-33; Dickson, p. 495.

[57] Sperling, *South Sea Company*, pp. 5-7; Carswell, pp. 30-59.

order to illustrate the relationship between banking and Tory politics.

Sir Francis Child (1642–1713), the founder of a banking house known for its Tory connections in the eighteenth century, was a belated Tory whose prominence in City Church-Tory circles by Anne's reign could not have been predicted at the time of the Revolution. A Common Council activist in 1682, Child had been viewed with suspicion by the loyalist party. In 1689–90 he was elected alderman and sheriff with Whig support. However, Child was really a moderate supporter of the Revolution rather than a revolutionary Whig. He was also a major Old East India investor whose association with that company eventually divided him from his erstwhile friends among the Whig magistrates. In 1698 the prospect of his mayoralty was greeted by them with little enthusiasm because, according to one observer, 'the Bank and the new East India Company have spoiled Sir Francis for a good Whig'.[58] A Church-Tory MP for Devizes in five parliaments between 1698 and his death, Child was also a City MP from 1702 to 1705, and was promoted as City MP on two other occasions. The careers of three of his sons overlapped with his own. Two of them were Tory MPs in Anne's reign. One of these, City leader Sir Robert Child, succeeded his father as the Tory Alderman of Farringdon Without, and a third son was involved in the early history of the South Sea Company.[59]

Sir Charles Duncombe (1648–1711) was satirized by Defoe in *The True-Born Englishman* and *Reformation of Manners* as the personification of rapacity and ingratitude.[60] Duncombe's opportunistic pursuit of wealth and public influence earned him a reputation for untrustworthiness that accords with Defoe's poetic strictures. Once a banker to the Earl of Shaftesbury, Duncombe served Charles II and James II in the 1680s as Excise cashier, amassing a fortune of £300,000–400,000. A loyalist alderman and Commons member before the Revolution, he nevertheless enjoyed the friendship after 1688 of such important Whigs as the Earl of Monmouth and the Duke of Bolton. Again Excise cashier and MP under William, Duncombe was also a private lender to the government;

[58] James Vernon, *Letters Illustrative of the Reign of William III from 1696 to 1708 addressed to the Duke of Shrewsbury, by James Vernon Esq.*, ed. G. P. R. James (1841), ii. 186.

[59] *DNB*; Woodhead, p. 46; Walcott, MPs tempus Anne; Dickson, pp. 442–3; Carswell, p 276.

[60] *POAS* vi. 302–8, 409–10.

but he was a lender greatly distrusted by Charles Montagu, the Junto patron of the Bank. Duncombe's position in London politics as a leading City Tory and Bank antagonist was clarified in the second half of William's reign. In 1695 he was rumoured to have encouraged an unsuccessful run on the Bank, and in 1696 he was a prominent backer of the abortive Country-Tory land bank scheme. In 1697 Duncombe was edged out of his Excise office. In 1698 Montagu launched a parliamentary attack upon him for official complicity in the false endorsement of Exchequer bills. When he was expelled from the Commons Duncombe's estate was saved from a bill of pains and penalties by the vote of a single peer. Smarting from these wounds, he turned again to the City as an appropriate arena for his political resuscitation, and after the fall of the Junto he reportedly figured in a scheme to lend the government some £4,000,000 at 5 per cent in order to pay off both the Bank and the New Company. Re-elected alderman in 1700, Duncombe failed, despite his extravagant and self-advertised charities, to gain a Commons seat as a City Tory candidate in the three parliamentary elections of 1701-2. In Anne's reign he was a notable patron of the High Church cause.[61]

Another early and persistent Bank critic was Sir Richard Hoare (1648-1719). The son of a Smithfield horse dealer, Hoare had joined the ranks of the City's leading financiers by the time of the Revolution. An important government lender in the 1690s, he was also reported to have circulated tracts in opposition to the Bank at the time of its creation. In 1708, shortly before the renewal of the Bank's charter, Hoare was again suspected of hostile intentions, and he found it necessary to issue public disclaimers of having sought to initiate a run on the Bank. An alderman from 1703 and a friend of Sir Charles Duncombe, Hoare was unsuccessfully promoted by the London Tories as MP in 1705 and 1708. On the occasion of his first failure to obtain a City seat, Hoare informed a friend that 'better must not be expected on any future Elections unless ye members of the New Company and Bank are restrained from concerning themselves'.[62] Finally gaining a City

[61] Henning, ii. 242-3; HMC *Portland MSS* iii. 606; HMC *Cowper MSS* ii. 388; Luttrell, *Brief Relation*, iv. 694; Dickson, pp. 369, 415-16; Horwitz, *Parliament, Policy and Politics*, pp. 61, 182, 230-5; Holmes, *British Politics*, p. 482 n. 20; Holmes, *Sacheverell*, pp. 70n., 240. I am indebted to Dr Eveline Cruickshanks for information about Duncombe.
[62] H.P.R. Hoare, *Hoare's Bank, A Record* (1955), pp. 21-2.

seat in 1710, he retained it in 1713. Excluded from Treasury
business by Godolphin, Hoare's family bank gained a major
remittance contract from Harley in 1710. Sir Richard was a
logical choice for the 1711 directorate of the South Sea Company,
and as a High-Churchman he was also named a commissioner in
the act for building fifty new churches in and around London.[63]

5. Domestic Traders and Industrial Employers

The domestic traders and industrial employers among the City
leaders of the late Stuart period were greatly outnumbered only
by the merchants. Although the persons grouped in this category
pursued a variety of business activities, most may be included in
two occupational clusters. The careers of 21, many of whom were
drapers and mercers, were tied to the cloth trades. Nineteen
others may be described as industrial employers. The latter
cluster included 8 brewers, 3 munitions manufacturers, 3 ironmongers, 2 London builders, a soap-maker, a joiner, and an
upholder. As a group, these City leaders were more heavily involved in corporate enterprise than the financiers. Several of the
brewers and clothiers among them had sizeable estates, and the
great ironmonger Sir Ambrose Crowley was worth at least
£200,000, if not considerably more. All the same, the more
modest estates of most City leaders from domestic commerce or
industrial backgrounds left them generally with somewhat less
stature in London politics. Only two London Commons members
of the period were drawn from their ranks.

City leaders from domestic and industrial trades were both
more numerous and more active among the Tories than among
the Whigs. Far more of the Tories were elected to, or nominated
for, magisterial office. Eight of the Tories, but only three of the
Whigs, sat in a late Stuart parliament. Most of the City leaders in
this occupational group were stock investors, and their interests
were similar to those of the overseas traders. The Tories among
them were tied to the older stocks and to the South Sea Company,
while eight of the Whigs served as directors of the Bank of

[63] *Whereas there hath been several false and Malicious reports . . . reflecting on Sir Richard Hoare*
(1708); Daniel Defoe, *The Anatomy of Exchange-Alley* [1719], pp. 29–30; *Post Boy* no. 2004,
18–20 Mar. 1708; Walcott, *MPs tempus Anne*; Sperling, *South Sea Company*, p. 6;
Carswell, pp. 41, 50, 297; W. Marston Acres, *The Bank of England from Within, 1694–1900*
(1931), i. 98.

England, of the New Company, or of the Million Bank. The leading City clothiers considered here were almost evenly divided between the parties, but thirteen of the nineteen leading City industrial employers were Tories. Moreover, the Tory proclivities of the industrial employers appear to match the Tory proclivities of the freemen and liverymen who were involved in the manufacturing and industrial occupations of this 'pre-industrial' urban society. This correspondence points to another important social fracture in London politics. Just as the financiers were City spokesmen for working Tory goldsmiths, so the City's large-scale Tory industrial employers seem to have been recognized as spokesmen by the City's small-scale manufacturers and 'mechanick' freemen. Occupational solidarities which cut across social lines of class and wealth gave large industrial employers the status of leadership among labouring freemen.

The evidence for this argument is twofold. First, all the leading Tory industrial employers who were aldermen or aldermanic candidates were first elected or nominated in wards with heavy concentrations of resident freemen in industrial employments. These wards included four peripheral ones, and they included five on the Thames with occupational topographies that reflected the presence of quays, wharves, warehouses, shipyards, and river traffic.[64] Secondly, in the parliamentary polls of 1710 and 1713, those livery companies that were most heavily Tory were also companies with liveries largely devoted to industrial occupations.[65] As this suggests, the Tory sentiments of most leading industrial employers expressed more than their economic differentiation from and their social rivalry with the leading Whig merchants. The Church-Tory politics of these leaders also reflected a strong ideological reaction of London's small producers and manufacturers against the 1690s' marriage between City trading and investing interests and City whiggism.

Each of the brewers who were Tory City leaders could be mentioned as an example of the connections among industrial entrepreneurship, Tory politics, and electoral geography. The most interesting of them were Peter Monger, Sir John Parsons (1639–

[64] The four peripheral wards were Aldersgate, Bishopsgate, Cripplegate, and Portsoken. The five Thames-side wards were Castle Baynard, Queenhithe, Dowgate, Bridge, and Tower.

[65] The political preferences of the guilds will be discussed in detail in section six of this chapter.

1717), and Sir John Lade (c.1662–1740). Peter Monger, whose family had been involved in London brewing for a century, and his partner John Hawkins, were common councilmen for Portsoken, the City's easternmost ward, which shared an industrial economy with adjacent Whitechapel and Ratcliff. Monger was unsuccessfully promoted in 1710 as Alderman of Queenhithe, a riverside ward. His ambiguous loyalties provoked a government indictment against him in 1715 at the time of the Jacobite disturbances in London's eastern extremities.[66] Sir John Parsons sat in the Commons for Reigate in eleven parliaments between 1685 and 1717, and he was also twice a Tory candidate for City MP. A victualling commissioner from 1683 to 1690, Parsons was a beer contractor in Anne's reign. He was also alderman for thirty years beginning in the reign of James II, and he was suspected of Jacobitism in his later years. Parsons was succeeded in business and in politics by his son Humphrey, a long-serving Portsoken alderman and a leader of the popular City opposition to Walpole.[67] Finally, Sir John Lade was a High Church Tory and a Southwark MP who trimmed his Jacobite sails before the end of Anne's reign. A noted patron and supporter of Henry Sacheverell, Lade was an unsuccessful aldermanic candidate in 1711 for Bridge, the nearest ward to his Southwark brewhouses. He was the only leading City brewer deeply involved in corporate enterprise, and he served as a South Sea director after the Bubble.[68]

Two other Tory City leaders in this category who deserve mention are Sir Ambrose Crowley (1659–1713) and Sir Samuel Ongley (1663–1726). Crowley has been described as the greatest industrial ironmaster in early eighteenth-century Europe, and Ongley was arguably the most successful London linen-draper of the period. Their careers converged in the early history of the South Sea Company.

The son of a Quaker nail-maker, Crowley owned extensive ironworks in Durham and a large shipping fleet, and he was a principal naval contractor in Anne's reign. He entered Corporation affairs in William's reign as a common councilman for Dowgate, the ward of his residence and the site of the City's steel-

---

[66] *Post Boy* no. 2358, 22–4 June 1710; Ryder, *Diary*, p. 156; 'Minutes of a Whig Club', p. 37; Peter Mathias, *The Brewing Industry in England 1700–1830* (Cambridge, 1959), p. 259n.

[67] Henning, iii. 208–9; Sedgwick, ii. 326–7; Mathias, pp. 7–11, 199, 335.

[68] Sedgwick, ii. 195; Holmes, *Sacheverell*, pp. 56–63, 254.

yard. In 1709 he was an unsuccessful aldermanic candidate for Queenhithe. The Tory triumph of 1710 was also a triumph for Crowley. A holder of large quantities of depreciated paper, he was one of the South Sea projectors and an original 1711 director with some £56,000 of stock. He joined the City magistracy in 1711 as alderman for Dowgate, and he was named a commissioner in the act to erect fifty new London churches. In the year of his death, Crowley was elected to the Commons for Andover and was associated with others in advancing the government £130,000. His son and heir was arrested as a Jacobite during the Hanoverian Succession crisis.[69]

Like Crowley, Samuel Ongley had reason to rejoice in 1710. He had been active in the City since the Revolution, serving as a Cornhill common councilman in the early 1690s and as an Old East India Company director in the mid-1690s. Not until Harley assumed the reins of the Treasury, however, did Ongley really gain City influence commensurate with his wealth. He was knighted and named the original deputy governor of the South Sea Company, and he also served as a commissioner for the government lottery of that year. Elected MP for Maidstone in 1713, Ongley was suspected of Jacobitism by the City Whigs in 1715.[70]

6. Wealth and Politics: The Parties and the People, 1682–1722

The foregoing analysis points to the complexity of the relationships between party politics and wealth in late Stuart London. Simply stated, Whig leadership in the Corporation overlapped significantly with City leadership among stock investors and directors. Tory leadership in the Corporation, on the other hand, overlapped with the leadership of all those investing, trading, and professional interests whose traditional civic power was threatened by the financial revolution. Once established, these patterns of party leadership endured for the remainder of the period. However, the fact must again be emphasized that these leadership patterns became clearly apparent only in the first years after the

---

[69] *Daily Courant* no. 2470, 23 Sept. 1709; *Spectator* no. 299, 12 Feb. 1712; Dickson, p. 65; Sperling, *South Sea Company*, pp. 3–6; Holmes, *British Politics*, p. 157; Michael Flinn, *Men of Iron: The Crowleys in the Early Iron Industry* (Edinburgh, 1962). I am indebted to Dr Eveline Cruickshanks for information about Crowley.

[70] 'Minutes of a Whig Club', p. 21; Walcott, MPs tempus Anne; Sedgwick, ii. 308; Carswell, pp. 52, 282.

Revolution. The acquisition of notably divergent leaderships by the parties in William's reign was quickly accompanied by other important changes. Indeed, because the character of each party's new leadership was somewhat at odds with its old constitutional ideas, the ideologies of both the City Whigs and the City Tories were bound to change.

The large extent to which the parties moderated their ideas and their style of politics to match a changing electoral situation is the concern of chapters five and six. Here, another question requires consideration. The parties could not have experienced ideological change as easily and as quickly as they did unless their new patterns of leadership were matched by corresponding changes in their social followings. Indeed, the relationship between wealth and politics cannot be understood fully unless it is approached from below as well as from above. Wealth and status—or a lack of wealth and status—were just as likely to affect the electoral choices of persons at the bottom of London's guild society as those of persons at the top. How then did London Whig electors and London Tory electors differ in their social and economic attributes in the first age of party? Prosperous and middling electors seem to have gravitated towards the party commanded by trading wealth, and marginal, mechanic, and artisan electors seem to have gravitated towards the party of City opposition. This socio-economic division of the electorate formed another fracture in London's late Stuart political life. Moreover, like the developing dichotomy in party leadership, this division of the electorate apparently was a post-Revolutionary development rather than a pre-Revolutionary one.

A complete examination of the relationship between the parties and the people could be provided only through exhaustive analysis of the City electorate with the aid of surviving poll books and tax rolls. Two alternative methods will be employed here to answer the question of how people of differing wealth and status aligned themselves along the party divide. First, the electoral preferences of liverymen in four City polls will be analysed in order to demonstrate that companies whose liveries came to incline towards the Whigs or towards the Tories also differed in social character. Secondly, the differing electoral preferences of geographical clusters of wards which also differed greatly in the social composition of their rate-paying populations will be analysed.

Bodies of electors will therefore be examined in place of individual electors, a procedure that necessarily obscures the numerous individual exceptions to the patterns introduced above. As the parties acquired their divergent socio-economic followings, many wealthy electors remained or became obstinate Tories, just as many poor electors remained or became obstinate Whigs.

A. *The Liveried Electorate*

If Whig magisterial and parliamentary candidates attracted greater support than their Tory counterparts from the more substantial electors, one would expect to find evidence of this in the quality of guild companies whose liveries preferred Whig candidates. Table 4.9 analyses the partisan majorities of the London livery companies in the mayoral poll of 1682 and in the parliamentary polls of 1710, 1713, and 1722. Seventeen sizeable guilds which included a significant proportion of merchants and other professionals on their liveries have been designated 'substantial' companies and distinguished from the remaining 'artisan' companies, many of which possessed smaller liveries.

In 1682, the liverymen of the substantial companies did not on the whole incline noticeably towards either party. The liveries of over half the substantial companies were split between Whig and Tory mayoral candidates in that year. On the other hand, Whig candidates did attract support then from more of the artisan companies than did the Tories. Indeed, twenty of the twenty-three companies whose liverymen inclined towards the Whigs were composed mostly of artisans. This finding accords with contemporary Tory observations that the party of exclusionist opposition was also the party of the 'mechanicks'. By the last four years of Anne's reign, however, the alignment of the guilds between the parties' parliamentary candidates had altered remarkably. In the polls of 1710 and 1713, the liveries of ten of the seventeen substantial companies favoured the Whigs, and the number of artisan companies inclined towards the Tories had almost doubled since 1682. That these results point to long-term trends rather than to temporary circumstances is demonstrated by the party breakdown of the livery companies in the 1722 parliamentary poll. At that election, two-thirds of the liveries that favoured the 'whig' candidates were from the substantial companies. The 'tory' candidates failed to attract a majority of votes from any of the

Table 4.9 The Livery Companies and the Parties, 1682–1722

	1682	1710/13	1722
Whig majorities:			
Substantial companies	3	10	14
Artisan companies	20	12	7
Tory majorities:			
Substantial companies	5	4	0
Artisan companies	13	24	29
Divided:			
Substantial companies	9	3	3
Artisan companies	5	7	8
All companies	55	60	61

Table 4.9 is based on the recorded votes of the London liverymen by company in the following sources: Bodl., *A List of the Poll of the Several Companies of London for a Lord Mayor* (1682); *The Poll of the Livery-Men of the City of London, at the Election of Members of Parliament* (1710); *A List of the Poll for . . . Hoare . . . Withers . . . Cass . . . Newland* (1713); *A List of the poll for . . . Ward . . . Scawen . . . Heysham . . . Godfrey* (1714); *The Poll of the Livery-Men of the City of London . . . April the 10th, 1722* (1722). Companies have been considered to have had a Whig or Tory majority in 1682 and 1722 if 55 % or more of their voting liverymen favoured the candidates of that party. Companies have also been so considered for 1710 and 1713 provided that 55 % or more of their voting liverymen favoured one party in either election, and provded that at least a simple majority favoured the same party in the other election. I have followed W. A. Speck and W. A. Gray in their usage of party labels for the 1722 election in 'Londoners at the Polls under Anne and George I', *Guildhall Studies in London History*, 1 (1975), 253–62. Only two companies that were Whig or Tory in 1710/13 reversed their partisanship in 1722. The following companies have been regarded as substantial companies here:

Apothecaries Goldsmiths Pewterers
Brewers Grocers Salters
Cloth-workers Haberdashers Scriveners
Drapers Ironmongers Skinners
Dyers Mercers Stationers
Fishmongers Merchant-taylors

All other companies have been regarded as artisan companies. Six artisan companies gained liveries at various dates after 1682 and have been considered in the first appropriate parliamentary poll.

substantial companies, but they claimed majority support from two-thirds of the artisan companies. This finding accords with the historical judgement that the City opposition to the Hanoverian

Whigs was especially strong among lesser tradesmen, shop-keepers, and craft manufacturers.[71]

This analysis of the party preferences of the liverymen by company may be faulted for exaggerating the trends it establishes. Sizeable minorities of Tory liverymen were found in all the substantial companies between 1710 and 1722, and most of the artisan companies also included significant numbers of Whig pollers. The same trends are nevertheless observable in the analysis of actual voters presented by proportion in Fig. 4.1.

In 1682, when almost half the total party poll came from the substantial companies, so did 48 per cent of the Whig voters and 51 per cent of the Tory voters. Thereafter, as the proportion of the total poll drawn from the artisan companies increased to over three-fifths, the proportion of the Tory voters drawn from those companies increased to 72 per cent in 1722. As the proportion of the voting livery from the substantial companies declined, Whig candidates could not carry elections without attracting considerable support from the artisan companies. Indeed, in every election considered here, slightly more than half the Whig voters came from the more numerous artisan companies. However, in the elections of 1710–22, a disproportionate share of the Whig voters came from the substantial companies. In other words, the success of Whig candidates was dependent upon their strength among the substantial companies, and the success of Tory candidates was dependent upon their strength among the artisan companies. The qualifications that need to be made to this interpretation of the relationship between the liveried electors and the parties require that it be advanced with some caution, but the qualifications support no alternative interpretation.[72] The conclusion that pros-

[71] Rogers, 'Resistance to Oligarchy', pp. 4–7.

[72] For instance, the dichotomy between substantial companies and artisan companies only crudely expresses the diversity of pre-industrial occupations pursued in the City. Moreover, the correspondence between some guild names and the actual occupations of their members is well known to have been little more than approximate. The liverymen of the substantial companies were not all substantial citizens, and neither were the liverymen of the artisan companies all of artisan stature. Nevertheless, the substantial companies include all but one of the 'great companies' whose prestigious traditions attracted members from the bourgeois ranks of London society, and although the occupational consistencies of the substantial companies were therefore weak, many of the artisan companies remained fellowships of craft practitioners. Furthermore, although wealth qualifications for admission to the livery were not strictly observed, most of the substantial companies required an estate of £1,000 after 1697, but all save one of the artisan companies required an estate of only £500.

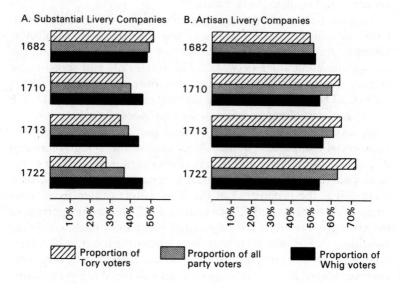

Figure 4.1 The Parties and the Liverymen, 1682–1722

Fig. 4.1 is based on the votes of the London liverymen in the poll records cited in note to Table 4.9. Individual liverymen in the three parliamentary polls have been considered Whig or Tory according to the following criteria. In 1710 and 1713, each liveryman who polled for four Whig candidates or for four Tory candidates has been counted as a Whig or a Tory. Liverymen who polled for three Whig candidates or for three Tory candidates have also been counted as Whigs or Tories regardless of whether, or how, they utilized their fourth vote.

The 1722 poll was a contest between three 'whig' candidates and three 'tory' candidates and is described by Speck and Gray in 'Londoners at the Polls'. Liverymen who voted for the three 'whig' candidates or for the three 'tory' candidates in 1722 have here been counted as 'whigs' or 'tories' regardless of whether or how they utilized their fourth vote. The analysis of the 1722 poll presented here rests, therefore, upon figures somewhat different from those employed by Speck and Gray. Liverymen who split their vote between candidates in any other manner have been omitted from consideration in all respects.

perous and middling electors inclined on the whole towards the Whigs, and that less substantial electors inclined on the whole towards the Tories, finds additional support in the behaviour of London's ward electorates.

B. Ward Electorates and the Common Council

Partisan patterns in Common Council elections corresponded to a socio-geographic division of the City's wards, as was mentioned in the discussion of dissent and politics. The electoral geography of the Corporation may be considered more fully here by reference to Figs. 4.2 and 4.3. The inner city, the middle city, and the city without the walls encompass clusters of wards characterized by contrasting populations in the seventeenth and eighteenth centuries. This can be demonstrated through the use of any of several London assessments such as those of the 1692 poll tax, which will be employed here.[73] The returns of the 1692 poll tax rate the housekeepers of London in three crude wealth

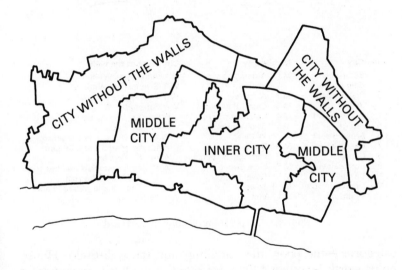

Fig. 4.2 Corporation of London: Inner City, Middle City, City Without the Walls

---

[73] The socio-geographic division of the wards within the walls is also apparent in a 1638 survey of London rents and in assessments of 1680 and 1695: Emrys Jones, 'London in the Early Seventeenth Century: An Ecological Approach', *London Journal*, 6 (1980), 123-33; Roger Finlay, *Population and Metropolis: The Demography of London 1580-1650* (Cambridge Geographical Studies, 12), Cambridge, 1981, pp. 70-82; Smith, pp. 408-10; *London Inhabitants Within the Walls 1695*, ed. David V. Glass (London Record Society Publications, ii), 1966.

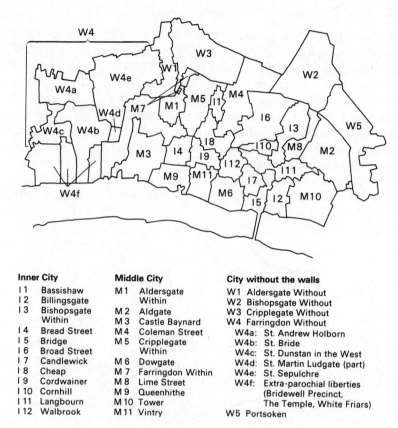

Inner City	Middle City	City without the walls
I 1 Bassishaw	M 1 Aldersgate	W 1 Aldersgate Without
I 2 Billingsgate	Within	W 2 Bishopsgate Without
I 3 Bishopsgate	M 2 Aldgate	W 3 Cripplegate Without
Within	M 3 Castle Baynard	W 4 Farringdon Without
I 4 Bread Street	M 4 Coleman Street	W 4a: St. Andrew Holborn
I 5 Bridge	M 5 Cripplegate	W 4b: St. Bride
I 6 Broad Street	Within	W 4c: St. Dunstan in the West
I 7 Candlewick	M 6 Dowgate	W 4d: St. Martin Ludgate (part)
I 8 Cheap	M 7 Farringdon Within	W 4e: St. Sepulchre
I 9 Cordwainer	M 8 Lime Street	W 4f: Extra-parochial liberties
I 10 Cornhill	M 9 Queenhithe	(Bridewell Precinct,
I 11 Langbourn	M 10 Tower	The Temple, White Friars)
I 12 Walbrook	M 11 Vintry	W 5 Portsoken

Fig. 4.3 Corporation of London by Ward

categories—the poor, the middling, and the well-to-do. House-holds worth less than £300 were rated at the basic assessment of one shilling per head per quarter. Housekeepers worth more than £300 paid a ten shilling surtax in addition to the basic assessment. All merchants, brokers, barristers, physicians, gentlemen, and wealthy women paid a surtax of one pound or more.

In each of the twelve inner city wards (or parts of wards), 45 per cent or more of the ratepaying housekeepers were liable for the 1692 poll tax surcharges. Indeed, in many of these wards the proportion of housekeepers who paid the surcharges was much higher; overall, 58 per cent of the inner city housekeepers were assessed in the higher rating categories. These figures reflect the residence of large numbers of overseas merchants in some inner city wards, such as Walbrook and Candlewick, and they reflect the residence of many substantial shopkeepers and domestic traders in other wards, such as Cheap and Cornhill.

In each of the eleven middle city wards (or parts of wards), on the other hand, 55 per cent or more of the ratepaying population paid only the basic poll tax assessment in 1692. Moreover, in most middle city wards the proportion of housekeepers who paid only the basic tax was much higher; overall, 68 per cent of the middle city housekeepers were so assessed. These figures reflect the residence of many persons engaged in Thames-side industrial employments in some wards, such as Castle Baynard and Queen-hithe, and they reflect large concentrations of ruder tradesmen and artificers in other wards, such as Cripplegate Within and Aldersgate Within.

The five sprawling wards and parts of wards outside the walls were undoubtedly the poorest in the City, although Farringdon Without contained a band of middling habitations stretched along Fleet Street and concentrations of élite settlement near Holborn and Temble Bar. Overall, however, 80 per cent of the house-keepers without the walls paid only the basic rate in 1692, a figure that reflects the preponderance of depressed artisans, transient labourers, and tenement dwellers within the population of each exterior ward.

The electors of the inner city wards, and the electors of the middle city wards, came to differ as strikingly in their political preferences as in their socio-economic profiles. This is indicated in Figs. 4.4 and 4.5.

As measured by the partisanship of common councilmen returned from inner city wards, the rather bourgeois inner city electorate came to provide the City Whigs with their strongest base of support. Obversely, the high proportion of Tories among the middle city common councilmen suggests that the more plebeian middle city electors became the City Tories' most reliable ward constituency. The lack of reliable data for much of William's reign precludes a precise dating of this development.[74] However, the composition of the Common Councils of 1681–3 strongly suggests that neither party had yet taken firm root in

[74] Few wardmote presentments survive for 1694-9.

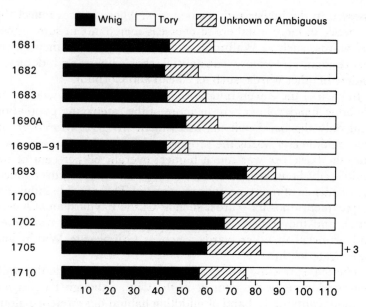

Fig. 4.4 Inner City Common Councilmen, 1681–1710 (various dates)

The Common Council designated 1690A is that chosen at the December 1689 wardmotes and dominated by the Whigs. The Common Council designated 1690B–91 is that chosen at the extraordinary June 1690 wardmotes. It sat for eighteen months and was heavily Tory. Analysis of the common councilmen of 1681–3 is based on party identifications by ward in Smith, pp. 404–7. Analysis of the common councilmen of 1690A–1702 is based on partisan identifications in De Krey, 'Trade, Religion, and Politics', iii. 623–71. Analysis of the common councilmen of 1705 and 1710 is based on the author's unpublished partisan identifications to 1720.

either electoral zone during the Exclusion Crisis and its aftermath.[75]

By 1700, on the other hand, the inner city was demonstrably a Whig inner city, and it largely remained so through the following decade. Obversely, the middle city was demonstrably a Tory middle city, and it also largely remained so thereafter. Although allowance must again be made for qualifications,[76] the likelihood

[75] The number of inner city Tories exceeded the number of inner city Whigs on the Common Councils of 1681–3, and although the Whigs lost middle city seats between 1681 and 1683, the numbers of Whig and Tory middle city common councilmen were almost equal in the first 1690 Common Council.

[76] For instance, freemen in comfortable or in straitened circumstances cannot simply be converted into Whig and Tory electors, and wealth was only one of several factors that

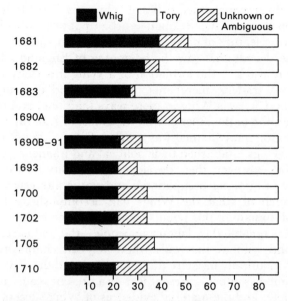

Fig. 4.5 Middle City Common Councilmen, 1681–1710 (various dates)

is that by Anne's reign middling and substantial ward electors inclined on the whole towards the Whigs, while economically
marginal ward electors inclined towards the Tories. The City
Whig leaders could not have enjoyed such consistent success in
the inner city unless they also enjoyed greater support than the
Tory leaders among the wealthier ratepaying freemen of those
wards. Neither could the Tory spokesmen have dominated middle city Common Council elections unless they had stronger ties
than the City Whigs to the poorer ratepaying freemen of those
wards. Finally, although the development of plebeian toryism in
the wards without the walls was retarded before 1705, those wards
were to become the section of the City most strongly attached to
the Tory party after 1710.

influenced the politics of individual freemen. Furthermore, some ward electorates in both
the inner city and the middle city fluctuated in their party preferences, and some wards
were divided between the parties. Neither the inner city electorate nor the middle city
electorate supported one party to the exclusion of the other. Indeed, in 1690B–91, when
the Tories gained a large Common Council majority, they did so by capturing many inner
city seats, and they succeeded in doing so again after 1710. Finally, if poorer ward electorates are to be associated with the Tories, the poorest wards—those without the
walls—did not conform to this pattern until after 1705. The correspondence between party
politics and the tripartite socio-geographic division of London was thus an imperfect one.

These divergent characteristics of Whig and Tory electors point to friction between two distinctive urban political subcultures as an enduring feature of party conflict in London after the Revolution. The decade that saw the beginning of England's financial revolution also saw the formation of a Whig inner city milieu of industrious traders, merchants, investors, and dissenters. The core of the City was Whig in more ways than one, and the over-representation of the inner city on the Court of Aldermen and the Court of Common Council was a major City Whig asset. As the London Whigs established their political and financial hegemony in London, however, there developed in the City a rival political ensemble of humbler occupational and status interests which rejected much of what the Whigs had accomplished. The geographical domain of this popular Tory following came to include those areas inhabited by labouring people—the 'industrial' wards within and without the walls where few merchants lived and where economically insecure tradesmen pursued their livelihoods. Destitution was either a present fear or a present reality for many such people, and the material evidences of Whig success became appropriate objects of popular Tory displeasure. The financiers, industrial employers, domestic traders, and opposition merchants who came to challenge the magisterial power of the new Whig oligarchy were quite responsive to the dissatisfactions of this popular Tory element in London society.

The party debate in the City was not, therefore, solely a polemical debate about the issues of religion, foreign policy, the succession, and trade. The parties also articulated in their rivalry the deep-seated social antagonisms that cleft the City electorate in twain. The Tory fracture was potentially the greater, and the development of that potential permitted the recovery of the City Tories from their post-Revolutionary paralysis and underpinned the Tory move to wrest control of the City from the Whigs in the last years of Anne's reign. How and why this electoral fracture developed in City politics may be further clarified by turning to the history of the Corporation after its revolutionary crisis.

V

The Results of Party Conflict in the City:
The Transformation of the Parties,
1690–1710

---

1. The Apostasy of the City Whigs

As a recent essayist reviewing the seventeenth-century English revolutions has remarked, the unexpected results of political conflict are often more dramatic than those actually intended by the proponents of revolutionary change.[1] After the Revolution of 1688–9, as the clouds of ideological confusion gradually receded, they revealed a political landscape marked not only by striking alterations in the pre-revolutionary parties but also by an astonishing growth in popular participation in politics. In London, as in the nation, the results of the resumption of party conflict after 1689 included unexpected adjustments in party polemics and a complex redefinition of the relationship between the parties and the people. The ultimate result of a generation of party conflict that culminated during the last years of Anne's reign was a violent political cataclysm that threatened to burst the constitutional bonds reforged at the time of the Revolution. By 1710, party warfare at Westminster had reached epic proportions, and the social harmony of the City was visibly fractured by ideological, religious, and economic tensions. Perhaps the most unexpected and startling result of party conflict in London was the ideological apostasy of the City's revolutionary Whig élite, a development that merits considerable attention.

The analysis of the City's revolutionary crisis presented in chapter two suggests that by 1690 the City Whig leaders had

---

[1] Lawrence Stone, 'The Results of the English Revolutions of the Seventeenth Century', in *Three British Revolutions: 1641, 1688, 1776*, ed. J.G.A. Pocock (Princeton, NJ, 1980), p. 49.

misgivings about their encouragement of popular involvement in Corporation politics. They had not yet begun actively to discourage such participation, but this was to become future Whig policy and is well known to have been the case after 1715. The Whig triumph in the Hanoverian Succession was then celebrated by the vigorous suppression of popular urban Jacobitism, by the passage of the Riot Act, and by the elimination of triennial parliamentary elections. The historian of the first of these developments has written that 'the Whig record was by 1717 transparently antilibertarian',[2] an argument that is equally applicable to the magisterial Whigs of the City and to the parliamentary Whigs of Westminster. In London, the Whig renunciation of popular liberties found its ultimate expression in the City Elections Act of 1725, which was designed both to narrow the wardmote franchise and to discipline Common Hall participants.[3] Although the act was the brain-child of Walpole, it found ready supporters among many Whig City magistrates whose families had been active in London's revolutionary politics a generation earlier. Nothing could be more astonishing than a juxtaposition of the Whigs' 1690 model for a civic commonwealth with their 1725 blueprint for civic oligarchy. What accounts for this remarkable volte-face? When and why did the London Whig leaders embark upon the political odyssey that ended with the anti-libertarian City Elections Act? The evidence suggests that by the mid-1690s the City Whigs had already set out on such a course, having first thrown over their popular principles of 1679–90 as so much ideological ballast. By the mid-1690s, the mercantile élite who provided the leadership of the Whig party had quietly shelved the cause of civic reform for the sake of the domestic stability made desirable by a war of unprecedented dimensions.

The political situation of the Whig magistrates after the City's revolutionary crisis encouraged their movement in this direction. To the Whigs' surprise, their promotions of politics out of doors and of populist revisions in the Corporation's constitution had seemingly contributed to the success of the City Tories in the 1690 parliamentary and Common Council elections. Although the

---

[2] Rogers, 'Popular Protest', p. 98.
[3] Ian Doolittle, 'Walpole's City Elections Act (1725)', *EHR* xcvii (1982), 504–29; Rogers, 'Resistance to Oligarchy', pp. 1–5; Plumb, *Growth of Political Stability*, pp. 184–5; Henderson, chapt. 4.

House of Commons had confirmed their rule in a back-handed fashion, the Whig aldermen were now confronted with the problem of seeking to govern in the face of residual grumblings from a strongly Tory Common Council. The Whigs' dilemma was not that their situation demanded an explicit sacrifice of principle, but rather that their erstwhile principles were unhelpful in advancing their current interests. The constitutional behaviour of the City Whig magistrates in the early 1690s points, therefore, to their unmistakable difficulties in adjusting the popular premises of their past to the present problems of Corporation government. In 1695 they publicly abandoned the attempt altogether, and in so doing they precipitated an open confrontation between themselves and populist liverymen that greatly transformed the character of City whiggism. The Whig retreat from populism is, however, somewhat clearer to the historian than it was to the Whig City leaders themselves. The Whig abandonment of libertarianism was convenient rather than contrived, the product of circumstances rather than design. This was a subtle apostasy much obscured by the Whigs' loud attachment to the Revolution. Indeed, the Whig magistrates perceived their new political posture rather as a defence of revolutionary objectives now accomplished than as a retreat from revolutionary objectives not attained.

The adjustment of Whig rhetoric to the pragmatic dictates of government began in May 1691 when the Whig magistrates confirmed the traditioned aldermanic right to prior review of all matters considered in Common Council.[4] The decision re-established the authority of the Whig-dominated bench over a Tory-dominated Common Council that still excluded all Whig aldermen from the Corporation's standing committees. The Whigs' decision was also an effectual renunciation of that clause of their late draft statute that had so strongly elevated the status of Common Council. The prerogatives of office now took precedence over the Whigs' often stated interest in enhancing the liberties of the 'commons' of London. Still, a few weeks later, as the time approached for the annual shrieval election, the Whigs expressed a continuing regard for their libertarian ideological heritage. At a poorly attended Common Council, they carried a vote to abolish the by-law permitting the Lord Mayor to choose one of the two sheriffs, a practice that

---

[4] Repertory 95, fos. 280–1.

had provoked more disputes than any other City issue in the early 1680s. The Whigs' proposal was lost, however, when those common councilmen who were opposed to it deprived the Court of its quorum by withdrawing.[5]

With their position much enhanced by their come-back in the December 1691 Common Council elections, the Whigs had greater opportunity in 1692 to consider the rights of the City electorate. Two incidents of that year reveal the Whig leaders still juggling their evolving magisterial interests with the liberties of the people. Less self-serving was another attempt, again frustrated in Common Council, to pass an act for the popular election by Common Hall of both sheriffs.[6] More ambiguous was the successful passage of an act to enforce the traditional exclusion of unfreemen from wardmote elections. The subject of a heated Common Council debate, this proposal seemed, on the surface at least, to divide the City parties on familiar grounds. The bill was strongly promoted by Alderman Wildman, long a friend to the rights of 'freeborn Englishmen', and half the committee that drafted it had been sponsors of the 1690 proposal for radical changes in the City constitution. Opposition to the measure was led by Thomas Langham, Deputy Alderman for Bishopsgate and a leading City Tory, whose visibility during the persecutions of the 1680s was still sadly remembered by the London Whigs. The Tories complained that the act would disfranchise many 'Eminent Merchants and Traders' not free of the Corporation but nevertheless accustomed to participating fully in the affairs of their wards.[7]

In reality, however, this dispute was not merely a replay of the old quarrel between Whig populism and Tory élitism. Examined more closely, the positions of the parties were quite otherwise. Two years earlier, the City Whigs had attempted to extend the wardmote suffrage to all housekeepers paying scot and lot, regardless of whether they were free of the Corporation. But the effect of the 1692 act was officially to exclude from participation

[5] Ibid., fo. 298; Journal 51, fo. 83; Luttrell, *Brief Relation*, ii. 249–50.

[6] Repertory 96, pp. 216, 244; Journal 51, fo. 179. The Whigs nearly achieved control of the Common Council in 1692. However, not until 1693 did they obtain the actual majority of Common Council seats that they continued to enjoy until 1704.

[7] Journal 51, fos. 187, 193, 209–11; BL Add. MS 34096, fo. 197, R. Yard to Sir William Colt, 28 Oct. 1692 and Add. MS 61690, fos. 60–1; KAO Chevening MS 78, R. Yard to A. Stanhope, 13 Sept. 1692; *The Case of the City of London* [1692]; *An Account of . . . the Exploits of Don Thomazo Pharmacopola* [1692].

some persons—perhaps many persons—who habitually assumed the rights of citizenship on St. Thomas's Day. Although old radicals like Wildman perceived the act as consistent with the principles of the Revolution, it actually created a reduced ward electorate and, as some may have hoped, a more manageable ward electorate. This the Tories opposed. Moreover, although the Tories lent respectability to their arguments by pitching upon the plight of the rich unfree, they were certainly aware that the act excluded as many poorer housekeepers as 'eminent traders' from the wardmotes. In other words, some two years after the City's revolutionary crisis the party leaders were beginning to redefine their relationship with the people. Still learning from the experiences of 1688–90, the Whigs had incorporated into the City's laws their discovery of how unhelpful popular involvement in politics could prove in the quest for political stability. Some Tory leaders, on the other hand, with their electoral successes of 1690 in mind, were already aware of the opportunities presented to them by popular political expectations.

The new orientation of the City Whig leaders became more apparent still in 1694–5 when they subordinated their old interest in the reform of shrieval election procedures to the pressing need of replenishing the chamber of the Corporation. Compelled to find new sources of revenue after parliament's assignment of many existing funds to the City orphans' debt,[8] the Whig leaders seized upon the potential bonanza of securing the shrieval elections of wealthy citizens likely to pay the customary fine of £400 to avoid office. In deciding to go 'a-birding' for sheriffs, the aldermen were adopting a time-honoured solution to the Corporation's financial difficulties that had sometimes yielded dozens of fines.[9] Moreover, they hoped to kill two birds with one stone by abolishing the unpopular mayoral prescription of one sheriff as well. The two magisterial objectives, were evident in an act drafted shortly before the 1694 shrieval election and readily adopted by the Whig Common Council majority.[10]

Those liverymen were to be disappointed, however, who expected a freer voice in choosing sheriffs after the elimination of both the Lord Mayor's shrieval prerogative and the requirement

[8] John R. Kellett, 'The Financial Crisis of the Corporation', ii, 220–7.
[9] Pearl, *London and the Puritan Revolution*, p. 65 n. 86.
[10] Journal 51, fos. 299–300, 318.

that sheriffs be elected from among the junior aldermen. The intention of the aldermen to accept fines from sheriffs-elect posed a new obstacle to the free election of sheriffs that replaced those removed by the 1694 act. Furthermore, by manipulating the 1694 and 1695 shrieval elections for the advantage of the City chamber, the Whigs seriously impaired their old rapport with the City's electors. By violating a popular freedom they had championed for so long, they drove an ideological wedge between themselves and many liverymen who resented this abridgement of their electoral privileges in Common Hall. Not without reason, the Whig magistrates were perceived by some long-time supporters as treading with ill-becoming grace in the steps of their anti-populist Tory predecessors.

The events of the 1694 and 1695 shrieval elections require brief summary before an interpretation of these affairs is presented. The 1694 election proved to be something of a dress rehearsal for the Common Hall controversy that erupted in 1695. In the former year, the Common Hall balked when its initial choices for sheriff were fined and excused by the Court of Aldermen. Lord Mayor Sir William Ashurst dissolved a second meeting of Common Hall when the liverymen again refused to poll, this time on the grounds that the aldermen had ignored their right to make binding elections. When summoned subsequently, Common Hall proved more pliant. The election turned into a summer-long farce in which the liverymen were called together at irregular intervals to elect new sheriffs as quickly as those previously elected had fined. The names of new candidates, apparently, were promoted by Whig leaders who selected citizens unlikely to want the office. The prominent goldsmith banker John Sweetapple and salter William Coles, both of dissenting sympathies, at last accepted office after the collection of £5,200 in fines.[11] Although the election had proved a great boon to the City chamber, its conduct raised many questions about the electoral integrity of Common Hall and made desirable another City act explicitly sanctioning the acceptance of seriatim fines. The adoption of such an act three days before the Midsummer's Day election of 1695 served notice to the liverymen that another fine campaign was in the offing.[12]

[11] Journal 52, fos. 7–8; Repertory 98, pp. 357–8 ff.; BL Loan 29/287, fo. 303, Robert Harley to Sir Edward Harley, 15 Sept. 1694; Bodl. MS Carte 79, fo. 544, James Vernon to Thomas Wharton, 28 June 1694; KAO Chevening MS 78, R. Yard to A. Stanhope, 3 July 1694.

[12] Journal 52, fos. 31, 47, 54–5.

The magistrates were much less successful in 1695. With both a foretaste and a forewarning of what the aldermen intended, the liverymen and their spokesmen adopted a variety of techniques to express their opposition to a perceived misuse of the shrieval election. Many liverymen stayed away from the four Common Halls that were necessary to complete the election, and among those who did attend were many who refused to poll. This was especially the case at the Common Halls of 2 July and 5 July, each of which was summoned after the aldermen accepted the fines of the sheriffs elected on 24 June. On the first occasion, when Lord Mayor Sir Thomas Lane announced the need for another choice, the liverymen 'made so great a Noyse that nothing could be heard or done', and the tumult was stilled only by dissolution of Common Hall. The proceedings of 5 July were preceded by an unsuccessful appeal to the aldermen for a fortnight's adjournment in order to discuss the issues, and they were further disturbed when a written protest was presented on the hustings. When a poll was nevertheless announced, it was greeted with thunderous cries of 'No, No, No.' Many citizens 'forebore to poll', and the announced results of the election revealed that fewer than one in ten of the liverymen had participated. The aldermen were troubled at their next meeting by the appearance of a delegation of dissident liverymen who threatened to petition parliament or to bring the matter before King's Bench. The aldermen were also disappointed of their fine money when one of the new sheriffs-elect, Edward Wills, a dissenting draper, sided with the aggrieved liverymen and declared his willingness to accept office. Surprised and somewhat alarmed by this unexpected outburst of opposition, the Lord Mayor and aldermen delayed for ten weeks before summoning another Common Hall in mid-September. The angry scenes of the summer were then repeated before a colleague was finally found for Wills in the person of Alderman Sir Owen Buckingham, the dissenting tobacco merchant.[13]

This account of the shrieval controversy suggests that the Whig élite showed a remarkable degree of indifference to the electoral

[13] Bodl. Newdigate Newsletters, LC 2490-3, 27 June-9 July 1695; Bodl. MS Carte 239, fos. 26 and 28, James Vernon to Thomas Wharton, 4 and 6 July 1695; KAO Chevening MS 78, R. Yard to A. Stanhope, 4 and 16 July, 10 and 24 Sept. 1695; *At a Common-Hall, July 5, 1695; The Present Case of the Common-Hall in their Election of Sheriffs* (1695); *Post Boy*, 12-14, 17-19, and 19-21 Sept. 1695.

scruples of the liverymen. Magisterial Whig indifference may better be understood by emphasizing that the 1695 Common Hall
episodes coincided with a momentous change in the outlook and
interests of that party's City leaders. The controversy shortly
followed the massive investment of City Whig money in the Bank
of England and in other long-term government borrowing schemes
of 1693-4. Moreover, it coincided with the initial signs of the financial instability of 1695-6, and fears about the security of investments and loans may have stimulated magisterial conservativism.
Indeed, as the City Whig leaders became the City guardians and
the prospective beneficiaries of the Junto's financial innovations,
they found their pedigree of civic populism a somewhat anach-
ronistic heritage. Openly compromising their credibility as advocates of electoral rights in 1695, they provoked an impassioned
and widespread public reaction against themselves. This reaction
occurred because the question of shrieval fines, which the Whig
aldermen regarded primarily as an administrative matter, revived
important constitutional issues that the Whig leaders had largely
avoided since 1690.

These issues were raised in the pamphlet literature of 1695,
which needs now to be analysed in order to understand the bearing
of the shrieval controversy on the changing relationship between
the Whig élite and the electorate. The anti-magisterial tracts
reveal that the dispute was entirely within the old Whig camp, or,
as one of the authors put it, between 'Men . . . who have always
stood up for the Rights of the City'. The London Tory leaders
seem not to have entered the fray, although they reportedly were
'laughing in their Sleeves' at the discomfiture of the Whigs.[14] The
argument rather arose between the pragmatic sitting Whig aldermen and common council leaders and many of their erstwhile
popular supporters, or, as a spokesman for the magistrates omin-
ously wrote, 'between the Government and the Governed'.[15] The
pamphlets and broadsides exposed the painful fact that these
Whig elements no longer shared the same political assumptions.
As in the course of other revolutions, those who had become

[14] William Atwood (?), *The Rights and Authority of the Commons of . . . London in their Common Hall* (1695), p. 3; *A Friendly Dialogue between a Livery-Man and a Freeman* [1695], p. 5.

[15] *A Modest Essay in Vindication of the . . . Lord Mayor . . . Aldermen, and Common Council*
(1695), p. 1. Although the Whig City leaders were apparently not all equally enthusiastic
about the fines, those who may have had private reservations gave no public encouragement to the livery.

satisfied with a new regime were divided from those who wished
to see revolution carried further. In other words, the shrieval issue
openly revealed the social and ideological contradictions that had
developed within the City's successful revolutionary party. The
informed observer could see that the commercial leadership of the
Whig party was now satisfying its desire for political supremacy in
the Corporation at the expense of the party's traditional following
among the *artisanat*. Furthermore, although they were mindful of
the revolutionary credentials of the Whig élite, libertarian liverymen were no longer willing to accept those credentials as sufficient
justification for the magistrates' high-handed conduct. Instead, the
livery spokesmen reminded the Whig leaders, who now pointedly
belaboured their pre-revolutionary sufferings, 'at what door all
that Mischief entered, if it were not by breaking in upon the
Rights and Privileges of the Common Hall'.[16]

What then did the radical liverymen of 1695 want? They wanted
not only the immediate elimination of shrieval fines, but also the
immediate establishment of a participatory civic polity like that
promised by the Whig leaders in 1690. The livery spokesmen condemned the aldermanic discharge of sheriffs-elect as 'contrary to
the *common*-Law Right of the *Electors*'.[17] By defining the issues in
these terms of abstract right, the Common Hall advocates also
brought into question the legitimacy of the entire constitutional
apparatus that supported fines. No mere change in the personnel
of the magistracy could secure the rights of the London citizenry.
That could be accomplished only by clarifying the constitutional
principles of City government. Such a clarification was now offered
for the second time since the Revolution, and it was offered in
even more radical language than that of 1690.

In the Whig constitutional draft of 1690, Common Council was
conceived as the institutional centre-piece of a popular Corporation regime; but the polemicists of 1695 placed the supreme authority in the City in the hands of the 'people' or the 'Great Body of
the Commonalty', as represented in Common Hall. One broadside baldly asserted that 'Common-Hall is the most antient Court,
and highest authority in *London*', and another writer perceived
this claim as entirely consistent with the purposes of the Revolution: 'As no Prince, who is not truly popular himself, can be

---

[16] *Present Case of the Common-Hall.*   [17] Atwood (?), p. 12.

pleas'd to have Power lodg'd in any great Body of his People; the Common Hall could not, in any Reign but this, have expected to bring on their Cause without great Disadvantage.'[18] The 'cause' of the Common Hall was, more specifically, to safeguard the rights of the electors by constitutionally subordinating the aldermen and common council to the anterior authority of the people. That authority included a popular right to override any acts of Common Council, such as those of 1694 and 1695, which encroached upon the liberties of the citizenry. According to the popular theorists, the right of the freemen to negate the legislation of Common Council was derived from the fact that the freemen, in whose name Common Council acted, had originally legislated on their own behalf: 'The *Rights* and Liberties of the City rest . . . in the whole Body of the *Freemen*: and the whole Body of them . . . regularly voted in making Laws, for the Benefit and Government of the City, before they had any charters, and since.'[19]

Arguing from a shared historical–constitutional perspective, the Common Hall writers proceeded to explain how legislative responsibility had been lodged in Common Council without detriment to the ultimate authority of the people. As the freemen had grown in numbers, they had conferred much of their power upon the 'publick' Common Hall, now composed of the liverymen of the City's companies. Similarly, as Common Hall had increased in size, it had authorized the establishment of a Common Council to act in a legislative capacity. But Common Hall had not thereby surrendered its power to oversee the legislative work of Common Council or to regulate the manner of choosing common councilmen. As one Common Hall protagonist explained at length:

Whatsoever the Power of a Common-Council is, it remains still subordinate and subject unto, and may have its Acts both questioned and superseded by a Common-Hall: For the former being a Creature of the latter, and only instituted and erected by it, for . . . ease and conveniency . . . it is not to be supposed but that the Free-men reserved a Jurisdiction unto themselves in their General Meetings, both of controlling and annulling such Acts as should be found to the Prejudice of the Corporation and Society.'[20]

---

[18] *Present Case of the Common-Hall*; Atwood (?), p. 3.   [19] Atwood (?), p. 19.

[20] R.H., *A Letter to a Livery-Man of London, truly stating . . . the Right of the Citizens . . . to Elect Sheriffs* (1695). Also see *The Antient Manner of Electing Sheriffs of London and Middlesex* (1695); *Cautionary Advice to the Livery-men of London* (1695); *The Right of the Citizens of London to elect Sheriffs in their Common-Hall* [1695].

Other writers defended this argument as no different from that developed by the City's counsel at the time of the *quo warranto* case in the effort to explain why the Corporation should not be held accountable for the misconduct of Common Council. Moreover, Common Council was depicted as a much less representative institution than Common Hall. Contending that half the freemen now resided outside the incorporated wards which returned common councilmen, the spokesmen for Common Hall argued that these non-resident citizens were actively represented in Corporation affairs solely by the liverymen. The 1695 case for civic democracy concluded with the assertion that the liverymen were not without means to enforce their authority. Any high office-holder who exercised his magisterial power in violation of electoral rights might be disfranchised by Common Hall.

The populist vision of the Corporation articulated by these spokesmen for the London livery differed in detail from that of the earlier radical draft statute. The intention of the two programmes, that of making the government of the City more responsible to the people, was the same, but the 1695 writers went beyond the earlier constitutional draft as they wrestled with a problem not considered by their Whig predecessors. Essentially, the livery spokesmen were defending an institutional device for preventing elected office-holders from ignoring the rights of those who elected them. They found the solution to this problem in the livery's continuing surveillance of the legislative acts of the aldermen and the Court of Common Council. In elaborating upon this model, they conceived of the Corporation as a participatory association of citizens who protected their individual liberties as active electors and as potential legislators. Simply put, the Corporation was the people in politics.

No definitive answers can be given to the questions of who the spokesmen for Common Hall were or of how representative their ideas were of the thinking of the liverymen.[21] Both the number of apologies for the Common Hall position and the cautious tactics of the magistrates after the initial protests suggest that dissatisfaction with the Whig leaders was widespread among the liverymen.

[21] The seven pieces in defence of Common Hall were each written anonymously. The most sophisticated of them has been attributed to the Lockean propagandist William Atwood, later a controversial Chief Justice of New York. Donald Wing, comp., *Short-title Catalogue . . . 1641–1700* (New York, 1945), i. 87.

Regardless of how many citizens actively opposed the aldermen, the arguments of the popular propagandists of 1695 reflect assumptions that were probably commonplace among the *artisanat*. The pamphleteers against shrieval fines described the Corporation, just as many London craftsmen wanted it described, as a corporate and consensual public organism that existed for the sake of its individual members. The pamphleteers pictured the city 'from the bottom up' in a fashion that accorded well with the civic ideals of those many Londoners who regularly participated in managing the affairs of their wards and guilds or of their precincts and parishes. These citizens experienced government as springing from the people, and like the pamphleteers they often forgot that the Corporation existed by virtue of a royal grant before the Revolution and a parliamentary grant thereafter. The popular political culture of late Stuart London was thus inherently libertarian, and it was to remain so even as the parties exchanged their principles.

If the revolt of the livery posed a libertarian challenge to the character of Whig rule, the response of the Whig magistrates is best interpreted as an explicit divorcement from their past promotion of popular political participation. Unfortunately, less is known about what the Whig leaders were thinking in 1695. One of two surviving pamphlets written on behalf of the magistrates appears to have been sponsored officially, but it does little more than collate quotations from Corporation records in defence of Common Council's authority to make binding by-laws.[22] The anonymous *Friendly Dialogue between a Livery-man and a Freeman* was privately offered, but it provides a more suggestive guide to the reaction of the Whig leaders. The author of this tract found the chief obstacle to good Corporation government in the unruly behaviour of Common Hall. He attacked the composition of that body on a variety of grounds, each of which betrayed his hostility to extensive popular involvement in electoral politics. Too many persons had been admitted to the livery, according to the *Friendly Dialogue*. Too many of the liverymen had only a mean estate, and too many lived outside the City. As a body, the liverymen did not adequately reflect the interests and trades of the whole number of freemen. Why, the author puzzled, should the election of important civic

[22] *Modest Essay in Vindication of the . . . Lord Mayor.*

officers be delegated to such 'a mixt Multitude of unknown Persons, such as *Weavers, Glovers, Coopers, Curriers, Blacksmiths, Cordwainers, & cum multis aliis* Mechanicks?'[23]

The *Friendly Dialogue* was also distinctly unfriendly to the contitutional arguments of the popular pamphleteers. Condemning the passionate devotion of some liverymen to 'every little Nicety and Punctillo' of past constitutional practice, the author outlined his own major constitutional revisions for the future. He proposed to eliminate entirely the exclusive electoral privileges of the City's liverymen. In place of the existing Common Hall composed of the livery, the writer of the *Friendly Dialogue* recommended one composed of Common Council sitting with two electoral representatives chosen by the freemen of each precinct.[24] In numerical terms, this alteration would have replaced 8,000 or more liveried electors with a Common Hall numbering fewer than 800. This vastly reduced and reconstituted Common Hall would be charged with the election of the City officers chosen by the existing body, including the City's representatives in parliament. Attacking tumultuousness at its root, the author was prepared to reduce London's parliamentary electorate by nine-tenths. Moreover, the small, reformed Common Hall he proposed, with the entire Common Council included, might have been far more susceptible to influences and electoral suggestions from the magistracy.[25]

Did these inflammatory recommendations, which would have disfranchised thousands of liverymen, actually reflect the perspective of the Whig aldermanic élite? The printed propaganda does appear to express the spirit, if not the actual letter, of the magisterial position. The testimony of one of the Common Hall pamphleteers suggests that the Whig aldermen were open to constitutional revisions somewhat similar to those proposed by the *Friendly Dialogue*. Reporting a Common Council debate on a possible transfer of the shrieval election to a body of single representatives from each ward, the writer feared that '26 Deputies shall appoint our Sheriffs, and so deprive thousands of Citizens of their Right to elect'.[26]

[23] *Friendly Dialogue between a Livery-Man and a Freeman*, pp. 8–9.

[24] Ibid., pp. 17–24.

[25] An electoral scheme resembling this one had been adopted by the Corporation in 1650–1. Farnell, pp. 175–83; Webb and Webb, *English Local Government . . . Part Two* (1908), p. 616 n.

[26] R. H., *Letter to a Livery-Man of London*. No record of such a debate has been preserved in the Journals.

The magistrates were thus perceived by their articulate opponents as harbouring designs against the London electorate. Moreover, the Whigs were in agreement with the dialogue-maker's goal of subordinating electoral independence to stable administration, although they may not have been prepared to pursue his specific means for achieving electoral order. Taunted with their own rhetoric refurbished, the Whig leaders were certainly embarked upon a complete ideological retreat. The full extent of their reaction against the popular protests of 1695 became apparent two years later when the Court of Aldermen adopted a new restrictive regulation governing admissions to the livery. This directive fell short of the Draconian measures of the *Friendly Dialogue*. Nevertheless, it revealed a desire to limit the liveried electorate and to elevate its social character in the expectation of making the liverymen more respectable and perhaps more manageable.

Adopted in July 1697, the magisterial order had been mooted the previous year when six aldermen were appointed to prepare it, among whom were the Whig Lord Mayor of 1695 and three other former supporters of radical revisions in the City's electoral procedures.[27] The order provided for a new wealth test to be applied by all the City's companies in calling persons to their liveries. Members of the twelve 'great' companies were to possess an estate of £1,000 in order to qualify as liverymen, and members of the remaining companies were to be worth at least £500. The effect of the order was to limit future electoral participation in Common Hall to the upper 25 to 30 per cent of the City's ratepaying population. The rationale that accompanied the order dwelt upon the declining quality of the livery rather than upon implications for the Common Hall franchise. Nevertheless, the measure was clearly aimed against the 'mechanick' liverymen complained about so strongly by the author of the *Friendly Dialogue* in 1695. The Whig City leaders had apparently come to the conclusion that the smaller tradesmen and artisans, or rather the greater part of them worth less than £500, endangered the political harmony of the City and the social harmony of their guilds. The political effect of the 1697 order was to freeze a majority of the *artisanat* below the line that separated ordinary freemen from those entitled to choose MPs and other high Corporation officers. Likewise, the

[27] Repertory 100, fo. 206; Repertory 101, fos. 115, 310–11.

order restricted the Common Hall franchise to propertied rate-payers, including the respectable 'middling sort' and the overseas merchants, among whom the urban Whigs were now finding their predominant social constituency. Just as the Common Council act of 1692 had reduced the ward electorate in the wake of the 1688–90 crisis, so the 1697 order was designed to curtail the Common Hall electorate in the wake of the 1695 shrieval uproar.

The years from 1695 to 1697 were a watershed, therefore, in the development of the London Whigs. A parting of the ways now occurred within a disjointed party that had previously sought to combine, however tenuously, the disparate socio-political interests of commercial entrepreneurs and an urban 'commons' of petty tradesmen and handicraft producers. The Common Hall controversy had forced the Whigs to act in accordance with developing reservations about popular political involvement that had originated in their post-revolutionary electoral disappointments of 1690. By 1695–7 the Whig leaders were no longer just lukewarm about the people in politics—they were positively frightened of the people in politics. What they had seen in 1695 was the formation of an opposition 'party' that drew its strength from the populist electorate and that showed much familiarity with the extra-constitutional political devices previously developed by the Whigs themselves. In 1690 the Whigs had learned how fickle the people could be in politics; in 1695 they witnessed how dangerous the people could be to the political stability of the City. By 1697, 'official' Whig thinking had changed from revolutionary libertarianism to an oligarchic philosophy of social control. As the electorate was again drawn into the conflict between the parties, the London Whig élite came to see popular liberties as nuisances rather than as the inviolate fruits of revolution.

2. The Rise of a Popular Tory Opposition, 1695–1710

A. The Recovery of the City Tories

As the Whig leaders revealed these new colours, their popular opponents of 1695 gained full title to an abandoned libertarian legacy. These opponents were also left with the bitter taste of defeat at the hands of a party leadership they had previously respected. Popular dissatisfaction with the Whig magistrates gave the City's Tory leaders an audience ripe for a new style of Tory politics. However, the development of a popular Tory opposition became only gradually apparent in London politics. Not until the second half of Anne's reign did the City again see the clear-cut competition between a 'popular' party and a 'magisterial' party that had been the case under reversed names from 1679 to 1690. Nevertheless, the evolution of Tory populism began in 1695, and it contributed to the revival of Tory strength in the Corporation that was apparent in the interval between the war that ended in 1697 and the war that began in 1702. This Tory revival was facilitated not only by the political disillusionment of artisans with the Whigs, but also by the economic woes of the decade and the appearance of new Tory leaders.

Popular dissatisfaction with high-handed magisterial tactics during the 1695 shrieval controversy may well have been aggravated by new economic strains experienced by craft manufacturers, tradesmen, and labourers. The 1690s were clearly years of hardship for many in the City, and that hardship was more difficult to bear because it followed the fifteen years of plentiful harvests and low food prices that had preceded 1688. A war-time depression of commercial and maritime employments overlapped with the dismal 'seven ill years' of 1693 to 1700, a period of poor harvests and high food prices that were possibly exacerbated by the introduction of export bounties on grain. The harvest of 1693 was the worst save one since the abysmal last years of Elizabeth's reign a century earlier. In 1696, wheat reached its highest price level for the entire period from 1660 to 1714, and between 1696 and 1699 wheat prices averaged over twice the level maintained from 1688 to 1691.[28] In those years, the Common Council and the Court of Aldermen were confronted both with popular complaints about the 'oppressions' of the farmers of the City markets and with complaints about the high prices of coal and bread. The funding of a new 'corporation for the poor' by Common Council in 1698 and the establishment of a new Bishopsgate workhouse

---

[28] Thomas Tooke and W. Newmarch, *A History of Prices* (1928), i. 30, 34; Max Beloff, *Public Order and Popular Disturbances, 1660–1714* (1938), p. 63 et seq.; Donald C. Coleman, *The Economy of England, 1450–1750* (1977), pp. 95, 102, 112; R. B. Rose, 'Eighteenth Century Price Riots and Public Policy in England', *International Review of Social History*, 6 (1961), pp. 281, 290.

constituted official acknowledgement of the extent of urban distress.[29]

War-necessitated taxation also added to the burdens of the poor and the hard-pressed. Although the detested hearth tax was removed at the beginning of the reign, poll taxes became a staple of Williamite finance and were levied no fewer than five times between 1690 and 1698. Excise duties were gradually extended over a broad range of popularly consumed items including salt, leather and leather goods, coal, glassware, soap, and paper. Moreover, in 1694–5, after the passage of an ingenious levy on burials, births, and marriages, the London guildsman was pursued by the tax collector even to his grave. The urban craftsman certainly had as much cause to complain about the extraordinary costs of war as did the country gentleman pinched by the annual land tax.

Urban social distress was most acute in mid-decade, from 1695 to 1696, when food prices reached their zenith and when a sudden inflation was broken by the sharp deflation and specie shortage of the recoinage crisis.[30] Elsewhere in England these were years of corn riots and tax riots. In London, the year 1695 saw both the opening of an ideological rift between the Whig magistrates and many of their former guild followers, and the first notable outbreak of popular urban Jacobitism in a Drury Lane riot.[31] The corporate and consensual political ideas espoused by the popular writers in the shrieval controversy therefore probably expressed the feelings of many liverymen who saw both their livelihoods and their privileges frustrated by the Revolution's disappointing denouement. Anxious guildsmen who faced an erosion of their living standards were understandably quick to detect magisterial arrogance in the aldermanic manipulation of Common Hall. In 1696 the 'freemen of Portsoken' not only complained to their common councilmen about taxation and the mismanagement of City funds, but also placed those grievances in the context of the 'Eminent Danger' to the 'Liberties, Properties and Priviledges of the Freemen of this City'.[32]

[29] Journal 52, fos. 178, 191–2, 228–31; Repertory 103, fos. 43–6; *A Copy of the Report of the Committee of Common Council, appointed to Consider of the Abuses committed by the Farmers of the City Markets* (1696); *A Copy of the Address of the Free-Men of the Portsoaken-Ward* (1696).

[30] J. Keith Horsefield, *British Monetary Experiments 1650–1710* (Cambridge, Mass., 1960). pp. 3–19.   [31] Luttrell, *Brief Relation*, iii. 483–4.

[32] *Copy of the Address of the Free-Men of Portsoaken.*

The Whig magistrates were now unmasked as no more sensitive to popular liberties than the old Tories had been. Worse still, the Whig-mercantile-dissenting élite that had gained power in the City after the Revolution actually derived numerous benefits from the war and from the taxation that cost other social elements so much. Indeed, by war's end the old corporate insitutions of urban government that attracted popular civic loyalties were either overshadowed or obstructed by the new complex of corporate commercial institutions whose directorates interlocked with the aldermanic bench. Although the bite of urban economic distress passed with the turn of the century, the sting long remained. The coincident experiences of economic hardship and civic disappointment may well have had lasting effects on the political attitudes of artisans and plebs. Moreover, although the economic consequences of the war of Anne's reign were not immediately as severe, another interval of high prices coincided with the increase in party tensions after 1707.[33] By that time, the revolutionary alliance of élite Whigs and articulate artisans was but a dim memory.

Whether the genesis of Tory populism owed more to an instinctive reaction of the *artisanat* against the Whig magistrates, or to the cultivation of such a reaction by artful Tory leaders, is difficult to say. Both developments were noticeable by the end of William's reign, and each encouraged and reinforced the other. Previous analysis of the Tory City leaders has demonstrated that the occupations and investments of many made them natural spokesmen for a party opposed to the new Whig corporate empire and to the nonconformist revival. Moreover, just as the deaths or superannuation of radical Whig leaders facilitated the Whigs' transition to oligarchy, so the deaths and superannuations of old prerogative-minded royalists facilitated the Tories' transition to civic populism. Surprisingly, though, the most successful practitioner of 'Tory democracy' in William's reign had also been among the most successful royalist plutocrats of the reigns of Charles and James. The political career of Sir Charles Duncombe was marked by a singular measure of opportunism and egotism, but he nevertheless exemplified the changing style of Tory leadership, albeit in exaggerated form.

[33] See references in note 55 below.

Duncombe's inveterate opposition to the Whig Junto and to their City projects has been recounted elsewhere, but the populist character of his opposition deserves mention here. Beginning in 1699, Duncombe was perhaps the most publicly conscious Tory politician in London. His well-informed associate, Dr Charles Davenant, reported that Duncombe's shrieval candidacy of 1699 was launched 'as a just rebuke to those invaders of property', the Junto Whigs.[34] The London liverymen found in Duncombe a sheriff to their liking, one whose dramatic gestures were calculated exhibitions of a new Tory regard for the feelings and frustrations of the London *artisanat*. Duncombe inaugurated his shrievalty by touring the London prisons, freeing fifty persons imprisoned for debts, satisfying their creditors, and sending them all home in his own coach! His continuing and well advertised largess to unfortunate freemen was reported by the Tory *Post Boy* to have amounted to some £5,400 by the end of his term as sheriff, and he also made liberal contributions to the newly endowed Bishopsgate workhouse.[35]

Public reaction to these benefactions probably contributed to Duncombe's election to the aldermanic seat of Bridge in June 1700. He then made clear that he intended not only to relieve indigent freemen but also to relieve the freemen's indigent Corporation, and he offered to build the City a permanent mayoral mansion at his own expense. Hoping to occupy this projected civic edifice himself, the City's newest sitting alderman entered the October 1700 mayoral contest with additional promises to 'lay out £40,000 for the good of the city'.[36] Despite 'the great affection of the people in General to him', and despite his lead in the mayoral poll, Duncombe and his popular supporters lost the mayoralty when the Whig magistrates secured the office for the alternative Common Hall designee. A year later, Duncombe advised the 'worthy Livery Men' in the press of another attempt to secure the mayoralty on their behalf, but his campaign for the office was again frustrated by the Whig magistrates.[37]

---

[34] HMC *Cowper MSS* ii. 388.

[35] *Post Boy*, 2–4 Apr. 1700. Also see *Post Boy*, 6–8 Feb. 1700; *London Post*, 9–11 Oct. and 1–3 Nov. 1699; *Flying Post*, 10–12 Oct. 1699 and 30 Dec. 1699–2 Jan. 1700.

[36] Luttrell, *Brief Relation*, iv. 692, 660, 667. Duncombe had previously been Alderman of Broad Street, 1683–6.

[37] *London Post*, 30 Sept.–2 Oct. 1700; *Post Boy*, 23–5 Sept. 1701.

Although Duncombe's public charities received much notice in the London news-sheets, little is known about the public interpretation of them. Defoe was swift to point out the self-serving ends of his benefactions,[38] but the several thousand liverymen who polled for Duncombe for Lord Mayor, or who supported him in the three parliamentary elections of 1701–2 may have accepted in good faith his protestations of regard for the citizenry and their civic institutions. Moreover, Duncombe was not the only Tory City leader to extend a munificent hand to the indigent or to respond to the Corporation's financial embarrassment. In 1703 the two senior Tory aldermen beneath the chair were recommended to the liverymen before the mayoral election as worthy civic patrons. Sir John Parsons had promoted an act to discontinue the mayoral sale of two lucrative Corporation offices and to divert the profits of those offices from the incumbents to the City chamber. Sir Thomas Cooke was similarly recommended for his private relief of poor foreign Protestant refugees. Some years later, ironmaster Sir Ambrose Crowley, who was seeking the aldermanic seat of Queenhithe in 1709, offered a free cauldron of coals to each poller on his behalf and public monuments for the ward.[39]

Arising from a mixture of philanthropic and political motives, the benefactions of these City Tories revealed a transformation in the strategy of Tory electioneering. If the Tory leaders had once dwelt upon the respect owed by the people to authority, they now dwelt upon the respect for the people of those seeking authority. In other words, through their charities, Tory politicians in the City showed a regard for the 'commons of London' in the expectation that the 'commons of London' would reciprocate that regard. Whig City leaders may also have been public benefactors, but the charities of the Tories were those that captured public attention. Moreover, although too much should not be made of the politics of philanthropy, several City Tories like Sir John Cass were also lavish patrons of the charity school movement.[40] A reputation as patrons of the poor clearly served the Tory leaders

---

[38] Daniel Defoe, *The True-Born Englishman* (1701).

[39] *Daily Courant* no. 439, 13 Sept. 1703; no. 451, 27 Sept. 1703; and no. 2470, 23 Sept. 1709.

[40] *Post Boy* no. 2464, 24–7 Feb. 1711; Mary Gwladys Jones, *The Charity School Movement: A Study of Eighteenth Century Puritanism in Action* (Cambridge, 1938), pp. 110–14; Sidney J. Farthing, *Sir John Cass and his School* (1910).

well in electoral clashes with Whig magnates who were tied to the 'moneyed interest'.

Several other signs of the convergence of Church-Tory politics and of popular interests were evident in the years following the 1695 Common Hall fracas. At the time of that dispute, a Tory political society was founded at the Castle tavern in the middle city ward of Farringdon Within. This organization, subsequently known as the 'Centenary Club', enjoyed a continuous existence throughout the eighteenth century, and its membership was active in the City opposition to Walpole in the 1720s and the 1730s.[41] The club's sixty late Stuart members were largely professionals and retail traders, and half of them were common councilmen for Far-ringdon Within and Castle Baynard at various dates between 1695 and 1715. These wards were the strongest Tory wards in the City by 1700, and they were among the four wards within the walls with the poorest populations. Although loyalist clubs had also flourished in the City at the time of the Exclusion Crisis,[42] the club that met at the Castle tavern marked a novel departure in the history of the London Tories. As representatives of wards with heavy populations of hard-pressed artisans and 'mechanicks', the members of this club were active in the Tories' populist fusion of Church and crown loyalism with respect for the privileges of the electorate and for the independence of Common Council.

New links between the Tory party and the *artisanat* may also be found by comparing the wealth and occupations of Whig and Tory common councilmen first elected in the years after 1695. If the Tory leaders developed a stronger following among plebeian freemen and artisans at this time, one would expect to find sup-porting evidence in the calibre of persons returned to Common Council as Tories. The large size of Common Council and the annual reselection of its members made that body the most responsive of all Corporation organs to popular political impulses. The analysis in Tables 5.1 and 5.2 of the relative wealth and of the occupations of common councilmen first chosen between 1695 and 1703 reveals that Tory common councilmen were, on the whole, of somewhat lesser stature than their Whig rivals. The Tories were better able to speak for the City *artisanat* because

[41] GL MS 544/1, Centenary Club, Register of Members, 1695–1806. I am indebted to Nicholas Rogers for sharing his interpretation of the Centenary Club's history with me.
[42] David Allen, 'Political Clubs in Restoration London', *HJ* xix (1976), 561–80.

Table 5.1 Real Wealth of new Common Councilmen, 1695-1703

	Percentage	
	Whigs	Tories
Over £80 p.a.	13	8
£41-£80 p.a.	54	41
£40 p.a. or less	32	51

Table 5.1 is based upon the 151 new common councilmen of known party, 1695-1703 (76 Whigs and 75 Tories), whose real wealth can be established. The real wealth of these individuals was calculated from the second quarter assessments of the 1694 parliamentary aid: CLRO Assessment Boxes; De Krey, iii. 623-71.

Table 5.2 Occupations of new Common Councilmen, 1695-1703

	Percentage	
	Whigs	Tories
Overseas Merchants	34	16
Professional Services	11	10
Domestic Wholesale and Retail Trades	19	19
Victualling Trades	17	12
Manufacturing and Industrial Trades	19	43

Table 5.2 is based upon the 122 common councilmen of known party and known occupation first elected in this period (64 Whigs and 58 Tories). The occupational identifications have been derived from several sources but principally from the 1692 assessments for the 1691 poll tax, first, second, and fourth quarters: CLRO; Assessment Boxes; De Krey, iii. 623-71. A discussion of the grouping of actual occupations into these categories may be found in De Krey, 'Political Radicalism in London', p. 608 n. 70.

more of the Tory common councilmen were of unpretentious social status themselves.

Still another token of the advent of Tory populism may be found in elections to the aldermanic bench. Nine of ten aldermanic vacancies between 1694 and 1702 were filled by Tory nominees whose names were forwarded from the ward electorates to the full

Court of Aldermen. Seven of the nine new Tory aldermen were chosen from middle city wards or from wards divided between the middle city and the city without, and an eighth was chosen from a ward entirely without the walls. Although eight of the ten seats had previously been held by Tories, a moderate Tory (Sir William Hedges) was replaced by a staunch Tory, and two former Whig seats were now claimed by Tories. Only a single Whig, the dissenting Sir Owen Buckingham, was chosen alderman in this eight-year period, and he was returned for Bishopsgate, a ward that included several wealthy inner city parishes. In other words, in the second half of William's reign, Tory aldermanic candidates succeeded in gaining the same measure of approval from the middle city electorate, top-heavy with artisans and plebeian freemen, as did Tory common councilmen. Moreover, the Tory monopoly of middle city aldermanic seats deprived the Whigs of their magisterial ascendancy by the end of the decade. The Whigs' control of the aldermanic bench for most of the 1690s was derived from the co-operation of a few maverick Tories and the repeated absenteeism of several ageing royalists. The desertion of the mavericks and the replacement of older Tories by younger Churchmen deprived the Whigs of their aldermanic majority by 1700. In 1702, at the time of Queen Anne's succession, the party count among the aldermen was sixteen Tories and ten Whigs.

The succession of Tory triumphs in contested aldermanic polls in the second half of William's reign is also indicative of the revival of City Tory prospects and of the increase in party tension that then occurred in London. By 1698, the first full year of peace, the mid-decade abatement of party antagonisms had ceased. This development coincided with the parliamentary 'heats' after the Peace of Ryswick and with the national reaction against the Junto Whigs. In the City, party conflict was renewed along several of the fractures of London's political life. Populist electoral disenchantment with the Whigs' new oligarchic finery was one of these, and it was one greatly cultivated by the Tories. High-Church reaction against the flaunting show of occasional conformity by two Whig Lord Mayors was another. The conflict between the two East India Companies was a third.

The upswing in City Tory fortunes left the Whigs embattled from 1698 to 1701 and defeated in 1702. Some impression of the Whigs' enforced retreat from power may be gained by looking at

mayoral elections in those years. The Whig's retention of the
mayoral chair after 1698 was jeopardized by the shrinking number
of junior Whig aldermen, but the Tories suffered from the opposite
embarrassment. The promotion of successive Whig aldermen to
the chair through the 1690s, without respect for the greater
seniority of several Tories, eventually left the Whigs without a
supply of suitable candidates. In 1698, they acquiesced in the
mayoralty of Sir Francis Child, the formerly moderate goldsmith.
The mayoral election of 1700 saw the Common Hall intrusion of
Sir Charles Duncombe, who was returned by the liverymen with
the Presbyterian Sir Thomas Abney for consideration by the
Court of Aldermen. Although Abney had trailed Duncombe by
several hundred votes in the poll, the Whig aldermen secured a
majority for Abney, apparently by twisting the arms of Sir William
Gore and other Tory aldermen anxious about Duncombe's opportunistic past. In 1701, the Whig magistrates again frustrated the
mayoral nominees of the Church party but were unable to carry
the election for one of their own number. By that date, only the
junior-most Whig alderman, Sir Owen Buckingham, had not
served as mayor. The Whigs promoted Buckingham and Gore,
whose interest in the Bank made him palatable to them, and when
Common Hall returned Gore and Duncombe, the Whig
aldermen reciprocated Gore's favour of the previous year by
voting for him.[43]

Whig leaders were more successful in retaining the City's parliamentary seats, but not without broadening their appeal by
standing with cross-grained Tories. As has been explained
elsewhere, the City parliamentary elections of the second half of
William's reign were greatly complicated by the establishment of
the Bank and by the hostility between the rival East India concerns.
The politics of investment corresponded roughly, but not exactly,
with the politics of party, and this disparity explains why not one of
the four City parliamentary elections between 1695 and 1701 pitted
a foursome of Whigs against a foursome of Church-Tories. In 1695,
in 1698, and in January 1701, the Whigs succeeded in electing three
City members, but in each case they did so by convincing a

---

[43] Repertory 104, fos. 551, 555; BL Add. MS 40774, fo. 195, James Vernon to William
III, 29 Sept. 1699; Luttrell, *Brief Relation*, iv. 433, 563, 692, 694–5; HMC *Portland MSS* iii.
631–2; *Flying Post*, 1–4 Oct. 1698; *London Post*, 30 Sept.–2 Oct. 1700, 26–9 Sept. 1701, and
1–3 Oct. 1701.

maverick Tory to stand with their candidates. Only in November 1701 were the Whigs able to carry all four seats for their ticket of Bank and New East India Company directors. The Tory-Old Company interest strongly contested the two elections of 1701, cleverly but unsuccessfully promoting tickets that included the popular Duncombe, moderate Tories still respected by some Whig pollers, and even a Whig alderman with major Old Company investments. Although the Tory candidates were defeated, they nevertheless dramatized the encroachment upon Corporation politics of the emerging dissenting-Bank-New Company interest.

Bitterly contested elections were one manifestation of the waxing of party spirit late in William's reign. Party 'heats' in the City were further inflamed by the keen interest of many Londoners in the Westminster debate about the prospects of war or peace. The king's cautious acceptance of a Country-Tory ministry late in 1700 was a further blow to the London Whigs' increasingly precarious grip on the City magistracy. The 1701 efforts of the City Whigs to embarrass the new ministry also served to demonstrate the erosion of Whig power in the Corporation. This was especially apparent in May of that year. The Whigs in London then acted in concert with Whigs elsewhere in the country in protesting against the ministry's impeachment of the Junto and against the ministry's reluctance to prepare for the possibility of another war. When the Commons imprisoned five Whig gentlemen who had presented an outspoken petition from the grand jury of Kent, the London Common Council appointed a committee to consider a petition to the crown 'concerning the circumstances of this Nation'. However, the preparation of the petition was halted at a subsequent Common Council by a vote of ninety-three to ninety-two. Both the closeness of the vote and the presence of such a large proportion of the common councilmen are indicative of the extent to which public opinion had been divided by the question. Especially galling to the Whigs was the fact that the casting vote against the petition was that of the Whig Lord Mayor, Sir Thomas Abney, who had come under strong pressure from the crown. The Whigs consoled themselves by feasting the Kentish petitioners upon their release and by illuminating the City with bonfires when the House of Lords rejected the articles of impeachment against Junto Lord Somers. The Whigs enjoyed greater success in September, when they secured Common Council adoption of an address to William condemning Louis XIV's recognition of James II's son.[44]

William's late 1701 dissolution of parliament, his rapprochement with the Junto, and the City Whigs' success in the second general election of 1701 seemed to put an end to the Tories' recovery in the Corporation, despite their acquisition of an aldermanic majority. The Whigs' hopes were quickly dashed, however, by the death of William and by Queen Anne's partiality for their opponents. Anne's reconstitution of the London Lieutenancy in July 1702 signalled to the Corporation electorate her endorsement of the City Tories, and the Tories quickly exploited that endorsement to their advantage. By the autumn of 1702 they had claimed the shrieval elections, the mayoral election, and three of the four City Commons seats. The Tory triumph was further sweetened by the queen's state appearance for the festive mayoral show of Sir Samuel Dashwood. The recovery of the Tories was marred only by the slight majority of Whigs among those common councilmen of known party loyalty.[45]

Thirteen years after the Revolution the Tories had finally bettered the Whigs in the City, and popular disillusionment with the Whig élite was certainly a very important factor in the Tory leaders' success. The Tory leadership had clearly responded to popular dissatisfaction, but the fusion of civic populism and Church-Tory partisanship had not yet been effected. Behaviour remained to be rationalized as principle. Anticipations of the subsequent articulation of Tory populism were apparent, but were still few. Duncombe's philosophical friend Charles Davenant was perhaps the most perceptive observer of the state of politics in the Corporation at the end of William's reign. He described the London Whigs 'who are now turned Tories' as 'those revolters from their old principles of liberty', and he implied that the privileges of the citizenry were now better protected by the Church party.[46] Similarly, the author of an anonymous 1701 satire of Common Council proceedings depicted the Whigs as enemies of popular liberties, but he was not yet certain whether those liberties were more safely entrusted to Tory hands.[47] The very success of the

---

[44] Journal 53, fos. 22, 123; BL Add. MS 40775, fos. 79, 221, James Vernon to William III, 19 Aug. and 30 Sept. 1701; Burnet, *History*, iv. 510–11; Horwitz, *Parliament, Policy and Politics*, p. 290.

[45] Luttrell, *Brief Relation*, v. 193; *Flying Post* no. 1168, 29–31 Oct. 1702; *Post Boy* no. 1165, 29–31 Oct. 1702.

[46] HMC *Cowper MSS* ii. 289.   [47] *A Common Council Journal. Anno 1701.*

Tory leaders by 1702 may have retarded the maturation of the new populist strains within the Tory creed. Those strains were the voice of opposition—not the voice of magisterial authority, which the Tories now possessed. The iconography and imagery of Tory electoral festivities in 1702 dwelt, therefore, not upon rights to be defended but upon blessings now achieved. The mayoral show of October and the state thanksgiving of November enunciated themes of domestic bounty and social harmony, military fortitude, and patriotic tradition. 'As threatening Spain did to Eliza bow, So France and Spain shall do to ANNA now', read one Tory-loyalist Ludgate banner of November 1702.[48]

B. The Metamorphosis of the City Tories

The years of Tory hegemony in the City proved to be both rather uneventful and rather brief. As the war of William's reign had dampened party strife in the City from 1691 to 1695, so the war of Anne's reign redirected the combativeness of Londoners towards an external enemy for some years. The London Churchmen had hoped to avoid another war, but when it came the City Tories— like the City Whigs—were 'Resolv'd t' Encourage War to Purchase Peace'.[49] Animosity between Whig and Tory City leaders was also eased for a time by the partial reconciliation of the two East India Companies. Only the question of religion and the issue of occasional conformity remained as especially visible signs of the city's abiding political division in the early years of the last Stuart monarch.

Furthermore, after a delay of several years, the format of shrieval elections was revised by a 1703 act of Common Council that permitted shrieval fines while affirming 'that the Right of Electing Sherriffes . . . is & Shall be in the Livery men . . . in Common Hall assembled'.[50] Through this language, the predominantly Tory magistracy of 1703 honoured its commitment to electoral rights, but the provisions of the bill permitted the Lord Mayor to make periodic shrieval nominations for several weeks prior to the Midsummer's Day Common Hall election. The Court of Aldermen was empowered to accept fines from nominees, and

---

[48] *Flying Post* no. 1174, 12–14 Nov. 1702.

[49] *The Restauration; or: a Change for the Better* (1702).

[50] Journal 53, p. 638; *An Act to Impower the Lord Mayor . . . to nominate one or more . . . persons to be Sheriff* (1704).

the Court of Common Council was empowered to discharge nominees from the office after the payment of fines. This formula
eliminated the shrieval election as a constitutional issue, sanctioned
nominations for the sake of fines, and also permitted both nominations and elections for the sake of party. The shrieval elections of
the early part of Anne's reign were fairly tame affairs, however, in
which the Corporation collected considerable sums of money and
in which personalities seem to have counted for more than party
principles. Most sheriffs who served between 1703 and 1709 were
Whigs; but little political significance should be attached to this
fact, because several other Whig leaders nominated or elected to
the office fined or sought to fine. Moreover, some of the Whigs
who served were initially nominated by Tory Lord Mayors.[51]

If the Tories acquiesced in the election of Whig sheriffs, the
Whigs acquiesced in the election of Tory Lord Mayors in the order
of their aldermanic seniority. A steady succession of Tories to the
mayoralty between 1702 and 1710 was interrupted only in 1704,
when Sir Owen Buckingham was chosen in accordance with his
seniority. No mayoral election was contested between 1703 and
1709, although the prospect of Sir Charles Duncombe's long-
awaited mayoralty in the fall of 1708 elicited one hostile broadside
and opposition from 'some great men'.[52] The lack of party spirit
in the London mayoral and shrieval elections of these years should
not be taken, however, to mean that party perspectives had faded
from civic memory. Beneath the placid surface of London politics,
developments occurred in 1704 and 1705 that were to mark
strongly the character of party conflict in the City, as it was
renewed thereafter with increasing vigour.

More known Tories than known Whigs were returned to the London Common Council in 1704 for the first time in over a decade.[53]
Although the Tory Common Council majority was at first a slim
one, it endured for the remainder of the first age of party and
subsequently increased, despite the efforts of the City Whigs
to reverse it. On the other hand, the Tory string of aldermanic

[51] The Journals and Repertories for these years contain a full record of shrieval
nominations, discharges, and elections.

[52] HMC *Portland MSS* iv. 503; *A Letter to a Citizen Concerning the Election of a Lord Mayor*
(1708).

[53] The Common Council of 1704 numbered 96 Whigs, 101 Tories, and 37 persons of
ambiguous or uncertain partisanship.

elections ended in 1702 and was followed by a run of Whig aldermanic elections which gave the Whigs a slight majority on the
bench by 1705. The Whig margin on the Court of Aldermen
also endured for the remainder of the first age of party and subsequently increased, despite the efforts of the City Tories to prevent
this. By 1705 the Whigs had gained two inner city wards from the
Tories, which gave them nine of thirteen inner city aldermanic
seats, and they had also captured two new middle city seats.
Although the Tory acquisition of a slight majority on the Common Council went virtually unnoticed at first, the March 1705
Broad Street aldermanic election that eliminated the Tories'
magisterial majority was strongly contested. This Tory loss was
further aggravated by the defeat, shortly thereafter, of the Tory
candidates in the 1705 parliamentary election.[54]

The events of 1704–5 presaged the institutional strengths that
the parties would enjoy and exploit for the remainder of Anne's
reign. The City Tories were to find a firm base in the Common
Council, and as the rhetoric of Tory populism emerged, it was to
do so around the defence and the extension of Common Council's
voice in Corporation affairs. On the other hand, the Whigs'
recovery of the magistracy and their strenuous exertions to retain
it again made the mayoral and aldermanic prerogatives the basis
of Whig strategy in the City. The Tories' new-found strength
within the Common Council was an outgrowth of the Church-
Tory sympathies of the less substantial electorate of the middle
city and the city without the walls, just as the Whigs' magisterial
success was chiefly owing to the low church–dissenting sympathies
of the more substantial inner city electorate. In other words, by
1705 the groundwork had been laid for a new 'rage of party', a
contest for power pitting the inner city against the rest of the city
and pitting the magisterial majority against the Common Council
majority. Still lacking in 1705, however, was a sufficiently vehement division over the issues capable of re-igniting the party con-
flagration.

By 1707–8 the issues of political conflict had revived, and by
1709–10 the City was again torn by bitter partisan animosities.
Several developments terminated the early war-time relaxation of

[54] *Daily Courant* no. 900, 5 Mar. 1705; *Post Man* no. 1405, 17–19 May 1705; *Rehearsal*, i.
no. 41, 5–12 May 1705; *Flying Post* no. 1565, 12–15 May 1705.

City strife. The 1707 defeat of the allied army at Almanza in Spain sparked the beginnings of the Tories' re-evaluation of the purposes of British participation in the war. By the end of the decade, war-weariness was spreading both among parliamentary Tories and among City Tories. In London, Tory reservations about the management and the goals of the war were stimulated by the reconstitution of the ministry in Whig hands after 1708. Popular enthusiasm for the Junto's commitment to 'no peace without Spain' was also severely strained by the late-decade rise in prices and by the accompanying shortages of corn, bread, and coal. Guildsmen afflicted by the twin scourges of rising prices and high taxes were further disturbed by the ministry's 1709 bill for the naturalization of foreign Protestants and by the sudden descent upon London of thousands of Palatine refugees. Feared as possible competitors in many employments, the 'poor Palatines' became a symbol of the Whigs' disregard for the native poor in the City's midst.[55]

Moreover, as the economic circumstances of some artisans and tradesmen deteriorated, the Whig-dissenting-mercantile complex was consolidating its position in the City's corporate enterprises. For instance, the charter of the Bank of England was renewed in 1709 despite vigorous Tory opposition, and a doubling of its subscription was authorized. The partnership of the Junto, who had assumed direction of the war, and of the Bank, which was favoured in the public finance of the war, redounded to the credit of neither in the eyes of City Tories like goldsmiths Sir Richard Hoare and Sir Francis Child.[56] Similarly, the East India animosity intruded upon City politics in a new guise after the consolidation of the two Companies in 1709. Former directors and investors of the New Company gained a majority voice in the directorate of the United Company, and the number of directors with Old Company ties thereafter decreased with each passing year. From its beginning, the directorate of the United Company was as heavily tied to the directorate of the Bank as had previously been the case with the New Company leadership. The union of these companies not

[55] Repertory 113, pp. 410–12; Repertory 114, pp. 220–1, 235–9; Burnet, *History*, vi. 34; *Post Boy* no. 2404, 7–10 Oct. 1710; Beloff, pp. 68–70; H. T. Dickinson, 'The Poor Palatines and the Parties', *EHR* lxxxii (1967), 473.

[56] Defoe believed that Hoare and Child had promoted a run on the Bank in 1708, *Anatomy of Exchange-Alley*, pp. 29–30; Holmes, *British Politics*, p. 173; W. Marston Acres, *Bank of England*, i. 98.

only simplified the East India trade but also simplified City politics by revealing the extent of the Whigs' joint-stock hegemony.

The religious division of the City was also revealed in several guises after 1707. The ecclesiastical provisions of the Act of Union were disturbing to London Churchmen long anxious about the strength of dissent in the City. High-flying divines who enjoyed the mayoral patronage of Sir Charles Duncombe and Sir Samuel Garrard sounded the 'Church in danger' alarums in 1708–9, when parliamentary Whigs considered a repeal of the sacramental test. Against this background, the ministry's prosecution of Doctor Sacheverell in 1709–10 triggered the active articulation in the City of many grievances and made Sacheverell a symbol of populist resentment of the Bank, of wealthy City dissenters, and of a Whig war policy that seemed to be undermining the domestic economy.[57]

Party strife in the City was again much in evidence after 1707. In June of that year the crown issued a new commission for the London Lieutenancy in which the Whigs gained a majority.[58] An obvious sign of the strengthening of Whig influence in the government, the alteration of the Lieutenancy commission was an incentive for Whig assertiveness in the Corporation and a provocation to the London Tories. Both Whig aggressiveness and dogged Tory resistance were especially apparent in subsequent aldermanic elections. Not satisfied with their narrow magisterial majority, the Whigs seemed bent on achieving a magisterial monopoly. Easily able to retain the three inner city seats that fell vacant between 1707 and 1710, Whig City leaders were also able to carry three of five middle city aldermanic elections. Moreover, the Whig aldermen took advantage of an unusual electoral situation in Portsoken which left that exterior ward without an alderman for over a year. By 1710, therefore, the Whigs had constructed a commanding magisterial majority of sixteen places to the Tories' nine.

The Whigs did not accomplish this without strenuous Church-Tory opposition and a strong Common Council reaction. Each of the Whig aldermanic victories outside the inner city in these years

[57] Repertory 112, p. 428; HMC *Portland MSS* iv. 507; Holmes, *British Politics*, pp. 92, 105; Holmes, *Sacheverell*, pp. 58, 61, 70n, 240; Holmes, 'The Sacheverell Riots'.
[58] CLRO, Transcript of names of 1707 London Lieutenancy from PRO State Papers 34.

is an illustration of partisan skill and determination. For instance, a 1709 vacancy in the middle city ward of Queenhithe gave the Whigs another aldermanic place, although no fewer than three polls were required to secure the seat. The Whig brewer Sir Benjamin Green first gained the support of the Queenhithe freemen in September 1709 by 'treating with good Venaison, Pastyes, and Claret'. His principal opponent, Tory Sir Ambrose Crowley, whose coal was offered to pollers in lieu of wardmote treats, was told by the electors that 'his Coals would not burn'.[59] Green's untimely death two months after his election gave the Tories an opportunity to recover the seat. This was the object of Lord Mayor Sir Samuel Garrard whose 'base tricks' were intended to prevent the election of another Whig. Only after the Whig aldermen voided Garrard's initial return was the High-Church Lord Mayor obliged to acquiesce in the wardmote nomination and the aldermanic election of Presbyterian John Fryer.[60]

The 1709 death of tobacco magnate Sir Jeffrey Jeffreys, alderman for the City's easternmost ward of Portsoken, also deprived the Tory party of a magisterial place. Whig candidates contested the Portsoken seat, but the wardmote gave a clear majority to Tory builder John Cass and to William Andrew, the ward's longtime Tory deputy alderman. The Whig aldermen gave their approval to Andrew rather than to Cass, the acknowledged Tory choice, and the Whigs may have done so well aware that Andrew neither desired the office nor possessed an estate sufficient to support it. Although Andrew repeatedly declined election on the latter ground, the Whig magistrates, after some study of the matter, repeatedly insisted that he assume office. This deadlock left the seat empty, prevented the election of John Cass or of any other popular Tory, and further enlarged the Whigs' aldermanic majority.[61]

Although the circumstances of the Portsoken election are not entirely clear, the result was obvious, and the election was perceived by the Tory Common Council majority as the last in a series of

[59] BL Loan 29/320, Dyer Newsletter, 24 Sept. 1709; *Daily Courant* no. 2470, 23 Sept. 1709.

[60] Repertory 114, pp. 67-8, 83-4; GL MS 12,017, fo. 27; BL Loan 29/320, Dyer Newsletter, 31 Dec. 1709.

[61] Repertory 114, pp. 12-13, 49-50, 114-16, 311; Journal 55, fo. 194; *Post Boy* no. 2256, 27-9 Oct. 1709; *Post Man* no. 1811, 29 Oct.-1 Nov. 1709.

abuses of magisterial power by the Whigs. For instance, the Whig aldermen had previously intervened in disputed Common Council elections in two wards after the St. Thomas's Day wardmotes of December 1707. These episodes marked the first occurrence of magisterial adjudication of Common Council electoral squabbles since 1692. A year later the magistrates demonstrated blatant partisan prejudice in responding to two wardmote disagreements occasioned by an unsuccessful Whig effort to reverse the Tories' Common Council majority. The Whig magistrates dismissed a petition of forty-five Tory freemen of Broad Street who complained of wardmote mismanagements by Whig Alderman Sir Joseph Woolfe. On the other hand, the Whig aldermen accepted a similar petition from the Whig freemen of a Portsoken precinct and voided the election of a Tory common councilman. These incidents were all seen as examples of Whig disregard for electoral privileges and for Common Council autonomy, and they sorely offended the constitutional sensitivities of Tory common councilmen that had matured since the beginning of Anne's reign.[62]

Common Council was in fact no longer the passive body that had dutifully followed the lead of the Whig magistracy in the 1690s. With encouragement from the Tory aldermen and from other Tory City leaders, the common councilmen had begun to assume the role once envisaged for them in the Whigs' revolutionary draft statute for restoring the Corporation. In 1695 Common Council had been pilloried with the aldermen by the popular writers in the Common Hall controversy, but in Anne's reign the evolving institutional pretensions of Common Council reflected the consensual and participatory civic notions of many London guildsmen. By 1710 the Tory common councilmen were acting as representatives of the commons of London, as champions of electoral privileges, and as spokesmen for the articulation of popular sentiment about issues of pressing importance. After 1710, the Tory common councilmen were to declare their institutional independence from aldermanic supervision, to assume the right to scrutinize aldermanic proceedings, and even to defy aldermanic decisions in the queen's courts.

The first step in the early eighteenth-century 'rise' of Common Council may have been the passage of the 1703 Corporation act

[62] Repertory 112, pp. 64–8; Repertory 113, pp. 65–6, 71–2, 81–4; Journal 54, p. 635; CLRO Misc. MS 64.3.

for regulating shrieval elections. By granting Common Council the ultimate right of discharging shrieval nominees and sheriffs-elect, the act ensured frequent Common Council meetings, and these meetings might easily become the occasions for discussion of other matters. Common Council met with much greater regularity in the first years of Anne's reign than had been the case in the last years of William's reign. As the Common Council majority passed from the Whigs to the Tories, the Tory Lord Mayors seem also to have attached greater importance to Common Council meetings, frequently reminding the aldermen of their duty of attendance.[63] However, by 1705, and perhaps earlier, the aldermen were no longer exercising a veto over Common Council decisions. Moreover, in both 1707 and 1708, Common Council polls on disputed questions were settled by a majority vote of those present, despite a preponderance of aldermanic votes on the losing side.[64] Further signs of Common Council assertiveness followed the Whig magistrates' biased adjudication of the December 1708 Common Council elections. The Tory majority retaliated in early 1709 by restating the right of ward electors to be represented by resident common councilmen, and they expelled the Whig deputy alderman for Vintry, a long-time member of the Court, for non-residence in his ward. The common councilmen also acted to prevent magisterial manipulation of their debates by reviving as a standing order the 'Antient Practice' that no member should speak more than three times at any meeting without leave. Finally, in March 1709, the Corporation clerks began to keep a separate journal of the minutes of several Common Council committees. Although it was discontinued in 1716, the new journal marked another step in Common Council's institutional maturation, and its dates coincide with the height of Tory Common Council independence from the late Stuart Whig magistracy.[65]

The activities of the Tory Common Council majority in 1710 point to the completed metamorphosis of the City Tories as the party of Common Council opposition and the party of electoral

---

[63] Formal notification to the aldermen of Common Council meetings is especially noticeable beginning with the 1705–6 mayoralty of Tory Sir Thomas Rawlinson. Repertory 110, passim.

[64] *Daily Courant* no. 1122, 17 Nov. 1705; Journal 54, pp. 626–7, 647–8.

[65] Journal 55, fos. 22, 28; CLRO MS 210.7.

reform. All Whig aldermen and common councilmen were excluded from four important committees, including that which prepared an address to the crown in the wake of the Sacheverell trial. The Common Council address of 5 April 1710 was among the most outspoken of the deluge of loyalist addresses orchestrated at that time by Church-Tory politicians hoping to force a ministerial alteration. With scant reference to the recent City tumults on behalf of Sacheverell, the address instead condemned 'daring and Insolent Attacks' made on the constitution and damned the 'Republican Notions' and 'Anti-Monarchical principles' spread by 'Seditious and Scandalous Books and pamphlets'. Immediately caricatured in the Whig press as the 'Mob's Address' and as a false show of loyalty by crypto-Jacobites, the address was adopted only after strong Whig objection. It was carried after a poll that revealed 80 per cent of the common councilmen in attendance, and it was carried over the protests of the Whig aldermanic majority.[66]

In July 1710, the common councilmen acted on the recommendation of another all-Tory committee and repealed part of a 1683 by-law that seemed to interfere with Common Council's surveillance of shrieval nominees. In the same month another committee of Tories was charged with a general review of all past acts of the Corporation to 'determine which were fit to be retained and which ought to be repealed'. Not since the revolutionary year of 1689 had the Common Council—then prompted by radical Whigs —created such a committee. Furthermore, in an unusual August meeting, Common Council responded to the Whig manipulation of the Portsoken election by passing a new act regulating procedures for aldermanic elections. This measure required the possession of a £15,000 estate for eligibility for the magistracy, and it established procedures to be followed in the event of the election of an individual not so qualified. It also required that aldermanic wardmotes be summoned within four days of the death or resignation of an incumbent in order to prevent undue expenditures by candidates. The latter proviso may have been in response to Whig 'treating' in recent elections, as the instance of Sir Benjamin Green suggests. Whatever the case, the Whig aldermen did not

---

[66] Journal 55, fos. 169–70; BL Add. MS 36722, fo. 5; *The Mobb's Address to My Lord M—* (1710); *Post Boy* no. 2328, 13–15 Apr. 1710; Holmes, *Sacheverell*, pp. 238–9.

accept the new act without first searching City records for precedents upon which to challenge it.[67]

A critical constitutional cleavage had thus again opened in
London politics on the eve of Harley's successful ministerial coup
and the Tories' parliamentary march of 1710. As the City Whigs
again asserted their devotion to the politics of social order, the
City Tories finally composed their opposition chorus of Stuart
loyalism, High-Church devotion, electoral privilege, and Common Council activism. The leading voices that enunciated these
themes in City politics were those of the money-lending and
manufacturing rivals of the Whig-dissenting moneyed interest.
These same themes found an articulate response among middle
city ratepayers, struggling artisans, and an urban plebs of mechanic artificers. The release of social tensions in the Sacheverell
affair indicated the convergence of the many London fractures that
made 'the four last years of the queen' years of perpetual crisis in
the City.

[67] Journal 55, fos. 191, 194, 209, 212; Repertory 114, pp. 337-8, 353-4; *An Act Concerning the Election and Discharge of Aldermen* (1710).

VI

The Results of Party Conflict in the City:
A Fractured Society

―――◆◆◆――――

1. Introduction: The Press and the People

THE metamorphosis of the London Tories prefaced and permitted
the bitter party struggle for control of the Corporation that marked
the 'four last years of the queen'. Beginning with the parliamentary
election of 1710, the Corporation was wracked by a climactic party
confrontation that waxed and waned in intensity, but continued
without interruption into the reign of George I. Reflecting all the
fractures of London's political life, that confrontation is the subject
of this chapter. Analysis of the issues and events that sustained this
party dispute may be introduced by a discussion of the role the press
had come to play in the politics of City and state by 1710. The elections of 1710 were preceded and accompanied by a torrent of
printed political words that gained their edge from the Sacheverell
affair and retained that edge for some time thereafter.[1] The circumstances that allowed printed media to become so critical an element
in London politics had originated in 1695, the year that also marked
the political separation of monied Whigs from populist artisans.

The lapsing of press licensing in May 1695 initiated a 'communications revolution' with as profound an impact upon London
political culture as the commercial revolution and the financial
revolution. Like those developments, this revolution was a long-
term one, although its implications for national political life were
not fully realized before the mid-eighteenth century. The end of
licensing permitted a freer circulation of newspapers, tracts, and

[1] Mary Ransome, 'The Press in the General Election of 1710', *Cambridge Historical Journal*, vi. (1940), 210–11; Mary Ransome, 'Church and Dissent in the Election of 1710',
EHR lvi (1941), 76–89.

occasional pieces, and by encouraging the entrepreneurship of commercial printers, it also provoked experimentation with new forms of political journalism. The increasing volume of London publications after 1695 reached a notable apex during the public events of 1710, and this sustained burst of print differed greatly from the journalistic boomlets of 1678-83 and 1688-90. The number of printing houses in London had doubled since the Exclusion Crisis, and political writers were more professional, more confident, and more acceptable. The number of commercial newspapers published in London had increased from none in 1695 to eighteen in 1709 (including one daily), and as many as 60,000 or more single newspaper copies were issued each week.[2] Moreover, the keen political interests of the late Stuart readership had created such national best-sellers as Defoe's *True-Born Englishman* (1701) and Sacheverell's 1709 sermon. Only in the revolutionary decades of the 1640s and the 1650s had politics and print been so closely connected, but few individual pamphlets or papers of those years matched the circulation of their best known early eighteenth-century successors. Indeed, as the historian of the 'information explosion' of the 1750s and the 1760s has observed, the individual sales of newspaper issues, tracts, and periodical essays in the latter years of Anne's reign were comparable to those of the troubled early years of George III's reign, although the politics of print had matured in several additional respects in the intervening years.[3] In view of these developments, the belief of many Tory MPs in 1712 that the press again required some form of regulation should occasion little wonder. The wonder is rather whether the Tories had not actually gained more, politically, than their adversaries from the 'license of the press'.

The flourishing late Stuart English newspaper and periodical press has been much studied by historians of politics and by students of literature, satire, and Grub Street. The utilization of

---

[2] J. A. Downie, *Robert Harley and the Press: Propaganda and Public Opinion in the Age of Swift and Defoe* (Cambridge, 1979), p. 10; Michael Harris, 'London Printers and Newspaper Production during the First Half of the Eighteenth Century', *Printing Historical Society Journal*, 12 (1977-8), 33 n. 2; James R. Sutherland, 'The Circulation of Newspapers and Literary Periodicals, 1700-1730', *The Library*, 4th Ser., xv (1934), 110-24; Jacob M. Price, 'A Note on the Circulation of the London Press, 1704-14', *BIHR* xxxi (1958), 215-24; Henry L. Snyder, 'The Circulation of Newspapers in the Reign of Queen Anne', *Library*, 5th Ser., xxiii (1968), 206-35.

[3] John Brewer, *Party Ideology and Popular Politics at the Accession of George III* (Cambridge, 1976), pp. 157-60.

the press by party politicians, the fortunes of particular publishing ventures, and the careers of learned essayists and commercial newsmongers are each subjects that have received attention.[4] That the English press of the early eighteenth century was essentially a London press and that Londoners made up a large proportion of its primary audience are points that have been made. However, the effects of the sudden mass circulation of printed political media upon an already politically sophisticated civic population have received less attention. By 1710 the London civic public was undoubtedly the most frequently informed public in Europe, and it was perhaps the best informed as well. The relationship between printed media and public consciousness is not one that lends itself to simple generalizations. Nevertheless, three arguments about this relationship may be advanced, each of which bears upon the volatile state of City political life from 1710 to 1715.

First, the emergence of an extensive newspaper press, which was permitted by the end of censorship, greatly facilitated the political education of Londoners. Secondly, the utilization of all varieties of printed media by writers who championed opposing political perspectives contributed to an ideological polarization of public opinion along party lines, a polarization that was greatly in evidence in London by 1710. Even more so than the circulation of newspapers, the propagation of the political essay and the proliferation of the satirical print stimulated and reinforced antagonistic and ideological partisanship. Thirdly, as the press began to exert its new impact upon the people of London, the *menu peuple* of the Tory party began to exhibit the effectiveness of popular Tory propaganda. The libertarian City opposition that sprang up in the labouring wards and the lesser guilds owed at least part of its distinctive *élan* to the vigour of Church-Tory journalism.

The single sheet newspapers that multiplied after 1695 will be examined first. They quickly became an integral part of London's political culture and a critical agent in providing the London electorate with information about politics. To be sure, the proportion of their print devoted to London happenings was smaller than

[4] Recent literature on the Augustan press, party propaganda, Grub Street, and print culture includes Downie; Harris; Herbert Atherton, *Political Prints in the Age of Hogarth* (Oxford, 1974); W. A. Speck, 'Political Propaganda in Augustan England', *TRHS*, 5th Ser., 22 (1972), 17-32; Pat Rogers, *Grub Street: Studies in a Subculture* (1972), abridged and republished as *Hacks and Dunces* (1980).

that devoted to foreign intelligence or to state affairs. Nevertheless, profit- and party-minded printers quickly developed the potential of their papers as purveyors of London news, and by 1702 the newspapers were certainly as instrumental in informing the London electorate as such traditional printed media as the handbill and the broadside.

By the end of William's reign, newspapers were contributing to the political education of Londoners in at least two different ways, each of which became even more apparent in subsequent years. First, some newsmongers sought to promote the electoral chances of magisterial and parliamentary candidates of one party. This first became evident in selective newspaper references to the names of mayoral, aldermanic, and parliamentary candidates of one party and in the frequent omissions by the papers of the names of candidates of the opposite party.[5] During the early part of Anne's reign, direct comment about London politics became quite common in Abel Roper's Tory *Post Boy* and in George Ridpath's Whig *Flying Post*, and commentary about London polls could also be found in the moderately whiggish *Daily Courant* and *Post Man*. Secondly, by drawing attention to London elections, the newspapers contributed to popular interest and involvement in City polls. From their inception, the newspapers regularly advertised the calendar of municipal elections, the names of party leaders and party candidates, and other political information. They added systematic printed notice of City elections to verbal notice and to the occasionally circulated candidates' tickets. Such reiterated printed announcements clearly stimulated attention to the dates and personalities of Corporation electoral events. Indeed, the increased dissemination of information at election times by all the newspapers may have had more profound political consequences in London than the more blatant attempts at partisan persuasion by particular newsmongers.

This purveyance of political information by the newspapers and its electoral consequences in London can be illustrated in several ways. From the late 1690s, the papers adopted the practice of giving advance notice of Common Hall polls, frequently

[5] De Krey, 'Trade, Religion, and Politics', ii. 411–14. A more cautious view is presented by R. B. Walker in 'The Newspaper Press in the Reign of William III', *HJ* xvii (1974), 708. Also see E. S. De Beer, 'The English Newspapers from 1695 to 1702' in *William III and Louis XIV: Essays 1680–1720 by and for Mark A. Thomson*, eds. Ragnhild Hatton and J. S. Bromley (Liverpool, 1968), p. 128.

announcing the approaching date as much as ten days earlier and repeating the announcement in the interval. The papers also alerted the ward electorates of approaching wardmotes, although these events rarely gained as much attention as polls of the livery. As electoral interest quickened in the late 1690s, the newspapers also adopted the habit of presenting candidates in print in party pairings or groupings. Although explicit party labels were almost always avoided, the names of mayoral, aldermanic, and parliamentary candidates who were standing together frequently appeared together both in London news segments and in advertising segments. While many readers may not have needed such cues to discern party tickets, all London news readers became accustomed to associating candidates mentally in terms of party slates by observing their names together in print. In this fashion, even the most impartial listing of candidates assisted party leaders in discouraging electors from distributing their votes among multiple candidates according to criteria other than partisanship. Indeed, the perception of candidates in party groupings was so ingrained by the end of Anne's reign that only about 9 per cent of the London parliamentary pollers of 1710 and 1713 failed to vote for all four Whig candidates or for all four Tory candidates.

Another descriptive feature of the late Stuart papers that was laden with political potential was the seriatim publication of partial results of polls in progress. Such information assisted London party leaders in arousing the active electoral participation of their supporters. Even without printed instructions, London readers who were parliamentary electors, and who had not yet polled, could judge the state of a contest from partial printed results and still act, if so inclined. Party leaders and partisan printers also soon became aware of the effectiveness of drawing attention to partial results explicitly in order to persuade voters. For instance, during the parliamentary poll of 1708, when partial printed results showed that one of the four Whig candidates had no chance of winning, the Whig leaders withdrew his name publicly in the press in order to steer voters towards the stronger Whig candidates.[6] Both through efforts at persuasion and through the dissemination of information, therefore, the London newspapers contributed to the political education of Londoners and to their electoral participation.

[6] *Daily Courant* nos. 1947-8, 14-15 May 1708.

Newspapers were not the only printed genre that inflamed London's politics and that strengthened the ideological attachments of electors. London readers also imbibed continuous advice, instruction, and party tonic from the mounting volume of printed pamphlets, journals, and controversia. The authors of this body of literature hoped to influence the informed 'public opinion' that was especially characteristic of the first age of party.[7] However, in London, public opinion (or the 'sense of the people') was neither a *tabula rasa* easily inscribed by partisan pens, nor was it the fickle, floating, and unpredictable force it may have been in some constituencies.[8] If London public opinion may be equated with the London electorate, it was increasingly fractured along party lines—so deeply fractured as to make the history of City elections in the latter part of Anne's reign a tale of two hostile cities. Without a doubt, the press contributed both to widening the ideological gulf between Whig and Tory electors and to limiting the size of the City's 'floating vote'.[9]

These ideological effects of the press upon the people are the second question that will be explored in this section. The press stimulated party antagonism and ideological polarization in London in two ways. First, by linking local and national issues, the press constantly transported the political fury of the national macrocosm into the civic microcosm. Secondly, the press trained the party-conscious London public to perceive politics as a Manichaean struggle between parties of political goodness and political madness.

Relationships between the constitutional crises of 1678–83 and 1688–90 and the coincident London 'heats' had previously been emphasized in print; but by 1710, the deliberate association of national and local issues was commonplace in acerbic papers like the *Post Boy* and the *Flying Post*. Such journals as Defoe's *Review*, Tutchin's and Ridpath's *Observator*, and Leslie's *Rehearsal* joined the newspapers in treating their readers to coloured impressions

---

[7] Geoffrey Holmes, *The Electorate and the National Will in the First Age of Party* (Lancaster, 1976), pp. 4–9.

[8] See W. A. Speck, *Tory and Whig: The Struggle in the Constituencies 1701–1715* (1970), pp. 76–9; W. A. Speck, W. A. Gray, and R. Hopkinson, 'Computer Analysis of Poll Books: A Further Report,' *BIHR* xlviii (1975), 66–90; Norma Landau, 'Independence, Deference, and Voter Participation: The Behaviour of the Electorate in Early-Eighteenth-Century Kent', *HJ* xxii (1979), 561–83.

[9] The 'floating vote' in London politics is further discussed below in section 5.

of London affairs. Not surprisingly, when a renewed constitutional cleavage opened in the politics of the Corporation in 1709–10, the London citizenry construed this dispute in terms of the national issues of religion, public credit, and constitutional security with which it was strongly associated in the prints. The confrontation that developed then between Whig magistrates and populist Tory common councilmen was perceived by readers of the London press as a City variation of the conflict between national party leaders who represented opposing principles of government in church and in state. In 1709–10, as the drizzle of printed propaganda thickened to a deluge, parliamentary and magisterial debates were together transferred 'out of doors' from parliament and Guildhall into the coffee-houses, the taverns, and the streets of London. No constituency in the country was so saturated by the new politics of print as London. Few electorates became as intensely divided over yoked issues as that of the Corporation, and in few other localities did the outbreak of rhetorical violence by 1710 match that of the City.

This polarization of public opinion became sharper still as it developed around reverse or mirror images of Whig and Tory politicians as agents of light or minions of darkness. Through sarcasm, satire, and billingsgate, writers of varied quality embellished printed stereotypes of the 'character of a Whig' and the 'character of a Tory'. The devotion of London electors to Whig or to Tory principles became steadily more passionate as these fearful and hyperbolic images were propagated. Compromise and rational political discourse became scarcely possible in a rhetorical environment overrun by the partisan monsters projected by Whig and Tory pamphleteers, cartoonists, and poetasters.

From what substance were these images fashioned? Disparate pejorative attributes of Whig and Tory character that had previously circulated in the press were clarified in the prints and verses that accompanied the Sacheverell trial and the general election of 1710. Drawing upon a dissenting pedigree of regicide and republicanism, Church-Tory spokesmen skilfully sketched scenes of slavery and tyranny under the rule of Cromwellian Whigs.

However, the Tories had no need to look as far back as the Commonwealth and the Protectorate for examples of arbitrary Whig behaviour or trespass upon property. They needed only to point to the credit monopoly of the Bank, the never-ending series of war-related taxes, and the ominous parliamentary presence of City moneyed men to depict a rising tyranny of wealth, corruption, and financial oppression. Whig polemicists paid similar attention to history and to current affairs in their reverse portrayal of the Tories as past and present enemies of life, liberty, and prosperity. 'Popery and arbitrary government' was a shibboleth that still raised such Court-Tory spectres as Laud and Strafford or Father Petre and Judge Jeffreys. The loss of the war to France and the triumph of the Jacks were a Whig apocalypse coloured with 'Gallick Fury, and Tyrannick Sway' and the alienation of landed property to returning hosts of monks and friars.[10]

By 1710, the literary rhetoric of the revived rage of party suggested to readers in London and elsewhere that the drama of politics was being played in the antechamber of hell. Individual electors may have varied in the credence they gave to such catastrophic visions of a Whig or Tory future, but such rhetorical scenarios could not have filled the London prints unless they found support and response in the fears and fantasies of party-minded electors. Furthermore, as has already been suggested of the newspaper press, the manner of political journalism was as important as its substance in encouraging a polarization of public opinion. Pamphlets written as rejoinders to pamphlets, doggerel that barked at doggerel, and prints that mimicked prints reminded readers and electors of the divided world of party politics. Similarly, the dialogue format of such journals as the *Rehearsal* and the *Observator* and the sharp exchanges between Whig and Tory publications accustomed readers to thinking in terms of polar political opposites.

A final issue raised by the impact of print upon the political culture of London is the role of the press in the shifting fortunes of the City parties at the hands of the people after 1695. Two related questions need to be raised in order to address this issue. First, how did the press affect the social composition of the London audience actively involved in politics? Secondly, how did the press contribute to the emergence of Church-Tory populism in the Corporation by 1710? In response to the first question, the argument may be made that the Augustan press greatly enlarged the

[10] British Museum, *Catalogue of Prints and Drawings*, ii. no. 1496, p. 176. On stereotypes and the maturation of Tory images of the Whigs, see Downie, pp. 8, 103-30.

London audience who participated in politics in electoral, extra-constitutional, or vicarious capacities. What was revolutionary about the communications revolution was not simply the volume or the variety of publications, but also the cheapness of publications.[11] The explosion of print in Anne's reign was an explosion that scattered printed materials of political interest into the hands of people from even the most humble social ranks. Newspaper and journal issues that sold for a penny or less were affordable to most 'mechanicks', and even political tracts that sold for four pence to ten pence could be purchased, if only occasionally, from the artificer's pocket-book.

If the cheapness of most publications contributed to their circulation, so did the public availability of newspapers and reviews in many of London's hundreds of coffee-houses, inns, and taverns. The *habitué* of a public house might actually have had little need to purchase those publications of most interest to him. Those London coffee-houses and alehouses that provided the socially humble with a convivial meeting place could also provide them with a forum for discussing the current prints that circulated within their doors. Tradesmen, apprentices, and artificers found cheap refreshment for both their natural and political appetites in these places. Moreover, the less articulate and those unable to read could find tutelage here from their better informed and better read acquaintances.[12]

In other words, in the first years after the lapse of licensing, printed political media may have had a more profound effect upon those elements of society formerly less familiar with print than upon those who had previously belonged to the polite reading audience. The initial London beneficiaries of the communications revolution may well have been those whose political participation had sometimes been either limited by electoral privilege or orchestrated by magisterial leaders. Moreover, the influence of print

[11] J.H. Plumb, 'The Commercialization of Leisure' in Neil McKendrick, John Brewer, and J.H. Plumb, *The Birth of a Consumer Society: The Commercialization of Eighteenth-Century England* (1983), p. 267; Speck, 'Political Propaganda', pp. 20–1.

[12] Brewer, pp. 148–9, 155; R.S. Schofield, 'The Measurement of Literacy in Pre-Industrial England' in *Literacy in Traditional Societies*, ed. Jack Goody (Cambridge, 1968), pp. 312–13. However, as Peter Clark has emphasized, the assumption that public houses frequented by plebs were hothouses of popular discontent is open to many qualifications. See his 'The Alehouse and the Alternative Society', in *Puritans and Revolutionaries*, eds. Donald Pennington and Keith Thomas (Oxford, 1978), pp. 47–72.

upon the people was reciprocated. Some of the excesses of early eighteenth-century propaganda may be attributed to the exploitation of a new social audience, just as some of the excesses of that new audience in the streets may be attributed to the increasing impact of printed imagery, rhetoric, and political cues on minds relatively unfamiliar with them.

If the widening circulation of the political press broadened political awareness among artisans and 'mechanicks', the argument may also be made that the City Tories reaped more of the political harvest nurtured by the press than did the City Whigs. This was not because the country lacked able Whig publishers and writers. Rather, the Junto Whigs of parliament and the magisterial Whigs of the City unswervingly followed a course after 1700 that enabled the Tory press successfully to exploitWhig connections with dissent, the stocks, and the increasingly burdensome war. Rising civic Tory populism crested in 1709–10 as these themes were trumpeted by the Harleyite Country-Tory propaganda and the Sacheverellite High-Church propaganda of those years. Much of that propaganda was deliberately aimed at the people 'out of doors', and its effectiveness was demonstrated in 1710 when the people closed the parliamentary doors on Whig candidates and challenged the Whig magistracy in London. As J.A. Downie has observed, the events of 1710 'proved once and for all that in the eighteenth century governments were subject to public opinion'.[13] Further, as contemporary observers noted, the electoral participation of the 'common people' contributed greatly to creating the heavily Tory parliament of 1710.[14] In London, the triumph of the City Tories in the 1710 parliamentary election owed much to the increased participation of liverymen from the lesser guilds and to the increased proportion of their votes claimed by the Church party candidates. The City Whigs could be in no doubt thereafter about the effect of Church-Tory propaganda upon the City commons. The language and trappings of the crowds of 1710 and 1715–16 graphically demonstrated the transferral of printed Tory propaganda into the opposition culture of urban popular protest.

---

[13] Downie, p. 115.
[14] HMC *Portland MSS* v. 649; Holmes, *Electorate and the National Will*, p. 11.

2. 'The Year of Wonders is arriv'd', 1710 [15]

The year 1710 was a watershed in the politics of London and of the nation. As the ministry of the duumvirate and the Junto collapsed in 1710, the war in the press lost all restraint. As Robert Harley began the formation of a new ministry, his hope of providing the queen with a government of moderate men was doomed by the escalating campaign of Tory propaganda that he himself had initiated—albeit in a Country rather than a High-Church vein. In London, the year 1710 saw an unusual degree of popular participation in politics both out of doors and at the polls. Although the Sacheverellite disturbances of March were short-lived, the popular mood of expectancy and the anticipation of extraordinary events long persisted. [16] Against this background, the issues of City politics remained combustible, and the citizens of London divided ever more deeply along the numerous fractures of urban society. The fundamental catalysts of party controversy in London—the nonconformist presence, the relationship between government and wealth, the role of the people in politics, the question of war and peace—together produced a chain reaction of partisan explosions comparable only to the violent 'heats' of the City's revolutionary crisis twenty years earlier. If 1710 was a 'year of wonders', the greatest wonder in London was the humiliation of the City's Whig leaders. As the Tory press and the Tory politicians successfully broke the Whigs' hold on ministerial and parliamentary power, the London Tories and their populist sympathizers worked towards the same goal in the Corporation. Although the City Whigs survived the remarkable elections of 1710 with their aldermanic majority still intact, the authority of the City magistracy had become an open question as the 'year of wonders' came to an end.

London also provided the country with one of its principal issues in the 1710 parliamentary election—the question of public credit. The issue was first raised in June when Anne dismissed the Earl of Sunderland from her government and thereby alarmed the Junto's City friends. Among the latter was Sir Gilbert Heathcote,

[15] This title is derived from the first line of Defoe's *Age of Wonders* (1710), which is reprinted in *POAS* vii, 465-72.

[16] Lee Horsley, '*Vox Populi* in the Political Literature of 1710', *HLQ* xxxviii (1975), 335-53.

who at the time was governor of the Bank and next in line for the mayoral succession. The news of Sunderland's dismissal prompted Heathcote and a delegation of Bank directors to seek an immediate audience with the queen. Their insistence that any further ministerial changes would harm public credit and Anne's apparent reassurances to them were subsequently developed in the Tory press as the most notorious example yet of the arrogance of the City's Whig magnates.[17] Moreover, as events quickly demonstrated, neither the credit of the government nor that of the Bank was safeguarded by the remonstrances to the queen of Heathcote and his colleagues.

By early August, the size of the government's floating debt, the uneasiness of foreign creditors and stock investors, and the inability of the Treasury to meet its remittance contracts, had combined to depress the public stocks. Heathcote and his fellow Bank directors then again intervened in state affairs, this time with results the opposite of those they intended. They informed Godolphin, the Lord Treasurer, that they could no longer make advances to the government without further assurances from Anne about the continuation of the current government and the current parliament. When Godolphin in turn sought such assurances from the queen, he quickly found himself out of office and Harley quickly found himself in.[18] Although Harley hoped for good relations with the Bank, he learned after the ensuing dissolution of parliament that the 'pique and revenge of Heathcote's . . . party' made this impossible for the time being.[19] Neither the declining credibility of the government's funds nor the declining share value of the public stocks was easily reversed, and the general election of 1710 was accompanied by partisan charges and countercharges about who was responsible for the 'sinking of credit'.[20]

---

[17] HMC *Portland MSS* iv. 545; B.W. Hill, p. 400; Holmes, *British Politics*, pp. 174, 290.

[18] B.W. Hill, pp. 401-2; James Brydges to Mr Sencerf, 17 Aug. 1710 in 'Letters on Godolphin's Dismissal in 1710', eds. Clara Buck and Godfrey Davies, *HLQ* iii (1940), 232-3. Clayton Roberts, 'The Fall of the Godolphin Ministry', *JBS* xxiii (1982), 83-5.

[19] HMC *Portland MSS* iv. 618.

[20] *Examiner*, i. no. 5, 24-31 Aug. 1710 and no. 10, 28 Sept.—5 Oct. 1710; *Review*, vii. no. 6, 15 Aug. 1710, nos. 116-18, 21-6 Dec. 1710; Defoe, *An Essay upon Public Credit* (1710); *The Bank of England's Most Loyal Address to her M*[ajest]*y* (1710); *Reasons for a Total Change of a Certain M*[inistry] *and the Dissolution of P*[arliament] (1710); Downie, pp. 120-1, 124-5.

As governor of the Bank and as the magisterial captain of the London Whigs, Sir Gilbert Heathcote became the most controversial candidate in the City's 1710 polls. A public foe of Sacheverell, he was scarcely greeted with enthusiasm as a prospective Lord Mayor by the London Churchmen. The logical choice for a rival mayoral candidate was goldsmith-banker Sir Richard Hoare, the senior Tory alderman beneath the chair. An outspoken critic of the Bank, Hoare headed a family concern that was already providing Harley with the financial assistance denied him by Whig lenders.

As the mayoral Common Hall of 29 September approached, three developments quickened interest in it. The first of these was the dissolution of the 1708–10 parliament with its Whig-dominated Commons on the 21st, an event greeted with 'Illuminations, Ringing of Bells, [and] Bonefires' in the City.[21] The second development was the announcement of a Tory ploy to ensure Heathcote's embarrassment as a mayoral candidate. Recognizing the superiority of Heathcote's claim to the office by virtue of his aldermanic seniority, the Tories decided to encourage voting for the second-most senior alderman, Sir Robert Beachcroft. Although he was a Whig, and although he was already being promoted with Heathcote by the City Whigs, Beachcroft outranked Hoare in seniority and therefore had a better claim to the office. The Common Hall contest was thus one between a Whig ticket of Heathcote and Beachcroft and a Tory ticket of Hoare and Beachcroft.[22] Thirdly, the Tories advertised the election as a popular referendum about the recent behaviour of Heathcote and the Bank directorate. On the eve of the mayoral Common Hall, the *Post Boy* recommended the candidacies of Hoare and Beachcroft, 'who, tho' not so near the Chair as ANOTHER . . . have never intruded into the Royal Presence to direct their *Sovereign* in State-Affairs, or the Choice of her own Servants'.[23]

When the liverymen assembled in Common Hall on 29 September, both Tory preparation and agitation were in

[21] *Post Boy* no. 2398, 23–6 Sept. 1710.

[22] This ensured that Beachcroft would head the poll, and perhaps, reasoned the Tories, the Court of Alderman would choose him Lord Mayor in preference to Heathcote. The Tories had no illusions about Beachcroft's politics. 'For their principles', wrote John Dyer of Beachcroft and Heathcote, 'you may shake them in a Bagg'. BL Loan 29/321, Dyer Newsletter, 30 Sept. 1710.   [23] *Post Boy* no. 2400, 28–30 Sept. 1710.

evidence. Sir Peter King, the City's Recorder and one of the managers of Sacheverell's impeachment, recommended the election of Heathcote on the grounds of seniority, but he was loudly hissed. When the names of the candidates were put to the liverymen, the Whig sheriffs declared Heathcote to have the majority of voices, but the Tories demanded a poll on behalf of Hoare and Beachcroft. Although Hoare finished last, the combined support of Whig and Tory electors gave Beachcroft some 2,000 votes more than Heathcote in a poll that attracted exceptional participation. As the poll ended, a Common Hall riot nearly erupted between Whig and Tory liverymen still present, amidst popular cries of '*No Whig Lord Mayor, No Forty One, No Murderers of the King*' and replies of '*No Pretender, No Wooden Shoes*'. Despite Beachcroft's lead, the Whig aldermanic majority declared Heathcote to be Lord Mayor.[24]

Heathcote and the Whigs had little time to savour the mayoral victory before the reassembling of Common Hall for the City's parliamentary election and the ensuing poll, which began on 10 October. Although confident of victory, the Whigs were dismayed by the ministerial announcement and publication on the very day the poll began of a new London Lieutenancy commission in which 'Tories were put in and Whigs were left out'. This announcement was obviously intended to damage the City Whig candidates.[25] With the crown's pleasure made clear, the London liverymen were also confronted with a startlingly clear choice between partisan candidates who reflected the many fractures in London's political life.

The four Whig candidates were Heathcote, Sir William Ashurst, Sir James Bateman, and John Ward. All four were overseas merchants long active in trade, and all four were aldermen, three of them sitting for inner city wards. Heathcote, Ashurst, and Ward had been City MPs in the previous parliament. Ashurst was a Presbyterian, Heathcote and Ward had dissenting connections, and Bateman came from a Dutch Calvinist family intermarried with leading London dissenters. Moreover, the Whigs could not have chosen four men more strongly associated with the moneyed interest. Heathcote and his three colleagues were all

---

[24] Journal 55, fo. 217; Repertory 114, p. 348; *Observator*, ix. no. 76, 4–7 Oct. 1710; *Post Boy* no. 2401, 30 Sept.–3 Oct. 1710; Luttrell, *Brief Relation*, vi. 635.

[25] Tindal, ii. 192; Burnet, vi. 16.

present or past Bank directors. Three of the four Whigs were former New East India Company directors, and Ward and Bateman had served as United Company directors since the East India merger.

The four Tory candidates were Hoare, Sir William Withers, Sir George Newland, and John Cass. Withers was both the only overseas trader among the Tory foursome and the only one who had previously held major joint-stock directorships. The occupations of the three other Tories mirrored the composition of the City Tory élite. As previously noted, goldsmith-banker Hoare was the Bank's arch City enemy. Newland was a Smithfield scrivener, and builder-carpenter John Cass was a leading industrial employer. Only Hoare and Withers were sitting aldermen, but three of the four Tory candidates were involved in the politics of middle city wards or wards without the walls. Withers and Newland were also principals in the populist Tory Common Council opposition to the Whig magistrates. Newland was among the best known City friends of Sacheverell, and Cass was establishing his reputation as a High-Church charity school philanthropist.[26]

The 1710 London parliamentary poll was conducted and concluded in an atmosphere of rhetorical and physical violence unmatched since the Revolution. The issues of the *Post Boy* and its *Supplement* that preceded the poll blasted the Whigs' dissenting interests and Heathcote's regard for the old ministry. Publisher Abel Roper also sounded the populist and pacifist themes of London toryism in his condemnation of the four Whigs as war-profiteers who valued the Bank's credit more than the well-being of the citizenry or the trade of the nation.[27]

As the poll continued through its five-day course, Whig and Tory papers competed in soliciting the votes of liverymen for the candidates they favoured. All four Whigs established sizeable leads on the first day of the poll, but thereafter a steady influx of Tory liverymen to Guildhall gradually gave victory to the Church candidates. If Daniel Defoe's description may be accepted, Whig pollers experienced increasing difficulty in recording their votes: 'A Lane of . . . *Furies* . . . plac'd themselves from the Entrance of the Hall, up to the Hustings . . . through whom . . . every Man

26 *Observator*, ix. no. 87, 11–15 Nov. 1710; Holmes, *Sacheverell*, p. 128.
27 *Post Boy* no. 2404, 7–10 Oct. 1710; *Supplement* no. 428, 9–11 Oct. 1710.

that came to Poll, was oblig'd to pass.' Among those insulted by these 'furies' was candidate and Lord Mayor-Elect Heathcote, who was jostled, hectored, and spat upon when he appeared to inspect the progress of the poll.[28]

The Whigs' insistence upon a time-consuming scrutiny postponed the final declaration of the Tories' victory for a month, but the London crowd celebrated the Churchmen's triumph at the close of the poll on the evening of 14 October. Some reports of the evening's disturbances suggest that the new Tory Lieutenancy commissioners were either unable or unwilling to interfere with the mob, and the fact that 14 October was also the birthday of James II gave rise to ominous Whig interpretations. Disturbances began in inner city wards near Guildhall, but the noise in the streets quickly spread westward into the large peripheral ward of Farringdon Without and the adjacent out-parishes. There the Sacheverell crowd had also accomplished much of its work, and if 14 October 1710 lacked the pyrotechnic displays of 1 March 1710, this night was not lacking in personal abuse and violence. The mob stopped coaches, rifled passengers, broke windows, and knocked down those who challenged their High-Church mottos. Even a sympathetic observer agreed that the crowd's extension of the parliamentary poll into the streets was without parallel: 'Ye Bells fell a Ringing for Joy as ye Church men would have pulled ye Steeples down. Ye Citty was illuminated with candles and Bonefires and there was such a mobb Runing to and frow— huzzaing & rejoycing that ye like has been hardly seen upon any occasion.'[29]

Riotously celebrated in the streets, the parliamentary poll was also celebrated enthusiastically in Tory prints and poems that heralded the Churchmen's victory as a presage of peace, the restoration of credit, and the easing of taxation.[30] Populist Tory pleasure at the election of 'Four Loyal-Members' was diminished

[28] *Review*, vii. no. 90, 21 Oct. 1710. *Post Man* no. 1927, 12–14 Oct. 1710; *Post Boy*, nos. 2405-6, 10–14 Oct. 1710; *Daily Courant* no. 2801, 14 Oct. 1710; Tindal, ii. 193. Of the four Whigs, John Ward, who trailed John Cass by only sixteen votes, came the closest to election.

[29] BL Loan 29/321, Dyer Newsletter, 17 Oct. 1710. *Observator*, ix. no. 79, 14–18 Oct. 1710 and x. no. 31, 14–18 Apr. 1711; *Review*, vii. no. 91, 24 Oct. 1710 and no. 116, 21 Dec. 1710; Tindal, ii. 193.

[30] British Museum, *Catalogue of Prints*, ii. no. 1549-50, pp. 336–40. See jacket illustration of this volume for 'Londons Happynes in Four-Loyal Members'.

only by the commencement of Heathcote's mayoralty and by the continued difficulty of MP-elect John Cass in securing the aldermanic seat of Portsoken. When Heathcote proceeded to Westminster on 30 October to be sworn, Tory aldermen absented themselves from his cavalcade, and those people out of doors for the occasion 'were so unmannerly and rude as to hiss & Scoff'.[31] Heathcote was also among those Whig magistrates who blocked John Cass's second aldermanic nomination by a Portsoken wardmote in October and who rejected a third 'unanimous' selection of the popular City builder in November. According to customary constitutional procedures, because three wardmote nominations had been turned down by the Court of Aldermen, the Court was now empowered to name an alderman of its own choosing for the vacant seat. The Whig aldermen failed to take such precipitous action, though, because their initial dismissal of Cass's name had prompted Common Council's recent act for the revision of aldermanic election procedures. Nevertheless, the case of John Cass, which was followed closely in Tory papers and newsletters, served to advertise the continuing magisterial obstruction of the electoral will.[32]

However, the Whig magistrates were themselves obstructed by the popular will when Common Council was selected on 21 December. The Whigs had good reason to be concerned about the composition of Common Council, given the populist tendencies exhibited by it earlier in the year. Their concern turned to panic after St. Thomas's Day, 1710. The wardmotes saw a turnover of almost 23 per cent in the membership of Common Council. This was roughly twice the average annual turn-over of 1700–9. The partisan break-down of the new Common Council suggests that an orchestrated eviction of sitting Whig common councilmen had taken place. Tory common councilmen numbered 141, an increase of thirty-one, and Whig common councilmen numbered only fifty-nine, a decrease of twenty-seven.[33] The Tories' Common Council victory extended even into the Whig-

[31] BL Loan 29/321, Dyer Newsletters, 21 Oct. and 31 Oct. 1710; Luttrell, *Brief Relation*, vi. 648.
[32] Repertory 115, pp. 52–3. Also see Repertory 114, p. 363; Repertory 115, pp. 8–9; *Post Boy* no. 2412, 26–8 Oct. 1710 and no. 2415, 2–4 Nov. 1710; BL Loan 29/321, Dyer Newsletters, 26 Oct. 1710 and 14 Nov. 1710.
[33] Of the remainder, twenty were of ambiguous partisanship, and the names or political preferences of fourteen are unknown.

dissenting inner city sanctum where, for the first time since 1690, Tories gained more seats than Whigs.[34] Still, the greatest strength of the Tories among the ward electorates remained in the middle city and the city without the walls. Of the 121 common councilmen returned for those wards in 1710, a mere fourteen were definitely Whigs. The Church-Tory sentiments of the artisans and 'mechanicks' who figured so largely in the electoral population of those wards could not have been revealed with greater clarity. Moreover, this Tory victory was also a victory for popular libertarianism. As one Tory observer wrote, 'now tis expected in ye first Common Concell that is held that they'll Repeal the By Law that putt ye Choice of an Alderman into ye hands of yt Court and will return it to themselves'.[35]

The Common Council election dramatically concluded London's 'Year of Wonders'. The year had seen the Junto fall, the party majority in the Commons reversed, the Whig magistrates checked, the dissenting interest repulsed, the Tory Common Council reinvigorated, and the City twice disturbed by tumultuous mobs. The general election of 1710 was followed by the articulation of Tory hopes for domestic concord, but the outlook for civic harmony in London was not auspicious. The institutional rift between the aldermen and the common councilmen had continued to widen, relations between the ministry and the City moguls of corporate finance and investment had never been worse, and even the London Tory leaders must have been surprised by the depth of popular distaste for the Whig magistrates.

3. The Parties and the City Constitution, 1710–13

Locked in a partisan confrontation by 1710, Whig magistrates and populist common councilmen engaged in a constitutional tug-of-war during the three years between the parliamentary elections of 1710 and 1713. In an attempt to preserve their authority in the Corporation, the Whig magistrates frequently exercised the prerogatives of their offices, sometimes doing so in a very heavy-handed fashion. Their behaviour elicited Tory charges that the

---

[34] Nevertheless, the steadfastness of Whig and dissenting inner city electors prevented a complete rout of the sitting Whig common councilmen. Forty-five of the surviving Whig common councilmen were returned for inner city wards.

[35] BL Loan 29/321, Dyer Newsletter, 21 Dec. 1710.

City had again fallen under 'arbitrary and despotick' rule. Moreover, Common Council responded by acting to defend its own power, to revise and reform further the procedures for City elections, and to champion the rights of the electorate. As these events occurred, constitutional authority in the City became almost as uncertain and ambiguous as it had been in 1690.

Central to this political and institutional contest were the outcomes of an unusual number of aldermanic elections. Twelve aldermanic seats fell vacant between 1710 and 1713, providing the City Tories with the welcome opportunity to gain aldermanic places on the strength of the popular rapport which they had demonstrated in 1710. Tory candidates gained election for seven of these twelve vacancies, but they were not as successful in acquiring former Whig inner city seats as in retaining former Tory seats for the middle city and the city without the walls. On the eve of the 1713 parliamentary election, the Whigs still possessed a magisterial majority of fifteen places to the Tories' eleven. However, several of the elections carried by Whigs produced extremely close polls, and some new Whig aldermen owed their seats more to magisterial manipulation than to electoral support. The most important of these disputed aldermanic elections will be reviewed briefly in order to establish the context for the Common Council opposition which they prompted.

These new disputes were preceded by one notable Whig effort at compromise. In January 1711, the Court of Aldermen finally accepted City MP John Cass as Alderman of Portsoken after his fourth nomination by the Portsoken inhabitants. Cass's election to the magistracy was balanced, however, by the simultaneous co-option to the bench of another Whig merchant prince as alderman for Bridge Without (Southwark). Chosen for this office was Francis Eyles, a Levant and colonial merchant and a former Bank governor. If the Whigs expected to receive popular credit for this trade-off, they were sadly mistaken.[36]

Some months later party tensions erupted anew over the choice of an alderman for Broad Street, a contest in which leading parts were taken by two of the principals in the 1710 City

---

[36] Repertory 115, pp. 71-3. Bridge Without was an unusual ward with no Common Council representatives, and the right of electing its alderman had been transferred from the Southwark inhabitants to the Court of Aldermen in the sixteenth century. Pearl, *London and the Puritan Revolution*, p. 28.

parliamentary election. Sir George Newland, the only City MP without an aldermanic place, was one of the candidates favoured by the ward's Tory inhabitants. Lord Mayor Heathcote, who presided at the Broad Street wardmote of 13 September 1711, placed his authority at the disposal of the rival candidates favoured by the Whig inhabitants. These included Gerrard Conyers, a Levant merchant and Bank director, and Sir John Scott, a long-time Presbyterian common councilman for the ward. An inner city ward, Broad Street nevertheless included several poor precincts adjacent to middle city and exterior wards, and the nonconformity of the Whig candidates aroused High-Church ire. Although the Tories carried a wardmote poll, Heathcote intervened in the scrutiny to ensure that Conyers's name was among those forwarded to the Court of Aldermen. The Court proceeded to elect Conyers in the face of Tory outrage in the ward, in the press, and in Common Council.[37]

The 1712 aldermanic poll in Langbourn, another inner city ward, followed a similar pattern. Like Broad Street, Langbourn was divided between wealthy retail precincts surrounded by other inner city wards and less wealthy precincts bordering on middle city wards. Sir Robert Beachcroft, who had succeeded Heathcote as Lord Mayor, presided over the wardmote of 9 July 1712. The Langbourn Whigs proposed the nominations of the Lord Mayor and of Peter Delmé, a Bank director and Levant and Iberian merchant with Huguenot, Dutch, and dissenting family connections. The Langbourn Tories preferred Sir Samuel Clark, recently designated a South Sea Company director, and Sir William Withers, City MP and a sitting alderman. As in Broad Street, the Tory candidates claimed a majority in the poll, but after a scrutiny Beachcroft declared results favourable to himself and to Delmé. At a Court of Aldermen held on 'an unusual day' in September, the Whig magistrates welcomed Delmé to their ranks. This action provoked an uproar at the next Court of Common Council and lent further credence to the *Post Boy* charge that 'such arbitrary Proceedings' were destroying the 'Rights and Privileges' of the London citizenry.[38]

[37] Journal 55, fos. 270, 288, 355–6; Repertory 115, pp. 398–402; Repertory 116, pp. 34–5, 81–90; *Post Boy* no. 2589, 13–15 Dec. 1711; *Supplement* no. 573, 12–14 Sept. 1711 and no. 591, 24–6 Oct. 1711; GL, *A True and Impartial Account of the Poll of the Inhabitants of the Ward of Broad Street . . . 13th of September, 1711.*

[38] Journal 55, fos. 338–41; Repertory 116, p. 312; CLRO Misc. MS 248.1; *Post Boy* no. 2671, 21–4 June 1712 and no. 2708, 16–18 Sept. 1712; Carswell, p. 276.

Given the mayoral conduct of Heathcote and Beachcroft, the London Tories had great cause for relief when Sir Richard Hoare was installed as Lord Mayor in October 1712. During his mayoralty, Hoare presided over wardmote nominations for four aldermanic places, and whether as a result of this influence or not, Tory candidates prevailed on each occasion. The most dramatic of these elections was that for Bishopsgate, a heavily populated ward divided by the wall between inner city and peripheral precincts. The Bishopsgate wardmote of 23 March 1713 was summoned on the day of the expiration of the three-year gag placed on Dr Sacheverell by the House of Lords. This event was an occasion for rejoicing among the doctor's popular London supporters, and it could not have failed to have an effect upon the Bishopsgate electors. Their nomination of a long-time Bishopsgate Tory common councilman, tobacconist Joseph Lawrence, produced a novel obstructionist manœuvre by the Whig aldermen. Ignoring the Lord Mayor's repeated summonses for a Court of Aldermen, the Whig magistrates deprived the Court of its quorum for six weeks. Not until mid-May did they reappear and acquiesce in the election of Lawrence, prompted perhaps by the appointment of a Common Council committee to examine the behaviour of 'Runaway Aldermen'.[39]

At no other time since the Revolution had the City Whigs shown such apparent disregard for the electorate as in these controversial aldermanic elections. The Whig aldermen clearly were straining the available mayoral and aldermanic prerogatives in flexing their magisterial muscle at the expense of ward electors. They may nevertheless have been convinced of the propriety of their behaviour for two reasons. First, decision-making in aldermanic selection had traditionally involved both ward inhabitants and the Court of Aldermen, according to an electoral formula that combined a debatable degree of popular consent with a debatable degree of magisterial authority. Secondly, and rather paradoxically, the formerly libertarian Whigs could easily rationalize their present anti-libertarian conduct as a defence of the Revolution they had endorsed in 1688–9. They believed that the security of that Revolution was imperilled by a disloyal ministry, an irresponsible Commons, a plague of high-flying clerics, and a misled

---

[39] Journal 56, fos. 44, 51–2; Repertory 117, p. 180 et seq.; *Post Boy* no. 2788, 21–4 Mar. 1713 and no. 2813, 19–21 May 1713; *Flying Post* no. 3353, 24–6 Mar. 1713.

urban plebs. Among the cries in the streets in October 1710 had been the announcement of 'A new Revolution!', and the City Whigs felt that this was a call for the effacement of their own Revolution. Moreover, among the magisterial candidates proposed by the City Tory electors were persons whose loyalty to the Hanoverian Succession was doubted by the Whig magistrates. Sir George Newland's Sacheverellite leanings bespoke a Jacobite family mentality, and Sir Samuel Clark's principles were also 'suspected'. Whig rhetoric about the Jacobite peril in the 'last four years of the queen' was decidedly more than electoral propaganda.[40]

The Whig magistrates' unmistakable disregard for the electoral liberties which they had once championed was grist for the populist mill now turned by the City's Tory leaders. Both the Common Council's actions of 1710 and the Tory cleansing of the Court in the 1710 wardmotes had been preparatory to a campaign for radical revisions in the Corporation's working constitution. Gaining additional incentive from repeated instances of magisterial belligerence, the Tory common councilmen embarked between 1710 and 1713 upon an implementation of the participatory conception of the Corporation's constitution that the revolutionary Whigs had favoured in 1690. The first Court of Common Council summoned after the 1710 wardmotes appointed a committee of Tories to prepare a new bill to regulate the election of aldermen. This bill received two readings in Common Council in May 1711, but precisely how radical its provisions were is uncertain. What happened when Common Council met to consider the bill for the third time is more certain, despite the clerk's cryptic minute that 'Nothing was done at this Common Councell.' The bill provoked an aldermanic veto which was twice approved over Tory objections at June aldermanic courts.[41]

A different bill about aldermanic vacancies was approved after much debate at a September Common Council. This measure struck at magisterial authority in aldermanic elections in two important respects, although it failed to provide for the direct elec-

---

[40] HMC *Portland MSS* v. 659; GL MS 12,017, fo. 28; *Observator*, x. no. 31, 14–18 Apr. 1711; 'Minutes of a Whig Club', p. 21; Sedgwick, ii. 293; H. T. Dickinson, 'The October Club', *HLQ* xxxiii (1969–70), 171–2.

[41] Journal 55, fos. 244–5, 249–50; Repertory 115, pp. 52–3, 111–12, 171–2, 244–5, 257.

tion of aldermen that the Tories probably desired. First, the 1711 bill curtailed the magistrates' freedom of choice by reducing the number of wardmote nominations from two commoners and two sitting aldermen to one nominee of each status. If the aldermanic nominee should decline to take the vacant seat, the Court of Aldermen was obliged to elect the single commoner. Secondly, the act stripped the aldermen of their freedom in filling the seat for Bridge Without, as they had recently done. It required that future vacancies for Bridge Without be offered to all sitting aldermen above the chair in the order of their seniority. In the event that no senior alderman desired the seat, the Alderman of Bridge Without was to be elected by Common Council according to the 'plurality of voices', a proviso that exempted such an election from any aldermanic veto.[42]

If Common Council's populist majority expected their new act to encourage magisterial restraint, they were sorely disappointed by the outcome of the 1711 Broad Street aldermanic election. Common Council again asserted its independence from aldermanic authority after receiving from aggrieved Broad Street inhabitants a petition that had been promoted by the ward's Tory common councilmen. The petitioners informed Common Council that they had initiated a motion for redress in Queen's Bench 'for the Supporting and ascertaining the Rights and Liberties of themselves and others citizens and Freemen of this City'. Requesting the approval of the Court of Common Council for this motion, the Broad Street petitioners were gratified by the initiation of a *quo warranto* suit against Heathcote by Common Council, by the appointment of a Tory committee to prosecute it, and by instructions that the cost of 'trying' the election of Gerard Conyers as alderman be met from the City chamber. Such a legal challenge to the jurisdiction of the Lord Mayor and Court of Aldermen was highly unusual, and its instigation was a measure of the resolution of the populist common councilmen to rescue electoral rights from magisterial trespass. The judges refused to issue an immediate mandamus against Heathcote, but the undismayed common councilmen thereafter yearly persisted with a suit against Conyers as the 'pretended' Alderman of Broad Street.[43]

[42] Journal 55, fos. 261–2; *An Act to Regulate the Elections of Aldermen* (1711).
[43] Journal 55, fos. 270, 335–6; CLRO Misc. MS 241.1; *Post Boy* no. 2582, 27–9 Nov. 1711.

Party passions in the City peaked again after the 1712 Langbourn election demonstrated that neither legal challenges nor acts of the Corporation were deterrents to Whig aldermanic determination to retain control of the magistracy. In September 1712, Common Council zealots were deprived of a resolution of two hours' debate about the Langbourn poll when presiding Lord Mayor Beachcroft suffered an incapacitating stroke in their presence. Not until the mayoral installation of Sir Richard Hoare did Langbourn Tory petitioners receive Common Council agreement with their claim that 'the Rights and Liberties of the Freemen of this City, are now, again, apparently invaded'. In November 1712 the common councilmen resolved to challenge the election of Whig Peter Delmé as Alderman of Langbourn, and in December they enacted another anti-magisterial act over Whig objections. Three provisions of this act require mention. It detailed extensive procedures for wardmote polls and scrutinies designed to preserve the rights of ward electors. It provided for public adjudication by the sheriffs of all objections to votes in Common Hall polls. It also discharged several deputy aldermen who were not common councilmen and required for the future that every alderman choose his deputy from the sitting common councilmen of his ward. This third provision of the act emphasized the importance of deputy aldermen as liaisons between ward officers and their aldermen, and it may have been intended to encourage the transit of populist Common Council leaders to the bench via the office of deputy alderman.[44]

Additional constitutional issues were raised by Common Council's reaction to the Whig magistrates' obstruction of the 1713 Bishopsgate aldermanic election. In May of that year, Common Council appointed a committee to investigate the extent to which the conduct of the Whig aldermen had been injurious to Corporation affairs, and in so doing the Tory common councilmen assumed that their Court enjoyed some measure of oversight of aldermanic conduct of routine Corporation business. The inspection of the town clerk's minutes of aldermanic courts by this Common Council committee was an affront to the traditional jurisdiction of the Court of Aldermen, which claimed the right to approve the minutes of the

[44] Journal 55, fos. 338-41, 346, 355-6; Repertory 116, pp. 320-1; Repertory 117, p. 41; *Post Boy* no. 2708, 16-18 Sept. 1712 and no. 2710, 20-3 Sept. 1712; *An Act for further regulating the Nominations and Elections of Aldermen and Common-Councilmen* (1712).

Court of Common Council. The end of the Whig aldermanic boycott terminated the work of this committee without diminishing Common Council's dissatisfaction with the magistracy. Sir Richard Hoare's mayoralty concluded with the appointment of another Tory committee with instructions to prepare a bill 'for restoring to the Freemen Inhabitants in the several wards of this City their antient Right of electing Aldermen'.[45]

As the Tory common councilmen asserted the rights of the City electors, they sought also to maintain the status of the freemen in the Corporation. Among the Tories' complaints about the Whig magistrates was their granting of too many freedoms to individuals not qualified by trade or by training. Among the Tories' complaints about Heathcote and Beachcroft was their connivance in the ward polling of strangers, foreigners, and unfreemen. When parliament deliberated the merits of the Whigs' 1709 Naturalization Act, the City Tories raised complaints about unfree and undenizened merchants who contrived to escape import duties owed to the crown and to the City chamber. In 1713, Common Council named a committee to review a popular petition complaining about abuses of the freedom. In other words, after 1710, the City Tories displayed much sensitivity to the guildsmen's conception of the Corporation as an organic association of independent craft practitioners whose possession of the freedom was also a claim to exclusive political and occupational liberties. Although the City Tories had expressed reservations about the reconfirmation of the freeman franchise in 1692, they were now clearly in favour of it. Already in political possession of those wards where the rich unfree were few, the Tories were troubled by the strength of the Whigs in the wards where the rich unfree were many. For the London Tories, ward democracy was an affair for the freemen only because the Tories found their supply of electoral support chiefly among the mass of labouring, 'meckanick', and artisan freemen.[46]

The decisions of the common councilmen between 1710 and 1713 just as surely measured the distance the City Tories had travelled since 1689–90 as the actions of the Whig magistrates measured their libertarian apostasy. The new Tory leaders who sponsored populist City by-laws had forgotten the old royalist cries that civic populism under Whig aegis would turn the Corporation

<hr />

[45] Journal 56, fos. 44, 51–2, 79; *Commune Concilium tentum . . . 30 Junii* (1713).
[46] Journal 55, fos. 324–5; Journal 56, fos. 7, 50–1, 76.

into a 'commonwealth'. Loudly proclaiming their loyalty to
queen and to Church, the London Tories were responsible for
acts that either implemented or implied the old radical Whig
model of participatory City government. They had put aldermanic elections upon a quasi-popular footing. They had shown
little regard for aldermanic vetoes or for aldermanic privileges
vis-à-vis Common Council. They had asserted Common Council's
right to adjudicate disputes about its own membership, and in
their Queen's Bench suits they denied the aldermen a similar
right over disputed aldermanic places. In all their actions, the
City Tories behaved as if Common Council was the proper centre
of Corporation government, and as if the Court of Aldermen was
merely the last bastion of 'a Factious and malitious party'. Not
since the mid-seventeenth century had Common Council so
strongly urged its authority against that of the magistracy. Moreover, by insisting upon the electoral rights of ward housekeepers
and by stressing the role of the deputy alderman as an inter-
mediary between each ward and its alderman, the Tories were
suggesting that magisterial authority was more strongly rooted in
the wards than in the continuity of the aldermanic bench.[47]

4. The London Parties and the Ministry, 1710–13: The Stocks, Peace, and Trade

City affairs were greatly affected by the actions of the new Tory
ministry and by those of the new Tory Commons in the interval
between the parliamentary elections of 1710 and 1713. As in the
years 1689–90 and 1699–1702, Westminster disputes contributed
significantly to disputes in the City and vice versa. The leadership
of the public stocks, the funding of the government debt, the making of peace, and the re-establishment of commercial relations
with France were all issues that fed the 'rage of party' in the City
and in parliament. In London, the struggle between magisterial
Whigs and populist common councilmen was accompanied in
1711 by a struggle for control of the stocks, and many of the principal combatants in the former arena were also participants in the
latter. Commercial uncertainties joined ideological disagreements
as causes of the deepening fractures in London politics during the
'last four years of the queen'.

[47] Journal 55, fos. 321–2.

The unexpected magnitude of the Tory upheaval of 1710 sent shock waves through the whiggish City complex of corporate enterprise, trade, and finance. Although some captains of City wealth made a quick accommodation to the new ministry, the strong ties of other moneyed men to the old ministry made accommodation on their part somewhat more difficult. Relations between the Bank and the Treasury improved after the election, but Harley continued to distrust many of the Bank's directors.[48] Moreover, when an internal reaction on the part of some Bank stockholders developed against Sir Gilbert Heathcote and his governing associates of 1710, Harley was happy to encourage such discontent. A similar rift developed in early 1711 between the directorate of the United East India Company and major shareholders dissatisfied with the directorate's Junto connections.

A rather quiet affair in most years, the election of directors in both companies in April 1711 became a referendum on the public behaviour and the political interests of the directors of 1710. In each company, an 'establishment' ticket of proposed directors was opposed by a rival ticket of major stockholders who enjoyed Harley's encouragement and who were pledged to his support. These 'ministerial' challengers to the Bank and East India establishments were largely unsuccessful, but Harley quickly found rewards for them. He had already made proposals in the Commons for incorporating the government's unfunded debt into a new joint-stock company, and when the South Sea Company received parliamentary blessing in May 1711, many of Harley's Bank and East India friends received directorates in the new stock.[49] The funding of the floating government debt into this new corporation solved the crisis of confidence in public credit that had plagued the Tory government from its beginning. However, the South Sea Company was not simply a Tory answer to the City Whig corporate establishment, and the 1711 divisions within the Bank and the East India Company were not simply contests betwen Whig and Tory tickets. Both contests need to be examined in order to understand the City's adjustment to the new ministry and the relationship between stock politics and party politics.

The disagreements within the Bank surfaced at a meeting of the General Court of stockholders on 5 April. A motion critical of

---

[48] B. W. Hill, pp. 406–11; HMC *Portland MSS* v. 651–2.
[49] Sperling, 'Division of 25 May 1711', pp. 194–5; Sperling, *South Sea Company*, pp. 6–7.

Heathcote and those directors who had visited the queen in 1710 was offered. This motion was 'suppress'd' in favour of a contrary one promoted by Whig Alderman John Ward, who was nevertheless among those sitting directors who had extended assurances to Harley. The choice of new directors on 13 April was animated by the appearance of Henry Sacheverell, a recent purchaser of stock, whose arguments on behalf of the ministerial ticket were angrily shouted down. Some 1,500 stockholders took part in a poll between opposing candidates for governor, deputy governor, and thirteen of the Bank's twenty-four directorships. Candidates for eleven directorships were acceptable to both sides, but all the ministerial candidates were defeated by a margin of about two-to-one.[50]

The successful Bank establishment ticket and the unsuccessful ministerial ticket differed in several respects. The establishment ticket was headed by Nathaniel Gould, candidate for Bank governor and one of the queen's 1710 visitors, and the list also included Sir Gilbert Heathcote. The ministerial ticket was headed by Sir James Bateman, who had made overtures to Harley. It also included John Blunt, one of the South Sea projectors, and Sir Theodore Janssen, a Treasury remitter under Godolphin who had agreed to serve Harley. Only one of the ministerial candidates other than Bateman and Janssen was a previous Bank director, but twelve of the fifteen establishment candidates had previously held the office. Including four sitting aldermen, the establishment ticket was also far more extensively tied to the City magistracy than the ministerial candidates were.

Some historians have described the ministerial ticket as a Tory ticket,[51] but this argument must be qualified. Five of the ministerial candidates were definitely Tories.[52] However, Bateman and Samuel Shepheard sen. were among six Whigs on the ministerial list, and the politics of four other ministerial candidates cannot be determined. Moreover, with only one exception, the eleven candidates agreed to by both sides were also Whigs.[53] The

[50] *Daily Courant* no. 2953, 7 Apr. 1711, no. 2958, 13 Apr. 1713, no. 2960, 16 Apr. 1711; *Post Boy* no. 2482, 7–10 Apr. 1711 and no. 2486, 17–19 Apr. 1711; Holmes, *Sacheverell*, p. 258.

[51] B. W. Hill, p. 410; Clapham, i. 75–6; Sperling, 'Division of 25 May 1711', p. 195.

[52] Three of these were the Tory City leaders Samuel Clark, Christopher DesBouverie, and Jeremy Gough.

[53] The one exception was October Club MP William Gore, the son of the Tory City leader of the same name.

Bank division was not primarily one between Whigs and Tories but rather one between established men with civic reputations and new men with civic aspirations. The fact that several prominent Whigs lent their reputations to the ministerial ticket does not indicate a political split among the leading City Whigs. They were divided only on the question of whether a rapprochement between the Bank and the new government required major changes in the leadership of the Bank. Whig leaders on the establishment ticket, like John Ward, thought not. Whig leaders like Sir James Bateman and Samuel Shepheard sen. thought so, and Whig leaders like Francis Eyles and Sir John Houblon, who were on both tickets, may have been of a divided mind.

The concurrent division in the United East India Company was more nearly, but not entirely, a Whig-Tory contest. It was also marked by a reappearance of past Old Company-New Company tensions. All but one of the twenty-four places on the Court of Directors were contested. The only name to appear on both the establishment ticket and the ministerial ticket was that of goldsmith-banker Robert Child, who was soon to replace his father as a leading Tory alderman. Child and nineteen of the establishment candidates, most of whom had been directors in 1710, were elected, as were four ministerialists. Unlike the Bank contest, however, the split in the East India Company was not primarily one between entrenched City figures and inexperienced challengers. The ministerial ticket included ten persons from Old East India Company families who had lost influence in the United Company, and it included eight persons presently or previously involved in the rapidly declining Royal African Company. The ministerial ticket also included several persons who had recently undertaken Treasury business or who had responded to overtures from Harley.[54] In keeping with these characteristics, the ministerial ticket was predominantly Tory. The rival establishment ticket was predominantly Whig, but not exclusively so.[55] The East India ministerial ticket is therefore best described as

[54] Among these were Matthew Decker, Samuel Ongley, Edward Gibbon, and Thomas 'Diamond' Pitt. HMC *Portland MSS* iv. 594, 617 et seq.; B. W. Hill, p. 403 n. 4; Carswell, p. 242.

[55] Ten individuals on the ministerial ticket whose politics are known were Tories, but among the five known ministerial Whigs were Sir Robert Beachcroft and Peter Godfrey. In addition to Tory Robert Child, the establishment ticket included Tory Alderman Sir John Fleet and the Tory merchant-investors Frederick and Nathaniel Herne.

being composed of persons whose City influence was jeopardized by the East India merger and the African Company collapse, many of whom apparently hoped to regain their corporate power through the Junto's demise and Harley's rise.

Largely disappointed in 1711, the 'ministerialists' in the Bank and the East India Company shortly found their reward. Eighteen persons or families on the ministerial tickets gained directorships in the South Sea Company before 1715.[56] However, the South Sea Company's parliamentary Tory sponsorship did not necessarily make it a City Tory stock, as the foregoing analysis has suggested. Its initial directorate reflected the varying shades of ministerial support in the City. Some of its directors were new Harleyite financiers like Janssen; others were City parvenus like John Blunt, George Caswall, and their associates in the Sword Blade Company. Some directors were populist Tory City leaders like Sir Richard Hoare, and several were Tory parliamentarians like Harley, his brother Edward, and Henry St. John. Some directors were leading City Whigs like Bateman and Shepheard, who were seeking to overcome their old Junto connections; others were Whig traders like Sir Robert Beachcroft, who had not previously held a joint-stock office.

Why, then, has the South Sea Company acquired so strong a Tory reputation in historical writing? This reputation is derived from the number of Tory politicians among its original directors and sponsors and from the parliamentary proviso that excluded sitting Bank and East India directors from holding office concurrently in the South Sea stock. Examined from a City perspective, however, the stock's Tory complexion becomes less remarkable. The City Whig element in the Company was noticeable, though not dominant, from the beginning, and it was maintained at the 1712 election of directors. Further, as has been noticed previously, among those City leaders who were South Sea directors between 1711 and 1715, Whigs slightly outnumbered Tories (Table 4.2). Moreover, the opposition of the Bank and the East India Company to the new enterprise weakened considerably by the time of its incorporation. In order to improve working relations with the Bank and East India directors, Harley gave them all the assurances he could that no harm was intended to their interests.

---

[56] See biographical appendix to Carswell, pp. 273–85.

Finally, although many City Whigs had reservations about the new company's prospects, they nevertheless became South Sea shareholders. Among the major subscribers of South Sea stock were numerous former Whig lenders to the government whose loans were incorporated into the company's shares.[57]

The floating of the South Sea Company did indeed ripple City waters somewhat, but its launching was much less divisive than the making of the peace from which the new stock was intended to derive its commercial opportunities. Although the City Whig establishment was able to make its financial peace with a Tory Treasury, the ministry's endeavours on behalf of a quick military peace gave the City parties a renewed issue in their civic strife. Many Whig lenders to the government viewed their loans since 1702 as pledges to secure easier trading access to Spain and its dominions, and nothing seemed more detrimental to those hopes than the Bourbon succession to the Spanish throne. If Spain was the *sine qua non* of City Whig enthusiasm for the war, neither the allied peninsular reverses of 1710 nor the signing of peace preliminaries with France in September 1711 could be regarded as hopeful signs. For this reason, the December 1711 parliamentary Whig attempt to wreck the Oxford ministry on Spanish shoals was strongly endorsed by Commons spokesmen for the City. Robert Walpole's motion against leaving the Spanish throne in Bourbon possession was supported by many prominent London Whigs before its defeat in the Lords.[58] As the Utrecht negotiations opened in January 1712, the City Whigs found some consolation in the concurrent English visit of Prince Eugene of Savoy, who came on behalf of Britain's anxious allies. Eugene succeeded in meeting the London Whig leaders who had previously raised money for him, but the magistrates' enthusiasm for the prince embroiled his City fête in protocol disputes with the

---

[57] Sperling, 'Division of 25 May 1711', pp. 194–5; BL Harleian MSS 7497–8, 'Lists of Subscriptions of £3000 or over to South Sea Stock dated 10 July 1711 and 8 August 1711'.

[58] Among Walpole's most vociferous backers in the Commons was the Corporation's Whig Recorder, Sir Peter King. Others who voted against the government in the Commons included Alderman and Bank magnate Sir Henry Furnese and his son Robert, Bank Governor Nathaniel Gould, Bank Deputy Governor John Rudge, and such major City investors as Robert Bristow, Philip Papillon, and Peter Gott. G. S. Holmes, 'The Commons' Division on "No Peace Without Spain", 7 December 1711', *BIHR* xxxiii (1960), 224–5, 233–4.

ministry.[59] Neither Whig manœuvres in parliament nor Whig opposition in the City deterred the government from negotiating a peace that left Louis XIV's grandson as King of Spain. If the ministry could count upon little support for its diplomacy from the Whig magistrates, it could count upon much support from the populist Common Council opposition. When the treaty preliminaries were released in June 1712, addresses from the Common Council and from the Tory Lieutenancy commissioners were among the earliest of a multitude of addresses orchestrated by Tory politicians. Opposed in Common Council by Aldermen Heathcote and Sir Charles Peers, the Corporation address was not only fulsome in its loyalty but also outspoken in its condemnation of Whig peace obstructions. The opposition common councilmen displayed their full enthusiasm in 1713 when the treaty of peace between France and Britain was signed at Utrecht and celebrated by London Tory crowds. Another Common Council address of April 1713 echoed that of 1712, and the state thanksgiving for peace at St. Paul's in July 1713 was a City Tory jubilee.[60]

Discomfited by the peace and the manner in which it had been made, the London Whigs nevertheless salvaged an issue from the ministry's diplomacy that aroused the fears of many City interests. This was the treaty of commerce with France that accompanied the treaty of peace, and that gave the London Whigs a strong ideological retort to populist Tory cries against an 'arbitrary and despotick' magistracy. Far from advancing English overseas commerce, the trade accord seemed to open Britain to French commercial penetration and to jeopardize the security of English cloth manufacturing. The treaty provided that British and French subjects should reciprocally enjoy the same trade privileges and customs treatment as subjects of the 'most favoured' nations in each state's commerce. It also provided for the end to several discriminatory British tariffs against French imports, most of which had been in effect for some time in order to protect different English trades.

Clothiers and cloth manufacturers from London and the provincial centres of the woollens industry were most outspoken in

[59] Repertory 116, fos. 61, 68-9, 81-2; *Post Boy* no. 2604, 17-19 Jan. 1712; Tindal, ii. 236-8.

[60] Journal 55, fos. 321-2; Journal 56, fo. 6; GL MS 186, London Lieutenancy Minutes, iii. 1473, 1501-2; *Post Boy* nos. 2834-6, 7-14 July 1713; *Flying Post* no. 3358, 4-7 Apr. 1713 and no. 3373, 9-12 May 1713; Tindal, ii. 273.

their dissatisfaction with the treaty's provisions, but it was also disliked on various grounds by many commercial elements associated with London whiggism. It was opposed by the Iberian wine importers, who feared competition from Bordeaux and Rochelle wines. The treaty aroused anxiety among Mediterranean merchants and among the élite Turkey traders, who had already experienced war-time French commercial advances in the Levant. It provoked a memorial from the East India Company, it was disliked by silk manufacturers in London, and it offended the strongly Whig City Weavers' guild. For all these London groups, the treaty raised the question of whether twenty-five years of commercial and military warfare had been for naught. The Tory ministry seemed to be selling short the country's trade in its hasty scramble for improved relations with France.[61]

The Anglo-French treaty of commerce also aroused unexpected Tory opposition in the Commons. It was not only the votes of Whig MPs but also those of Tory MPs—indeed those of many October Club members— that defeated the Commons bill to give effect to the treaty in June 1713. As the dazed ministry withdrew the treaty, Whig bonfires blazed in the City, and the Blackwell Hall factors and the Spitalfields weavers celebrated their victory. The bonfires announced that the London Whigs would make the security of trade the principal issue in the approaching parliamentary election, just as the Tories had made the security of public credit the issue in 1710. The City Whigs failed to acknowledge the fact that City Tory leaders deserved some credit for the demise of the commerce bill. Among the votes against the ministry were those of three of the four Tory City MPs and those of two other London Tory aldermen who sat for other constituencies.[62]

The preparations of the City parties for the parliamentary election were extensive and protracted. A conclave of Tory citizens endorsed the candidacies of the four City members of the previous parliament some seven weeks before the election. The Whigs

---

[61] *JCTP 1708-9 to 1714-15*, pp. 410, 414-15; *CJ* xvii. 333 et seq.; *Post Boy* no. 2874, 8-10 Oct. 1713; Tindal, ii. 314-20. Also see Geoffrey Holmes and Clyve Jones, 'Trade, the Scots, and the Parliamentary Crisis of 1713', *Parliamentary History*, 1 (1982), 47-77.

[62] Sir John Cass, Sir Richard Hoare, and Sir George Newland voted against the ministry, as did Sir William Lewen and Sir John Parsons. *A Collection of White and Black Lists* (1715), p. 29; *Flying Post* no. 3391, 20-3 June 1713; Dickinson, 'October Club', pp. 169-70.

required three meetings to agree upon their candidates, a situation that reflected their concern to find candidates who could stand as representatives of trade and manufacturing and who could siphon Tory votes from the old members. Confusion over whose candidacies would most effectively accomplish these purposes ended a few days before the October poll, when an assembly of Whigs, reportedly numbering 1,500 persons, plotted strategy for gaining a majority in Common Hall.[63]

The four Whig candidates were all merchants of considerable standing, but the Whig ticket was much better 'balanced' than that of 1710, which had been too obviously identified with the Bank and the magistracy. Thomas Scawen, a Bank director who had recently joined the aldermanic ranks, was a staunch magisterial Whig, but as the Dutch ambassador reported, the other three Whigs *'passent pour toris moderez'*.[64] Alderman John Ward was the only Whig candidate who had also stood in 1710. An independent Whig, Ward had been acceptable to the City Tories as a parliamentary candidate in 1708, but he had also opposed the ministerial ticket in the 1711 Bank and East India Company elections. Peter Godfrey's Whig family had been associated with the Bank from its beginning, and he had previously served as a director of the Bank, of the New East India Company, and of the United Company. In 1711, however, he had been one of the few individuals on the ministerial East India ticket elected to its directorate. Colonial trader Robert Heysham had impeccable *Tory* credentials as a long-time MP for his native Lancaster. Now entering Corporation politics for the first time, Heysham was clearly adjusting his political posture. He had recently been among the Commons members who spoke and voted against the French commerce bill.

Their candidates carefully and cleverly chosen, the City Whigs belaboured the Tory threat to the City's trade in a highly polemical election manifesto that exposed the anti-libertarian origins of City toryism. The Tories countered by insisting that their candidates were equally capable of promoting the City's trading and manufacturing interests. Sir William Withers was in

---

[63] BL Add. MS 17677GGG, fo. 354, Transcript of L'Hermitage dispatch to the States-General, 10/21 Oct. 1713; *Post Boy* no. 2853, 20–3 Aug. 1713; *Daily Courant* no. 3723, 18 Sept. 1713 and no. 3730, 26 Sept. 1713.

[64] BL Add. MS 17677GGG, fo. 354.

fact the only merchant among the four Tories. He had favoured the unpopular commercial treaty, but his September 1713 appointment to the Commission for Trade and the Plantations refurbished his City reputation.[65]

The election involved a protracted two-week poll with rowdy scenes reminiscent of 1710.[66] When the poll had become a dead heat, the Whigs flooded Guildhall with a crowd of weavers who 'caused much fighting and quarrelling in the street'.[67] In the end, though, it was the Tories who carried the poll with their 'reserve' among the artisan livery companies. Still, the contest was so close as to suggest that the liveried electors were almost evenly divided between the parties. Both magisterial London Whigs and populist London Tories now had every reason to believe that their institutional struggle within the Corporation would continue with renewed vigour. Ideological and social divisions over the constitution and religion had again been reinforced by commercial disagreements about the stocks, peace, and trade.

5. The People and the Parties, 1710–14

During the 'four last years of the queen', the party contest in London involved the people to a greater extent than had been the case since the City's revolutionary crisis of 1688–90. The relationship between the City parties and the London electorate had greatly matured since then, and popular politics 'out of doors' was becoming a companionate forum to the magisterial politics of Corporation government. The various means open to London citizens for expressing their political attitudes were each extensively utilized by them between 1710 and 1714. Moreover, the people displayed signs of independence to manipulation from above, although they also showed signs of abiding partisan commitments. Heavy-laden with partisan actions and with partisan words, London's political culture became, by the end of Anne's reign, an explosive and unstable civic amalgam. The Corporation's official calendar of public events was supplemented by a

---

[65] *Advice to the Livery-Men of London . . . to Chuse Merchants in Trade for their Representatives in Parliament* (1713); *Post Boy* No. 2867, 22–4 Sept. 1713.

[66] 'London Pollbooks 1713', pp. 62–3; *Post Boy* no. 2876, 13–15 Oct. 1713.

[67] BL MS Loan 29/8, Dyer newsletter, 20 Oct. 1713.

popular calendar of public happenings in the streets, and participation in politics out of doors was perhaps as habitual for some Londoners as participation in Corporation polls was for others. The fractures of City politics were deepened by the vehemence, the consistency, and the regularity of popular expressions of political sentiment. The relationship between the people and the parties will be discussed both by examining the political behaviour of the electorate and by following the accelerating rhythm of politics in the streets.

Electoral involvement in London parliamentary polls reached a climax in 1710 and 1713. This may be demonstrated through a comparison of the probable numbers of participants in those elections with the numbers who polled in other late Stuart London parliamentary contests for which reliable figures survive. As Table 6.1 suggests, a significantly larger number of liverymen polled in 1710 than in the keenly contested polls of 1701 and 1702. Participation in the 1713 poll reached a phenomenal level that demonstrates the extent to which the liverymen were aroused by constitutional, commercial, and religious issues. Participation of ward residents in aldermanic contests was also apparently considerable after 1710 and contributed both to the difficulty in judging close polls and to charges that some pollers were not qualified electors.

Among London's liveried electors, participation in parliamentary polls was not only rather high by the end of Anne's reign, but participants were also rather evenly divided between party candidates. As Table 6.2 suggests, candidates of the rival parties generally attracted fairly equal numbers of supporters in the parliamentary elections of 1702 to 1713 with the election of 1705 constituting the single major exception. The table shows the votes cast for the candidates of the losing party as a proportion of those cast for the candidates of the successful party, success here meaning the carrying of the most seats.

The alternation of Whigs and Tories in the City's Commons seats seems to have rested not upon large swings of the electorate from one party to the other, but rather upon quite modest swings. This generalization must be offered cautiously because of the deviations from 'straight' party tickets in some contests. Nevertheless, study of the behaviour of individual liverymen also indicates that voters who polled regularly also polled consistently, as

Table 6.1 Participation of London Liverymen
in Parliamentary Polls, 1690–1715

Year of Poll	Probable Number of Participants	Probable Proportion of Liverymen Participating (%)
1690	5,396	67
1695	4,986	62
1701	5,514	69
1702	5,805	71
1705	5,103	62
1707	6,039	74
1708	5,673	69
1710	6,638	81
1713	7,530	92
1715	6,375	77

Final poll results for all candidates were derived from the following sources: 1690: *London, the Fourth of March, 1689* [1690]; 1695: *Post Boy*, 24–6 Oct. 1695; 1701 (Jan.): Luttrell, *Brief Relation*, v. 10; 1702: *English Post* no. 280, 24–7 July 1702; 1705: *Post Man* no. 1405, 17–19 May 1705; 1707: *Post Man* no. 1853, 22–5 Nov. 1707; 1708: *Post Man* no. 1903, 13–15 May 1708; 1710: Speck and Gray, 'Londoners at the Polls', p. 254; 1713: 'London Pollbooks 1713', p. 63; 1715: Sedgwick, i. 279. The number of liverymen in William's reign has been taken as 8000. The number of liverymen in Anne's reign has been taken as 8200. For most elections, the number of participants has been deduced by dividing the total votes cast by four and by making a slight upward adjustment (based on the 1710 results) for participants who cast fewer than four votes. For the 1713 election, this procedure yields a greater number of pollers than that suggested by Speck and Gray in 'London Pollbooks 1713', p. 64. The total number of votes cast in 1713 suggests that the original compilers of the two 1713 poll lists missed or omitted some voters.

W. A. Speck and W. A. Gray have previously suggested.[68] For instance, about nine in ten of those liverymen who participated in both the 1710 and 1713 parliamentary polls showed consistent Whig or Tory partisanship. Moreover, despite important changes in the nature of City politics between 1713 and 1722, almost four in five of the Whig or Tory pollers in the 1713 poll who also polled in 1722 showed a consistent 'whig' or 'tory' preference. And altogether, three of every four liverymen who participated in all three polls between 1710 and 1722 showed a consistent partisan preference.[69] A 'floating vote' among experienced London

[68] Speck and Gray, 'Londoners at the Polls', pp. 260–2.
[69] These estimates are based upon a random sample of 10% of the 1713 pollers listed by Speck and Gray in 'London Pollbooks 1713'. The precise figures for electoral con-

Table 6.2 Probable Partisan Ratio of Parliamentary Votes, 1690–1715

Year of Poll	Ratio	City MPs Elected
1690	0.778	4 Tories
1695	0.857	3 Whigs, 1 Tory
1701	0.777	4 Whigs
1702	0.956	3 Tories, 1 Whig
1705	0.657	4 Whigs
1707	0.920	1 Tory
1708	0.922	3 Whigs, 1 Tory
1710	0.909	4 Tories
1713	0.965	4 Tories
1715	0.819	4 Whigs

Table 6.2 is based on poll results derived from the sources listed in the note to Table 6.1. The ratio for 1695 has been established by omitting the votes of maverick Tory Sir John Fleet, who was supported by most liverymen who voted for the three Whig candidates and by most liverymen who voted for the remaining Tory candidates. The ratio for January 1701 votes has been established by counting as Whig those votes cast for Tory Sir William Withers, who was put up with three Whig candidates against four Church-Tory candidates. The ratio for 1708 has been established by counting as Tory votes the votes cast for the independent Whig John Ward. Ward stood with three Tories against the official Whig foursome, and he certainly attracted some Whig votes, but how many is impossible to say. The figures are clearly more reliable for some polls than for others.

parliamentary electors did exist, but this 'floating vote' seems to have been less important in the reversal of partisan Common Hall majorities than the 'casual' vote of inexperienced parliamentary electors. Parliamentary candidates of each party could count upon solid blocs of committed supporters, but in order to carry

sistency yielded by this sample are 89% between 1710 and 1713, 81% between 1713 and 1722, and 75% between 1710 and 1722.

Although greatly indebted to their work, I differ from Speck and Gray in defining a party vote and a 'split ticket'. I have counted as a 'split ticket' only an equal division of votes between party candidates. In calculations for 1722 (an election between opposing slates of only three candidates), I have not eliminated the many 'whig' and 'tory' liverymen who voted for an extra (fourth) candidate or the few 'whig' and 'tory' liverymen who voted for two candidates of one grouping of three and a single candidate of the rival grouping. The relative merits of my procedures and those of Speck and Gray are debatable. However, in following individual voters by livery company through three different polls, I am convinced that pure party voting is too exclusive a standard for an indication of party preferences. Examples might be given of many Whig and Tory aldermen or common councilmen who could not be so designated using such an exclusive criterion.

elections they needed to outpoll their adversaries among occasional and first-time voters. This was the case because London
was a constituency characterized both by strong partisan attachments and by a heavy turn-over in the composition of its parliamentary electorate over time.[70]

The ward electorates of the Corporation also showed consistent
partisan preferences, as was suggested in chapter four. However,
the partisan division within the wards was both more complicated
and more favourable to Tory candidates. Although Whig
nominees could match or nearly match Tories in contests involving the more substantial liveried electorate through the end of
Anne's reign, this was decreasingly so among the ward electorates, which extended downwards through the ranks of the humbler
artisans and shopkeepers to the ranks of plebeian freemen. The
Tory sentiments of populist freemen virtually stripped the Whigs
of Common Council representation outside the inner city in the
years after 1710, and the Whigs floundered then even within the
inner city. The resort to electoral manipulation by Whig Lord
Mayors in aldermanic contests in inner city wards like Broad
Street and Langbourn was one demonstration of this. So was the
inability of the Whigs to recapture quickly a majority of the inner
city Common Council seats lost to the Tories. After the December
1711 wardmotes, Whig representation on Common Council
further declined to a mere forty-five of 234 places, and in that year
twice as many Tory common councilmen were returned from the
inner city as were Whigs. Thereafter, Whig Common Council
representation did grow marginally in each year, with recaptured
inner city seats accounting for most of the increase. Whig exertions were especially noticeable before the December 1713 wardmotes, but as one observer wrote of these efforts, 'the Mountain
Brought forth a Mouse'.[71] The party had elected only sixty-six
common councilmen, but fifty of these were chosen from inner
city wards where Whig representation on the Court did now equal
that of the Tories.

How are the difficulties of the Whigs at the hands of the people
in Common Council elections after 1710 to be explained? The
Whigs fared poorly in Common Council elections because only in

[70] For instance, among the sample of 1713 pollers employed here, only 49% were also
found as active pollers a decade later in 1722.
[71] BL Loan 29/8, Dyer newsletter, 24 Dec. 1713.

the inner city were plebeian and socially marginal electors out-numbered by the middling and the well-to-do. The Whigs retained control of several inner city wards with the smallest populations and with large numbers of merchants and substantial traders among their residents. Nevertheless, the fact that the Whigs suffered Common Council losses in other inner city wards with similar populations suggests a degree of slippage in their support among middling and upper bourgeois electors. Some disillusioned electors of means must have joined with the less well-to-do rate-payers of inner city wards in choosing Tory common councilmen devoted to populist principles. Moreover, the humbler electors of the inner city, who lived in the midst of concentrated wealth and concentrated nonconformity, had these very circumstances as particular inducements to the espousal of Church and Tory populism. High turn-outs for some wardmote contests in the inner city suggest that many more of these plebeian electors were participating in ward politics in the last years of Anne's reign.[72] Conversely, of equal importance in explaining the Whigs' inner city malaise was the number of substantial inner city residents who were either unfree of the Corporation or who found wardmote business bothersome. The disinterest of a considerable proportion of the wealthiest ratepayers in lowly ward affairs was the Achilles' heel of inner city whiggism. Still, as the Tories became the party of 'the people', the Whigs remained the party of most of the wealthier people. This was precisely the point of the author who in 1713 encouraged Whig electors to 'brag . . . of your Weight as well as your Numbers, shew your *Mercers*, your *Drapers*, your *Skinners*, instead of their *Glasiers* and *Blacksmiths*. . . . You have the Riches of the City on your Side'.[73]

The political and social cleavage between prosperous and humble London citizens was equally apparent in the arena of street politics, which became increasingly crowded between 1710 and 1714. These years between the Sacheverell riots and the anti-Hanoverian riots of 1715–16 constituted an interval of great importance in the articulation of popular political sentiments. If the

[72] For instance, 82% of the ratepaying inhabitants of Bridge appear to have polled in that ward's 1711 aldermanic contest, and 76% of the Langbourn ratepayers polled in the controversial aldermanic election of 1712. These figures have been established by comparing the number of ward ratepayers in the 1710 land tax returns (GL) with poll results in *Daily Courant* no. 2960, 16 Apr. 1711 (Bridge) and Journal 55, fos. 338–9 (Langbourn).

[73] *Advice to the Livery-Men of London*, p. 16.

former disturbances marked the birth of 'a tradition of independent street politics', the latter episodes marked its rather rapid establishment.[74] In the years between, tumultuousness became a regularly repeated element in London's political conflict. Nicholas Rogers has masterfully demonstrated the rich political lexicon of the 1715–16 crowds, the large measure of their independence from élite guidance, and the rather astonishing depth of their contempt for Whig magisterial and ministerial authority. Further light may be shed upon these crowd characteristics by an examination of the street experiences after 1710 that contributed to the self-confidence of plebeian protesters against the regime of the Hanoverian Succession.

These experiences included many popular embellishments of a rather full London calendar of public anniversaries and commemorations that was in place by 1710. These occasions began with the High-Church feast of Charles the Martyr, which was followed by the February, March, and April anniversaries of Anne's birth, accession, and coronation. The cycle also included the birthdays of Charles II and William III, and such time-honoured holidays as the anniversaries of the Gunpowder Plot and Queen Elizabeth's accession. Before 1710 this calendar was commemorated with little politicization and was marked by few popular disturbances of a political nature. However, after 1710 the commemorative calendar was expanded by some to include the birthdays of the Electress of Hanover and her son, and it was expanded by others to include the anniversaries of the Sacheverell riots and the doctor's 'restoration'. Indeed, as the strains within London politics intensified, the calendar of public événements was itself divided by adherents of the two parties, punctured by increasingly vehement initiative from below, and stained by angry political clashes out of doors.

The parliamentary election riot of October 1710 was the first in a series of popular disturbances in the streets that also greatly disturbed Whig magistrates in the City and Whig politicians at Westminster. Although these mêlées were not confined to the boundaries of the Corporation, only those that occurred within or partially within the City will be considered here. When and where they took place, who participated in them, and why they happened

---

[74] Rogers, 'Popular Protest', p. 70.

are all questions of relevance to the relationship between the people and the parties. The most frequent occasion for popular activities 'out of doors' was the day of the official observance of the queen's birth in early February. In 1711, for instance, the popular celebration of the royal birth cost Whig Alderman Sir John Houblon the repair of his glass coach after its windows and doors were deliberately broken, 'his 3 daughters being inside'. More serious trouble plagued the City Marshall and his constables in February 1712 when a 'Great Ryott' broke out near Guildhall and concluded with a crowd attempt to 'pull down the poultry Jaol', a principal place of detention for City plebs accused of offences.[75]

Chief among a dozen additional street affairs in these years involving popular crowds or gatherings were the unofficial celebrations of the coming of peace in 1713, which preceded the official celebration, and which appear to have been organized from below. When news of the signing of peace reached London on the evening of 3 April, a large crowd assembled in Gracechurch Street near the Three Tuns and Rummer tavern, a well-known Whig rendezvous. Demanding that the inhabitants illuminate their houses, the mob pelted the windows of those who failed to do so. According to the whiggish *Flying Post*, the crowd chanted '*James the Third, James the Third*' as it went about its business, and it was headed by a noted Jacobite who had led anti-Whig mobs on other recent occasions.[76] When the peace was officially proclaimed in May, some streets were again the sites of popular excesses. Fifteen persons were indicted for a riot in Fleet Street, and another crowd burned symbols of nonconformity in Long Acre. The official celebration of peace was staged at St. Paul's in July 1713, and it was accompanied by popular illuminations, bonfires, healths, and rowdiness.[77]

These and other popular disturbances in the City after 1710 occurred at various locations both within and without the walls. However, sites in the peripheral wards were the most frequent,

[75] CLRO Sessions files, 19 Feb. 1711, recognizance 7; 25 Feb. 1712, recs. 24–6.

[76] Flying Post no. 3358, 4–7 Apr. 1713. The leader of the crowd was identified as the son of a druggist named Farey, who was most likely the Tory Robert Farey of the nearby parish of St. Magnus. Glass, p. 103; 'London Pollbooks 1713', p. 85.

[77] CLRO Sessions files, 18 May 1713, recs. 15–18 and MS London Lieutenancy Minutes, 1696–1714, pp. 235–6; *Flying Post* no. 3373, 9–12 May 1713; *Post Boy* nos. 2834–6, 7–14 July 1713.

and the overwhelming majority of those accused before the City sessions of rioting were from middle city wards or exterior wards and out-parishes, as were their sureties. In both these respects, the lesser popular disturbances of 1711–14 were similar to the greater disturbances of 1710 and 1715–16. Moreover, as was true of the anti-Hanoverian rioters, the popular demonstrators of 1711–14 were overwhelmingly plebeian in their social status, in so far as their occupations and those of their sureties can be determined.[78] Although Whigs claimed that Tory common councilmen aided and abetted abuses in the streets, no individuals of social substance were among those accused of disturbing the peace. Unlike the case of the Sacheverell riots, no evidence points to sponsorship of street politics by Tory gentlemen behind the scenes. Such organization or pre-meditation as existed seems to have sprung from the same plebeian sources as the rioters themselves. Only the sluggishness of the watch in intercepting crowds, and the alleged Tory partiality of trained band regiments point to any degree of active liaison between populist demonstrators in the streets and populist Tories in ward or City offices.[79]

What, then, were the motives of plebeian demonstrators in the last years of Anne's reign? What were these protesters doing in the streets, and what meaning did they attribute to their doings? Immediate economic promptings were of little importance in these affairs.[80] The calendar of popular political disturbances coincided only with the commemorative calendar of national anniversaries. Gatherings in the streets were prompted by contempt for whiggism, contempt for the Whigs' war, and contempt for Whig City leaders. When personal violence and violence against property occurred—as it often did—it was primarily directed against individual Whigs (like Sir John Houblon), against City officials acting under Whig magisterial authority (like the City Marshall), or against places where Whigs gathered

[78] Only two liverymen can be identified among some fifty persons accused before the City courts of assault or riot on occasions or anniversaries associated with the expression of populist political sentiments.

[79] Rogers, 'Popular Protest', pp. 84–7; Holmes, 'Sacheverell Riots', pp. 75–81; *Flying Post* no. 3295, 8–11 Nov. 1712 and No. 3636, 23–6 Apr. 1715.

[80] The sole exception to this generalization was a riotous gathering of shoe-makers in Moorfields in early July 1714. It was prompted by parliamentary consideration of legislation affecting the exportation of leather, and it has not been regarded as a political demonstration here.

(like the Three Tuns and Rummer). Apolitical personal assaults and violence also occurred in the midst of plebeian anniversary celebrations, but the motives for such gatherings were nevertheless consciously political. The queen's birthday, for instance, was deemed an appropriate occasion for an attack upon a City gaol. In this episode, the attackers politically appropriated the authority of the monarch in defence of their behaviour. Hostile crowd gatherings on the occasions of Whig celebrations, which will be discussed below, also suggest that plebeian anniversary commemorations reflected the same populist sentiments that gave Common Council its strong Tory majority. Although the City Tory leaders gave little direct encouragement to street disturbances, popular protesters nevertheless drew some inspiration from the contemporary party heats in the Corporation and in the press.

Were the plebeian crowds that shouted '*No Whiggish Pretender*', '*No Hanover*', or '*James the Third, James the Third*' also Jacobitical?[81] Whig accounts of crowd epithets may exaggerate the conscious level of plebeian Jacobitism, but no reason exists to doubt that such sentiments were loudly expressed in the streets. What these sentiments meant to those who uttered them is more problematic. As the first quoted motto suggests, the crowd may often have deliberately inverted or reversed Whig political propaganda. Because Tory crowds detested the City Whig establishment, they also mocked and detested the political future so strongly desired by the Whigs. Well before 1714, the Hanoverian 'pretender' was strongly associated with an unpopular civic magistracy and was therefore rejected by some City plebs. Similarly, the Whig shibboleth 'James the Third' became an appropriate symbol of what the Tory crowd wanted. They wanted most of all an end to Whig hegemony, and an appreciation of that desire is essential to understanding the character of plebeian Jacobitism in London after 1710.

The City Whigs sought to impede the rise of plebeian opposition in the streets, just as they sought to combat populist opposition in Common Council. This was the motive of their sponsorship, together with parliamentary friends, of festive celebrations on the historic anniversaries of 4–5 November and 17 November. The

[81] *Flying Post* no. 3295, 8–11 Nov. 1712; no. 3334, 7–10 Feb. 1713; and no. 3358, 4–7 Apr. 1713.

celebrations of William's birth and landing, of the Gunpowder Treason, and of Elizabeth's accession were well-suited for an effort to reclaim some of the people for the Hanoverian cause. The Whigs intended to do this by appealing to popular patriotism and by advertising the evils that would accompany the success of the pretender. They hoped to reverse the popular urban drift towards toryism and Jacobitism through a counter-theatre rich in whiggish symbolism that had once been attractive to the people. However, the Whigs discovered that they were largely speaking to themselves. Their efforts at public persuasion prompted many angry exchanges with unconvinced plebs in the streets.

The first of these Whig celebrations was a pope-burning intended for 17 November 1711, which apparently was planned to some extent by the Earl of Wharton and other Junto Lords. Their plans were disrupted on the eve of Elizabeth's accession day by Lord Dartmouth, upon whose orders a large Drury Lane cache of Catholic effigies was confiscated. These were to have been burned at Temple Bar at the conclusion of an enormous procession through Westminster and the City, which was to have been adorned with streamers, anti-Catholic emblems, and representations of heroic Protestant figures. Frustrated in 1711 by ministerial over-reaction to the prospect of such a mass spectacle, the Earl of Sunderland and his City friends celebrated William's birthday in 1712 in a less extravagant manner at the Three Tuns and Rummer, Gracechurch Street. While this assemblage of some two hundred Whig gentlemen intoned 'Protestant songs' inside, their bonfire outside attracted a contrary popular crowd. These adversaries overpowered the guardians of the Whigs' flame, destroyed the windows of the tavern, and pursued departing Whig celebrants. Routed for the time being, the same party of Whigs rallied in February 1713 and turned the table on their detractors by celebrating the queen's birthday at the Three Tuns and Rummer in their own fashion. This time their bonfire received effigies of the pope, the devil, and the pretender. As these figures were consigned to the flames, the charge of a hostile Tory crowd was beaten off. Similar scenes were enacted at Charing Cross in Westminster, the site of another Whig gathering and pope-burning.[82]

[82] *An Account of the Mock-Procession of Burning the Pope and the Pretender, intended to be Perform'd on the 17th of November, 1711*; *Post Boy*, no. 2578, 17–20 Nov. 1711; *Flying Post* no. 3293, 4–6

These Whig celebrations were the visual accompaniament to printed Whig efforts to revive old fears of Catholicism. The polemical pages of the *Flying Post*, in particular, reiterated and embellished 1680s' stories of rights and liberties threatened by and rescued from popish tyranny. However, as Whig propaganda in the press and in the streets became more pronounced, so did Tory denunciations of Whig demonstrations as evidence of conspiratorial and republican designs. For instance, the Gracechurch Street gathering of 4 November 1712 was portrayed in the *Post Boy* as a 'Hellish Design of the English Republicans and Scotch Cameronians' whose festivities were led by disguised Oliverians. When Whig efforts in the streets finally inspired a seemingly popular and noisy Hanoverian gathering near Ludgate on the queen's 1714 birthday, the Tories likewise cried 'treason'.[83]

Whig attempts to counter Jacobitism out of doors seem, therefore, only to have convinced Tories of the sinister ends of the Whigs themselves. Tory propaganda rather than Whig propaganda prevailed with the popular participants in London politics. Moreover, counter-accusations of republicanism and Jacobitism fed the deepening ideological polarization of public opinion. Political street theatre and counter-theatre in London were by 1714 not simply an exhibition of deep partisan hatreds. They also became another cause of the vast measure of distrust that separated populist Tories from Whig and dissenting Hanoverians. Not without reason many Tory citizens feared that a Hanoverian Succession would also bring a republican and Presbyterian triumph over the established constitution in church and state. And not without reason many Whig citizens feared that Tory populism in the streets and in the wards was really inspired by disloyalty to the Protestant Succession. The numerous political tensions that fed London's party contest were as acute by 1714 as they had been at any time during the 1680s.

Nov. 1712 and no. 3334, 7–10 Feb. 1713; Abel Boyer, *Quadriennium Annae Postremum; Or the Political State of Great Britain*, 2nd edn. (1718–19), ii. 667–9, iv. 291–4, v. 90–2; Tindal, ii. 226; *POAS* vii. 514–19.

[83] CLRO Sessions of Gaol Delivery, 24 Feb. 1714, recs. 11, 21; *Post Boy* no. 2579, 20–2 Nov. 1711, no. 2730, 6–8 Nov. 1712, nos. 2927–8, 9–13 Feb. 1714; Boyer, *Political State*, iv. 295–6, vii. 184–6; Tindal, ii. 297.

The London Parties and the Succession Crisis, 1714–1715

THE critical period between the 1713 parliamentary election and the Jacobite rebellion of 1715-16 saw a climax in the partisan struggle for power that had been waged in London with such ferocity since 1710. The year of Queen Anne's final illness and death began with the renewal of efforts by populist Tory common councilmen to undermine the authority of the sitting Whig magistrates and to lay the groundwork for a future populist majority on the aldermanic bench. These were the intentions of the new formula for aldermanic elections adopted by Common Council early in 1714 in a libertarian revival of 'antient' constitutional practices. The Court's passage of this act and its renewal of legal challenges to the elections of Whig aldermen in two wards exhibited the enthusiasm and determination with which a confident City Tory party planned the demise of the City Whigs. Aptly described as 'beleaguered' by 1714, the London Whigs were far from destroyed, however. The party continued to enjoy the solid support of the more substantial elements of the City electorate and of the dissenting interest, as Whig parliamentary candidates had demonstrated with near success in 1713. For this reason, the renewed Tory assault on the magistracy provoked not a Whig collapse but rather a spirited and organized Whig design to shore up the party's electoral support and to assist national Whig leaders in protecting the Hanoverian Succession.

Convinced that the Succession was jeopardized by disaffected minsters, by disaffected common councilmen, and by disaffected City plebs, the London Whigs took much encouragement from the initially uncontested proclamation of the Elector of Hanover. However, the arrival of George I ended neither the uncertainty about the intentions of the pretender and his supporters, nor the

uncertainty about the future of City government. Although somewhat dispirited by the queen's death, the City Tory leaders were
prepared, for the most part, both to continue their struggle
against the civic Whig oligarchy and to affirm their allegiance to
the new king. The deep social roots of Tory populism were now to
prove the party's greatest asset. The Whigs, on the other hand,
stood to benefit from the greatest measure of royal and ministerial
favour they had ever enjoyed, and that favour permitted them to
regain the initiative in City affairs by 1715. As this happened, the
principal question in London politics became that of whether the
Whigs could successfully reverse the tide of popular toryism.
Despite much ingenuity and many exertions, events were to prove
that they could not regain either the streets or those wards outside the inner city. The fractures in London politics had become
too deep and too fixed. These fractures endured after the passing
of the Succession Crisis in London, and their endurance ensured
that London would frequently be troubled by social and constitutional disputes as the issues of Hanoverian politics were defined.

Common Council's move to establish the direct election of aldermen had long been anticipated and had again been announced by
the October 1713 appointment of a committee to prepare such a
bill. This new by-law appeared in its final form in April 1714, in
the midst of a furious row triggered by what the Tories regarded
as the most flagrant example yet of Whig magisterial trespass
upon the rights of electors and the status of Common Council. A
seemingly minor squabble over the return of the 1714 common
councilmen for the inner city ward of Cheap escalated until it involved and inflated all the constitutional issues that separated the
Court of Common Council from the Court of Aldermen. This dispute began when Sir William Humphreys, Alderman of Cheap,
declared the election of a ticket of Whig common councilmen after
a close poll with a rival slate of Church-Tories. Led by the brother
of the Archbishop of York, the defeated Cheap Tories initiated
Queen's Bench suits for their places, and they secured the
appointment of a Common Council committee of investigation.
When the committee requested the attendance of all the disput-
ants, the Cheap Whigs rejected Common Council's jurisdiction
and also threatened to 'take a shorter way, by going into
Westminster-Hall.'[1]

---

[1] Journal 56, fos. 86, 93, 103–5; CLRO Small MS Box 30, No. 9, Small MS Box 55,

The position of the Cheap Whigs was supported by the Whig magistrates, who presented Common Council in April with a copy of a Queen's Bench ruling staying all further proceedings on the suits initiated by the Cheap Tories. Interpreting these developments as affronts to the authority of their Court, the common councilmen responded with a spate of libertarian words and libertarian deeds. They first charged their committee of investigation with the additional responsibility of preparing a petition to parliament 'for the better settling the Rights of the Citizens of London, in their Elections at Common Halls, and Wardmotes'. Secondly, the common councilmen adopted the new bill about aldermanic elections. It provided that in future vacancies the freemen of each ward should choose 'one person only' to be their alderman, and it thereby transferred the ultimate right of election from the Court of Aldermen to the ratepaying freemen of each ward. Finally, a month later, Common Council expelled the Whig common councilmen for Cheap and seated their Tory challengers.[2]

The approval of direct aldermanic elections was the final word of Tory populists on the subject of electoral liberties prior to the queen's death. As a radical solution to the violation of those liberties from above, the act was an appropriate cap-stone to the populist programme that the Tories had adopted, with modifications, from the radical Whigs of the 1680s and the early 1690s. The by-law implied the same degree of magisterial accountability demanded by the radical framers of the 1690 draft London statute and by the 1695 spokesmen for the populist liverymen. However, in its Tory guise, the defence of electoral rights was also part of a broader defence of those institutions of political and religious governance that had been resecured at the Restoration. This ideological posture was made clear when the common councilmen, in their last important act under Stuart rule, addressed the queen in support of the Schism Act, a 1714 proclamation against the pretender, and the Hanoverian Succession.[3] Anglican, monarchical, and populist, the Tories affirmed their regard for royal authority in church and state and for the continuation of

No. 19, Misc. MS 136.23. Sir Joshua Sharp, a Cheap stationer, was the brother of Archbishop John Sharp.

[2] Journal 56, fos. 97–9, 105; Repertory 118, pp. 227–36.
[3] Journal 56, fo. 128.

that authority in the Hanoverian line. Although 'James III' had become a symbol for the expression of plebeian discontent, many City Tory leaders actually perceived the pretender as a threat to the institutions of City and national government that they had laboured to preserve. Jacobitism and republicanism were for them the extremities to be rejected in favour of their own *via media* of electoral rights and royal authority.

The London Whigs and the dissenting interest saw things quite differently. They so strongly identified their own success with that of Hanover that they could only interpret their defeats in the streets and in the wards as evidence of Jacobite conspiracy. The Tory Common Council triumphs of April and May 1714 were therefore followed by Whig responses of extraordinary novelty. The first of these responses was the immediate organization of a City 'Hanover Society'.[4] This body was to become a City Whig steering committee that assumed numerous tasks of political importance, the first of which was the preparation of projected lists of the entire London electorate by livery company and by precinct. From its beginning, the Hanover Society sought also to promote improved communications among Whig activists in different parts of the City. With this in mind, the organizers of the club recruited members from two-thirds of the City's wards.[5] The importance of the society may be further judged from the calibre of its active early membership of nineteen. Although it originally included no sitting Whig magistrates, the club numbered among its founders some persons closely connected to the Whig magistracy and other persons who had personal ties to Whig parliamentary grandees. Half of the attenders were present or past common councilmen. John Eyles and John London were MPs at the time of the organization of the club, Robert Baylis had sat in the 1708-10 parliament, and Charles Cooke was returned to the Commons for Grampound in 1715. Eyles and Baltic merchant Henry Lyell were directors of both the Bank and the East India Company in 1714, and Richard Houblon, who occasionally

---

[4] As Geoffrey Holmes has also suggested, the most likely meaning of the initials 'HS', by which the club's secretary referred to it, is 'Hanover Society'. See his review of *London Politics 1713-1717* in *Parliamentary History*, 2 (1983), 244-7. Other scholars have interpreted 'HS' to mean the 'Honourable Society' or the 'Hanoverian Succession' club. Horwitz, 'Introduction' to 'Minutes of a Whig Club', pp. 2-3; Doolittle, 'Government Interference in City Elections 1714-16', *HJ* xxiv (December, 1981), 945.

[5] 'Minutes of a Whig Club', pp. 11-15.

attended the club, was also a Bank director of prominent lineage.

Both the purposes and the personnel of the Hanover Society made it the most sophisticated local political club of its era. Not since the days of the Levellers had any political element in London devised such an ambitious agency to effect its purposes. The dedication of the club to the Protestant Succession is further indicated by the involvement of several of its members in another London organization which was also jolted into novel actions by the 1714 behaviour of City and parliamentary Tories. This was the Honourable Artillery Company, a genteel citizens' society for the private exercise of arms, whose several hundred members annually chose their own officers.[6] It had become embroiled in the City's political quarrels when its leadership was snatched from the Tories by Whig magistrates in 1708. In 1711 and again in 1712, Sir William Ashurst, Sir Gilbert Heathcote, and Sir Charles Peers retained the company's principal executive offices against the opposition of Sir William Withers, Sir Richard Hoare, and Sir John Cass. Both parties obviously attached great importance to control of the Honourable Artillery Company. Whig possession of its leadership prevented the Tories from gaining a complete monopoly of military resources in London after the 1710 Lieutenancy alteration. Moreover, as the license of Tory crowds increased, even in the presence of the trained bands, the City Whigs came to see the company as a potential remedy to Jacobite ochlocracy in the streets. By 1713, the London Whigs regarded the company as a Hanoverian militia, and all the places on its Court of Assistants were held by reliable persons.[7]

The City leaders who dominated the Honourable Artillery Company may have been among those approached early in 1714 by Generals James Stanhope and William Cadogan, who were then plotting Whig military measures to counter any threats to

---

[6] The company had previously gained political importance in the early 1640s when its ranks were swelled with parliamentary Puritans. Pearl, *London and the Puritan Revolution*, pp. 170-3.

[7] *Post Man* no. 2110, 20-2 Mar. 1712; *Flying Post* no. 3369, 30 Apr.-2 May 1713; John Blackwell, 'A Brief Historical Account of the Honourable Artillery Company' in *A Compendium of Military Discipline as it is practiced by the Honourable Artillery Company* (1726), viii; Anthony Highmore, *The History of the Honourable Artillery Company of the City of London* (1804), pp. 165-6; G. Gould Walker, *The Honourable Artillery Company 1537-1947*, 2nd edn. (Aldershot, 1954).

the Succession.[8] In any case, after parliamentary wranglings about the security of the Succession and after the new populist advances in Common Council, the Artillery Company's governors resolved in June 1714 to establish a collateral company of grenadiers. As the company's whiggish clerk recalled a decade later, this decision 'served to rouse up many . . . and many Gentlemen entered themselves Members of the Company on purpose the better to . . . fight for their Liberties and Properties'.[9] In the City's revolutionary crisis twenty-five years earlier, the London Whigs had sought to protect their Revolution by organizing a private military company. Convinced that their Revolution was again threatened, the City Whigs were similarly prepared to use forcible measures in 1714. The opposition of a Whig Artillery Company to a Tory Lieutenancy added a military rivalry to the already numerous fractures within London's political life.

The City Whigs' military preparations for the Hanoverian Succession proved unnecessary in the short-run. The queen's death and the proclamation of George I were not attended by the immediate disturbances the Whigs had anticipated. Instead, they found themselves bidding for royal attention against their Tory opponents, who were determined to vindicate publicly their recent political behaviour and their understanding of the civic constitution. The City Tories undertook every effort to make their voices heard in the chorus that welcomed the king.

A flurry of Common Council activity preceded the king's progress through the City on his way to St. James's on 20 September. That event was the most lavishly staged public procession in twenty years, and the Tory common councilmen were determined to utilize the occasion to advertise their self-proclaimed constitutional status. Breaking all precedents for ceremonial protocol, they twice resolved that the entire Court of Common Council should appear in the procession to balance the appearance of the aldermen. Their decision was blocked, however, by the Earl Marshall on behalf of the Lords Justices, who feared that the appearance of all the common councilmen would produce unseemly 'Confusion and Disorder'. This humiliation was made the greater by the highly visible part taken in the procession by the grenadiers of the Artil-

---

[8] Tindal, ii. 347; Basil Williams, *Stanhope: A Study in Eighteenth-Century War and Diplomacy* (Oxford, 1932), pp. 143–5.
[9] Blackwell, viii–ix.

lery Company. Nevertheless, the City Tories tried again in October to infuse civic ceremony with constitutional drama. Invitations to the king and to the Prince of Wales to attend the mayoral installation of Whig Lord Mayor-Elect Sir William Humphreys were issued by the Tory Common Council. A committee preparing the royal entertainment was also ordered to see that the entire Court of Common Council was accommodated at a Guildhall banquet in the presence of the king. This time the Tories were able to represent the constitutional credentials of Common Council through the Court's corporate appearance at the mayoral banquet, but the common councilmen's appearance completely failed to make the desired impression.[10]

The City Tories quickly discovered that their Whig adversaries enjoyed the respect of the new ministry. This became clear in the royal distribution of offices and favours in late 1714 which, as in the past, alerted the London electorate to changes in the government's confidence in the City's political leaders. The City Whigs basked in a stream of preferments, but only two Tory aldermen gained so much as a knighthood.[11] Their stature emphasized and enhanced by numerous signs of royal and ministerial approval, the London Whigs eagerly prepared for the December 1714 wardmotes and for the January 1715 City parliamentary election. Whig efforts in the wards, which included a whispering campaign against the most outspoken Tories and the publication of a critical broadside, yielded an increase in Whig seats.[12] However, Tory common councilmen still greatly outnumbered Whigs, and in at least three wards, sitting Tories triumphed over challengers in well attended polls. The *Post Boy* exulted 'that the *Old Members* are not to be despis'd; notwithstanding the unprecedented Artifices,

---

[10] Journal 56, fos. 132-4, 150-1; Repertory 118, pp. 393-5; BL Loan 29/8, Dyer newsletter, 14 Aug. 1714.

[11] Knighthood was conferred on Tory Aldermen Robert Child and Joseph Lawrence. Knighthoods were also granted to Whig Aldermen John Ward, Thomas Scawen, Gerrard Conyers, and Peter Delmé. Lord Mayor Humphreys, Alderman John Fryer, and Alderman Francis Eyles were among the first Hanoverian baronets. Recorder Sir Peter King became Chief Justice of Common Pleas; Alderman Sir William Ashurst became an Excise Commissioner; Alderman Sir Charles Peers was named a Customs Commissioner; and Charles Cooke was named a Commissioner for Trade and the Plantations. Finally, a new London Lieutenancy commission top-heavy with Whigs (including over half the active membership of the Hanover Society) was issued in November.

[12] *December, 1714. The following Proceedings of the Common Council, are Offer'd to the Consideration of the Citizens of London, against their next Election of Common Council-Men.*

Promises, and Menaces, to constrain Persons to poll against them'.[13]

The first parliamentary contest of the Hanoverian era saw the Whigs advance the same moderate candidates who had fallen just short of election in 1713. As in the previous election, they emphasized their standing as active merchants, and they condemned supporters of the late ministry for their disregard of trade. The Tories again put up Sir William Withers and Sir John Cass, but the death of Sir George Newland and internal Tory debates about electoral strategy produced two new parliamentary candidates. These were Aldermen Sir William Stewart and Sir George Merttins. They had both sat upon populist Common Council committees, and they joined their colleagues on the Tory ticket in proclaiming their libertarian credentials. The Whig slate carried a poll that was characterized by a large margin of victory (Table 6.1). However, the notable decline in the number of pollers between 1713 and 1715 may have been a sign of the limitations of electoral enthusiasm for the Whigs (Table 6.2).[14]

Although the London Whigs had succeeded in regaining the initiative from their City adversaries in the first six months of the new reign, indications of resistance to their success were also obvious by early 1715. The Tory common councilmen had been embarrassed but not subordinated to the magistracy. The Whigs could point to enthusiastic crowds at Hanoverian celebrations in the City, but words of disaffection had also been shouted in the streets. Both Common Council populism and plebeian Jacobitism were perceived by the Whigs as blemishes on the fruits of the Succession. If both had been regarded as incompatible with securing the Revolution before 1714, each became even more unsightly to Whig activists after the arrival of George I. The City Whig leadership therefore considered the Succession itself incomplete until the populist opposition in Common Council and in the wards had been subdued. The early months of 1715 saw the opening of a Whig offensive to reverse the populist advances of 1710 to

[13] *Post Boy* no. 3064, 25–8 Dec. 1714. For polls in Tower, Farringdon Within, and Bread Street see *Post Boy* no. 3062, 21–3 Dec. 1714 and no. 3069, 6–8 Jan. 1715. The partisan break-down of the 1715 Common Council was 134 Tories, 79 Whigs, 13 persons of ambiguous party loyalties, and 8 persons of undetermined partisanship.

[14] *Post Boy* no. 3074, 18–20 Jan. 1715; *Post Man*, 20–2 Jan. 1715 and 29 Jan.–1 Feb. 1715; Boyer, *Political State*, ix. 82–7; William Maitland, *The History of London* (1756), i. 518–19.

1714. The outcome of this offensive was critical because upon its success or failure rested the meaning of the Succession for the City. The outbreak of rebellion during 1715 and the escalation of popular protests in the streets gave the Whigs additional reasons for pursuing their new programme. As they did so, the Whig leaders demonstrated the ease with which they could assimilate anti-populist actions to the Hanoverian rhetoric of liberty and property rescued from tyranny.

The strongest indication of the beginning of this Whig drive was the recruitment after the parliamentary election of a considerably enlarged membership by the City Hanover Society. The club now attracted the participation of such magisterial Whigs as Lord Mayor Humphreys and Alderman Heathcote, and Postmaster General James Craggs also developed intimate contacts with its members. The enlargement of the society's membership also pointed to an expansion in the range of its activities which placed it firmly in the centre of City politics for the next year. Among the club's most desired objectives was the elimination of the freeman franchise, an important institutional support of Common Council populism. In a survey of the likely political results of opening the ward franchise to unfreemen, the club projected Whig benefits in most inner city wards and in those middle city wards with large numbers of unfree merchants or unfree Quakers. One of the society's most active members was also party to a King's Bench suit initiated after the 1714 Tower wardmote, when several prospective Whig common councilmen were disappointed by the disqualification of unfree pollers. This suit became a Whig probe for testing judicially the freeman franchise. The Hanover Society began to collect money from its membership on behalf of the Tower appellants some months later, and in November the club resolved to prosecute the suit itself.[15]

If broadening the ward franchise to include wealthy unfree residents likely to support the magistracy was one element of City Whig calculations, narrowing the franchise to exclude less well-to-do freemen was another. Differences over the ratepaying

[15] 'Minutes of a Whig Club', pp. 4–5, 16–17, 22–3, 26, 28, 32; CLRO Misc. MS 64.3 Hanover Society member Richard Lechmere appears to have been the prime mover in the King's Bench suits of the Tower Whigs. Earlier intimations of Whig dissatisfaction with ward electoral qualifications came in the wake of the adoption of direct aldermanic elections. Repertory 118, p. 435; Repertory 119, pp. 25–6.

qualification for voting that had arisen by 1715 made this clear. An anti-magisterial pamphleteer of that year claimed that Whig aldermen had replaced the qualification of paying church and poor rates in their wardmotes with a more restrictive qualification that included the payment of several additional City assessments.[16] This Whig interpretation of the ratepaying qualification for the ward franchise assumed that marginally qualified electors were also largely populist electors.

As the City Whigs raised these challenges to the ward franchise, they also seriously considered incorporating changes into a parliamentary bill 'for Quietting Disputes' about aldermanic and Common Council elections. Both Whigs and Tories had threatened a political resort to Westminster in 1714, and the City Whigs' decision to pursue this course in 1715 was another indication of the seriousness of their resolve to recover control of the Corporation quickly. However, the City Tories easily obstructed this anticipation of magisterial objectives that found ultimate expression in the 1725 City Elections Act. Acting in defence of the 'validity of several acts of Common-Councell . . . brought into Question' by Whig manoeuvres, the populist common councilmen defeated a resolution for the drafting of an elections bill to be submitted to parliament.[17]

The Whig assault on the franchise had, therefore, further disturbed the City rather than quieting it. For this reason, and probably also because the promotion of major constitutional changes seemed inadvisable in the midst of the Fifteen, the formal Whig effort to revise the franchise was eventually shelved. Nevertheless, the Whigs and their populist opposition had clearly articulated different attitudes towards it, and the issue of the ward franchise was to be raised almost annually in the disputed elections that continued through the next decade.

Other 1715 initiatives undertaken by the Whigs came at the suggestion of Postmaster Craggs. The Hanover Society assumed oversight of appointments of minor government place-holders in London, and it prepared ward surveys of disaffected persons as fears of Jacobite plotting were realized. However, the most important element of the Whigs' anti-populist crusade was their renewed

---

[16] Webb and Webb, p. 632.
[17] Journal 56, fo. 164. Also see Webb and Webb, p. 632 and n. 4, p. 633 and n. 1.

drive to evict Tories from Common Council in the December 1715 wardmotes. The earlier moves against the ward franchise were probably intended as a preliminary to this endeavour. The Hanover Society was again the nerve centre of Whig planning, which included the solicitation of candidates in the Whig interest in many wards, the distribution of sums of government money on behalf of Whig nominees in most wards, and the application of personal influence upon voters susceptible to such blandishments.[18]

Although the Whigs failed to meet their goals in the 1715 wardmotes, the election nevertheless marked the apex of Whig success in Common Council affairs in the early eighteenth century. The nearly one hundred Whig common councilmen on the 1716 Court composed the largest body of Whig representatives on Common Council between 1704 and 1720. However, the results also demonstrated again the limitations of Whig electoral prospects in the wards. Two-thirds of the Whig common councilmen were elected from the inner city. No Whig common councilmen were returned in December 1715 from any of the populous exterior wards, a situation that remained unchanged as late as 1720. In preparing for the 1716 wardmotes a year later, many Hanover Society members lamented that no further improvements could be made in the representation from their wards. The apparent demise of the Whig club early in 1717, after fruitless wardmote efforts, may have represented an acknowledgement that Common Council could not be regained from the civic opposition. Moreover, despite the Whigs' conviction that Tory populism represented a rejection of the Revolution, the behaviour of most City Tory leaders during the Rebellion had given the lie to Whig rhetoric. Although the Whigs had better grounds for complaining of disloyalty in the streets, they largely had themselves, rather than the City Tories, to thank for that.[19]

The London Whigs were, therefore, unable to break the spirit of the populist Common Council opposition that had been forged under Church-Tory banners in Anne's reign. The reasons for this failure reflected all the political fractures that had shaken the stability of the Corporation. First, the apostasy of the City Whigs

[18] Horwitz, 'Introduction' to 'Minutes of a Whig Club', pp. 5-9; Doolittle, 'Government Interference in City Elections', pp. 945-8.

[19] Journal 56, fo. 195; 'Minutes of a Whig Club', pp. 42-5.

from the libertarian principles which they had once promoted deprived them of the popular support that they had enjoyed at the time of the Revolution. Secondly, the political success and the trading acumen of the sizeable dissenting minority had contributed to a deep popular reaction against a party in which nonconformists took so important a part. The disregard of so many Whigs for the established religious institutions of the country encouraged the belief that the political institutions of civic government were also unsafe in Whig hands. Thirdly, the connections between the magisterial party and the great stock companies had strengthened an alternate City leadership drawn from those trading, investing, and commercial interests which were dismayed or dislodged by the financial revolution. These Tory leaders had adroitly responded to popular suspiciousness of a new financial and political élite that seemingly pursued its interests in trade and foreign policy with little regard for fiscal burdens imposed upon other social ranks. Finally, the civic *artisanat*, which was drawn from London's lesser guilds and poorer wards, had taken raw offence at the Whigs' behaviour and had thus become all the more devoted to the active exercise of electoral rights. Widely disseminated and inculcated through the new politics of print, the feelings and attitudes that had supported the late Stuart rise of Tory populism could not easily be effaced from London's political culture.

The significance of the Succession Crisis for London politics was, therefore, that it confirmed both the entrenchment of a popular opposition in Common Council and the entrenchment of the Whig-mercantile élite in the magistracy. The collapse of the Fifteen and the studied loyalism of populist Common Council leaders lessened, without eliminating, the political tensions that still divided the City. Only by inducing some Tories to co-operate with the magistracy and by avoiding sensitive issues could the Whigs create a semblance of civic harmony. However, the fractures in London politics could not easily be obscured by Whig charades. The tensions that had produced these fractures occasionally again brought to the surface the fiery words of the last four years of the queen. The aldermen's unsuccessful reassertion of their Common Council veto in 1717 was one episode attended by such disagreements. The contrived 1719 enquiry by the House of Lords into Common Council's expenses on *quo warranto* suits was another, and several disputed ward elections produced additional heat.[20] On the other hand, the passage of the Septennial Act, which long deprived the London parties of a major parliamentary contest, also prevented the release of much of the political tension generated by their distrust of each other. The extended interval between the parliamentary elections of 1715 and 1722 provided the parties with much time for reorganization, redefinition, and the recruitment of new leaders. The eventual discharge of political hostility in the 1722 City parliamentary election was, however, far from exhaustive. Instead, it was a major rumbling in another building civic cataclysm that Robert Walpole sought to contain with much skill but with little ease.

[20] Journal 57, fo. 22; Repertory 121, p. 159; Repertory 123, pp. 210-15, 223, 242, 401; CLRO MS 77.3, Misc. MS 64.3, Misc. MS 146.9; *LJ* xxi. 72, 145-9; Maitland, i. 521-5; Reginald R. Sharpe, *London and the Kingdom* (1894-5), iii. 12-27; Webb and Webb, pp. 633-4.

BIBLIOGRAPHY

I. Manuscript Sources

Angus Library, Regent's Park College, Oxford
  MS   Minute Book of Bagnio Court Baptist Church, 1689–1723
Bank of England, Archives Section
  MS   Index to the Book of Subscriptions, 1694
Baptist Union Library
  MS   Barbican Church Minute Books: Turners Hall, 1695–9; Paul's
    Alley, Barbican, 1699–1739
  MS   Little Wild Street Church Book, 1700–15
Bodleian Library, Oxford
  Carte MSS
  Newdigate Newsletters (Microfilm)
  Rawlinson MSS
British Library
  Loan 29   Papers of Robert Harley, Earl of Oxford
  Additional MSS
  4460
  5752
  17677GGG   L'Hermitage Dispatches to the States-General (tran-
    scripts)
  32057
  33512
  34096
  36722
  40774
  40775
  42952
  61690   Blenheim MSS (Sir John Wildman Papers)
  Harleian MSS
  7497–8   Lists of Subscriptions of £3000 or over to South Sea Stock
    dated 10 July 1711 and 8 August 1711.
  Sloane MSS
  203
  Stowe MSS
  354
Cambridge University Library
  MS Sel. 3.232[81]   A Coppy of a Printed Paper which was Published in
    Guild-hall on Wednesday ye 24. June 1691.

Congregational Library
  MS   Account of the Congregational Church of Christ which meets
    . . . on the Pavement, Moor-fields
  Records of the Church worshipping at the King's Weigh House,
    1699–1794 (transcript)
  MS   Register of all the Names of the Members of the Church of
    Christ . . . Bury Street in Duke's Place
Corporation of London Records Office
  MSS 40/35–40/71   Corporation loans to the Crown, 1689–97
  MS 77.'3
  MS 210.7
  Misc. MSS
  34.5
  64.3
  136.23
  141.10 no. 9   Draft Clauses for Inclusion in the Act reversing the
    Quo Warranto, 1689–90
  146.9
  169.17   Draft Statement . . . in answer to the Petition made by cer-
    tain Members of the Common Council to the House of Commons
    [1690]
  199.11   Little Moorfields Papers
  241.1
  248.1   Scrutiny Books for the Election of 2 nominees for Alderman
    for Langbourn Ward, 1712
  Assessments Boxes   1692 Poll Tax Returns
    1694 4/- Aid Returns
  MS   Lists of Common Councilmen of London, 1660–1880, 2 vols.,
    by ward and alphabetically.
  MS   Common Serjeant's Books.
  Conventicles Boxes 1 and 2, Certificates of Convictions, 1682–6
  Inventory Boxes
  Journals of the Court of Common Council
  Lieutenancy Court Minute Books, 1684/5–1714
  London Inhabitants Without the Walls (alphabetized transcript of
    names from the 1694 4/- Aid returns)
  Repertories of the Court of Aldermen
  Sessions Files
  Sessions of Gaol Delivery Files
  Small MS Boxes 30, 55
  Ward Presentments
Devonshire Square Baptist Church, Stoke Newington
  MS Minutes, *Libs.* A and B

Dr Williams's Library
  Congregational Fund Board Minutes, vols. i–ii (1695–1704)
  John Evans' List of Dissenting Congregations, 1715–29
  Hand-Alley Congregation membership in John Evans' List
  Presbyterian Fund Board Minutes, vol. i (1694–1722)
  Roger Morrice's MS Ent'ring Books, Q and R
  MS Salters' Hall Lecture Accounts, 1696–1737
Goldsmiths Company
  Court Minute Books, vols. ix–x (1682–1708)
Guildhall Library
  MS 186   Minutes of the Commissioners of the Militia of London, vols. ii–iii, 1677–1714 (transcript of original at CLRO)
  MS 544/1   Centenary Club, Register of Members, 1695–1806
  MS 557   Church Book of the Meeting-house in Lime Street (afterwards removed to Miles's Lane), 1728–64
  MS 592   Proceedings of the Church of Protestant Dissenters Called General Baptists meeting in White's Alley, Moorfields, vols. i–ii, 1681–1708
  MS 3083   Minutes of the Dissenting Deputies, vol. i, 1732–67
  MS 3589
  MS 4962   Founders Hall Chapel (Scottish Presbyterian), Record Book of Proceedings, 1717–71
  MS 5099   A collection of minute books chiefly relating to the 'Charter Bill', 1688.
  MSS 7930, 7952   Minutes and Miscellaneous Records of the New England Company
  MS 9060   Archdeaconry of London, Assignation Book in Respect of Proceedings taken against Dissenters, 1683–4
  MS 9579   Diocese of London, Certificates Requesting Construction of Nonconformist Churches under the Toleration Act
  MS 10,823   Boddington Family Papers
  MS 11,741   Russia Company Court Minute Books, vols. ii–iii, 1683–1707
  MS 12,017   Holograph Autobiography of Sir John Fryer
  Chronological Index to Broadside Collection
  Dale, Thomas Cyril, comp., Typescript index to the Liverymen of London in 1700 (1933)
  Film 171   New England Company Letterbook, 1688–1760
  Land Tax Returns, 1710
  Noble Collection
  Stocken Collection

History of Parliament Trust
  Robert Walcott, 'MPs Tempus Anne' (Microfilm of unpublished
    biographical notes)
House of Lords Record Office
  MS 154 (h), (l), (m) Names of London liverymen removed and restored
    1687–88
India Office Library
  Home Miscellaneous Series, vols. i-iii, Old East India Company,
    Lists of Adventurers, 1691–1702

  Minutes of the Court of Directors of the New East India Company,
    1698–1708 (B/42, B/45, B/47, B/49)

  Minutes of the Court of Committees of the Old East India Company,
    1688–1708 (B/39–41, B/43–44, B/46, B/49)

  Minutes of the Court of Committees of the United East India Com-
    pany, 1708–15 (B/49–53)

  Parchment Records 54A, 54B   Two Books of Original Subscriptions
    to the £2 million, 14–16 July 1698
Kent Archives Office
  Chevening MSS
  Papillon MSS
Public Record Office
  C 114/14/1   Million Bank: Minutes of the General Meetings of the
    Subscribers, 1695–1702
  C 114/15/1
  C 114/16   Autograph List of Million Bank Subscribers, 1695–1700
  PROB 11   Prerogative Court of Canterbury, Wills
  State Papers
    Series 34   Domestic, Anne
    Series 105/153–56   Levant Company: Court Minute Books, 1669–
      1706
  T 52/19, fos. 1–25   National Land Bank: Commission for Taking
    Subscriptions, 1 May 1696
  T 70/188   Royal African Company: Journals, 1691–3
  T 70/189   Royal African Company: Stock Ledger, 1696–9
  T 70/191   Royal African Company: Stock Ledger, 1703–4
Society of Friends' Library
  Devonshire House Monthly Meeting MSS, Men's Minutes, Regular
    Meetings, vol. i, 1689–1707

  MS   Minutes of the Six Weeks Meeting for London and Middlesex,
    vols. ii-v (1683–1710)

II. Printed Sources

The place of publication is London, unless otherwise stated.

A. Newspapers and Reviews

The Daily Courant (1702–1715).
The English Post (1700–1703).
The Examiner (1710–1714).
The Flying Post (1698–1715).
The London Courant (1688–1689).
The London Mercury (1688–1689).
The London Post (1699–1705).
The Observator (1702–1712).
The Post Boy (1695–1715).
The Post Man (1695–1715).
The Rehearsal (1704–1709).
The Review (1704–1713).
The Spectator (1711–1712).
The Supplement (1708–1712).
The Tatler (1709–1711).
The Universal Intelligence (1688–1689).

B. Pamphlets, Broadsides, and Sermons

An Account of the Mock-Procession of Burning the Pope and the Pretender, intended to be Perform'd on the 17th of November, 1711.
An Account of Some Few of the Exploits of Don Thomazo Pharmacopole [1692].
An Act concerning the Election and Discharge of Aldermen (*1710*).
An Act for further regulating the Nominations and Elections of Aldermen and Common-Councilmen (1712).
An Act to Impower the Lord Mayor . . . to nominate one or more . . . persons to be Sheriff (*1704*).
An Act to regulate the Elections of Aldermen (1711).
Advice to the Livery-Men of London, in their Choice of a Lord-Mayor, on Michaelmas Day, 1692 (1692).
Advice to the Livery-Men of London . . . to Chuse Merchants in Trade for their Representatives in Parliament (1713).
The Allegations of the Turkey Company and Others against the East-India Company (1681).
The Antient Manner of Electing Sheriffs of London and Middlesex (1695).
At a Common-Hall, July 5, 1695 (1695).
Atwood, William (?), *The Rights and Authority of the Commons of . . . London in their Common Hall* (1965).
The Bank of England's Most Loyal Address to her M[ajest]y (1710).

The Case of the City of London [1692].

The Case of Dowgate and Aldergate Wards, and the matters in question between the Court of Aldermen, and the Common Council thereupon (1690).

The Case of the Lord Mayor and Aldermen of London, upon the petition of some of the Common-council men, presented to the . . . House of Commons (1690).

A Caution to the Inhabitants of Every Ward (1690).

Cautionary Advice to the Livery-Men of London: with some thoughts on the proceedings at the last Common-hall, Tuesday July 2, 1695.

A Common-council Journal, Anno 1701

Commune Concilium tentum . . . 30 Junii (1713).

Considerations upon the Act of Parliament, for reversing the Judgment in a Quo Warranto against the City of London (1690).

Considerations upon the Bill for better Discovery of Clippers (1694).

A Copy of the Address of the Free-Men of Portsoaken-Ward (1696).

A Copy of the Report of the Committee of Common Council, appointed to Consider of the Abuses committed by the Farmers of the City Markets (1696).

The Corporation of Weavers at London and Canterbury (1689).

December, 1714. The following Proceedings of the Common Council, are Offer'd to the Consideration of the Citizens of London, against their next Election of Common Council-Men.

Defoe, Daniel, *The Anatomy of Exchange-Alley* [1719].

—— *An Essay upon Public Credit* (1710).

—— *The True-Born Englishman* (1701).

A Friendly Dialogue between a Livery-Man and a Freeman of the City of London concerning the late proceedings at Guild-hall [1695].

H, R, *A Letter to a Livery-Man of London . . . proving that the Right of the citizens both to elect sheriffs . . . and to admit them to, or refuse them to be discharged by fine* (1695).

Howe, John, *Sermon Preached on the Day of Thanksgiving* (1697).

Leslie, Charles, *The Snake in the Grass*, 3rd ed. (1698).

A Letter from a Country Gentleman, to an Eminent but Easy Citizen, who was unhappily misguided in the fatal election of Sir John Moore for the Lord Mayor of London, at Michaelmas 1681 (1692).

A Letter to a Citizen Concerning the Election of a Lord Mayor (1708).

A Letter to a Friend in the Country. Giving an Account of the Proceedings of the Election of Parliament-Men for the City of London, etc. (1690).

London, the Fourth of March, 1689 [1690].

Milbourne, Luke, *The People not the Original of Civil Power . . .* (1707).

—— *A Sermon preached at St. Ethelburga's . . .* (1708).

The Mobb's Address to My Lord M— (1710).

A Modest Essay in Vindication of the . . . Lord Mayor . . . Aldermen, and Common Council (1695).

A New Years Gift for the Tories, alias rapperrees (1690).

A Petition to the Petitioners: or some queries put to the managers of the famous City Petition (1691).

The Present Case of the Common-Hall in their Election of Sheriffs (1695).

Reasons for a Total Change of a Certain M[inistry] and the Dissolution of P[arliament] (1710).

Reasons humbly offered, for the Lords ready Concurrence with the House of Commons, in the Bill for reversing the Judgment in the Quo Warranto, and restoring the City-charter in statu quo, etc. [1690].

Reflections Upon the Late Famous Petition, and the Well Timing of It (1691).

The Restauration; or: A change for the Better (1702).

[Ridpath, George], *A Dialogue betwixt Jack and Will* (1698).

The Right of the Citizens of London to Elect Sheriffs in their Common-Hall [1695].

The Rights and Authority of the Commons of the City of London in their Common Hall Assembled (1695).

A Rowland for an Oliver (1698).

Sacheverell, Henry, *The Perils of False Brethren, both in Church, and State* (1709).

—— *The Political Union* (1702).

A Seasonable Caution to all Loyal Subjects against Antimonarchical Principles (1690).

Some Queries concerning the election of Members for the ensuing Parliament (1690).

The State of the City of London (1690).

Swift, Jonathan, *A Tale of a Tub* in *The Prose Writings of Jonathan Swift*, ed. Herbert Davis (Oxford, 1957).

To the Honourable, the Knights, Citizens, and Burgesses, in Parliament . . . the humble petition of the members of the Common-council . . . hereunto subscribing (1690).

True Account of the Proceedings of the Common-hall (1689).

Whereas there hath been several false and Malicious reports . . . reflecting on Sir Richard Hoare (1708).

C. Other Primary Sources in Print

The Bagford Ballads: Illustrating the last years of the Stuarts, ed. Joseph Woodfall Ebsworth, Ballad Society Publications, nos. 14–17, 20 (Hertford, 1878).

Besse, Joseph, *A collection of the Sufferings of the People Called Quakers*, 2 vols. (1753).

Blackwell, John, *A Compendium of Military Discipline as it is practiced by the Honourable Artillery Company* (1726).

Boyer, Abel, *Quadriennium Annae Postremum; Or the Political State of Great Britain*, 2nd edn., vols. ii–v (1718–19).

Burnet, Gilbert, *Bishop Burnet's History of his Own Time*, 2nd edn., 6 vols. (Oxford, 1833).

Calamy, Edmund, *An Historical Account of My Own Life*, ed. John Towill Rutt, 2 vols. (1829).
—— *Memoirs of the Life of the late Rev. John Howe* (1724).
Calendars of State Papers, Colonial Series.
Calendars of State Papers, Domestic Series.
Chamberlayne, Edward, *Angliae Notitia*, 19th and 20th edns. (1700, 1702).
A Collection of White and Black Lists (1715).
Collett, Joseph, *Private Letter Books*, ed. H. H. Dodwell (1933).
Crosby, Thomas, *History of the English Baptists*, 4 vols. (1740).
Dalrymple, Sir John, *Memoirs of Great Britain and Ireland*, 3 vols. (1790).
Dunton, John, *Life and Errors*, 2 vols. (1818).
Fox, George, *Short Journal and Itinerary Journals*, ed. Norman Penny (Cambridge, 1925).
Glass, David V., ed., *London Inhabitants Within the Walls 1695*, London Record Society Publications, ii (1966).
Grey, Anchitell, *Debates of the House of Commons, 1667–1694*, 10 vols. (1769).
Hazard, Samuel, *Annals of Pennsylvania, 1609–82* (Philadelphia, Pa., 1850).
Highmore, Anthony, *The History of the Honourable Artillery Company of the City of London* (1804).
Historical Manuscripts Commission:
—— *Cowper MSS*, ii.
—— *Dartmouth MSS*, i.
—— *Downshire MSS*, i.
—— *Finch MSS*, i–iv.
—— *Hastings MSS*, ii.
—— *House of Lords MSS*.
—— *Portland MSS*, iii–v.
Journal of the Commissioners for Trade and Plantations from April 1704, to February 1708–9 (1920).
Journal of the Commissioners for Trade and Plantations from February 1708–9 to March 1714–5 (1925).
Journal of the Commissioners for Trade and Plantations from March 1714–5 to October 1718 (1924).
Journals of the House of Commons.
Journals of the House of Lords.
Lampson, Sophie Felicité Locker, *Quaker Post-Bag* (1910).
Lapthorne, Richard, *The Portledge Papers*, ed. Russell J. Kerr and Ida Coffin Duncan (1928).
'Letters on Godolphin's Dismissal in 1710', eds. Clara Buck and Godfrey Davies, *Huntington Library Quarterly*, iii (1940), 225–55.
List of All the Adventurers in the Mine-Adventure (1700).

A List of the Commissioners of Lieutenancy of the City of London (1690).

A List of the Names of All the Proprietors in the Bank of England (1701).

A List of the Names of All the Proprietors in the Bank of England (1705).

A List of the Names of All the Subscribers to the Bank of England [1694].

A List of the Names of the Field-Officers, Captains, Lieutenants and Ensigns in the Auxiliaries of the City of London (1690).

List of the Names of the Subscribers of Land and Money towards a Fund for the National Land-Bank (1695).

List of the Names of the Subscribers to the Land-Bank (1695).

A List of the Names of the Subscribers to a Loan of Two Millions [1698].

A List of the Poll for . . . Hoare . . . Withers . . . Cass . . . Newland (1713).

A List of the poll for . . . Ward . . . Scawen . . . Heysham . . . Godfrey (1714).

A List of the Poll of the Several Companies of London for a Lord Mayor (1682).

The Little London Directory of 1677 (1863).

'London Pollbooks 1713', eds. W. A. Speck and W. A. Gray in *London Politics 1713-1717*, London Record Society Publications, xvii (1981).

Luttrell, Narcissus, *A Brief Historical Relation of State Affairs*, 6 vols. (Oxford, 1859).

Maitland, William, *The History of London*, 2 vols. (1756).

The Marlborough–Godolphin Correspondence, ed. Henry L. Snyder, 3 vols. (Oxford, 1975).

Middlesex County Records (Old Series), ed. John C. Jaeffreson, 4 vols. (1965).

'Minutes of a Whig Club 1714-1717', ed. Henry Horwitz in *London Politics 1713-1717*, London Record Society Publications, xvii (1981).

Moens, William J. C., ed., *The Marriage, Baptismal and Burial Registers 1571-1874 . . . of the Dutch Reformed Church, Austin Friars, London* (Lymington, 1884).

New Jersey Archives, 1st Series, vol. ii (Newark, NJ, 1881).

The Pepys Ballads, ed. Hyder Edward Rollins, 8 vols. (Cambridge, Mass., 1929-32).

Poems on Affairs of State: Augustan Satirical Verse, 1660-1714, eds. William J. Cameron and Frank H. Ellis, vols. v–vii (1970-75).

The Poll of the Livery-Men of the City of London, at the Election of Members of Parliament (1710).

The Poll of the Livery-Men of the City of London . . . April the 10th, 1722 (1722).

The Registers of the French Church of Thread-needle Street, Huguenot Society of London Publications, xvi (1906).

Rich, Edwin E., ed., *Hudson's Bay Copy Booke of Letters Commissions Instructions Outward*, 1688-1696, Hudson's Bay Record Society, xx (1957).

Rokeby, Sir Thomas, 'A Brief Memoir of Mr. Justice Rokeby', *The Publications of the Surtees Society*, xxxvii (1861), 1-71.

Ryder, Dudley, *Diary 1715-16*, ed. William Matthews (1939).

Sampson, Henry, 'Day-books', in *Gentleman's Magazine*, NS, xxxv (April, 1851), 381–8 and (July, 1851), 11–17; and *Christian Reformer or Unitarian Magazine and Review*, NS, xviii (April, 1862), 235–47.

Speck, W.A., ed., 'An Anonymous Parliamentary Diary, 1705–06', *Camden Miscellany*, xxiii (Camden Society, 4th Ser., vii, 1969), 29–84.

Statutes of the Realm, vol. vi (1819).

'A Supplement to the London Inhabitants List of 1695', *Guildhall Studies in London History*, ii (1976), 77–104, 136–57.

Taubman, Matthew, *London's Great Jubilee* (1689).

Tindal, N., *The Continuation of Mr. Rapin de Thoyras's History of England*, 2nd edn., 2 vols. (1751).

A True and Impartial Account of the Poll of the Inhabitants of the Ward of Broad Street . . . 13th of September, 1711 (1711).

Vernon, James, *Letters Illustrative of the Reign of William III from 1696 to 1708 addressed to the Duke of Shrewsbury, by James Vernon Esq.*, ed. G.P.R. James, 3 vols. (1841).

III. Secondary Sources

The place of publication is London, unless otherwise stated.

Acres, W. Marston, *The Bank of England from Within, 1694–1900*, 2 vols. (1931).

—— 'The Directors of the Bank of England', *Notes and Queries*, clxxix (1940), 38–41, 57–62, 80–3.

Allen, David F., 'The Crown and the Corporation of London in the Exclusion Crisis, 1678–81' (Cambridge Univ. Ph. D. thesis, 1977).

—— 'Political Clubs in Restoration London', *Historical Journal*, xix (1976), 561–80.

Ambrose, G.P., 'The Levant Company, 1640–1753' (Oxford Univ. B. Litt. thesis, 1933).

Ashley, Maurice P., *England in the Seventeenth Century*, Hutchinson University Library (1978).

—— *John Wildman, Plotter and Postmaster* (1947).

Atherton, Herbert M., *Political Prints in the Age of Hogarth* (Oxford, 1974).

Bailyn, Bernard, *The New England Merchants in the Seventeenth Century* (New York, 1964).

Beaven, Alfred B., *The Aldermen of the City of London temp. Henry III–1908*, 2 vols. (1908, 1913).

Beloff, Max, *Public Order and Popular Disturbances, 1660–1714* (1938).

Bennett, G.V., *The Tory Crisis in Church and State 1688–1730: The Career of Francis Atterbury, Bishop of Rochester* (Oxford, 1975).

Bolam, Charles G., *et al.*, *The English Presbyterians From Elizabethan Puritanism to Modern Unitarianism* (1968).

Braithwaite, William C., *The Second Period of Quakerism* (1919).

Brenner, Robert, 'The Civil War Politics of London's Merchant Community', *Past and Present*, 58 (1973), 53-107.

Brewer, John, *Party Ideology and Popular Politics at the Accession of George III* (Cambridge, 1976).

British Museum, Department of Prints and Drawings, *Catalogue of Prints and Drawings in the British Museum. Division 1. Political and Personal Satires*, 11 vols. (1870-1954).

Browning, Andrew, *Thomas Osborne*, 3 vols. (1951).

Burke, Peter, 'Popular Culture in Seventeenth-Century London', *London Journal*, 3 (1977).

Cannon, John, 'Poll Books', *History*, xlvii (1962), 166-9.

Carswell, John, *The South Sea Bubble* (Stanford, Calif., 1960).

Chaudhuri, K. N., *The Trading World of Asia and the English East India Company, 1660-1760* (Cambridge, 1978).

Clapham, Sir John, *The Bank of England: A History*, 2 vols. (Cambridge, 1944).

Clark, Peter, 'The Alehouse and the Alternative Society', in *Puritans and Revolutionaries*, eds. Donald Pennington and Keith Thomas (Oxford, 1978).

Coleman, Donald C., *The Economy of England, 1450-1750* (1977).

—— 'London Scriveners and the Estate Market in the Later Seventeenth Century', *Economic History Review*, 2nd series, iv (1951), 221-30.

Colley, Linda, 'Eighteenth-Century English Radicalism Before Wilkes', *Transactions of the Royal Historical Society*, 5th series, 31 (1981), 1-19.

—— *In Defiance of Oligarchy: The Tory Party 1714-60* (Cambridge, 1982).

Cressy, David, *Literacy and the Social Order: Reading and Writing in Tudor and Stuart England* (Cambridge, 1980).

Davies, Kenneth G., 'Joint-Stock Investment in the Later Seventeenth Century', *Economic History Review*, 2nd series, iv (1952), 283-301.

—— *The Royal African Company* (1957).

Davis, Ralph, *Aleppo and Devonshire Square: English Traders in the Levant in the Eighteenth Century* (1967).

—— 'English Foreign Trade, 1660-1700', *Economic History Review*, 2nd series, vii (1954), 150-66.

De Beer, E. S., 'The English Newspapers from 1695 to 1702', in *William III and Louis XIV: Essays 1680-1720 by and for Mark A. Thomson*, eds. Ragnhild Hatton and J. S. Bromley (Liverpool, 1968).

De Krey, Gary S., 'Political Radicalism in London after the Glorious Revolution', *Journal of Modern History*, 55 (1983), 585-617.

—— 'Trade, Religion, and Politics in London in the Reign of William III' (Princeton Univ. Ph.D. thesis, 1978).

Dickinson, H. T., 'The October Club', *Huntington Library Quarterly*, xxxiii (1969-70), 155-73.

—— 'The Poor Palatines and the Parties', *English Historical Review*, lxxxii (1967), 464–85.

Dickson, P.G.M., *The Financial Revolution in England: A Study of the Development of Public Credit, 1688–1756* (1967).

Dictionary of National Biography.

Doolittle, Ian, 'Government Interference in City Elections 1714–16', *Historical Journal*, xxiv (1981), 945–8.

—— 'Walpole's City Elections Act (1725)', *English Historical Review*, xcvii (1982), 504–29.

Downie, J.A., *Robert Harley and the Press: Propaganda and Public Opinion in the Age of Swift and Defoe* (Cambridge, 1979).

Dunn, Richard S., *Sugar and Slaves: The Rise of the Planter Class in the English West Indies, 1624–1713* (Chapel Hill, NC, 1972).

Ehrman, John, *The Navy in the War of William III, 1689–97* (Cambridge, 1953).

Evans, John T., *Seventeenth-Century Norwich: Politics, Religion, and Government, 1620–1690* (Oxford, 1979).

Fairholt, Frederick W., *Lord Mayors' Pageants*, 2 vols. (1843).

Farnell, J.E., 'The Politics of the City of London, 1649–1657' (Univ. of Chicago Ph. D. thesis, 1963).

Farthing, Sidney J., *Sir John Cass and his School* (1910).

Finlay, Roger, *Population and Metropolis: The Demography of London 1580–1650* (Cambridge, 1981).

Fisher, H.E.S., *The Portugal Trade: A Study of Anglo-Portuguese Commerce 1700–1770* (1971).

Flaningam, John, 'The Occasional Conformity Controversy: Ideology and Party Politics, 1687–1711', *Journal of British Studies* xvii (1977), 38–62.

Flinn, Michael W., *Men of Iron: The Crowleys in the Early Iron Industry* (Edinburgh, 1962).

Foster, William, 'Sir John Fleet', *English Historical Review*, li (1936), 681–5.

Fox, Dixon R., *Caleb Heathcote, Gentleman Colonist* (New York, 1926).

Foxcroft, H.C., *The Life and Letters of Sir George Savile, Bart.*, 2 vols. (1898).

'Free Society of Traders in Pennsylvania', *Pennsylvania Magazine of History and Biography*, xi (1887), 175–80.

Furley, O.W., 'The Pope-Burning Processions of the Late Seventeenth Century', *History*, xliv (1959), 16–23.

Goldie, Mark, 'The Revolution of 1689 and the Structure of Political Argument: An Essay and an Annotated Bibliography of Pamphlets on the Allegiance Controversy', *Bulletin of Research in the Humanities*, 83 (1980), 473–564

—— 'The Roots of True Whiggism 1688-94', *History of Political Thought*, 1 (1980), 195-236.

Gordon, Alexander, *Freedom After Election*, Publications of the Univ. of Manchester, cxiv (Manchester, 1917).

Greaves, Richard L., and Zaller, Robert, eds., *Biographical Dictionary of British Radicals in the Seventeenth Century*, vols. 1-2 (1982-3).

Haley, K. H. D., *The First Earl of Shaftesbury* (Oxford, 1968).

Harris, Michael, 'London Printers and Newspaper Production during the First Half of the Eighteenth Century', *Printing Historical Society Journal*, 12 (1977-8), 33-51.

Henderson, Alfred J., *London and the National Government, 1721-1742; A Study of City Politics and the Walpole Administration* (Durham, NC, 1945).

Henning, Basil D., *The House of Commons 1660-1690*, 3 vols. (1983).

Hill, B. W., 'The Change of Government and the "Loss of the City", 1710-11', *Economic History Review*, 2nd series, xxiv (1971), 395-413.

Hill, Christopher, *Society and Puritanism in Pre-Revolutionary England*, 2nd edn. (New York, 1967).

Hinton, R. W. K., *The Eastland Trade and the Common Weal in the Seventeenth Century* (Cambridge, 1959).

Hoare, H. P. R., *Hoare's Bank, A Record* (1955).

Holmes, Geoffrey, *British Politics in the Age of Anne* (1967).

—— 'The Commons' Division on "No Peace without Spain", 7 December 1711', *Bulletin of the Institute of Historical Research*, xxxiii (1960), 223-34.

—— *The Electorate and the National Will in the First Age of Party* (Lancaster, 1976).

—— *Religion and Party in Late Stuart England* (1975).

—— Review of *London Politics 1713-1717*, London Record Society Publications, xvii (1981) in *Parliamentary History*, 2 (1983) 244-7.

—— 'The Sacheverell Riots: The Crowd and the Church in Early Eighteenth Century London', *Past and Present*, 72 (1976), 55-85.

—— *The Trial of Doctor Sacheverell* (1973).

—— and Jones, Clyve, 'Trade, the Scots, and the Parliamentary Crisis of 1713', *Parliamentary History*, 1 (1982), 47-77.

Hood, Henry G., Jr., 'A Study of the Occasional Conformity and Schism Acts, their Effects, and the Agitation for their Repeal' (Univ. of Pennsylvania Ph.D. thesis, 1956).

Horsefield, J. Keith, *British Monetary Experiments 1650-1710* (Cambridge, Mass., 1960).

Horsley, Lee, '*Vox Populi* in the Political Literature of 1710', *Huntington Library Quarterly*, xxxviii (1975), 335-53.

Horwitz, Henry, 'The East India Trade, the Politicians, and the Constitution: 1689-1702', *Journal of British Studies*, xvii (1978), 1-17.

—— 'The General Election of 1690', *Journal of British Studies*, xi (1971), 77–91.

—— *Parliament, Policy and Politics in the Reign of William III* (Manchester, 1977).

—— *Revolution Politicks: The Career of Daniel Finch, Second Earl of Nottingham, 1647–1730* (Cambridge, 1968).

Hurwich, Judith J., '"A Fanatick Town": The Political Influence of Dissenters in Coventry, 1660–1720', *Midland History*, 4 (1977), 15–47.

Jacob, Margaret C., *The Newtonians and the English Revolution 1689–1720* (Ithaca, NY, 1976).

Jenkins, Philip, *The Making of a Ruling Class: The Glamorgan Gentry 1640–1790* (Cambridge, 1983).

Johnson, Richard R., 'Politics Redefined: An Assessment of Recent Writings on the late Stuart Period of English History, 1660 to 1714', *William and Mary Quarterly*, 3rd series, 35 (1978), 691–732.

Jones, D. W., 'London Merchants and the Crisis of the 1690s', in *Crisis and Order in English Towns 1500–1700*, eds. Peter Clark and Paul Slack (1972).

—— 'London Overseas Merchant Groups at the End of the Seventeenth Century, and the Move against the East India Company' (Oxford Univ. D. Phil. thesis, 1971).

Jones, Emrys, 'London in the Early Seventeenth Century: An Ecological Approach', *London Journal*, 6 (1980), 123–33.

Jones, J. R., *The First Whigs: The Politics of the Exclusion Crisis, 1678–1683* (1961).

Jones, Mary Gwladys, *The Charity School Movement: A Study of Eighteenth Century Puritanism in Action* (Cambridge, 1938).

Jones, P. E., and Judges, A. V., 'London Population in the Late Seventeenth Century', *Economic History Review*, vi (1935), 45–63.

Joslin, David M., 'London Private Bankers, 1720–85', *Economic History Review*, 2nd series, vii (1954), 167–86.

Kellaway, William, *The New England Company, 1649–1776* (1961).

Kellet, John R., 'The Breakdown of Guild and Corporation Control over the Handicraft and Retail Trade in London', *Economic History Review*, 2nd series, x (1958), 381–94.

—— 'The Financial Crisis of the Corporation of London and the Orphans' Act, 1694', *The Guildhall Miscellany*, ii (1963), 220–7.

Kenyon, J. P., *Revolution Principles: The Politics of Party 1689–1720* (Cambridge, 1977).

Kishlansky, Mark A., *The Rise of the New Model Army* (Cambridge, 1979).

Lacey, Douglas R., *Dissent and Parliamentary Politics in England, 1661–1689* (New Brunswick, NJ, 1969).

Landau, Norma, 'Independence, Deference, and Voter Participation:

The Behaviour of the Electorate in Early-Eighteenth-Century Kent',
Historical Journal, xxii (1979), 561–83.

Leder, Lawrence H., *Robert Livingston, 1654–1728, and the Politics of Colonial New York* (Chapel Hill, NC, 1961)

Levin, Jennifer, *The Charter Controversy in the City of London, 1660–1688, and its Consequences* (1969).

Loughead, P., 'The East India Company in English Domestic Politics, 1657–88' (Oxford Univ. D. Phil. thesis, 1981).

Macaulay, Thomas B., *The History of England from the Accession of James II*, ed. C. H. Firth, 6 vols. (1913–15).

Madan, F.F., *A Critical Bibliography of Dr. Henry Sacheverell*, ed. W.A. Speck, University of Kansas Publications—Library Series, 43 (Lawrence, Kansas, 1978).

Manning, Brian, *The English People and the English Revolution, 1640–1649* (1976).

Mathias, Peter, *The Brewing Industry in England 1700–1830* (Cambridge, 1959).

Melton, Frank T., 'London and Parliament: An Analysis of a Constituency, 1661–1702' (Univ. of Wisconsin Ph.D. thesis, 1969).

Pearl, Valerie, 'Change and Stability in Seventeenth-Century London', *London Journal*, 5 (1979), 3–34.

—— *London and the Outbreak of the Puritan Revolution* (Oxford, 1961).

Plomer, Henry R., *A Dictionary of the Printers and Booksellers who were at work in England, Scotland and Ireland from 1688 to 1725* (1922).

Plumb, J.H., 'The Commercialization of Leisure', in McKendrick, Neil, Brewer, John, and Plumb, J.H., *The Birth of a Consumer Society: The Commericialization of Eighteenth-Century England* (1983).

—— *The Growth of Political Stability in England 1675–1725* (1967).

Pomfret, John E., *The Province of East New Jersey, 1609–1702* (Princeton, NJ, 1962).

—— *The Province of West New Jersey* (Princeton, NJ, 1956).

Price, F. G. Hilton, *A Handbook of London Bankers* (1890–1).

Price, Jacob M., *Capital and Credit in British Overseas Trade* (1980).

—— 'A Note on the Circulation of the London Press, 1704–14', *Bulletin of the Institute of Historical Research*, xxxi (1958), 215–24.

—— *The Tobacco Adventure to Russia* (Transactions of the American Philosophical Society, NS, li, Philadelphia, Pa., 1961).

Priestley, Margaret, 'Anglo-French Trade and the Unfavourable Balance Controversy, 1660–1685', *Economic History Review*, 2nd ser., iv (1951), 37–52.

—— 'London Merchants and Opposition Politics in Charles II's Reign', *Bulletin of the Institute of Historical Research*, xxix (1956), 205–19.

Raistrick, Arthur, *Quakers in Science and Industry* (New York, 1968).

Ransome, Mary, 'Church and Dissent in the Election of 1710', *English Historical Review*, lvi (1941), 76–89.

—— 'The Press in the General Election of 1710', *Cambridge Historical Journal*, vi (1940), 209–21.

Rich, Edwin E., *The History of the Hudson's Bay Company, 1670–1870*, 2 vols. (Hudson's Bay Record Society, xxi–xxii, 1958–9).

Richey, Russell E., 'Effects of Toleration on Eighteenth-Century Dissent', *Journal of Religious History*, 8 (1975), 350–63.

Roberts, Clayton, 'The Fall of the Godolphin Ministry', *Journal of British Studies*, xxiii (1982), 71–93.

Rogers, Nicholas, 'Money, land and lineage; the big bourgeoisie of Hanoverian London', *Social History*, 4 (1979), 437–54.

—— 'Popular Protest in Early Hanoverian London', *Past and Present*, 79 (1978), 70–100.

—— 'Resistance to Oligarchy: The City Opposition to Walpole and his Successors', in *London in the Age of Reform*, ed. John Stevenson (Oxford, 1977).

Rogers, Pat, *Grub Street: Studies in a Subculture* (1972), abridged and republished as *Hacks and Dunces* (1980).

—— 'Matthew Prior, Sir Henry Furnese and the Kit Cat Club', *Notes and Queries*, New Series, xviii (Feb., 1971), 46–9.

Rose, R. B., 'Eighteenth Century Price Riots and Public Policy in England', *International Review of Social History*, 6 (1961), 277–92.

Sachse, William L. 'The Mob and the Revolution of 1688', *Journal of British Studies*, iv (1964), 23–40.

Schofield, R. S., 'The Measurement of Literacy in Pre-Industrial England', in *Literacy in Traditional Societies*, ed. Jack Goody (Cambridge, 1968).

Schwoerer, Lois G., *The Declaration of Rights, 1689* (Baltimore, Md., 1981).

—— 'Press and Parliament in the Revolution of 1689', *Historical Journal*, 20 (1977), 545–67.

—— 'Propaganda in the Revolution of 1688–89', *American Historical Review*, 82 (1977), 843–74.

Scott, William R., *The Constitution and Finance of English, Scottish, and Irish Joint-Stock Companies to 1720*, 3 vols. (Cambridge, 1910–12).

Scouloudi, Irene, 'Thomas Papillon, Merchant and Whig', *Proceedings of the Huguenot Society of London*, xviii (1947), 49–72.

Sedgwick, Romney, *The House of Commons 1715–1754*, 2 vols. (1970).

Sharpe, Reginald R., *London and the Kingdom: A History derived mainly from the Archives at Guildhall*, 3 vols. (1894–95).

Sherman, Arnold A., 'Pressure from Leadenhall: The East India Company Lobby, 1660–1678', *Business History Review*, 50 (1976), 329–55.

Smith, Arthur G., 'London and the Crown, 1681–85' (Univ. of Wisconsin Ph.D. thesis, 1967).

Snyder, Henry L., 'The Circulation of Newspapers in the Reign of Queen Anne', *The Library*, 5th series, xxiii (1968), 206–35.

—— 'Party Configurations in the Early Eighteenth-Century House of Commons', *Bulletin of the Institute of Historical Research*, xlv (1972), 38–72.

Speck, W.A., 'Political Propaganda in Augustan England', *Transactions of the Royal Historical Society*, 5th series, 22 (1972), 17–32.

—— *Tory and Whig: The Struggle in the Constituencies 1701–1715* (1970).

—— and Gray, W.A., 'Londoners at the Polls under Anne and George I', *Guildhall Studies in London History*, i (1975), 253–62.

—— Gray, W.A., and Hopkinson, R., 'Computer Analysis of Poll Books: A Further Report', *Bulletin of the Institute of Historical Research*, xlviii (1975), 66–90.

Sperling, John G., 'The Division of 25 May 1711, on an Amendment to the South Sea Bill: A Note on the Reality of Parties in the Age of Anne', *Historical Journal*, iv (1961), 191–217.

—— *The South Sea Company: An Historical Essay and Bibliographical Finding List* (Boston, Mass., 1962).

Stone, Lawrence, 'Literacy and Education in England, 1640–1900', *Past and Present*, 42 (1969), 69–139.

—— 'The Results of the English Revolutions of the Seventeenth Century', in *Three British Revolutions: 1641, 1688, 1776*, ed. J.G.A. Pocock (Princeton, NJ, 1980).

Sutherland, James R., 'The Circulation of Newspapers and Literary Periodicals, 1700–1730', *The Library*, 4th series, xv (1934), 110–24.

Sutherland, Dame Lucy S., 'The City of London in Eighteenth-Century Politics', in *Essays Presented to Sir Lewis Namier*, eds. Richard Pares and A.J.P. Taylor (1956).

Thorpe, Malcolm R., 'The Anti-Huguenot Undercurrent in Late Seventeenth-Century England', *Proceedings of the Huguenot Society of London*, xxii (1976), 569–80.

Tolles, Frederick B., *Quakers and the Atlantic Culture* (1960).

Tooke, Thomas, and Newmarch, W., *A History of Prices and of the State of the Circulation from 1792 to 1856*, 4 vols. (1928).

Troyer, Howard W., *Ned Ward of Grubstreet* (Cambridge, Mass., 1946).

Underwood, Alfred C., *History of the English Baptists* (1947).

The Victoria History of the Counties of England, *A History of Oxfordshire*, vol. viii (1964).

Walcott, Robert, 'The East India Interest and the General Election of 1700–1701', *English Historical Review*, lxxi (1956), 223–39.

Walker, G. Gould, *The Honourable Artillery Company 1537–1947*, 2nd edn. (Aldershot, 1954).

Walker, R.B., 'The Newspaper Press in the Reign of William III', *Historical Journal*, xvii (1974), 691–709.

Webb, Sidney, and Webb, Beatrice, *English Local Government from the Revolution to the Municipal Corporations Act: The Manor and the Borough, Part Two* (1908).

Western, John R., *Monarchy and Revolution: The English State in the 1680s* (1972).

Whitley, William T., 'A Baptist Governor of Madras in 1716', *Baptist Quarterly*, vii (1934–5), 123–37.

—— *The Baptists of London, 1612–1928* (1928).

Williams, Basil, *Stanhope: A Study in Eighteenth-Century War and Diplomacy* (Oxford, 1932).

Wilson, James Holbert, *Temple Bar: The City Golgotha* (1853).

Wilson, Walter, *The History and Antiquities of Dissenting Churches and Meeting Houses in London, Westminster, and Southwark*, 4 vols. (1808–14).

Wing, Donald, comp., *Short-title Catalogue of Books Printed in England, Scotland, Ireland . . . 1641–1700*, 3 vols. (New York, 1945–51).

Wood, Alfred C., *A History of the Levant Company* (Oxford, 1935).

Woodhead, J.R., *The Rulers of London 1660–1689* (1965).

Worden, A.B., 'Introduction' to Edmund Ludlow, *A Voyce from the Watch Tower*, Camden Society Fourth Series, vol. 21 (Royal Historical Society, 1978).

Walsh, K. ..., *The Poor ...*, ... London, 1980.

Watts, D. ... and Webb, R. ..., ... *Economic History*, ... (1971).

Watson, James ..., *A Survey of ...* ... ... (1972).

Webster, William C. ..., *A History in economic ...* ... ... *Economic History*, ... 1935.

—— *The History of banks* (1935-1939?).

White, Keith Sutton, *A ...* ... ... Paris, (Harvard) (Oxford, 1931).

White, James Boston, *A Rural ...* ... *The Economic History*.

Wilson, Walter, *The History of England* ... ... Journal of *Modern History*. ... ... *London*, 1905-1907.

Wong, Donald, Canton, *Foreign Commerce* ... ...

Scottish Journal of Political Economy, ... (1955-58).

Wood, Alfred C., *A History of ... London* ... (1932).

Wrightson, J. F., ... *Journal of ...* ... (1931) and (1945).

Yonge, A. J., *Introduction to Education* ... ...

Past and Present, ... (1972-1973). (Oxford, 1974).

INDEX